MEDIA DIVERSITY AND LOCALISM

Meaning and Metrics

MEDIA DIVERSITY AND LOCALISM

Meaning and Metrics

Edited by

Philip M. Napoli
Associate Professor, Schools of Business
Director, Donald McGannon Communication Research Center
Fordham University

Routledge
Taylor & Francis Group
NEW YORK AND LONDON

First published by Laurence Erlbaum Associates 2007
10 Industrial Avenue, Mahwah

Routledge
711 Third Avenue, New York, NY 10017
2 Park Square, Milton Park, Abingdon, Oxfordshire OX14 4RN

Routledge is an imprint of the Taylor & Francis Group, an informa business

First issued in paperback 2012

Cover design by Tomai Maridou

Library of Congress Cataloging-in-Publication Data

Media diversity and localism : meaning and metrics / edited by Philip M. Napoli.
p. cm. — (New directions in communication disorders research, integrative approaches)

Includes bibliographical references and index.

1. Mass media—Ownership. 2. Local mass media. 3. Mass media and minorities. 4. Mass media policy. I. Napoli, Philip M. II. Series.
P96.E25M39 2006
302.23—dc22 2006003198
CIP

ISBN 978-0-8058-5548-7 (hardback)
ISBN 978-0-415-65003-8 (paperback)

Contents

II: CONCEPTUAL AND METHODOLOGICAL ISSUES IN ASSESSING MEDIA DIVERSITY AND LOCALISM

III: MINORITIES, MEDIA, AND DIVERSITY

IV: CONTEXTUALIZING MEDIA DIVERSITY AND LOCALISM: AUDIENCE BEHAVIOR AND NEW TECHNOLOGIES

List of Contributors

Peter J. Alexander, Federal Communications Commission
Christine M. Bachen, Santa Clara University
Leonard M. Baynes, St. John's University
Sandra Braman, University of Wisconsin, Milwaukee
Mark Cooper, Consumer Federation of America
Brendan M. Cunningham, United States Naval Academy
Peter DiCola, University of Michigan/Future of Music Coalition
Ellen P. Goodman, Rutgers University, Camden
Alexander Halavais, State University of New York at Buffalo
Allen S. Hammond, IV, Santa Clara University
Eszter Hargittai, Northwestern University
Matthew Hindman, Arizona State University
Robert B. Horwitz, University of California, San Diego
Jenghoon Lee, Florida State University
Stephen D. McDowell, Florida State University
Philip M. Napoli, Fordham University
Catherine J. K. Sandoval, Santa Clara University
Stefaan G. Verhulst, Markle Foundation
Joel Waldfogel, University of Pennsylvania
James G. Webster, Northwestern University
Steven Wildman, Michigan State University

Preface

The purpose of this volume is to bring a wide array of perspectives to bear on what has become increasingly contested terrain—the concepts of diversity and localism and their appropriate meaning and application in communications policymaking. This volume arose out of the turmoil surrounding the Federal Communications Commission's (FCC's) controversial June 2003 decision to relax a wide range of media ownership regulations, as well as out of the associated discussion of what role research could—or should—play in this area. Out of these discussions, it became increasingly clear that the concepts of diversity and localism—and their place in communications policymaking—were being addressed by researchers across a wide range of disciplines. Unfortunately, work across these disciplines had seldom been brought together in a single resource. This volume is an effort to address that gap, and to provide a basis on which future interdisciplinary research can develop.

This volume is intended to serve a broad audience, including scholars across a wide range of disciplines with relevance to communications policymaking, including law, economics, sociology, political science, and communication, as well as graduate students in all of these areas. It is also intended to serve as a resource for the policymaking and policy advocacy communities, who often express the desire for accumulations of relevant current literature on specific policy topics. Hopefully this volume will serve that need as it pertains to the diversity and localism principles.

The first section of this volume includes chapters that directly address the issue of media ownership in relation to the diversity and localism principles, as it is the issue of media ownership around which the principles of diversity and localism most frequently become entwined. This section begins with a chapter by Joel Waldfogel that addresses the fundamental question of whether we should regulate media ownership, as well as the many thorny issues associated with answering that question. Waldfogel's chapter is followed by a comprehensive historical treatment by Robert Horwitz of the diversity principle and its place in the media concentration debate. Three more empirically oriented pieces follow Horwitz's contribution, including the following: a piece by Peter DiCola that examines the potential employment effects of consolidation of ownership in the radio industry, a unique analysis by Peter Alexander and Brendan Cunningham of the relationship between ownership concentration and news content diversity in television news, and, finally, a methodologically creative approach to assessing the potential impact of common ownership of newspapers on newspaper content by Alexander Halavais that employs textual analysis to address the ownership policy issue.

The second section focuses specifically on conceptual and methodological issues surrounding the diversity and localism principles. Stefaan Verhulst begins this section with an exploration of the role of mediators in the communication process, the ways that new communication technologies are changing (and not changing) this role, and the implications of these developments for communications policymaking. Sandra Braman then addresses the possibility that there has been an overemphasis on diversity as a policy goal, particularly in relation to the activities of the public interest and advocacy communities, such that other important policy goals that are equally central to the role that the media play in a democracy may be neglected. Braman's piece is followed by a detailed analysis and critique of the FCC's ill-fated Diversity Index by Steven Wildman that includes a detailed discussion of how a better mousetrap (from a Diversity Index standpoint) might be built. The final two contributions to this section include an overview by Stephen McDowell and Jenghoon Lee of how existing publicly available data might be better utilized to analyze broadcast stations' commitment to localism and a thorough exploration by Mark Cooper of how best to analyze media markets in ways that account for the realities of the dynamics of citizens' media usage.

The third section of the volume focuses specifically on issues of minority media and minority representation, which underlie many diversity-focused communications policies—although far fewer today than in years past. Leonard Baynes details the underrepresentation and misrepresentation of minorities in prime-time network television, as well as the potential policy ramifications of such underrepresentation and misrepresentation. Christine Bachen, Allen Hammond, and Catherine Sandoval provide a thorough treatment of the rationales (both theoretical and empirical) for minority ownership of media outlets.

The contributions in the final section address the diversity and localism principles within the contexts of audience behavior and new media technologies, in an effort to address the increasingly important need to enhance our understanding of exactly how new technologies are changing the dynamics of media usage. James Webster explores the concept of diversity of exposure, using television ratings data to address the extent to which the enormous channel capacity of the contemporary television environment is indeed, as many suspect, leading to increasingly narrow content consumption habits for the typical audience member. Matthew Hindman then provides a cross-media analysis of the distribution of audience attention, in an effort to provide important comparisons in terms of which media are in fact the most concentrated from the standpoint of the allocation of audiences. Eszter Hargittai focuses on the dynamics of audience behavior online, in an effort to better understand how the online environment may impact the type of content that citizens access. Finally, Ellen Goodman considers how communications policymaking might better account for the dynamics of media usage patterns, the changing nature of the distribution of media content, and the often-times discouraging dynamics of consumer demand for different types of media content.

A number of individuals and organizations helped make this book possible. First and foremost, tremendous thanks are due to Becky Lentz, Program Officer for the Ford Foundation's Electronic Media Policy Program, who provided the grant for the conference from which this volume grew, and who has continued to support the activities of the Donald McGannon Communication Research Center at Fordham University. Professor Everette Dennis, Area Chair for Communications and Media Management in the Schools of Business at Fordham, and Sharon Smith, former Dean of the Schools of Business, both merit thanks for providing me with the teaching release time that has allowed me to devote time to McGannon Center activities such as this book project and the conference that preceded it. Thanks also are due to the McGannon Center's Advisory Board, particularly Professor Nancy Busch, who chairs the board, and John Hollwitz, former Vice President of Academic Affairs at Fordham, for their strong support for the McGannon Center's activities. Sarah Walker and Adrienne Shiffman, my graduate administrative assistants at the McGannon Center over the past 2 years, provided outstanding editorial assistance, as did McGannon Center research assistant Nancy Gillis. Without their help, this project would have taken even longer to complete than it did. I am of course also eternally grateful to all of the authors who contributed to this volume, who took the time to prepare thoughtful and well-written pieces of work that I believe provide a compelling and wide-ranging portrait of the various theoretical and methodological perspectives that can be brought to bear on the concepts of media diversity and localism. Tremendous thanks also are owed to Linda Bathgate, my editor at Lawrence Erlbaum, for her enthusiasm for this project and her valuable advice as it moved forward, and to Karin Wittig Bates at Lawrence Erlbaum for her expert handling of the production process. Finally, I owe my greatest debt to my wife Anne, for her continued support and enthusiasm for my work. This book is dedicated to her.

—*Philip M. Napoli*

Introduction: Media Diversity and Localism—Meaning, Metrics, and Policy

Philip M. Napoli
Fordham University

Questions of the quality of media performance or the effectiveness of media policymaking often revolve around the extent to which the media system fulfills the values inherent in the diversity and localism principles. Those concerned about the current state of our media system often focus on issues such as the inadequate representation of minority groups on television programs (e.g., Baynes, 2003), or the concentration of ownership of media outlets (e.g., Bagdikian, 2000), or the failure of media outlets to provide adequate local news and public affairs programming (e.g., Media Access Project/Benton Foundation, 1998), as evidence of the failings of our media system. Concerns such as these all arise from the expectation that our media system serve the values inherent in the diversity and localism principles. And, to varying degrees, concerns such as these have become central to media policymaking, as policymakers are faced with the challenge of crafting a regulatory structure that both preserves and promotes diversity and localism (Napoli, 2001).

This challenge is particularly well illustrated by the Federal Communications Commission's (FCC's) ongoing efforts to reassess a wide range of media ownership regulations (Federal Communications Commission, 2003b). Central questions in this reassessment have included the following: (a) Is there sufficient diversity and localism in the current media environment to justify the relaxation of ownership regulations? (b) Is there a meaningful relationship between ownership and diversity and localism? and (c) How should diversity and localism be defined and operationalized for use in policymaking and policy analysis?

These questions are reflected in the FCC's virtually unprecedented effort to strengthen the empirical record on the relationship between the diversity and localism principles, media ownership, and media policy. In the fall of 2002, the FCC released a series of 12 studies in conjunction with the ownership proceeding, many of which addressed the diversity and localism principles in some way. For instance, one study examined the relationship between various television station ownership characteristics and the provision of local news and public affairs programming (Spavins, Dennison, Frenette, & Roberts, 2002). This study took the provision of such programming as a key indicator of the extent to which a station fulfilled the values inherent in the localism principle. Another study examined the relationship between market structure in local radio markets and the diversity of the song playlists of stations in those markets (Williams, Brown, & Alexander, 2002). Another study examined whether cross-ownership of newspapers and television stations within individual markets bore any relationship to the diversity of viewpoints reflected in the content of those media outlets (Pritchard, 2002). These and other studies (e.g., Einstein, 2002) conducted for the ownership proceeding represented an important step forward in terms of analyzing the dynamics of the diversity and localism principles and in terms of integrating such analyses into the policymaking process.

Unfortunately, these studies were forced to build on a disappointing paucity of previous research addressing such issues. Indeed, the tradition of empirical inquiry into the nature of the diversity and localism principles is both brief and not particularly well-developed (Napoli, 2001). This is part of what makes the challenge of formulating and evaluating policies that can potentially impact diversity and localism particularly daunting. Moreover, Congress requires that the FCC reassess its ownership regulations every 4 years. Consequently, the analysis of the relationship between media ownership, market conditions, and diversity and localism has become an institutionalized process, one in which each new inquiry must build upon the advances of the previous inquiry.

These inquiries, as well as any other inquiries pertaining to policies related to the diversity and localism principles (such as Equal Employment Opportunity policies or public interest obligations), face the twin challenges of developing thorough and specific definitions of these principles, and then translating these principles into valid and reliable performance metrics. Given the complexity inherent in the diversity and localism principles, and their relationship to the foundations of our democratic process (Napoli, 2001), it is essential that these activities be informed by a broad range of institutional and disciplinary perspectives. It is this imperative that helped motivate the assembling of this collection of work. This collection draws on scholarship across a wide range of disciplines, including law, political science, communication, sociology, and economics, in an effort to bring together cutting-edge thinking from across the various disciplines grappling with these challenging issues. Moreover, this collection addresses not only the empirical dimensions of the diversity and localism principles, but also these principles' conceptual and historical underpinnings. Efforts to develop systems of assessing diversity and localism must emerge from a sound foundation in terms of how these concepts have been conceptualized and applied over the years—and many of the contributions to this volume work to strengthen this foundation.

Policymakers' desire to gain a deeper understanding of the meaning of the diversity and localism principles and their place in media policymaking and policy analysis is well-illustrated by events that took place both leading up to and after the FCC's June 2003 media ownership decision. First, in May of 2003, a month before the FCC's ownership decision, then-FCC Chairman Michael Powell announced the creation of a Federal Advisory Committee on Diversity in the Digital Age (Federal Communications Commission, 2003a). This advisory committee (composed primarily of media and telecommunications industry executives) was charged with a number of tasks, including making recommendations to the FCC "regarding policies and practices that will further enhance the abilities of minorities and women to participate in telecommunications and related industries" (Federal Communications Commission, 2003a, p. 1). Coinciding with the creation of the Advisory Committee was the issuance by the FCC's Media Bureau of a Public Notice seeking comment on the issue of potential barriers to female and minority ownership of media and telecommunications outlets, and also seeking data or studies relevant to this issue (Federal Communications Commission, 2004a).

On the localism front, in August of 2003, 2 months after the ownership decision, then-Chairman Powell created the Localism Task Force, a group of Commission personnel charged with a variety of tasks, including conducting "studies to measure localism and the efficacy of the Commission's localism rules" and advising the Commission on "legislative recommendations to Congress that would strengthen localism" (Federal Communications Commission, 2003c, p. 1). The creation of this task force has subsequently led to the issuance by the FCC of a Notice of Inquiry on Broadcast Localism (Federal Communications Commission, 2004b), in which the FCC sought information on the extent to which broadcasters are serving the informational needs and interests of their local communities, and comment on whether modifications to the existing regulatory requirements designed to preserve and promote localism are necessary.

This flurry of activity in recent years underscores the challenges policymakers face in effectively reflecting the diversity and localism principles in their policymaking and policy analysis and the opportunity (and need) for the scholarly community to contribute relevant research. The need for information, innovative thinking, and systematic data in these subject areas is tremendous. The work collected in this volume represents a small part of what needs to become a larger and more concerted effort by the scholarly community to help meet these needs.

One of the key challenges the FCC and its various committees and task forces face is developing agreed-on standards and metrics for assessing the current state of diversity and localism. Certainly, the abstraction and complexity that are inherent in concepts such as diversity and localism mean that developing reliable performance metrics is a difficult task. However, other normative principles—some of them of arguably greater complexity—have proven amenable to empirical assessment. Consider, for instance, the large body of literature that has developed around the measurement of the concept of democracy (see Beetham, 1994). Research in this vein has facilitated longitudinal analyses of national development, international comparative analyses, as well as explanatory research into the factors that both contribute to and hinder the development of democracy (Beetham, 1994). Similar efforts have been directed at developing performance metrics for more media-specific concepts such as freedom of the press (Freedom House, 2003) and media sustainability (International Research and Exchanges Board, 2002).

Of course, in the face of growing efforts to develop rigorous and reliable performance metrics for the diversity and localism principles, one could argue that these principles need not—and, in fact, should not—be subject to empirical assessment. It could be argued that these principles exist on a normative plane in which policies initiated on their behalf need not be assessed in ways that ultimately involve reducing the richness and complexity of these principles into fairly simplistic performance metrics. An underlying concern of this argument is that the difficulties in translating complex concepts such as diversity and localism into empirical measures ultimately may produce results that undermine the role of these principles in media policymaking rather than support them. That is, if research fails to indicate significant relationships between particular media structures or policies and the diversity and localism principles, then such presumed diversity—or localism-enhancing structures or policies, will be undermined—although it is possible that these structures or policies had value that social science research was unable to capture.

This is a very compelling argument that rests on the legitimate point that there are limits to what research can effectively capture. However, the contemporary policy environment is one in which an opposing consideration must be taken into account. Specifically, the nature of both judicial decision making and media policymaking have been evolving in such a direction over the past 3 decades that empirical evidence is becoming increasingly central to the decision-making process. The courts have been particularly demanding that the FCC provide evidence that policies designed to preserve or promote diversity or localism effectively accomplish these objectives (Napoli, 2001). Thus, to assert today that principles such as diversity and localism are above and beyond the realm of empirical assessment is to ignore the realities of the contemporary policymaking environment and potentially subject these principles to even greater jeopardy. Thus, in the contemporary legal and policymaking environment, empirical evidence is increasingly necessary to support policies believed to preserve or promote diversity and localism. It is hoped that the ideas presented in this volume will advance the thinking and research in this area.

REFERENCES

Bagdikian, B. H. (2000). *The media monopoly* (6th ed.). Boston: Beacon.

Baynes, L. M. (2003). White out: The absence and stereotyping of people of color by broadcast networks in prime-time entertainment programming. *University of Arizona Law Review, 45,* 293–370.

Beetham, D. (Ed.). (1994). *Defining and measuring democracy.* London: Sage.

Einstein, M. (2002). *Program diversity and the program selection process in broadcast network television* (FCC Media Ownership Working Group Paper No. 5). Retrieved August 31, 2005, from http://www.fcc.gov/ownership

Federal Communications Commission. (2003a). Diversity FAC. Retrieved October 1, 2005, from http://www.fcc.gov/DiversityFAC

Federal Communications Commission. (2003b). *2002 Biennial Regulatory Review, Report and Order and Notice of Proposed Rulemaking,* 18 FCC Rec. 13620.

Federal Communications Commission. (2003c). *Localism Task Force.* Retrieved July 20, 2005, from http://www.fcc.gov/localism.

Federal Communications Commission. (2004a). *Media bureau seeks comment on ways to further Section 257 mandate and to build on earlier studies.* Public Notice, MB Docket No. 04–228, DA 04–1690 (MB June 15, 2004).

Federal Communications Commission. (2004b). *Broadcast localism. Notice of Inquiry,* 19 FCC Rec. 12425.

Freedom House. (2003). *Freedom of the press 2003.* New York: Author.

International Research and Exchanges Board. (2002). *Media sustainability index.* Washington, DC: International Research and Exchanges Board.

Media Access Project/Benton Foundation. (1998). *What's local about local broadcasting?* Retrieved August 1, 2005, from http://www.radiodiversity.com/localbroadcasting.html

Napoli, P. M. (2001). *Foundations of communications policy: Principles and process in the regulation of electronic media.* Cresskill, NJ: Hampton.

Pritchard, D. (2002). *Viewpoint diversity in cross-owned newspapers and television stations: A study of news coverage of the 2000 presidential campaign* (FCC Media Ownership Working Group Paper No. 2). Retrieved August 1, 2005, from http://www.fcc.gov/ownership

Spavins, T., Dennison, L., Frenette, J., & Roberts, S. (2002). *The measurement of local television news and public affairs programs* (FCC Media Ownership Working Group Paper No. 7). Retrieved August 15, 2005, from http://www.fcc.gov/ownership

Williams, G., Brown, K., & Alexander, P. (2002). *Radio market structure and music diversity* (FCC Media Ownership Working Group Paper No. 9). Retrieved June 24, 2005, from http://www.fcc.gov/ownership

I

Media Ownership and Media Diversity and Localism

1

Should We Regulate Media Ownership?

Joel Waldfogel
The Wharton School, University of Pennsylvania

Why regulate media ownership? To many this seems a stupid question because the answer is completely self-evident. The mere thought that "big companies" might be buying more media outlets sparks concern in some. No discussion or research is needed—it is obviously bad, and political action is justified to prevent further growth in ownership concentration. A problem with self-evident answers, however, is that opposite answers are often just as self-evident to others. So it is with media regulation. One group fears ownership concentration whereas another group says that (a) we already regulate mergers, and besides, (b) the "public interest" standard means nothing; or nothing useful anyway. Ownership regulation is just an avenue for allowing mischief into policy-making. The media ownership debate seems to amount to an argument between "the sky is falling" versus "we have a working missile shield" viewpoints.

To move a discussion of media ownership regulation beyond fear-mongering or misplaced complacency it is necessary to define what outcomes we might seek to affect through regulation. Academics are constrained to play by "Marquis of Queensbury" rules and can only deem something good or bad to the extent that it can be linked to mechanisms and outcomes that policymakers decide are good or bad. This has two separate parts. First—and this is the part where social science can help—is the question of whether media ownership affects particular outcomes. Second, there is the philosophical, or at least political, decision of whether the control of those outcomes is warranted by media ownership regulation.

The federal government recently completed a broad review of its media ownership regulations, resulting in an attempt at substantial relaxation of ownership, and cross-ownership, rules. The deregulation was controversial and the Federal Appeals Court, in a June 2004 ruling, found that the Federal Communications Commission (FCC) had not adequately justified its decision. This was a large—and surprising—victory for the activist community, and it left many wondering what prompted the activist opposition to the proposed deregulation. FCC Commissioner Copps's remarks given at the University of Pennsylvania in the spring did little to clarify the reasoned opposition to deregulation animating policymakers.

Although less evidence surfaced than I might have hoped in the recent discussions of media ownership rules, there is a significant body of research suggesting possible effects of deregulation. The purpose of this brief essay is to share the research findings relevant to the development of sensible policy and explore what those findings say about regulating media ownership.

The FCC has traditionally been charged with regulating in the "public interest," a lofty but ill-defined goal. Recently, the FCC has sought to create bright-line regulations on media consolidation that are informed by evidence. The implicit model utilized by the FCC is the HHI analysis, also employed by antitrust regulators in assessing proposed mergers (Department of Justice & Federal Trade Commission, 1997). The HHI is essentially a size-weighted measure of the number of firms in a product market. Antitrust regulators are primarily concerned about the effects of mergers on prices paid by consumers, and an accumulated body of evidence shows that prices are higher as there are fewer sellers in a market. Although a "big is bad" view holds sway in the popular imagination, the actual standards employed by antitrust regulators largely concern harmful effects of mergers on consumers via prices paid for products.

Yet, the analogy of media ownership regulation to antitrust is incomplete. Antitrust regulators limit increases in concentration achieved through mergers to keep prices low. The analogy to media regulation fails—at this point—because regulators have not articulated what outcomes they would control in the public interest. The public interest extends beyond the outcomes countenanced by antitrust regulation, the prices paid by advertisers, and the costs borne by media firms. The public interest surely also includes consumers of media content, in other words, "citizens."

In thinking about whether media products should be regulated, one needs to consider two features that make them special. First, media products have two sets of customers, advertisers and users, and in some cases only the advertisers pay. As a result, some programming intensely desired by small groups will not be provided, even if it should be provided (Berry & Waldfogel, 1999).[1]

Second, one's consumption of media products affects both one's self and others. How? There are two kinds of media products, those providing entertainment and those providing information, such as news and weather. People watch the Weather Channel more to obtain necessary information, in this case to help choose appropriate apparel for their children, than for entertainment. Similarly, people watch news mainly because it helps them obtain the necessary news information to conduct their lives as citizens, to help them determine how and whether they should vote.

Given this conception of media markets, what do we know that would help inform regulation? First, as documented in the work of Oberholzer-Gee and Waldfogel (2001), the availability of media products targeting particular groups affects an extremely important outcome—the decision whether to vote. Just as the prices paid by consumers for products are the important outcome potentially affected by antitrust policy, civic engagement may be the important aspect of the public interest. If media ownership regulation affects whether people vote—my research indicates that it does—then one might construct a reasonable argument for regulating media ownership with the promotion of this important outcome in mind.[2]

Beyond civic engagement, it is reasonable to ask whether program targeting also affects other civic and social outcomes, for example public health measures. We know that media outlets carry information through both advertising and health-related content (how to prevent AIDS, availability of prenatal care, etc). Again, if media targeting affects these kinds of outcomes—and if ownership regulation can affect the targeting giving rise to these outcomes— then this too would provide a guide to ownership regulation. Research to determine the range of outcomes affected by media is a necessary condition for developing sensible regulation. It is, however, frankly, not sufficient. We need a political determination that regulation is warranted for their control.[3]

Second, we know that the mix of media products available is sensitive to population size. The preferences for different media content exhibited by Blacks and Hispanics differ sharply from majority preferences, and both groups are relatively small in most local markets. As a result, there is minimal programming designed to appeal to these two groups.[4] Many markets have little or no minority-targeted programming. Given that media product availability affects voting, regulations affecting program targeting are potentially very important to minority communities.

Third, it is known that outlet ownership affects program targeting, at least in the case of Black-owned radio stations. Siegelman and Waldfogel (2001) document that reducing the number of Black or Hispanic-owned radio stations in a market reduces the total number of minority-targeted stations, relative to what the number would have been otherwise. This evidence completes a logical chain that might be used to justify a public interest rationale for media regulation: Ownership regulations can affect who owns which outlets, which, in turn, affects the mix of programming available, which, in turn, affects civic engagement of various communities.

However, research shows that not all effects of consolidation are bad. From a theoretical perspective, one might expect consolidation to reduce program duplication. Recent studies of consolidation in radio and daily newspaper markets show that increased concentration actually increases product variety by some measures (Berry & Waldfogel, 2001).

If all the information contained in this essay up to now is true, does that mean the government should nationalize the media in an attempt to ensure that all sorts of citizens receive equal amounts of information, or equal inducements to vote? It is worth noting before moving on that in many contexts, government policy does seek to overcome market under-provision of products to particular, usually small, groups. In addition to the public radio broadcasting context mentioned earlier (Berry & Waldfogel, 1999), we also do this in pharmaceutical markets through Orphan Drug laws that subsidize the development of drugs aimed at conditions experienced by small populations (Lichtenberg & Waldfogel, 2003), as well as the government's provision of residential mail delivery services at the same price, regardless of one's decision of where to live. In many markets, government regulation promotes provision of products to groups that might otherwise face fewer, or no, options.

So why not nationalize the media? The 2001 article by Djankov, McLiesh, Nenova, and Shleifer provides many reasons. A return to our antitrust analogy provides some guidance on regulation short of nationalization. Policy seeks to protect consumers from high prices, and high ownership concentration (extreme form: monopoly) causes high prices. Yet, regulation does not prohibit monopolies that are lawfully obtained (via the proverbial "better mousetrap," for example). Rather, regulation prevents mergers that increase ownership concentration sufficiently so that they would be expected to substantially raise prices. How is this helpful to our question on the regulation of media? It suggests that here, as in antitrust generally, one might regulate media by prohibiting changes in ownership that substantially harm people in their capacity as citizens.

But, to return to an original point, sensible media regulation requires articulation, first, of what aspects of public interest are affected by media, and second, evidence that ownership affects these things. The research summarized in this chapter helps provide the latter. Is there a body of evidence that could form a sound basis for media merger guidelines? Even with a consensus that the stimulation of civic participation was an appropriate goal of media regulation, there is a need for more evidence. Should media be sharply deregulated in the meantime? That is not so clear. There is enough evidence that ownership matters for outcomes we care about to warrant deep study before permitting large changes.

NOTES

[1]In principle, government can play a role in providing programming that markets cannot provide. In practice, rather than targeting underserved minorities, much public broadcasting in the United States is a close substitute for commercially provided classical music.

[2]The Marquis of Queensbury rules compel me to issue an important caveat here: it is not self-evident to all social scientists who think about such things that society is better off with higher voter turnout. Whether a particular individual votes has a definite cost (the time spent voting that can no longer be spent doing other things) and almost certainly no effect on the outcome. That said, if a proposed change in ownership structure were going to reduce the amount of content targeted to, say, Black citizens, one could predict reduced Black voter turnout. Winners and losers from such a change could "do the math" themselves and might find reasons to care.

[3]This need not be an impossibly high standard. Recall that the goal of antitrust policy is to prevent consumers from paying high prices. If aspects of media that policy can control could prevent outcomes at least as socially harmful as paying, say, 10% more for gasoline, then such regulation could be equivalently justified.

[4]The relative paucity of content targeting minority citizens is documented for radio in Joel Waldfogel (2003), "Who Benefits Whom in Differentiated Product Markets?" for daily newspapers in Lisa George and Joel Waldfogel (2003), "Who Affects Whom in Daily Newspaper Markets?" and for television in Joel Waldfogel (2004), "Who Benefits Whom in Local Television Markets?"

REFERENCES

Berry, S., & Waldfogel, J. (1999). Public radio in the U.S.: Does it correct market failure or cannibalize commercial stations? *Journal of Public Economics, 7,* 189–211.

Berry, S., & Waldfogel, J. (2001). Do mergers increase product variety? Evidence from radio broadcasting. *Quarterly Journal of Economics, 116,* 1009–1025.

Department of Justice & Federal Trade Commission. (1997). 1997 Merger Guidelines [Electronic version.]. Retrieved July 1, 2005, from http://www.usdoj.gov/atr/hmerger/11251.htm

Djankov, S., McLiesh, C., Nenova, T., & Shleifer, A. (2001, May). *Who owns the media?* (NBER Working Paper No. 8288). Cambridge, MA: National Bureau of Economic Research.

George, L., & Waldfogel, J. (2003). Who affects whom in daily newspaper markets? *Journal of Political Economy, 111,* 765–784.

Lichtenberg, F., & Waldfogel, J. (2003, June). *Does misery love company?: Evidence from pharmaceutical markets before and after the Orphan Drug Act* (NBER Working Paper No. 9750). Cambridge, MA: National Bureau of Economic Research.

Oberholzer-Gee, F., & Waldfogel, J. (2005, April). Strength in numbers: Group size and political participation. *Journal of Law and Economics, 98,* 73–91.

Siegelman, P., & Waldfogel, J. (2001). Race and radio: Preference externalities, minority ownership, and the provision of programming to minorities. In M. R. Baye & J. P. Nelson (Eds.), Advertising and differentiated products (pp. 73–108). Cambridge, MA: Elsevier.

Waldfogel, J. (2003). Who benefits whom in differentiated product markets? *RAND Journal of Economics, 34,* 557–568.

Waldfogel, J. (2004). Who benefits whom in local television markets? *Brookings-Wharton Papers in Urban Affairs, 3,* 257–284.

2

On Media Concentration and the Diversity Question*

Robert B. Horwitz

Department of Communication, University of California–San Diego

Corporate mergers and the consolidation of ownership in the American communications arena have long been sources of concern. The perception of a direct relationship between democracy and a vibrant communications system of diverse sources and owners is near universal (or, at least, is given universal lip-service), as is, for the most part, the converse fear that a communications system which rests in just a few hands will corrupt the freedom of speech, impair the practice of democracy, and impress an ideological pall on society. The Supreme Court's reasoning in the case of *Associated Press v. United States* (1945) expresses the issue plainly. In language that has since assumed a kind of talismanic status in discussions about the First Amendment and corporate power, the Court stated the following:

> [The First] Amendment rests on the assumption that the widest possible dissemination of information from diverse and antagonistic sources is essential to the welfare of the public, that a free press is a condition of a free society. Surely a command that the government itself shall not impede the free flow of ideas does not afford non-governmental combinations a refuge if they impose restraints upon that constitutionally guaranteed freedom. Freedom to publish means freedom for all and not for some. Freedom to publish is guaranteed by the Constitution, but freedom to combine to keep others from publishing is not. Freedom of the press from governmental in-

terference under the First Amendment does not sanction repression by private interests. (p. 20)

Distrust of government control of media is, of course, an elemental principle of American politics, encoded, among other places, in the First Amendment. But because the press could itself stifle freedom of speech through its business practices (in the *Associated Press* case, restrictive membership regulations), the First Amendment did not preclude government from applying the antitrust laws to that medium. A few years earlier in 1934, apprehension about private power in the then new medium of broadcasting saw Congress embed within the mandate of the Federal Communications Commission (FCC), broadcasting's new regulatory body, a general command to preserve competition in commerce in the broadcast medium and a specific directive to refuse a station license to any person adjudged guilty of unlawfully monopolizing or attempting unlawfully to monopolize radio communication. Congressional fears of radio's potentially dangerous concentration of political power in part underlay the Act's prohibition against any joint ownership of radio and wired systems as reflected in Sections 313 and 314 of the Communications Act (1934). In the period immediately following the second World War, the Commission on Freedom of the Press, conducting probably the most important study of mass media in the United States (undertaken by a distinguished group of intellectuals under the leadership of the famed educator, Robert Maynard Hutchins), rearticulated these concerns. Seeing in the ownership patterns of the postwar media system a distinct danger of concentration, the Hutchins Commission worried that such concentration undermined the press's crucial roles as conveyer of information, government watchdog, and educator (see Commission on Freedom of the Press, 1947).[1] In recent years, many Americans have become apprehensive as they watch a cascade of mergers among already very large media corporations.

In short, although fear of governmental power and government control of media is central to American politics, the dismay over the concentration of private power in media is a very strong undercurrent. U.S. regulatory and antitrust policy traditionally attempted to address the dangers of concentrated media power by securing a "diversity of voices" structurally, largely through rules regarding ownership. This chapter examines the history and logic of media ownership rules in the United States, and analyzes why, even as media corporations are becoming larger and presumably more powerful, ownership regulations are being rescinded or struck down. To this end, the analysis of the concept of diversity is a central focus. The framework of the chapter is as follows: The first part introduces the concept of diversity within the framework of the First Amendment and examines some of the problems in empirically assessing the efficacy of ownership rules. The second part presents the lineaments of the recent debate over whether media are, in fact, concentrated, and in so doing contrasts the antitrust mandate of the Department of Justice's Antitrust Division with the public interest touchstone of the FCC. The third part displays the main media ownership rules and their basis in regulatory theory and practice. The fourth part reviews the historical relationship between the FCC and the federal appellate courts, highlighting the courts's pressure on the FCC to issue more stringent ownership rules, particularly when the linkage was made between the diversity of voices to issues of race. Analysis of the majority and minority opinions in the important case of *Metro Broadcasting v. FCC* (1990) is a key focus. The fifth part follows the logic of Justice O'Connor's *Metro Broadcasting* dissent into several recent appellate court rulings that have struck down FCC ownership rules, and moreover, require the FCC to engage in "nonconjectural" empirical analysis to support its regulations in the ownership area. The sixth part concludes the chapter, ending with a suggestion that the First Amendment metaphor of marketplace of ideas is misplaced and how our thinking about media ownership and diversity might be better served by the metaphor of a mixed media system.

DIVERSITY WITHIN THE FIRST AMENDMENT FRAMEWORK

Traditionally, the dangers of ownership concentration in the communications industry were addressed by a combination of antitrust and regulatory policies that attempted to attend to the amalgamation of corporate power, but of course, did not question private power itself. The logic of government policy generally derived from the juxtaposition of the antitrust laws and regulatory practice with free speech jurisprudence. The First Amendment arguments are pretty familiar by now: The robust clash of opinions unimpeded by government is the prerequisite of democracy, that is, of self-government; an uninhibited exchange of diverse ideas yields better public choices, decisions, and policies; a free press provides a vital checking function on government actions and possible abuses; freedom of expression is a condition of being a human subject, enabling individuals to learn, grow, and realize their autonomy; the social system functions better when space is made for people to dissent or blow off steam publicly. The First Amendment literally forbids government from abridging the freedom of speech or press (in fact, the language literally forbids only Congress from abridging that freedom). Absent such abridgement, the speech marketplace is expected to secure the benefits listed earlier. The "marketplace of ideas," formulated by Justice Holmes in the dissent in

Abrams v. United States (1919), typically is the guiding metaphor in free speech jurisprudence.[2]

But the concentration of private power in the communications media may skew, if not undermine, the presumed free marketplace of ideas. To stay with the metaphor, concentrated media ownership tends to corrupt the marketplace and renders it dysfunctional. At the most basic level, concentrated ownership constricts the number and kinds of speakers. Owners of the communication systems that deliver content can erect bottlenecks that favor certain content providers and thwart others. In more pointed analyses that link the ownership question to the predominantly advertiser-supported structure of U.S. media, concentrated mass media are understood to shape content in ways that reproduce the prevailing structures of power and dominant cultural norms. At the very least, a commercially based media system is structurally biased toward content connected to marketable products and services, and, related, is biased away from content valued by the poor. Content that cannot attract commercial sponsorship tends not to see the light of day. To rectify these problems, Congress, the antitrust agencies, and the FCC enacted a set of policies over the decades designed to address media concentration by separating communication industries from each other and restricting common ownership. These policies were pursued under the general rubric of a concept of safeguarding a "diversity of owners" or "maintaining a diversity of voices." In some instances, such as those concerning telephone companies and broadcast outlets in the same market, or newspaper and broadcast outlets in the same market, common ownership was directly prohibited. Under the same diversity logic, the FCC also set ceilings on the numbers of broadcast outlets any single person or corporation could own. These limits, and the FCC's authority to make them, were upheld, occasionally even compelled, by the federal appellate courts.[3] In the early years "diversity" was not explicitly articulated as the theory that legitimated government policy on media ownership, but the theory always underlay the policy, and in recent decades, the word itself has become preeminent.[4]

In spite of the long-standing concern over the concentration of ownership, the efficacy of government interventions in American mass media area is hard to assess. It is difficult to know whether and to what degree Justice Department or Federal Trade Commission antitrust actions or FCC ownership rules safeguarded or promoted a free and diverse marketplace of ideas. A central problem here is what is meant by diversity, and how we should assess it. Should we understand diversity by the number of owners of media outlets, or rather (perhaps in addition) by the number of sources that provide content,[5] or by the number of different perspectives conveyed in information content, or, to take the question out of the dimension of the purely informational and political, by the number of distinct audience segments or demographics appealed to by various content providers, a measure that examines program formats? Or should we understand diversity by the varied racial composition of a media outlet's workforce?

Philip Napoli has written astutely on the varieties of diversity. In a useful typology, Napoli (1999) identifies source diversity as encompassing ownership (within which there is a subset distinction between the ownership of outlets and the ownership of content, a distinction very pertinent to cable television, for example, and the basis for the Financial Interest and Syndication Rules for broadcast) and workforce composition (the theory, connected to Equal Employment Opportunity policies, that a diverse workforce within any given media outlet would inherently stimulate interactions, the effects of which would diversify content and viewpoints). Content diversity encompasses format or program-type diversity, demographic diversity (particularly whether minority groups and other demographic groups are portrayed on television in reasonable proportion to their prevalence in society, a metric that has not been central to policymakers, but has been important to communication studies), and of course, idea-viewpoint diversity. Exposure diversity, in Napoli's view a neglected dimension, considers the diversity of content "as received," in the sense of actual media selection by audiences.[6] The FCC and Congress usually soft-pedaled the conceptual difficulties associated with diversity, sticking to generic praise of the policy, and assuming that a diversity of owners would translate to a diversity of formats, viewpoints, and audience segments catered to. But the assumption is part of the problem. Can ownership rules, concentration limits, and minority licensing preferences actually bring about desired changes in media content when they are applied in the context of the broader economic structure and sets of incentives and constraints inherent to an advertiser-supported media system? And if these rules, limits, and preferences did secure diverse media content, would audiences avail themselves of it?

There are two issues here. First, much evidence points to the strength of commercially rooted incentives and constraints. Owners, even diverse owners, may have particular ideological proclivities or programming visions, but the significant public goods features of media products, the economics of competition (with respect to the number of outlets and structure of existing audience preferences), and the bias toward content linked to marketable products and services, make it difficult for owners to follow through with those proclivities and visions.[7] Most empirical studies of the effects of ownership rules and other diversity remedies on media content and format are inconclusive at best—a fact that has always left hopeful media reformers somewhat disappointed.[8] Only the FCC's minority preference rules show some clear relationship between (minority) owners and altered content.[9] Conversely, there are some data that show an increase in diversity at the level of program formats as a result of deregulation and new entry.[10] The example that many commentators like to highlight (to some degree because of its paradoxical nature) is the Fox television network. Fox, the first new broadcast television network in 50-odd years, was made possible in part due to the expansion of independent television stations and cost reductions in satellite program distribution, but also ostensibly to the rollback of FCC rules on vertical integration (the Fin/Syn and Prime Time Access rules). Discovering an unmet market niche, Fox markedly increased the amount of Black-oriented entertainment programming on television (Farhi, 1994).

I referred to a second issue about ownership rules. If policy remedies are perceived as bringing about the desired changes in content, that is, if they are perceived as directly effective or even reflect the government's intention to be effective, do they violate the First Amendment's content neutrality doctrine?[11] Because the desire of government to bring direct changes in media content flirts uncomfortably close to the possible abrogation of the literal First Amendment, the usual phraseology is geared toward the more abstract and grandiloquent formulation of "enhancing the marketplace of ideas." Government ownership policies are meant not to secure specific changes in media content, but rather to alter the structure so that different kinds of owners have the opportunity to offer different content.

In the wake of the Telecommunications Act of 1996 and the wave of mergers subsequent to that legislation, and the explosive growth of the Internet, the concern about media concentration remains stronger than ever, but there is reason to believe that the question of diversity has become more complicated than ever. Three interrelated forces are at play. First is the combination of technological convergence in communications and the ideological triumph of liberalization or deregulation. If the traditional regulatory regime was devoted to the separation of elements of the communications industry, defined for the most part according to medium and technology, digitalization has undermined the technical basis of many of those separations. Indeed, a key impetus for the Telecommunications Act of 1996 was the dismantling of regulation-imposed separations, and fostering the ability for previously separated media and communications corporations to compete on each other's turfs (see Aufderheide, 1999).[12] With technological convergence and liberalization, and the growth of the Internet as an open delivery system, come new questions about the application of conventional antitrust tools, such as the identification of clear-cut product and geographic markets—the traditional building blocks in the determination of what's concentrated or not.[13] Some of this questioning is statutorily required. The Telecommunications Act instructed the FCC to eliminate one ownership rule and to revise five others. In view of this changed environment, second, the federal appellate courts, increasingly skeptical of congressional or regulatory assertions of media concentration and imposition of specific ownership rules, insist on a new concentration metric based on "nonconjectural" empirical evidence of anticompetitive behavior and verification of the efficacy of regulatory remedies. Third, this trend in communications law has been abetted by the way that a new conservative formalism in equal protection law has become attached to First Amendment jurisprudence. These jurisprudential developments underscore the enduring historical connection between the civil rights movement and media regulation. As has been mentioned, diversity analysis in mass media has always been a part of the regulatory mandate of the FCC, albeit in a general way. Diversity analysis attained significantly more bite when, in the late 1960s, civil rights litigation provided diversity a much more specific definition. In the media ownership arena, diversity's star, as it were, got hitched to the success of the legal logic of civil rights and affirmative action. After the 1960s, diversity in broadcasting and other communications industries under the authority of the FCC was assessed essentially by how accessible media were to minority, particularly racial minority, participation. As affirmative action and its jurisprudential logic have lost favor over the past 15 years, the principle of diversity in communications likewise has come under fire. This is best seen in a line of cases starting with Justice O'Connor's dissenting opinion in *Metro Broadcasting v. FCC* (1990). In this, the courts have brought to the media ownership debate a formalistic reading of the First Amendment, the upshot of which is sympathy for the arguments asserting the free-speech rights of corporations and increasing skepticism of the role of government in promoting diversity in mass media. Corporations have successfully used the new formalism to challenge media ownership policies as not meeting heightened First Amendment scrutiny.[14] So even as media corporations are becoming larger and presumably more powerful, ownership regulations are being rescinded or struck down.

ARE THE MEDIA CONCENTRATED?

Are American media concentrated, particularly in the light of the merger activity following the Telecommunications Act of 1996? One prominent line of argument responds in the negative. Whereas one finds a notable number of large mergers and combinations in the communications industry over the past 20 years or so, one also finds tremendous overall sectoral growth. Eli Noam (in press), for example, contrasts the early 1980s, when three television networks collectively controlled 92% of TV viewership, one company (AT&T) controlled 80% of local telephone service and nearly 100% of the long distance market, and another company (IBM) accounted for 77% of the computer market, to the mid-1990s, when, after the deregulation of cable television and the breakup of AT&T, the networks accounted for barely more than 50% of TV viewership, AT&T served 55% of the long distance market and had virtually no local customers, and no computer manufacturer supplied more than 12% of the microcomputer market. Noam explains that the long period of limited media, characterized by few players and government regulation to limit their market power, had given way to a period of multichannel communications that greatly expanded the overall media market. The market for broadcast, cable, print, and content grew from $151 billion in 1979, Noam notes, to $367 billion in 1993—an increase of 21% in constant dollars. And if the computer industry is included in this figure, the market grew from $168 billion in 1979 to $615 billion in 1993—83.5% growth in constant dollars. So, although there has been significant merger activity, the huge overall growth of the industry has alleviated any danger of concentration (also see Waterman, 2000). Moreover, the current multichannel communications environment, fueled by a technological juggernaut and now, with the 1996 Telecommunications Act, a procompetition policy structure, will enable the broad convergence of delivery platforms for telecommunications, mass media, and computer data distribution. Under these conditions, although there are particular, delimited, instances of market power, these will tend to erode as existing firms adapt and new firms enter the market.

Benjamin Compaine (2000) makes a similar argument. Notwithstanding recent megamergers, such as AOL-Time Warner and Viacom-CBS, media markets are in fact no more concentrated, according to traditional antitrust measures, than in previous decades. When the standard Herfindahl-Hirschman Index (HHI) of industry concentration is applied to the media industry, the change in concentration between 1986 and 1997 is trivial.[15] In fact, in some media subsectors, such as television broadcasting, the HHI was lower in 1997 than in 1994—before the wave of mergers commenced. Arguing that the appropriate unit of analysis for concentration measurement purposes is now the media industry *as a whole* rather than constituent market segments, Compaine (2000, pp. 560–561) finds that its HHI score of 268 reveals a remarkably unconcentrated industry. The shift to viewing the industry as a whole reflects the fact that changing patterns in technology and consumer media uses complicate the traditional geographic and product market distinctions pivotal to antitrust analysis. The Justice Department, FCC, and the appellate courts have now largely accepted the concept of "substitutes," that the product offered by, say, cable television, broadcast television, and video rentals, is essentially the same. Thus, under many circumstances, companies previously understood as individual media segments operating in separate product markets in fact compete and therefore should be included in the same product market for antitrust purposes.[16] When the product market is understood in that fashion and the communications industry evaluated as a whole, the industry does not appear concentrated; indeed, despite mergers, there is more competition than ever before. Finally, changes in delivery systems, in particular the nature and growth of the Internet, enable local radio and local newspapers to be delivered anywhere. Compaine and others argue that the Internet's capacity to erode old bottlenecks and blur lines between traditional media further complicates the traditional antitrust thinking about geographical markets, and thus requires us to move toward evaluating the media industry as a whole.

The overall growth of media (and the particular growth of the Internet) has important bearing on how to think about diversity and regulation. Economic models show that as the number of substitutable outlets increases, the audience fragments, and minority-interest content becomes economically viable, a fact that is born out empirically when the programming of, for instance, large cable television systems is monitored. In a limited media system, such as the old broadcast system, it might make sense to regulate vertically, that is, require that any individual outlet air a broad and diverse mix of programming; in an extensive media system, doesn't it make sense to look at the diversity question horizontally, that is, across all substitutable outlets? If so, and that market shows no troublesome concentration, government intervention is not needed, and is, in fact, pernicious. Simple vigilance on the antitrust front will safeguard diversity.

Opposed to this relatively sanguine position on media concentration is a critique that rests less on conventional ownership concentration ratios per se than, rather, the recognition that the media are situated within the wider relations of power. In particular, the analysis of mergers is embedded within a critique of the commercial structure of American media. Ben Bagdikian (1983, 1997), perhaps the dean of contemporary critics of media concentration, insists that the great mergers of communications firms over the past two decades have grave effects on the type and diversity of information available. Writing in 1983 in the first of several editions of *The Media Monopoly*, Bagdikian argued that not only do a smaller number of owners have possession of larger and larger numbers of media properties, but for the first time in the history of American journalism, news and public information have been integrated formally into the highest levels of financial and nonjournalistic corporate control. In Bagdikian's analysis, media mergers have reduced the number of controlling corporate players from approximately 50 in 1984 to 10 in 1996. In an age when face-to-face communication is far less important for politics than mass-mediated communication and information, media power is, baldly, political power. Bagdikian (1997, p. ix) writes in the 5th edition, "… [T]he communication cartel has exercised stunning influence over national legislation and government agencies, an influence whose scope and power would have been considered scandalous or illegal twenty years ago." As communication scholar James Curran (2000) succinctly puts it, the issue is no longer simply that the media may be compromised by their links to big business; the media *are* big business. This makes the old "democratic watchdog on power" claim rather time-worn. The concentration of media ownership has led to more controlled information, fewer and less diverse sources of information, and thus less "real" information despite a purported information overload. The ownership of communication media by large corporate conglomerates creates greater likelihood that the old firewalls between news and advertising, between news and entertainment, and between entertainment and rank product placement, erode. Conglomerated corporate ownership also means treating communication media as economic properties pure and simple, without the traditional conflicted balance between profit and public service experienced by stand-alone publishers or broadcast groups. That balance may have been a piece of self-legitimating ideology of traditional news organizations, but the very existence of the discourse meant that there were grounds for criticism and sites through which to exercise pressure both within and without media organizations. The high prices paid for media properties in this most recent wave of acquisitions means heavy financial pressures for each media property, including news and journalism outlets, to be profitable. The widely noted cutbacks in broadcast news divisions and instances of commercial conflicts of interest at even quality newspapers in the 1990s would appear to confirm Bagdikian's point (see Downie & Kaiser, 2002; Hamilton, 2004).

Edward Herman and Robert McChesney (1997), among others, expand Bagdikian's argument to a worldwide focus and examine the remarkable vertical integration of international media holdings that has occurred over the last few years. The vaunted "synergies" of such integration, where a large national cable system operator may combine with a movie production studio, which already has television station holdings in several nations, magazine publishing, and an Internet portal, result in packaged news and entertainment product characterized by self-promotion and the celebration of the capitalist system of which they mediate. For Herman and McChesney, this isn't just transnational control over exported media content (the earlier form of Western media hegemony) so much as increasing transnational corporate control over media distribution and content within nations, in which formerly public media systems are transformed into commercial systems based on advertising. This ownership structure has unmistakable consequences on media content: a concentration of attention on the stock market rather than poverty and inequality, on business rather than labor, on celebrity rather than social movements and pressing social problems.[17] Advertising values, for the most part, rule over media content, imparting an ethic of consumption and hedonism. The market generally underproduces certain kinds of content, pointedly including content with positive externalities, such as investigative journalism and public affairs analysis, whose watchdog impacts affect far more people than actually consume the specific media product (Baker, 2001). As has been noted for decades, the market ordinarily fails to represent and serve minorities. Contrary to the canard of the liberal media, mainstream commercial media generally avoid presenting political viewpoints of the left, largely due to the left's intrinsic critique of commercialism and corporate power. Synergies of common ownership, especially when they are news outlets, become the vehicle for the outlets to promote, not compete with, the other outlets. Notwithstanding that there may be more communication outlets than ever before, the critics argue, more is actually less. It is not the total number of outlets that matters, but the number of owners (see Cooper, 2003).

Exacerbating these trends is a propensity of industry competitors to enter into cooperative agreements regardless of ownership, and the fact that consolidations of distributors and content creators invariably lead to concentrated information systems (see Benkler, 1999; Hill & Landro, 2000; Tunstall & Machin, 1999; Wysocki, 2000). The Internet, for all its wonders, is at risk of being dominated by the same entities that dominate other media and which threaten to destroy its open architecture (see Bar et al., 1999; Lessig & Lemley, 1999).[18] Finally, contrary to the argument that more outlets create substitutes, in actuality, substitution effects are rather weak because people value content differently, especially with regard to news and information. Relying simply on antitrust to safeguard media diversity is misplaced, because for antitrust purposes, the product market for (much) media is advertising, whereas the underlying basis of diversity revolves around content.[19] The advertising market thus cannot be a simple surrogate for content, because the concern about ownership concentration in media cannot rest just on possible economic harm and the ability to practice price discrimination; the concern about media concentration focuses on the access to receive and produce information. Hence any antitrust theory that focuses solely on market power over pricing will be too limited in its consideration of the negative features of media concentration (see Baker, 2002; Consumers Union, Consumer Federation of America, Civil Rights Forum, Center for Digital Democracy, & Leadership Conference on Civil Rights and Media Project, 2002; Cooper, 2003). Concentrated ownership in the communications media yields diminished editorial voice, the decline of journalistic values, diminution of the press's watchdog function, reduction in the diversity of ideas, and, as a consequence, thwarts democratic deliberation.

To some degree, the stark differences between these perspectives on media concentration reflect a long-standing divergence among scholars and lawyers regarding the purpose of antitrust laws, and, more generally, a market economics versus social value perspective on communications policy. Media mergers, like all industrial combinations, require scrutiny by the Department of Justice (DOJ) and Federal Trade Commission (FTC). Section 7 of the Clayton Antitrust Act (1914) requires the DOJ and FTC to evaluate the anticompetitive ramifications of mergers, but also their potential efficiencies as well in terms of bringing economies of scale, lower transaction costs, technological synergies, and so forth. An exclusively economic focus on allocative efficiency, the society's total wealth, is fairly characteristic of the Chicago School approach to antitrust. The dominant concern is that mergers should not be permitted "to create or enhance market power or to facilitate its exercise" by enabling firms to "impose at least a 'small but significant and nontransitory' increase in price" (U.S. Department of Justice and the Federal Trade Commission, 1992). In this view, the purpose of antitrust is to promote economic efficiency, not equitable distribution, making results (not actions) the criteria for legal judgments. But antitrust law also encompasses other than economic concerns, including, for instance, preventing the loss of communities's local economic independence to large absentee corporations, protecting small business, and preserving the social and civic ties that bind communities, as embodied in the Celler-Kefauver Amendment (1950) to the Clayton Act. This emphasis on the social and political values of antitrust law is championed by the Multivalued approach to antitrust.[20] Those values are part and parcel of the Federal Communications Commission's charge. Because of the special role that the communications media play in a democracy, especially, perhaps, at the local level, media mergers must be approved by the FCC. In light of the DOJ and FTC's proclivity toward looking primarily at efficiency concerns, the FCC in many respects has a broader charge in the media merger area. The FCC must determine whether a proposed merger is consistent with the public interest, convenience, or necessity, which traditionally has been interpreted as, among other things, whether the merger promotes competition and the diversity of voices, and whether it poses special dangers to diversity in the local setting. Indeed, the public interest standard in principle compelled the FCC to act in advance of specific antitrust problems. If, generally speaking, the aim of antitrust is to prevent "restraint of trade," a principal aim of the 1934 Communication Act came to be interpreted by the FCC as the prevention of "restraint of trade in ideas" over the airwaves. The FCC's policy of promoting diversity is distinct from the goal of promoting competition.[21] It may be too strong to state that the Noam and Compaine position is tied to the Chicago School of antitrust and the market economics perspective on communications policy, whereas the Bagdikian and Herman and McChesney position is tied to the Multivalued antitrust approach and social value perspective on policy, but the proclivities of the former to economic efficiency and the proclivities of the latter to social and political values seem pretty clear.

MEDIA OWNERSHIP RULES

Let us proceed by returning to fundamentals. As has been mentioned, Congress and the FCC typically addressed antitrust issues by separating communication industries from each other and restricting common ownership. One of the most important separations, enacted at the beginning of federal regulation, was that between broadcast and common carrier. A broadcaster could not operate as a telephone provider, and effectively, could not own the delivery system that linked broadcast stations in a network. The broadcaster was explicitly responsible for the content aired over the station. Telephone companies provided access to the wired delivery system on a nondiscriminatory basis, and, as common carriers, were not responsible for the content sent over the system. This essentially encoded into law and policy a division of industry hammered out among the principal corporate players in 1926 (Barnouw, 1966). The FCC endeavored to foster diversity and forestall monopolization in broadcasting by a series of (vague) content and behavioral regulations that, in the wake of the Report on Chain Broadcasting (1941), were augmented by structural regulations. Structural regulations established ceilings on the number of broadcast stations an entity could own nationally, forbade (in theory) the dominance of a local market through cross-ownership restrictions and a rule that an entity could own just a single outlet in a local area, and effectively dictated that broadcast networks must be owned by different entities. Some structural rules were designed to enhance competition and cultivate new programming. The 1970 Financial Interest and Syndication Rules, which barred television networks from owning the firms that provided their programming, were enacted in an attempt to increase programming diversity by separating production from distribution in broadcast television. The Prime Time Access

Rule, also enacted in 1979, cleared out an hour of television prime time from network control so that local stations would air their own programming. Specific content rules, such as the Fairness Doctrine and associated rules of section 315 of the Communications Act, were enacted to ensure that broadcasters would present issues of concern and controversy in their programming, guarantee access to stations by candidates for political office, and ensure that informational and editorial programming was aired with a degree of fairness and balance. Other content rules included various regulations against indecent programming. The FCC also developed more specific behavioral rules, such as requiring that broadcasters meet with community groups in their broadcast market to ascertain their concerns and interests. The public interest—understood in terms of the maintenance of diverse viewpoints, some degree of local control and local program orientation, a general balance of programming (including of controversial topics), and equitable treatment of political candidates—was the ultimate linchpin of oversight.

The main ownership rules in electronic mass media were historically as follows:

- Dual network rule prohibited broadcast stations from affiliating with any entity that maintained more than a single network.—One of the earliest rules on ownership, the rule grew out of the FCC's investigation on "chain broadcasting" and was applied to radio in 1941, then to television in 1946. The rule was eliminated with regard to radio in 1977. The Telecommunications Act of 1996 revised the rule for television to prohibit a party from affiliating with an entity if that entity controlled more than one of the four largest networks—ABC, CBS, Fox, and NBC—or with an entity that controlled one of these four networks and either of two emerging networks (UPN and WB). In 2001, the FCC amended the rule to permit one of the four major television networks to own, operate, maintain, or control the UPN or the WB network.
- One-to-a-market rule prohibited the common ownership of a radio and a television station serving substantial areas in common (although waivers were routinely granted).—Waivers were routinely granted in part because in the early years of television, the FCC encouraged radio licensees to obtain TV licenses to spur the growth of the new medium. Only later did the FCC see a problem in common ownership. Since 1989, the FCC generally waived the rule in the top 25 markets if, after the combination, there remained at least 30 separately owned independent voices (including radio and TV stations, and certain local newspapers and cable stations) in the market.
- Television duopoly rule prohibited common ownership or control of television stations with overlapping Grade B signal contours, dating from

1964. As a rule, the FCC considered anyone with an interest of at least 5% in the media company as an owner. (But Local Market Agreements, through which an owner turned over programming to other broadcast owners, undermined the rule.)—The rule was replaced in 1999 so that a company may own two television stations in the same Nielsen designated market area (deemed more appropriate than the Grade B signal contour measurement) if one of the stations is not among the four highest ranked stations in the market, and so long as eight independently owned, full-power, operational television stations remain in the market after the merger.

- National multiple ownership rules limited the total number of television and radio stations an entity could own nationally, irrespective of location.—As originally promulgated in the early 1940s, the rules prohibited common ownership of more than three television stations. Between 1953 and 1985, the number was seven AM radio, seven FM radio, and seven television stations (with a maximum of five in the VHF band). In 1984, the FCC increased the ceiling to 12-12-12, and in 1992, the FCC raised the national radio ownership limits to 30 AM and 30 FM. The rise in ownership caps in part accompanied expansions in the bands and in the number of licensed stations. The Telecommunications Act of 1996 repealed all national ownership limits for radio; locally a company may now own five to eight radio stations in a single market, depending on the size of the market. The Act also repealed the 12-station national cap for television, preventing a single company from owning stations that reach more than 35% of the nationwide television audience.
- Television networks could not own shares of the firms that provided their programming (Financial Interest and Syndication Rules).—The FCC implemented the rule in 1970 in an attempt to increase programming diversity by separating production from distribution in broadcast television. The FCC relaxed the Fin-Syn rules in 1991 and appeals courts later relaxed the rules even further, in essence eliminating all traces of Fin-Syn by 1995.
- Cable horizontal ownership: Pursuant to the requirements of the Telecommunications Act of 1996, the FCC adopted rules prohibiting any one entity from having an attributable interest in cable systems reaching more than 30% of cable homes passed nationwide.—The FCC changed the method by which the horizontal ownership cap was to be calculated in 1999, effectively raising it from 30% to 36.7%. The cap in general was found not suitably justified in *Time Warner v. FCC* (2001).
- Cable vertical ownership: Pursuant to the requirements of the Telecommunications Act of 1996, a cable company could not have any ownership affiliation with more than 40% of the programming that it carried on

any of its cable systems with up to 75 channels. On systems with more than 75 channels, 45 channels were required to be reserved for nonaffiliated programming.—This cap was found not suitably justified in *Time Warner v. FCC* (2001).

- Broadcast and newspaper cross-ownership rule: Although concern over such combinations surfaced at the FCC as early as the 1930s, an appellate court decision declared in dicta that the FCC could not prohibit newspaper publishers, as a class, from receiving licenses to operate broadcast stations (see *Stahlman v. FCC,* 1942). Adopted in 1975, the FCC prohibited the same company from owning a newspaper and a broadcast station in the same market.—The FCC "grandfathered" almost all historical combinations.
- Broadcast networks and cable systems cross-ownership rule: Adopted in 1970, the FCC prohibited the same company from owning a broadcasting network and a cable system.—Relaxed in 1992, the rule was eliminated by the 1996 Telecommunications Act.
- Broadcast and cable cross-ownership rule: Adopted in 1970, the FCC prohibited the same company from owning a cable system and a broadcast television station in the same local market. Congress codified the policy in 1984.—The 1996 Telecommunications Act eliminated the statutory cross-ownership restriction but retained the FCC rule. Thus, cross-ownership is at the FCC's discretion.
- Cable and telephone cross-ownership rule: Adopted in 1970 with the intention to protect cable television from telephone companies, the FCC prohibited the same company from owning a cable system and a telephone system in the same market.—The rule was eliminated by the 1996 Telecommunications Act.
- Finally, the Telecommunications Act of 1996 (Sec. 202[h]) requires the FCC to review each of its ownership rules every 2 years to "determine whether any of such rules are necessary in the public interest as a result of competition," directing the Commission to "repeal or modify any regulation it determines to be no longer in the public interest."

The legitimation of most of the FCC's structural and many of its behavioral and content rules were weaved in and around a diversity rationale that was itself premised on the proper role of government in licensing applicants of a scarce public resource. The scarcity theory, that broadcast frequencies were inherently physically (or "naturally") scarce and thus required government to assign them—the standard accepted constitutional basis for the regulation of broadcasting—has come under considerable fire in recent years. Many courts and commentators have cast doubt on the continued relevance of the scarcity rationale, particularly given the recent growth of the medium.[22] But the rationale for the regulation of broadcasting, as C. Edwin Baker (1995) and others have argued, was never premised simply on the basis of natural scarcity, but of scarcity ensconced within a problem of the commons and a fear of radio's potential to focus political power. As every standard history of broadcasting recounts, before the licensing of frequencies in 1927, interference plagued the airwaves. The limited availability of a valuable resource, combined with the absence of some form of governmental or social allocation of usage rights, resulted in overuse, making the resource worthless to everyone. Natural scarcity exists when there is no legal definition of rights. In the language of the Court of Appeals in *National Citizens Committee for Broadcasting v. FCC* (1977):

> The need for some regulation of the airwaves became clear in the 1920's when there was none. 'With everybody on the air, nobody could be heard' (quoting *National Broadcasting Co. v. U.S.*, 1943). In order to ensure the public's ability to hear some speakers, the rights of other potential speakers were curtailed. The hard choice was between forcing free speech to bend or watching it break. (p. 948)

In other words, the private system of allocation was unable to solve the problem of the commons. The government responded with a licensing regime that, because licenses were given away without charge, inevitably created a second scarcity. Could or should the government have created a standard, exclusionary private property right in the spectrum? Again, as any standard broadcast history will tell, that possibility was recognized and rejected in 1927 as embedding a "right of selfishness" in the medium (*Red Lion Broadcasting Corp. v. FCC,* 1969, p. 376, n. 5, quoting the House sponsor of the 1927 Radio Act, Representative Wallace H. White). The reasons for rejecting private property rights in the spectrum were unanimously affirmed by the Supreme Court in *Red Lion*. Noting broadcasters's claim to have unlimited choice in respect to the use of their licenses, that is, their ability to treat the license like private property, the *Red Lion* Court cited *Associated Press* (1945) that the "First Amendment does not sanction repression of that freedom by private interests" (p. 392). The Court rejected the print model of private First Amendment rights for broadcasting. In C. Edwin Baker's (1995) words, the Court in *Red Lion* "essentially held that the government has the power to structure the media in a manner that the government thinks will promote the best communications environment" (p. 104). Whether or not this is the Court's understanding of itself, when presented an explicit opportunity in 1994 to repudiate the scarcity doctrine, the Court "declined to question its continuing validity" (*Turner Broadcasting v. FCC,* 1994).

The diversity argument essentially flowed from this logic. Through the licensing process, government grants broadcast frequencies to private parties. To make sure that a robust marketplace of ideas prevails in the broadcast medium, the government sets limits on how many stations a single private entity may own, made sure, for example, that a single voice would not monopolize a local community through the common ownership of broadcast and newspaper, and required a broadcast licensee to open up its frequency to other viewpoints. This set of interventions had its limits, of course. Government could not censor programs and government could not direct content. Indeed, the Fairness Doctrine, adopted in 1959 to formalize the expectation that broadcasters should air contrasting viewpoints, vested in the broadcaster the power to initiate debate and to select the mode for producing viewpoint balance. It was these fundamental limits on government that prompted the FCC to pursue its primary strategy for fostering diversity through ownership regulations.

Diversity was always a concern of the FCC, although in the early years it was implicit, wrapped within the problem of getting broadcasters to fulfill their public interest responsibilities. The public trustee status of broadcast licensees meant that they were to serve a public, rather than a purely private function, which, in turn, meant that they were in principle obliged, within reason, to air a varied set of programs, including news, religious programs, weather, and other types of local productions, to a range of audiences. This was what we now call format diversity, understood vertically, that is, within each broadcast outlet. It must be acknowledged, of course, that this regulatory effort was undertaken within an advertiser-supported broadcast structure and in a political context subject to the exigencies of institutional bias and influence peddling, in which various incarnations of the FCC issued license grants to commercial and corporate broadcasters in the early years and to political cronies in succeeding years (see, among others, Rosen, 1980; Schwartz, 1959). When the FCC (and in its earlier incarnation as the Federal Radio Commission) wasn't giving away frequencies to favored constituents, it struggled, contrarily and with limited success, to formulate policies that would encourage broadcasting in the public interest against the strong constraints established by a commercially based broadcasting system. As the consequences of broadcasting's commercial structure and the FCC's largely corporate license grants became clear, the FCC initiated some structural policies to deal with what was then termed *the problem of monopolization* (Report on Chain Broadcasting, 1941), and behavioral policies to induce broadcast licensees to air, among other things, more public affairs, educational, and locally oriented programming (Network Programming Inquiry, 1960). In 1953, the FCC promulgated the first of its multiple ownership rules on the logic that the "fundamental purpose" of the rules was "to promote diversification of ownership in order to maximize diversification of program and service viewpoints" (Amendment of Sections 3.35, 3.240, and 3.636 of Rules and Regulations Relating to Multiple Ownership of AM, FM, and Television Broadcast Stations, 1953). A 1964 amendment to those rules stated that "the greater the diversity of ownership in a particular area, the less chance there is that a single person or group can have an inordinate effect in a ... programming sense, on public opinion at the regional level" (Amendment of Sections 73.35, 73.240, and 73.636 of Commission's Rules Relating to Multiple Ownership of AM, FM, and Television Broadcast Stations, 1964, p. 1482). Diversification of ownership was one of the comparative criteria used by the FCC to assess applicants competing for a broadcast license (Policy Statement on Comparative Broadcast Hearings, 1965).

Diversity per se became a more explicit concern of the FCC as broadcasting issues and the African American civil rights struggle intermingled. The famous WLBT case *(Office of Communications of the United Church of Christ v. FCC, 1966)*, whose political import was the expansion of the legal doctrine of standing (thus opening up regulatory agencies and courts to parties without direct economic interest in any given controversy), illustrated that broadcasters were not just ignoring huge portions of their audience, but in that instance routinely aired racist programming and practiced workplace discrimination as well (Horwitz, 1997). The Kerner Commission Report on the causes of the racial unrest of the 1960s noted that American media presented an almost totally White world (National Advisory Commission on Civil Disorders, 1968). The broadcast reform movement of the 1960s, very often linked to and fueled by the civil rights struggle, challenged broadcasters to air content pertinent to minority audiences and to hire minorities at the stations, and pressed the FCC to enforce the public interest standard of the Communications Act (Fife, 1984). The FCC accommodated some of these demands under the conceptual rubric of diversity. The negligible presence of minority and ethnic groups in broadcasting—whether in ownership, programming, or station employment—was a major element behind the FCC's behavioral regulations such as the requirement for licensees to "ascertain" the communities to which they broadcast and to air programming relevant to these ascertained local community concerns (Chapman Radio and Television Co., 1970; Primer on Ascertainment of Community Problems by Broadcast Applicants, 1971). The promulgation of equal opportunity regulations in station employment was another example of the influence of the civil rights movement on the FCC's agenda (Nondiscrimination in the Employment Policies and Practices of

Broadcast Licensees, 1976; Petition for Rulemaking to Require Broadcast Licensees to Show Nondiscrimination in their Employment Practices, 1968).[23] By the 1970s, this movement began to affect policy on ownership, as well, largely via pressure from the courts.

THE FCC, MINORITY OWNERSHIP POLICIES, AND THE FEDERAL COURTS

Although the diversification of ownership was one factor of several in the mix of elements considered by the FCC in comparative hearings for broadcast license applications before 1973, minority ownership was not. The FCC, arguing that the Communications Act was "colorblind," would take an applicant's race into account only to the extent that the applicant could show that his or her race would likely lead to better, more diverse programming in the particular instance. In 1973, in a case called *TV9, Inc. v. FCC,* the D.C. Circuit Court of Appeals ruled that the racial identity of an African American applicant for a radio license was a relevant consideration in choosing between and among applicants. There was no justification of minority preference as remedial to past discrimination; the court reasoned that minority ownership could result in diverse programming. In the wake of the *TV 9* decision, the FCC formulated a policy that gave evaluation enhancement in comparative hearings to minority ownership and participation in station management by members of minority groups.[24] The FCC's Review Board subsequently extended this enhancement to women (Gainesville Media, Inc., 1978). However, women's enhancement was less than that of racial minorities, because women, in the FCC's view, have "not been excluded from the mainstream of society" due to prior discrimination (a statement that did insert a notion of minority preferences as remedial, but in a general way, not specific to broadcasting; Mid-Florida Television Corp., 1978). Included in the FCC's Statement of Policy on Minority Ownership of Broadcasting Facilities (1978) were a minority tax certificate program (which provided incentives to owners of existing broadcast properties to sell their properties to minorities) and a distress sale program (which allowed a broadcast licensee whose license had been designated for a revocation hearing to sell his station to a minority-controlled entity at 75% or less of the station's fair-market value). The tax certificate program allowed the seller to defer any gain realized on the sale if the property was sold to a minority purchaser, and the gain was rolled over into a qualified replacement broadcast property.

In 1984, the D.C. Circuit Court of Appeals affirmed the legality of the minority preference in comparative hearings under the Communication Act's public interest standard. The court argued that the *TV 9* decision "required" the FCC to assume that Black owners would present distinctive programming valuable not just for Black audiences but for all audiences by exposing them to new ideas and points of view. Proof of actual connection between minority or female ownership and diversity in program content was not required (*West Michigan Broadcasting Co. v. FCC,* 1984). And in 1985, the FCC amended its multiple ownership rules, allowing a nonminority owner to take a noncontrolling interest in an additional 2 minority-controlled television stations, making for a TV ownership limit of 14 stations (in contrast to the then normal limit of 12), if the aggregate audience of all its stations did not exceed 30% of the national audience. The aim was to foster minority ownership (Amendment of Section 73.3555 of the Commission's Rules Relating to Multiple Ownership of AM, FM, and Television Broadcast Stations, 1985).

The legitimization of these policies was premised on the presumed connection between ownership diversity and the program and viewpoint diversity it would bring. "Full minority participation in the ownership and management of broadcast facilities results in a more diverse selection of programming. In addition, an increase in ownership by minorities will inevitably enhance the diversity of control of a limited resource, the spectrum," wrote the FCC in its Statement of Policy on Minority Ownership of Broadcasting Facilities (1978, p. 981). The expected viewpoint diversity was woven into a broader argument on the particularly beneficial consequences of equal employment opportunities in the broadcast industry, "which could 'contribute significantly toward reducing and ending discrimination in other industries' because of the 'enormous impact which television and radio have upon American life'" (*Metro Broadcasting v. FCC,* 1990, p. 555, quoting Nondiscrimination in the Employment Policies and Practices of Broadcast Licensees, 1976). Roughly similar preference programs were applied to cable television and enacted in wireless spectrum lotteries and auctions, for which Congressional legislation directed the FCC to give minority groups and women bidding credits (Policies and Rules Regarding Minority and Female Ownership of Cable Television Facilities, 1982). In the wireless area, the viewpoint diversity argument was not relevant, of course. The bidding credits policy partook of the general affirmative action logic of ensuring that minority groups and women would not in any way be excluded from the competitive bidding process for spectrum.[25]

It is probably the case that viewpoint diversity was always the ultimate aim in these broadcast ownership policies from the 1970s—although other manifestations of diversity, such as source, format, workforce, and audience (or demographic) diversity assumed both independent and instrumental importance, especially because of the intersection of civil rights and broadcasting. In some of its documents, the FCC directly stated that the diversity of ownership of outlets and sources was merely a means to promote the diversity of viewpoints (see, e.g., Review of the Commission's Regulations Governing Television Broadcasting: Further Notice of Proposed Rulemaking, 1995). It is viewpoint diversity that lies at the heart of the "profound national commitment to the principle that debate on public issues should be uninhibited, robust, and wide-open," embodied in First Amendment jurisprudence and famously articulated in *New York Times v. Sullivan* (1964, p. 270)—itself a case rooted in the civil rights struggle. But because any direct pursuit of viewpoint diversity butts up against First Amendment content neutrality doctrine and the provision against censorship in the Communications Act, a more indirect set of strategies, calling on assumed and logically linked, but often unproved, assumptions were employed. In this regard, the diversity of ownership was assumed to translate into format, demographic, and, down the line, viewpoint diversity. The train of logic went something like this: Putting a ceiling on the ownership of stations not only safeguarded the broadcast medium from being dominated by a single or a few owners, but also ensured the likelihood that different owners would have commitments to distinct broadcast formats and thus reach different audiences. The diversity of owners and formats would translate into a diversity of viewpoints. Similarly, the diversity of broadcast station workforces was expected somehow to infuse the content and viewpoint of broadcast stations. This was understood as especially true in the case with racial minority groups, inasmuch as minority audiences, a series of FCC studies concluded, were not programmed to by traditional (White) station owners and their White employees (Ascertainment of Community Problems by Broadcast Applicants, 1976; *Office of Communications of the United Church of Christ v. FCC,* 1966; Public Service Responsibility of Broadcast Licensees, 1946).

In general, the diversity rationale received strong approval in both judicial and congressional forums for the roughly 20 years between 1970 and 1990. In *National Citizens Committee for Broadcasting v. FCC* (1977), quoting Second Report and Order (1974; emphasis added), for instance, the Court of Appeals upheld an FCC rule forbidding the future formation or transfer of colocated newspaper-broadcast combinations. The court restated with vigor the FCC's assertion that, "If our democratic society is to function, *nothing can be more important* than insuring that there is a free flow of information from as many divergent sources as possible" (p. 946). Indeed, in this case, the court vacated and remanded the portion of the FCC's rule that limited divestiture to egregious cases of effective monopoly essentially on the grounds that the limitation eroded the diversity motive. The court, in short, considered the FCC's divestiture policy too meek: "... [W]e believe precisely the opposite presumption is compelled, and that divestiture is required except in those cases where the evidence clearly discloses that cross-ownership is in the public interest" (p. 966). Congress acknowledged the link between minority ownership and diversity in programming in 1982, when it directed the FCC to employ a minority-ownership preference in the newly authorized lottery program for the selection of applicants for any medium of mass communications (House of Representatives Conference Report, 1982).

The minority preference diversity logic reached its high-water mark in a Supreme Court ruling upholding the constitutionality of the FCC minority preference policies in comparative hearings and the minority distress sale program in broadcasting—but by a narrow 5 to 4 margin cobbled together by Justice Brennan. *Metro Broadcasting v. FCC* (1990) found that programming diversity represented an "important" governmental interest and that the FCC minority preference policies were substantially related to the achievement of that objective. In First Amendment terms, this meant that the affirmative action regulations triggered only intermediate scrutiny, because

> benign race-conscious measures mandated by Congress—even if those measures are not "remedial" in the sense of being designed to compensate victims of past governmental or society discrimination—are constitutionally permissible to the extent that they serve important governmental objectives within the power of Congress and are substantially related to achievement of those objectives. (pp. 564–565)

Relying on Justice Powell's formulation in *Regents of the University of California v. Bakke* (1978), that just as a "diverse student body" contributing to a robust exchange of ideas is a "constitutionally permissible goal" on which a race-conscious university admissions program may be predicated, the Court majority in *Metro Broadcasting v. FCC* (1990) determined that the diversity of views and information on the airwaves serves important First Amendment values. The intermediate scrutiny standard was consistent with previous decisions involving affirmative action plans sponsored by the federal government under Congress's powers in accordance with paragraph 5 of the 14th Amendment (*Fullilove v. Klutznick*, 1980).[26] The minority ownership policies primarily reflected Congress and the FCC's goals to promote programming diversity, said the majority in *Metro Broadcasting v. FCC* (1990, p. 566, quoting H.R. Conf. Rep., 1982), but it also indicated that the policies had some remedial purpose ("Congress found 'that the effects of past inequities stemming from racial and ethnic discrimination have resulted in a severe underrepresentation of minorities in the media of mass communications'"; 1990, p. 566). But there is no factual record that the underrepresentation of minorities in broadcasting was due to discrimination on the part of the FCC, an important distinction in equal protection claims against government. In keeping with prevailing doctrine on judicial review, particularly when a program employing a benign racial classification is adopted by an administrative agency at the explicit direction of Congress, the Court majority found that Congress's fact-finding and the FCC's expertise on the nexus between minority ownership and programming diversity should be given great weight. The *Metro Broadcasting v. FCC* (1990, n. 16) majority favorably quoted the FCC to the effect that "ownership carries with it the power to select, to edit, and to choose the methods, manner and emphasis of presentation" (p. 570). And in the majority's judgment, those data showed a substantial relationship between broadcast diversity and minority preferences.[27]

It may be, however, that the real importance of *Metro Broadcasting v. FCC* was Justice O'Connor's strong dissent, as that opinion laid out the jurisprudential framework for the series of cases reversing minority preferences and casting doubt on the logic of the diversity rationale in broadcasting. In fact, O'Connor's dissent in *Metro Broadcasting v. FCC* reflected a battle that had been simmering throughout the 1980s between an FCC, now reflecting Reagan administration ideology, and a more liberal Congress, and between judges of the District of Columbia Circuit Court of Appeals (itself part of the battle between liberal and conservative jurists in that circuit over the nature of judicial review of regulatory decisions; see Horwitz, 1994). In *Steele v. FCC* (1985), for example, a three-judge panel struck down the FCC's gender enhancement policy in comparative license hearings. The majority argued that there was no evidence that women owners would manifest a distinctly female viewpoint (raising questions about what a female viewpoint is and underscoring the problematic essentialism that sometimes pervades the analysis of difference), and further, implied that the government's assumption that a station owner's heritage will determine his or her interests was to engage in the kind of stereotyping that the law forbade. The case subsequently was heard by the D.C. Circuit *en banc,* which vacated the panel's opinion and judgment. In supplemental briefs, the FCC (1984), now dominated by Reagan appointees under the chairmanship of Mark Fowler, claimed that the link between its preference schemes and increased diversity of viewpoints had no factual support, and declared that the race and gender preference policies were contrary to both the Communications Act and the Constitution. When the Commission initiated an inquiry calling for public comments on the preference policies, Congress ordered it to desist (and even forbade the FCC to analyze the data it had gathered in its effort to scuttle the minority preference rules) in a rider to the Continuing Appropriations Act for Fiscal Year 1988 (1987). A divided appellate panel from the D.C. Circuit struck down the Commission's distress sale program as unconstitutional in *Shurberg Broadcasting, Inc. v. FCC* (1989), whereas a divided panel upheld the Commission's comparative licensing program for racial and ethnic minorities on statutory and constitutional grounds in *Winter Park Communications, Inc. v. FCC* (1989).

These issues came to the Supreme Court in *Metro Broadcasting v. FCC* (1990), and the opinions in that case reflected the conflicts that had been churning in the D.C. Circuit. Justice O'Connor's dissent in *Metro Broadcasting v. FCC* pivoted on the level of scrutiny required of racial preferences. She argued that intermediate scrutiny would not do. All racial classifications, even "benign" ones, required the Supreme Court to apply a strict standard of scrutiny, because such classifications inherently "endorse race-based reasoning and the conception of a Nation divided into racial blocs," contrary to the Constitution's guarantee of equal protection that "Government must treat citizens 'as individuals, not as simply components of a racial, religious, sexual or national class'" (pp. 602, 603). Indeed, she argued that a "benign" racial classification "is a contradiction in terms," because there is no way to determine which classifications are benign and which are motivated by illegitimate notions of racial inferiority (p. 609). Thus, only congressional measures that seek to remedy identified past discrimination do not presumptively violate equal protection.

As for the FCC's minority preference policies, O'Connor argued, these were not designed as remedial measures and were in no sense narrowly tailored to rectify identified discrimination. In O'Connor's view, not only does the *Metro Broadcasting v. FCC* majority's assertion of diversity as an "important" government interest not rise to the proper level of scrutiny, but the very assumption that minority broadcast station owners will engage in minority programming or viewpoints itself constitutes an impermissible supposition equating race with thoughts and behavior: "The policies impermissibly value individuals because they presume that persons think in a manner associated with their race" (p. 618). And at the same time, in a kind of damned if you do, damned if you don't observation, Justice O'Connor asserted that the FCC presented no credible evidence that a nexus exists between the owners's race and resulting programming. Although her argument focused on the specific question of the nexus between the owners's race and programming, it clearly cast doubt on the general long-standing logic of an assumed relationship between a diversity of ownership and a diversity of viewpoints. Because "... the market shapes programming to a tremendous extent," the diversity logic has a fatal flaw (p. 626). The FCC cannot direct viewpoints; it can shape the structure of broadcasting to encourage a general diversity of viewpoints. Yet the FCC is unable to show empirically that there in fact is a viable connection between ownership policy and actual viewpoint diversity. Although the Supreme Court has recognized an interest in obtaining diverse broadcasting viewpoints as a legitimate basis for the FCC to adopt measures designed to increase the number of competing licensees and encourage licensees to present varied views on issues of public concern, the Supreme Court, according to Justice O'Connor, has never upheld a measure designed to amplify a distinct set of views or the views of a particular class of speakers (p. 617). Moreover, the dissenting opinion in another closely divided case, *Turner Broadcasting v. FCC* (1994), shows that at least four members of the Supreme Court believe that government regulation designed to ensure access to a multiplicity of voices is based on content and is thus constitutionally suspect.

Justice O'Connor essentially suggested that if the FCC wanted to pursue diversity (given her equal protection analysis, it's doubtful she would even contemplate a category of "minority programming"), the FCC should return to its old methods: develop an effective ascertainment policy, or evaluate applicants on their ability to provide, and commitment to offer, whatever programming the FCC believes would reflect underrepresented viewpoints—but do so on a race-neutral basis (*Metro Broadcasting v. FCC,* 1990). Of course, there is widespread agreement that these methods didn't really work in the past. And the closer the FCC gets to requiring broadcasters to program specific material, the closer it gets to violating the First Amendment's content neutrality doctrine.

COURT RULINGS SUBSEQUENT TO *METRO BROADCASTING*

Justice O'Connor's *Metro Broadcasting v. FCC* (1990) dissent in effect provided a wedge for the conservatives on the D.C. Circuit to attack FCC minority preference and diversity policies by way of the new equal protection analysis. In *Lamprecht v. FCC* (1992), a divided panel again struck down the FCC's gender enhancement policy in the comparative licensing process. (The gender policy had not been an issue before the Court in *Metro Broadcasting v. FCC.*) In *Lamprecht v. FCC,* the D.C. Circuit majority (in the last opinion written by Clarence Thomas before he was elevated to the Supreme Court) ruled that the FCC's gender preference was not substantially related to achieving the diversity of viewpoints because there was no evidence offered to demonstrate a link between ownership by women and any type of underrepresented programming. Moreover, reasoned the majority, an assumed nexus—unsupported by evidence—between women owners and "a female viewpoint" engaged in a form of stereotyping normally denounced by the Supreme Court.

By 1995, in *Adarand v. Pena,* the reasoning in Justice O'Connor's *Metro Broadcasting v. FCC* dissent had become the majority's opinion. *Adarand v. Pena* concerned a subcontractor compensation clause in federal agency contracts, which gave a prime contractor a financial incentive to hire subcontractors certified as small businesses controlled by socially and economically disadvantaged individuals. The policy required the contractor to presume that such individuals include minorities or any other individuals found to be disadvantaged by the Small Business Administration. Adarand Constructors, which submitted the low bid on a Department of Transportation project, but was not a certified business, filed suit claiming that the race-based presumptions used in the subcontractor compensation clauses violated the equal protection component of the Fifth Amendment's due process clause. The Supreme Court agreed. Writing for a 5 to 4 majority, Justice O'Connor expanded on the logic of her *Metro Broadcasting* dissent, arguing that all racial classifications, including "benign" ones, imposed by whatever federal, state, or local government actor, must be analyzed under strict scrutiny. To the extent that *Metro Broadcasting v. FCC* was inconsistent with that holding, and to the extent that its embodiment of a different standard of review for federal, as opposed to state and local, racial classifications placed the law in an unstable condition, it was overruled. But, although *Adarand* overruled the intermediate scrutiny standard used in *Metro Broadcasting v. FCC,* the Court did not address whether the diversity rationale of *Metro Broadcasting v. FCC* was still permissible. Read narrowly, *Adarand v. Pena* did not undermine either the importance of the policy goal of viewpoint diversity from a constitutional perspective, or non-race-based ownership regulation as a means to achieve that goal. But between Justice O'Connor's opinions in *Metro Broadcasting v. FCC* and *Adarand v. Pena,* the question was implicitly raised about how non-race-based diversity policy would be treated, especially given the dismissal of the data asserting a nexus between ownership and viewpoints.

The post-*Adarand v. Pena* rulings on race-based remedies are slightly mixed, although they mostly follow the logic that only policies addressing past governmental discrimination meet the strict scrutiny test.[28] And where the issue of media diversity was considered directly, in *Lutheran Church-Missouri Synod v. FCC* (1998), the Court of Appeals held that the FCC's equal employment opportunity (EEO)-related diversity rules did not rise to the level of a compelling governmental interest. The FCC found that the Lutheran Church, licensee of two radio stations in Clayton, Missouri, had not abided by EEO regulations that forbid stations to discriminate in employment and require stations to adopt an affirmative action program targeted to minorities and women. The stations, one with a noncommercial religious format, the other a commercial classical music format with some religious programming, hired few minorities because their hiring criteria stipulated knowledge of Lutheran doctrine and classical music training, thus narrowing the local pool of available minorities.[29] The FCC, identifying "diversity of programming" as the interest behind its EEO regulations, found the Church's hiring preferences too broad; that it was not necessary for receptionists, secretaries, engineers, and business managers to have knowledge of Lutheran doctrine. The Church filed suit, arguing that the FCC violated both its religious freedoms and the equal protection component of the Fifth Amendment.

Following *Adarand v. Pena*'s stipulation of strict scrutiny of racial classifications, the court sided with the Church. Apart from *Adarand v. Pena* doctrine, the court delved into the FCC's logic and found it both contradictory and objectionable. The FCC had argued that the Church could not prefer Lutheran to non-Lutheran secretaries because low-level employees would have little or no effect on the broadcast of religious views, yet the FCC defended its affirmative action recruiting policy by arguing that all employees affect a station's programming. "How, the Church asks, can the FCC maintain that the religion of a secretary will not affect programming but the race of a secretary will? After all, religious affiliation, a matter of affirmative intellectual and spiritual decision, is far more likely to affect programming than skin color" (*Lutheran Church-Missouri Synod v. FCC,* 1998, p. 350). Relying extensively on Justice O'Connor's *Metro Broadcasting v. FCC* dissent, the court argued that encouraging the notion that minorities have racially based views is antithetical to equal protection and antithetical to our democracy. Finally, the court chastised the FCC for "never defin[ing] exactly what it means by 'diverse programming,'" yet suggested that "any real content-based definition of the term may well give rise to enormous tensions with the First Amendment" (*Lutheran Church-Missouri Synod v. FCC,* 1998, p. 354):

> Perhaps this is illustrative as to just how much burden the term 'diversity' has been asked to bear in the latter part of the 20th century in the United States. It appears to have been coined both as a permanent justification for policies seeking racial proportionality in all walks of life ("affirmative action" has only a temporary remedial connotation) and as a synonym for proportional representation itself. It has, in our view, been used by the Commission in both ways. (*Lutheran Church-Missouri Synod v. FCC,* 1998, p. 356)

In sum, the court verged on attacking the diversity rationale *in toto*.

What is striking in this rehearsal of court cases is how strongly FCC policies were affected by the civil rights movement, to the extent that the traditional, relatively desultory diversity policy took on much sharper focus in the 1970s on issues of racial and ethnic representation in the media. The conjoining of minority ownership policies with broadcast diversity policies clearly energized the latter. Diversity was no longer a matter that a broadcast station should air a catholic mix of programs or that the FCC should prevent a corporation from operating more than one broadcast network, but that licensees should represent minority communities and minority audiences in programming, hiring, and ownership. Indeed, minority ownership was valued as a way to secure the diversity of programming and viewpoints. But did it? A central question was whether racial diversity in media ownership enhances political viewpoint diversity, which is, after all, the real concern of Bagdikian, Herman, and McChesney, and other critics of American media.

This question was addressed obliquely at first, then head-on in the courts. As the Reagan revolution made its way through appellate court appointees, the attack on affirmative action by way of equal protection clearly began to confront the new diversity logic, to the extent that very little of the supposed nexus between ownership and programming or viewpoint will be taken on faith, yet when that nexus is asserted, it risks judicial denunciation as an invidious stereotype if racially based, and may raise First Amendment content neutrality problems if the nexus appears too strong. This has led to hard questions for media diversity policy in general. At the risk of numbing the reader with another litany of cases, it is worth briefly noting recent cases in which the longtime premises of diversity policy have been met with a distinct lack of judicial sympathy. In *Schurz Communications v. FCC* (1992), the Court of Appeals for the 7th Circuit struck down the FCC's revised Fin-Syn rules as arbitrary and capricious, in large part because the FCC did not explain how the rules would accomplish the stated goal of enhancing diversity in programming. In an opinion written by noted law and economics proponent Judge Richard Posner, the opinion evinced strong skepticism that increases in source diversity could be presumed to lead to increases in program diversity. By the time the court of appeals heard a nonbroadcasting, but diversity-related ownership limitation case, the attack on diversity took on a knife-like empirical edge. In *Time Warner v. FCC* (2001), the Court of Appeals struck down FCC regulations that had prevented the largest cable companies from growing larger and carrying more of their own networks and programs. Congress had directed the FCC in the Cable Television Consumer Protection and Competition Act (1992) to set two types of limits on cable operators to promote diversity in ideas and speech and to preserve competition. Accordingly, the FCC enacted a horizontal rule imposing a 30% limit on the number of subscribers that could be served by a cable multiple system operator, and a vertical rule that reserved

60% of channel capacity for programming by nonaffiliated firms. Because, according to the court, the promotion of diversity and preservation of competition were statutorily intertwined, the FCC had to defend its rules with evidence supporting a "nonconjectural risk of anticompetitive behavior" in the horizontal limit. Engaging an antitrust-based economic modeling logic, the court ruled that the FCC had not done so. With regard to the vertical limit, the court ruled that the FCC failed to justify the rule as not burdening substantially more speech than necessary under intermediate scrutiny. The rules thus violated the Time-Warner's First Amendment rights to reach new audiences and to control its programming "speech."

In *Fox Television Stations v. FCC* (2002), the Court of Appeals vacated the cable and broadcast cross-ownership rule and remanded to the FCC the national television station ownership (NTSO) rule for further consideration. In the case of the cross-ownership rule, the court claimed that the FCC's diversity rationale for retention of the rule was so "woefully inadequate," that it accepted the petitioner's arguments *in toto* and vacated the rule. With regard to the national television station ownership rule, the court asserted that although the rule was not unconstitutional, the FCC's decision to retain it was arbitrary and capricious because the FCC failed to give an adequate reason for its decision. In remanding the rule, the court wrote forcefully that the FCC had "adduced not a single valid reason to believe the NTSO Rule is necessary in the public interest, either to safeguard competition or to enhance diversity" (*Fox Television Stations v. FCC,* 2002, p. 1043). Similarly, in a case that challenged the FCC's television duopoly rule—allowing common ownership of two television stations in the same local market if eight independently owned television stations remain after the merger (referred to afterward as the "eight voices exception")—the Court of Appeals remanded the exception because the FCC failed to demonstrate that its exclusion of nonbroadcast media from the exception is necessary for ensuring the appropriate level of broadcast diversity (*Sinclair Broadcast Group v. FCC,* 2002).

The new Bush administration FCC, under the chairmanship of Michael Powell, seemed to have entered into a kind of alliance, even one-upmanship, with the District of Columbia Circuit Court of Appeals in paying obeisance to corporations's First Amendment rights and removing traditional ownership limitations. Because the social science data on the nexus between ownership policies and programming are weak, most ownership or structural regulations were being read as violations of the speech rights of corporations. In December 2001, the FCC permitted Comcast to purchase AT&T's cable holdings, giving Comcast 20% of the nation's cabled homes. The FCC also amended the old dual network rule, permitting one of the four major television networks to own, operate, maintain, or control the UPN or the WB television networks (Amendment of Section 73.658[g] of the Commission's Rules—The Dual Network Rule, 2001). In September 2002, the FCC announced a Notice of Proposed Rulemaking (2002) on six ownership rules.[30] As expected, the FCC, on a party-line vote, rescinded in June 2003 the broadcast-newspaper cross-ownership rule, the local multiple television ownership limit, and the national television station ownership rule.[31] What was unexpected was the public firestorm the FCC's rulemakings precipitated. In July, the U.S. House of Representatives voted 400 to 21 to roll back the FCC's national television ownership rule; the Senate took a similar stand in September on a 55 to 40 vote. And in September, the Third U.S. Circuit Court of Appeals, siding with a coalition of media access groups that claimed its members could suffer irreparable harm if the rules went into effect as scheduled, issued an emergency stay of the new rules (*Prometheus Radio Project v. FCC,* 2003). The court subsequently remanded the case back to the FCC, finding that the FCC had not adequately defended its relaxation of the ownership rules as being in the public interest (*Prometheus Radio Project v. FCC,* 2004). At this writing, it is unclear whether Congress will restore the old rules or whether legislation doing so could withstand a threatened presidential veto.[32]

CONCLUSION

In an essay published in the *Journal of Communication,* Robert Entman and Steven Wildman (1992) made the case that the market economics and social value approaches to communication policy for too long have ignored the other's arguments and evidence. Market economics, taking as axiomatic the normative superiority of allowing individuals to choose what they like best, and of using public policy (sparingly) to nudge the market toward that end, tended to neglect externalities that are not quantifiable and do not fit well into the standard economic cost–benefit calculus. As former FCC Chairman Mark Fowler and his legal counsel Daniel Brenner (1982) once baldly and simplistically declared, "the public's interest ... defines the public interest" (pp. 3–4). But it is clear that a market-governed media system underproduces certain kinds of content, especially content essential to democratic deliberation and self-government. The social values school, focusing on the spread of knowledge, encouraging democracy, or appropriate content for children, tended to ignore the strength of consumer preferences and the limited effects of regulatory interventions on audiences's consumption of the school's favored content. In addition, the social values school's conceptual dichotomy between information and entertainment, ensconced within a critique of the overwhelming entertainment focus of American media, failed to acknowledge that important ideas may come through entertainment content and that collective understandings and value conflicts are debated and revised in part through media entertainment.[33] Entman and Wildman attributed the general problem to both schools's faulty understanding of diversity and to their shared, misplaced attachment to the First Amendment metaphor of the marketplace of ideas.

I take seriously the authors's entreaty to bridge the divide between the schools, even as the market economics approach seems to have trumped the social values school at the FCC and in the courts. Let us grudgingly concede that the court conservatives got it right: Despite the longstanding and strongly asserted connection between diverse ownership and diverse content, the evidence generally *has* been weak. The primary reason, as Justice O'Connor noted in her *Metro Broadcasting v. FCC* (1990) dissent, is that "the market shapes programming to a tremendous extent" (p. 626). Acknowledging the power of market forces is not to say that such forces are so commanding that ownership is irrelevant and that the concern with who owns the media is fundamentally misguided. After all, the evidence of format variety brought by minority ownership of broadcast stations is modest but significant, and the argument offered by Robert Entman (1989) and others about the crucial importance of philosophy of publishers with regard to the quality of newspapers is surely relevant.[34] Ownership does matter. The proclivities and commitments of the Sulzbergers at *The New York Times* or Katherine Graham at *The Washington Post* point to the importance—and the room for maneuver—of individual publishers of newspapers (see Downie, Jr. & Kaiser, 2002; Graham, 1997; Tifft & Jones, 1999). (To what extent we can generalize about newspapers's room for maneuver to broadcasters and cable operators is another question; newspapers tend to monopolize their markets.) The argument is rather that market forces—the amalgam of advertiser pressure; the coercion of Wall Street expectations; high debt service on pricey, newly acquired media properties; the wish for high profit margins; and yes, audience preferences—create very strong constraints and incentives. The long and largely disappointing history of FCC policies to induce broadcast licensees to program in the broad public interest and contrary to their narrow economic interests is a testament to the power of market forces. The sway of such forces continues to be underscored, for example, by sober accounts of the economic failure at efforts to air quality local television news even in an era of television abundance (see Kaniss, 1991; Winerip, 1998).

Deregulation and markets do appear to abet some degree of *format* variety. Market-driven format variety, and especially the formats brought by minority ownership, is not to be belittled. Market-driven format variety has enhanced consumer preference (recognizing, of course, that choice is prestructured by the conditions of economic competition). And the broadened representation in the mass media of racial and ethnic minorities as a result of FCC minority preference policies has had positive consequences for important issues of access, identity, and visibility. Beyond the cultural politics of representation, these issues have political ramifications inasmuch as representational invisibility often means political invisibility as well.[35] But, notwithstanding the augmentation of consumer preference and the modest broadening of racial and ethnic representation in media, format variety does not often reach the core of viewpoint diversity. Rap and Latin jazz radio formats, for example, fill a need and a niche, but their entertainment orientation goes only so far in terms of the articulation of different viewpoints, especially political viewpoints. Different viewpoints and overt attention to public affairs are in some fashion taken up by *public* television and radio, a fact that points to the significance of their different organizational mandates, and, equally important, the different mode of their financing. This brings me to my key, if in some respects, pedestrian, and, in this day and age, seemingly pie-in-the-sky point. Between deregulation and court rulings, market economics now reign supreme in American media. As this chapter has argued, markets bring some format variety, but are unlikely to beget other forms of diversity. To bring diversity, we need a more mixed system of mass media with different mandates and different modes of financing. It is some combination of a mixed system of media and curbs on media concentration that will best secure a diversity of viewpoints and content. James Curran (2000) has proposed such a scheme as a mixed system approach, wherein the media system is designed to promote the expression of diversity by organizing its constituent parts in different ways, and which connect to different parts of society.

In Curran's model, a core media sector constituted by general interest TV channels that reach a mass audience would be entrusted to public service organizations, governed by fairness and access rules and financed by a universalist funding mechanism. This core sector, as the embodiment of the traditional public service media mandate, fulfills the republican function of being in principle open to everyone's participation in the formulation of collective ideas and public goals. It is fed by peripheral media sectors, three of which are intended to facilitate the expression of dissenting and minority views. A "civic sector" consists of channels of communication linked to organized groups and social networks. Intended as partisan media, enabling social groups to constitute themselves and clarify their objectives, the sector fulfills liberal-pluralist functions. A "professional media sector" occupies a space wholly independent of both the state and the market in which professional communicators relate to the public on their own terms, with the minimum of constraints. A "social market sector" subsidizes minority media as a way of promoting market diversity and consumer choice. To this is added a conventional market sector, which relates to the public as consumers, and whose central rationale within the media system is to facilitate market preferences and to act as a restraint on the overentrenchment of minority concerns to the exclusion of majority pleasures. Obviously, such a model is more at home in European social democracies than in the United States, but it is important to acknowledge that the United States does recognize many of these principles, albeit in cribbed fashion. Our public broadcasting system doesn't approach the range or scope of European public service broadcasting, but the republican values are largely the same. The standard that some constituent part of the electronic media should be universally accessible was one of the bases of the Supreme Court's affirmation that cable systems "must carry" local over-the-air television broadcast signals (*Turner Broadcasting System, Inc. v. FCC,* 1994, 1997). Cable public access channels represent the principle that somewhere in the electronic media system, ordinary people and groups should have the access and ability to produce programming free from operator control over the content. The Supreme Court upheld the principle, even in the face of a challenge to protect audiences from indecent and offensive speech on such channels in *Denver Area Education Telecommunications Consortium, Inc. v. FCC* (1996).

Thus, although the prevailing legislative and judicial trends as described in the lion's share of this chapter appear quite hostile to the idea of establishing a mixed media system governed by structural rules and curbs on media concentration, there are clearly legitimate grounds for such a policy. That the principle of media diversity got tied to and now apparently has gone down with the equal protection rulings on minority preferences should not be grounds for undermining diversity analysis per se. The most charitable reading of recent Court of Appeals decisions on media diversity is that the court seems to believe that, in the absence of "nonconjectural" evidence of the relationship between structural rules and diversity, First Amendment scrutiny analysis requires government to withdraw in favor of the market. Part of the problem here is the metaphor of the marketplace of ideas. The problem with the metaphor is not that it is ill suited per se; the problem is that it has become the central metaphor in First Amendment thinking, effectively crowding out other metaphors and the explanations that give rise to metaphor. It is a particularly loaded metaphor because not only does it tie ideas to the market, but essentially conveys the sense that the marketplace is natural, neutral, and unproblematic. In its rhetorical deployment, the marketplace of ideas metaphor unites and reduces the manifold justifications of freedom of speech to a simple talisman that ignores the reality of the large, concentrated ownership of the electronic means of communication—a point that has been made by many commentators in recent years (see, among others, Baker, 2002; Fiss, 1996; Horwitz, 1991; Sunstein, 1993). We should give the marketplace of ideas metaphor a rest in favor of the metaphor of a "mixed media system." This metaphor is surely consonant with American tradition. We are a proudly mongrel nation; why not have a proudly mongrel media system? Freedom of speech has been discussed and defended with reference to several different arguments, the lineaments of which were noted in the beginning of this chapter. If we move off from the marketplace of ideas metaphor toward a mixed media system, we are better placed theoretically to act to guarantee diversity of viewpoints and the forums for democratic deliberation. Different kinds of media fulfill different functions in a democracy; creating structures that facilitate diverse media is both necessary and legitimate. Diversity can be secured not by ownership curbs alone—in a market-driven media system such curbs are likely to be of limited efficacy—but by some such limitations within a mixed media system.

NOTES

[1]Although the members of the Hutchins Commission generally shared the concern over ownership concentration, they disagreed among themselves regarding the proper remedy, especially about the wisdom of government intervention that went beyond conventional regulatory and antitrust policies. The compromise— advocacy of an ethic of professionalism and responsibility among journalists—laid the foundation for the "social responsibility" theory of the press that soon became a mainstay of journalism education, but did not directly address the broad questions of media ownership and access (see Siebert, Peterson, & Schramm, 1956).

[2]"But when men have realized that time has upset many fighting faiths, they may come to believe even more than they believe the very foundations of their own conduct that the ultimate good desired is better reached by free trade in ideas—that the best test of truth is the power of the thought to get itself accepted in the competition of the market, and that truth is the only ground upon which their wishes safely can be carried out" (*Abrams v. United States*, 1919, p. 630).

[3]The Supreme Court traditionally upheld the structural regulation of media against First Amendment challenge by corporate owners. *Associated Press v. United States* (1945) has already been mentioned. Other prominent cases include *National Broadcasting Co. v. United States* (1943), in which the Supreme Court ruled in favor of the Federal Communication Commission's (FCC's) "chain broadcasting" regulations; *United States v. Storer Broadcasting Co.* (1956), in which the Court upheld the FCC's limit on the number of broadcast stations a single entity could own nationally; and *FCC v.*

National Citizens Committee for Broadcasting (1978), in which the Supreme Court upheld the newspaper-broadcast cross-ownership prohibition.

[4]In early broadcast regulation, for example, the diversity principle was embedded within the Federal Communication Commission's (FCC's) "public interest" mandate. The Federal Radio Commission interpreted the public interest obligations of the broadcast licensee to be such "that the tastes, needs, and desires of all substantial groups among the listening public should be met, in some fair proportion, by a well-rounded program ..." (In the Matter of the Application of Great Lakes Broadcasting Co., 1929, p. 32). In comparative hearings for broadcast licenses, the FCC indicated that the diversification of control of the mass media is one of the most important criteria in ranking applicants (Policy Statement on Comparative Broadcast Hearings, 1965).

[5]Outlets and sources are interrelated, but they are not the same, as evidenced by the long struggle over Financial Interest and Syndication Rules in television broadcasting. Those rules, which were in force between 1970 and 1995, prohibited the television networks from owning shares of the firms that provided their programming, with the expectation that the policy would expand the sources of program production (Report and Order, 1970). Similarly, in *United States v. Paramount Pictures* (1948), the settlement required the movie studios to divest themselves of movie theaters, thus restricting the vertical integration between producer and distributors of motion pictures and their exhibition. The separation was rescinded in *U.S. v. Syufy Enterprises* (1989) on the logic that changes in technology warranted expansion of the product market beyond first-run exhibition to include subrun exhibition, as well as exhibition in ancillary markets of home video, cable, and pay-per-view TV.

[6]For earlier attempts to disentangle the many strands of diversity see, among others, Noll, Peck, and McGowan (1973) and Levin (1980).

[7]The public goods argument derives from specific features of media products. In economic terms, media products are nonrivalrous; one person's benefit often does not affect the benefit of others. Also, media products have high first copy costs, but adding distribution incurs essentially no marginal cost. Once a program has been broadcast, for example, there is no additional cost of adding another listener or viewer. These features create problems in pricing and of realizing price discrimination. Elements of this critique have been articulated by many scholars and in many documents for years, including the Federal Communication Commission's "Blue Book" (*Public Service Responsibility of Broadcast Licensees,* 1946), but they have been given recent elegant and pointed formulation by C. Edwin Baker (2001).

[8]For example, Harvey J. Levin (1970) was largely critical of the claims made for the group ownership rule in terms of its effects on competition and diversity (although he admitted to a paucity of good data on content diversity). J. C. Busterna (1988) found no significant relationship between the effects of TV and newspaper cross-ownership on the diversity of issues covered in the news. Writing in 1985, Waklshlag and Adams (1985) found that the introduction of the Prime Time Access Rule, enacted in 1970 by the Federal Communication Commission to encourage local television production, was largely responsible for a sharp decline in network program diversity. Most of the

programming that replaced network shows in the 7 p.m. to 8 p.m. hour were cheap (and generally agreed as dreadful) game shows and animal shows. These findings seem to underscore the power of market conditions.

[9]The most careful studies of the efficacy of Federal Communication Commission minority preference policies do register a noteworthy degree of change in format and in primary audience (see Congressional Research Service, 1988; Dubin & Spitzer, 1995; Waldfogel & Siegelman, 1999). Minority broadcast owners (and, according to Dubin & Spitzer, 1995, women owners) have a greater tendency to program differently than White (male) owners, although this diversity registers at the level of radio program formats—an important component of diversity, but not one that necessarily reaches directly to the core issue of different viewpoints. Moreover, these programming changes tend to be realized only under particular market conditions. They are much more likely to happen in markets with large numbers of minorities in the audience, where there are large numbers of broadcast stations, and where none of the stations are yet serving minority audiences. In markets that do not satisfy one or more of these conditions, the theoretical chance that a minority owner will program differently from a White owner declines (see Spitzer, 1991). A 2001 study suggests that the race or ethnicity of broadcast station owners enhances news and public affairs diversity, as well as format diversity (Mason, Bachen, & Craft, 2001). The study was based on a nationwide telephone survey with some 200 news directors at radio and television stations, and, although suggestive, is limited by the self-reporting and possible bias of the respondents, as the authors themselves note.

[10]See, for example, Beebe (1977), Steiner (1952), and Waterman (1992); but see, contrarily, Grant (1994). One recent empirical study (Berry & Waldfogel, 2001) found that the mergers in the radio industry consequent to the 1996 Telecommunications Act increased the number of formats available relative to the number of stations, and some evidence that the increased concentration increased variety absolutely. The logic underlying this phenomenon derives from the fact that multiproduct firms do not want their products to compete with each other, so mergers can lead firms to spread similar products apart. A serious problem in assessing the empirical studies, as Napoli (1999) suggests, is that the categories and the methodologies are not consistent. Another problem is that, for methodological ease, most studies focus on format (radio and cable TV) or program-type (television) diversity, most often assessed by categories employed by Arbitron or Nielsen or Duncan or the media industry itself. To some extent, this is perfectly understandable, because the categories seem stable and are hence measurable. After all, how can an empirically oriented social scientist measure viewpoint diversity? A perceptive reader can reasonably discern general differences of tone and coverage among *The Wall Street Journal, USA Today,* and *The Nation,* for instance. But, even in this comparison, does one analyze the coverage according to (a) some general reckoning or by particular item? (b) by news article or "op/ed" column? (c) over a comprehensive week or by random sampling? (d) and according to what kind of scale? If quantitative, does one analyze the coverage by the frequency an issue or event is covered or by column inches? If qualitative, what exactly does one look for when one conducts a content analysis? And this is news and opinion, presumably conducive to viewpoint analysis.

How does one evaluate the viewpoints embedded in entertainment programming? Even approaching that particular problem resurrects the quandary of who does the measuring: the content analyst scholar or the audience; at an overt level of messages and meanings, or a covert one? The ethnographic turn in audience research has, in complicated fashion, revisited the old "selective influence" model of communication, that different people often read different messages into and derive different values from the same entertainment (and news) content (see, among others, Lowery & DeFleur, 1995; Seiter, 1999). Thus it's not surprising that empirical social scientists trying to assess media diversity will gravitate to the stable, if less consequential, measures of format. The problem, of course, is that format or program diversity is just one of several gauges of diversity, yet commentators often leap to broad, general conclusions about the efficacy (or not) of the market in expanding diversity. Researchers attentive to this problem, such as Berry and Waldfogel (2001), make an effort to refer to "variety" rather than "diversity" when analyzing formats.

[11]"But, above all else, the First Amendment means that government has no power to restrict expression because of its message, its ideas, its subject matter, or its content" (*Police v. Mosley,* 1972, p. 95).

[12]The fact that such competition has not fulfilled expectations is another matter, and may be rooted in the economies of scale and scope that still impel communications toward oligopoly, a discussion I do not take up here.

[13]Merger analysis entails three steps: (a) define the relevant market, (b) estimate the merging firm's strength in the relevant market, and (c) examine industry and transaction specific factors. With regard to the first step, the key determinations are the "line of commerce," or the product market, and the "section of the country," or the geographic market. What exactly is the product that might be subject to too much market "power"? The more that products are reasonably interchangeable, the more likely it is that they should be considered the same product market. Traditionally, the geographic market may be a city, a region, or the entire country. What is the geographic scope of competition in the product market? For example, although it may be useful to aggregate overall market power of a newspaper or cable chain, the degree of competition at the local level needs to be considered separately (see Nesvold, n.d.).

[14]In an effort to formalize how judges should assess the balance between free speech rights and regulations that seek to safeguard the state's interests, the Supreme Court has adopted an approach known as levels of scrutiny. Scrutiny entails a weighted balancing, using a multitiered categorization approach. Strict scrutiny requires the state to show a "compelling" interest in regulating speech. Any content-based regulation will trigger strict scrutiny; to survive, the regulation must be "narrowly drawn" to fulfill only the compelling interest. Intermediate scrutiny requires the showing of a "substantial," "significant," or "important" state interest. To survive, the regulation must be content-neutral, be narrowly tailored to serve the state interest, and leave open ample alternative channels for communication of the information (see *United States v. O'Brien,* 1968).

[15]The Herfindahl-Hirschman Index (HHI) is used by the Department of Justice and the Federal Trade Commission to quantify the level of concentration in any given

market. The measure takes the market share of each firm, squares it, sums the result, and multiplies by 10,000. The resulting number is then broadly categorized as unconcentrated (HHI below 1,000), moderately concentrated (HHI between 1,000 and 1,800), and highly concentrated (HHI above 1,800; see U.S. Department of Justice and the Federal Trade Commission, 1992).

[16]For instance, in *Cable Holdings of Georgia v. Home Video, Inc.* (1990), the court of appeals upheld a merger between two cable companies under the logic that the relevant product market definition was all "passive visual entertainment," including cable television, satellite television, video cassette recordings, and free broadcast television. These were reasonable substitutes and hence constituted a single product market. One important question, however, is what is the "product" in an advertising-based media system—the content or the advertising (see Ekelund, Ford, & Jackson, 1999).

[17]Not only are advertising-based media outlets structurally biased toward content connected to marketable products and services, their predisposition to avoid content oriented toward the poor exacerbates the general phenomenon of poor people's lack of voice in American politics. A consistent and compelling theme of Ehrenreich (2001) is that poor people's dependence robs them of voice.

[18]The ability of Internet Service Providers (ISP) to direct the attention of their customers through branding (where the most likely links are the ones that have the most prominent display, fastest connection, best premiums, etc., and are those that benefit the ISP) or data management middleware (software resting between the user applications and the ISP servers and acting as a broker-facilitator-gateway that manages the flow of data in ways that privilege the ISP's offerings) worries some students of the Internet (see Aufderheide, 2002; Center for Digital Democracy, n.d).

[19]The Justice Department's current guidelines for radio mergers, for example, limit ownership to controlling more than half the advertising revenue in major markets. The operative "product market" for radio is advertising. The Department of Justice (DOJ) can review radio mergers on the grounds that they would potentially raise prices to advertisers. As Berry and Waldfogel (2001, p. 1015) submit, it is not clear whether the DOJ could review on grounds of product variety because there is no "price" paid by listeners.

[20]The argument that the protection of allocative efficiency is the paramount, even the only, concern of antitrust has gained ascendance over the last 25 years, to the point of reading the principle back into the drafting of the Sherman, Federal Trade Commission, and Clayton Acts as their sole legislative intent. This is the mode of Robert Bork's (1978) volume, for example. Yet any reasonable historian can discern that there were many principles embedded into the founding antitrust acts, not the least of which were fear of concentrated corporate power on social and political life and the concern over the distributional inequity resulting from firms with monopoly power extracting wealth from consumers (see Hofstadter, 1955; Lande, 1982; Millon, 1988). The shift to efficiency principles and the reverence accorded Bork's text must be located in the ideological ascendance, beginning in the 1970s, of the law and economics perspective.

[21]As a testament to how far the pendulum has swung toward viewing communications as just another industry and to conceiving antitrust as simply a matter of compet-

itiveness and efficiency (as well as revealing the nasty relations between the political parties in the 1990s), there was an effort in the Republican-controlled Congress to strip the Clinton Federal Communication Commission (FCC) of the power to evaluate media mergers. The gambit disappeared after the disputed 2000 presidential election was decided in favor of George W. Bush and effective control of the FCC would revert to the Republican agenda.

[22]The central critique is that there is no "natural" scarcity of broadcast spectrum. The scarcity in broadcasting was created by government itself in the process of establishing control over the resource. If there were a proper market in spectrum, so goes the critique, there would be no scarcity, as demand would meet supply at the right price. Like other commodities, there is no real physical or technological scarcity in broadcasting; rather broadcasting is characterized by a normal economic scarcity made problematic by government intervention. Ronald Coase (1959) was the originator of the theory that Congress erred by not adopting a property rights solution in the spectrum. Thomas Hazlett (1990) has argued that although property rights is the correct solution, Congress did not err; rather, lawmakers entered into a rent-seeking arrangement with incumbent broadcasters, both of whom would benefit from a regulatory regime. For a recent statement of the wrong-headedness of scarcity argument, from the Chairman of the Federal Communications Commission, see Powell (1998).

[23]The U.S. Commission on Civil Rights (1977) published a highly critical assessment of the television industry's treatment of minorities and women in 1977. Examining the portrayal of women and minorities on television and their employment in the industry, the study found that they were underrepresented on the work forces of television stations and were almost totally excluded from decision-making positions in the industry. This pressure led the Federal Communications Commission to tighten its equal employment guidelines.

[24]If and when a broadcast license came available, there were often several applicants for it. The Federal Communications Commission would conduct a comparative hearing to determine which applicant should be awarded the license. Evaluative criteria in comparative license applications traditionally included local ownership, the integration of ownership and management, past performance, broadcast experience, proposed programming, and diversification of control of media. With the 1978 minority ownership policy, minority applicants in comparative license hearings would receive "extra points," as it were, in the evaluation process (Statement of Policy on Minority Ownership of Broadcasting Facilities, 1978).

[25]The Federal Communications Commission formulated four policies to increase the ownership of broadcast licenses by racial and ethnic minorities: lottery preferences, comparative hearing preferences, distress sales, and tax certificates (Statement of Policy on Minority Ownership of Broadcasting Facilities, 1978).

[26]Paragraph 5 of the 14th Amendment states the following: "Congress shall have the power to enforce, by appropriate legislation, the provisions of this article." It has been generally taken to mean that Congress has special powers in the equal protection area and that federal legislation can be judged by somewhat different criteria than state and local legislation.

[27]Spitzer (1991) argues, correctly, that the *Metro Broadcasting v. FCC* (1990) majority accorded a very high degree of deference to Congress and the Federal Communications Commission's presentation of the nexus between minority ownership and diverse programming. There are some data showing that nexus (see endnote 9), but they are hardly strong.

[28]See *Hopwood v. Texas* (1996), *Police Association v. City of New Orleans* (1996), and *Contractors Association of Eastern Pennsylvania v. Philadelphia* (1996) as cases where set-asides or preferences were struck down as not satisfying strict scrutiny. In contrast, see *Wittmer v. Peters* (1996) and *Erwin v. Daley* (1996) as cases in which the rectification of past discrimination was not the only basis on which race can be taken into account. However, those have been limited to law-enforcement and correctional settings.

[29]In 1977, the Federal Communications Commission adopted explicit quantitative standards for workplace diversity. Broadcast stations with more than 10 full-time employees would have their license applications reviewed if minorities were not employed at a ratio of 50% of their overall availability in the labor force and 25% in the upper four job categories. The percentage of minority representation in the upper four job categories was raised to 50% in 1980 (Equal Employment Opportunity Processing Guidelines for Broadcast Renewal Applicants, 1980).

[30]The six included the Newspaper/Broadcast Cross-Ownership Prohibition (1975), Local Radio Ownership (1941), National TV Ownership (1941), Local TV Multiple Ownership (1964), Radio/TV Cross-Ownership Restriction (1970), and Dual Television Network Rule (1946).

[31]The key rule changes are as follows:

- Local TV multiple ownership limit—in markets with 5 or more TV stations, a company may own 2 stations, but only one of these can be among the top four in ratings. In markets with 18 or more TV stations, a company can own 3 TV stations. The Federal Communications Commission has a waiver process for markets with 11 or fewer stations in which 2 of the top 4 stations wish to merge.
- National TV ownership limit—a company can own TV stations reaching no more than a 45% share of U.S. TV households (had been 35%). The FCC maintains the historical UHF "discount": Stations in the UHF frequency band count only 50% for calculating the national television reach.
- Continuation of local radio ownership limit, but a change in the methodology for defining a radio market (replacing the signal contour method with a geographic market approach)—in markets with 45 or more radio stations, a company may own 8 stations; 30–44 stations: 7; 15–29 stations: 6; 14 or fewer: 5.
- Cross media limits—in markets with 3 or fewer TV stations, no cross-ownership is permitted among TV, radio, and newspapers. In markets with between 4 and 8 TV stations, combinations are limited to one of the following:

  A. A daily newspaper, one TV station; and up to half of the radio station limit for that market;

  B. A daily newspaper; and up to the radio station limit for that market (no TV).

C. Two TV stations; up to the radio station limit for that market (no newspapers).

[Report and Order, 2003].

[32]As for whether the Supreme Court's summer 2003 decision in the Michigan affirmative action cases will have any bearing on media matters, the majority opinion in *Grutter v. Bollinger* (2003) is so narrowly focused on university admissions that it seems very unlikely to affect the media diversity area.

[33]Entman and Wildman (1992) ask, "How do we distinguish 'The Cosby Show,' with its frequent overt and covert messages about racial prejudice, from the nightly news in terms of idea content?" (p. 11). The contemporary, even more jarring example because it is an irreverent cartoon, would be "The Simpsons," aired, ironically—because it is widely viewed as the most politically conservative and commercially vulgar television network—on Fox.

[34]Entman (1989) argues that, although the data are generally inconclusive, the philosophy and proclivities of the newspaper owner are at least as important as markets with regard to the quality of newspapers. It should be noted, however, that newspapers now largely operate under monopolistic competition where the workings of that market give owners more leeway. In the case of minority ownership and minority-oriented programming in radio, Spitzer (1991) suggests that minority owners might be partly able to buck market forces because minority group membership allows them to realize production cost advantages, particularly in knowing their audiences's tastes and in monitoring the performance of station managers. All the same, the specific features of the market limit the extent to which such owners will offer minority-oriented content.

[35]The importance of minority owners in this matter of representational or demographic diversity is noteworthy when the record of cable television is considered. One 1995 study found that new cable channels made no difference whatsoever in the frequency of representation of racial minorities, women, and any age group other than young adults on television (Kubey, Shifflet, Weerakkody, & Ukeiley, 1995).

REFERENCES

Abrams v. United States, 250 U.S. 616 (1919).

Adarand v. Pena, 515 U.S. 200 (1995).

Amendment of Section 73.3555 of the Commission's Rules Relating to Multiple Ownership of AM, FM, and Television Broadcast Stations. 100 FCC 2d 74 (1985).

Amendment of Section 73.658[g] of the Commission's Rules—The Dual Network Rule. MM Docket No. 00–108. Report and Order (2001).

Amendment of Sections 3.35, 3.240, and 3.636 of Rules and Regulations Relating to Multiple Ownership of AM, FM, and Television Broadcast Stations. Report and Order. 18 FCC 288 (1953).

Amendment of Sections 73.35, 73.240, and 73.636 of Commission's Rules Relating to Multiple Ownership of AM, FM, and Television Broadcast Stations, Report and Order. 45 FCC 1476 (1964).

Ascertainment of Community Problems by Broadcast Applicants. 57 FCC 2d 418 (1976).

Associated Press v. United States, 326 U.S. 1 (1945).
Aufderheide, P. (1999). *Communications policy and the public interest: The Telecommunications Act of 1996*. New York: Guilford.
Aufderheide, P. (2002). Competition and commons: The public interest in and after the AOL-Time Warner merger. *Journal of Broadcasting and Electronic Media, 46*, 515–531.
Bagdikian, B. (1983). *The media monopoly*. Boston: Beacon.
Bagdikian, B. (1997). *The media monopoly* (5th ed.). Boston: Beacon.
Baker, C. E. (1995). Turner broadcasting: Content-based regulation of persons and presses. In D. J. Hutchinson, D. A. Strauss, & G. R. Stone (Eds.), *The Supreme Court Review 1994* (pp. 57–128). Chicago: University of Chicago Press.
Baker, C. E. (2001). *Media, markets, and democracy*. New York: Cambridge University Press.
Baker, C. E. (2002). Media concentration: Giving up on democracy. *Florida Law Review, 54*, 839–919.
Bar, F., Cohen, S., Cowhey, P., DeLong, B., Kleeman, M., & Zysman, J. (1999). *Defending the Internet revolution in the broadband era: When doing nothing is doing harm* (Working Paper No. 137). Berkeley, CA: Berkeley Roundtable on the International Economy.
Barnouw, E. (1966). *A history of broadcasting in the United States*. New York: Oxford University Press.
Beebe, J. H. (1977). Institutional structure and program choices in television markets. *The Quarterly Journal of Economics, 91*, 15–37.
Benkler, Y. (1999). Free as the air to common use: First amendment constraints on enclosure of the public domain. *N.Y.U. Law Review, 74*, 354–446.
Berry, S., & Waldfogel, J. (2001). Do mergers increase product variety? Evidence from radio broadcasting. *The Quarterly Journal of Economics, cxvi*, 1009–1025.
Bork, R. H. (1978). *The antitrust paradox: A policy at war with itself*. New York: Basic Books.
Busterna, J. C. (1988). Television station ownership effects on programming and idea diversity: Baseline data. *Journal of Media Economics, 1*, 63–74.
Cable Holdings of Georgia v. Home Video, Inc., 712 F. Supp. 1389 (N.D. Cal. 1989), *aff'd*, 903 F.2d 659 (9th Cir. 1990).
Cable Television Consumer Protection and Competition Act, Pub..L. No. 102–385, 106 Stat. 1460 (1992).
Celler-Kefauver Amendment to the Clayton Act, 1950, Pub. L. No. 81–899, 64 Stat. 1125, codified at 15 U.S.C. § 18 (1994).
Center for Digital Democracy. (n.d.). *How broadband systems will narrow the net*. Retrieved September 17, 2004, from http://www.democraticmedia.org/narrownet.html
Chapman Radio and Television Co. (1970). 24 FCC 2d 282.
Clayton Antitrust Act. (1914). Ch. 323, 38 Stat. 730.
Coase, R. (1959). The FCC. *Journal of Law and Economics, 2*, 1–40.
Commission on Freedom of the Press. (1947). *A free and responsible press, a general report on mass communication: Newspapers, radio, motion pictures, magazines, and books*. Chicago: University of Chicago Press.
Communications Act, Pub. L. No. 416, 73rd Congress, S. 3285 (1934).
Compaine, B. M. (2000). Distinguishing between concentration and competition. In B. M. Compaine & D. Gomery (Eds.), *Who owns the media? Competition and concentration in the mass media industry* (3rd ed., pp. 537–581). Mahwah, NJ: Lawrence Erlbaum Associates.
Congressional Research Service. (1988). *Statistical analysis of FCC survey data: Minority broadcast station ownership and minority broadcasting*. Washington, DC: Library of Congress.
Consumers Union, Consumer Federation of America, Civil Rights Forum, Center for Digital Democracy, Leadership Conference on Civil Rights and Media Access Project. (2002). Com-

ments in the Matter of Cross-Ownership of Broadcast Stations and Newspaper (MM Docket No. 01-235) and Newspaper/Radio Cross-Ownership Waiver Policy (MM Docket No. 96–197). Retrieved September 17, 2004, from http://www.mediaaccess.org/filings/consumers_union_et_al_nbco_comments.pdf

Continuing Appropriations Act for Fiscal Year 1988, Pub. L. No. 100–201, 101 Stat. 1329 (1987).

Contractors Association of Eastern Pennsylvania v. Philadelphia, 91 F. 3d 586 (3rd Cir. 1996).

Cooper, M. (2003). *Media ownership and democracy in the digital information age: Promoting diversity with first amendment principles and market structure analysis*. Stanford, CA: Stanford Law School, Center for Internet & Society.

Curran, J. (2000). Rethinking media and democracy. In J. Curran & M. Gurevitch (Eds.), *Mass media and society* (3rd ed., pp. 120–154). London: Arnold.

Denver Area Education Telecommunications Consortium, Inc. v. FCC, 518 U.S. 727 (1996).

Downie, Jr., L., & Kaiser, R. G. (2002). *The truth about the news: American journalism in peril*. New York: Knopf.

Dubin, J., & Spitzer, M. L. (1995). Testing minority preferences in broadcasting. *Southern California Law Review, 68*, 841–884.

Ehrenreich, B. (2001). *Nickel and dimed: On (not) getting by in America*. New York: Holt.

Ekelund, R. B., Ford, G. S., & Jackson, J. D. (1999). Is radio advertising a distinct local market? An empirical analysis. *Review of Industrial Organization, 14*, 239–256.

Entman, R. (1989). *Democracy without citizens: Media and the decay of American politics*. New York: Oxford University Press.

Entman, R., & Wildman, S. (1992). Reconciling economic and non-economic perspectives on media policy: Transcending the 'marketplace of ideas.' *Journal of Communication, 42*(1), 5–19.

Equal Employment Opportunity Processing Guidelines for Broadcast Renewal Applicants. (1980). 45 Fed. Reg. 16335.

Erwin v. Daley, 92 F.3d 521 (7th Cir. 1996).

Farhi, P. (1994, November 29). A television trend: Audiences in Black and White; viewers split on racial lines as networks find diversity sells—but critics see cultural risks. *The Washington Post*, p. A1.

FCC. (1984). Brief for the FCC in *Steele v. FCC*. 1985. (D.C. Cir. No. 84–1176) (1985) (*en banc*).

FCC v. National Citizens Committee for Broadcasting, 436 U.S. 775 (1978).

Fife, M. (1984). *FCC policy on minority ownership in broadcasting: A political systems analysis of regulatory policymaking*. Unpublished doctoral dissertation, Stanford University, Stanford, CA.

Fiss, O. (1996). *Liberalism divided: Freedom of speech and the many uses of state power*. Boulder, CO: Westview.

Fowler, M., & Brenner, D. (1982). A marketplace approach to broadcast regulation. *Texas Law Review, 60*, 207–257.

Fox Television Stations v. FCC, 280 F.3d 1027 (D.C. Cir. 2002).

Fullilove v. Klutznick, 448 U.S. 448 (1980).

Gainesville Media, Inc. (1978). 70 FCC 2d 143, Rev. Bd.

Graham, K. (1997). *Personal history/Katherine Graham*. New York: Knopf.

Grant, A. E. (1994). The promise fulfilled? An empirical analysis of program diversity on television. *Journal of Media Economics, 7*, 51–64.

Grutter v. Bollinger, U.S. Supreme Court, Slip Opinion, No. 02–241, Decided June 23, 2003.

Hamilton, J. T. (2004). *All the news that's fit to sell: How the market transforms information into news*. Princeton, NJ: Princeton University Press.

Hazlett, T. (1990). The rationality of U.S. regulation of the broadcast spectrum. *Journal of Law and Economics, 33*, 133–175.

Herman, E. S., & McChesney, R. (1997). *The global media: The new missionaries of corporate capitalism*. Washington, DC: Cassell.
Hill, C., & Landro, L. (2000, January 12). Does everybody have to own everything? Behind the vast media octopus of AOL and Time Warner, there's a simpler strategy. *The Wall Street Journal*, p. B1.
Hofstadter, R. (1955). *The age of reform: From Bryan to F.D.R.* New York: Vintage.
Hopwood v. Texas, 78 F.3d 932 (5th Cir. 1996).
Horwitz, R. B. (1991). The first amendment meets some new technologies: Broadcasting, common carriers and free speech in the 1990s. *Theory and Society, 20*, 21–72.
Horwitz, R. B. (1994). Judicial review of regulatory decisions: The changing criteria. *Political Science Quarterly, 109*, 133–169.
Horwitz, R. B. (1997). Broadcast reform revisited: Reverend Everett C. Parker and the WLBT case [*Office of Communications of the United Church of Christ v. FCC*]. *The Communication Review, 2*, 311–348.
House of Representatives Conference Report. (1982). No. 97–765. 97th Cong., 2d Sess.
In the Matter of the Application of Great Lakes Broadcasting Co. (1929). 3 FRC Annual Report 32.
Kaniss, P. C. (1991). *Making local news*. Chicago: University of Chicago Press.
Kubey, R., Shifflet, M., Weerakkody, N., & Ukeiley, S. (1995). Demographic diversity on cable: Have the new cable channels made difference in the representation of gender, race, and age? *Journal of Broadcasting & Electronic Media, 39*, 459–471.
Lamprecht v. FCC, 958 F.2d 382 (D.C. Cir. 1992).
Lande, R. H. (1982). Wealth transfers as the original and primary concern of antitrust: The efficiency interpretation challenged. *The Hastings Law Journal, 34*, 67–151.
Lessig, L., & Lemley, M. (1999). Written ex parte of Professor Mark A. Lemley and Professor Lawrence Lessig in the matter of application for consent to the transfer of control of licenses MediaOne Group, Inc. to AT&T Corp. FCC, CS Docket No. 99–251. Retrieved September 17, 2004, from http://www.fcc.gov/Bureaus/Miscellaneous/Public_Notices/Exparte/1999/exa91207.doc
Levin, H. J. (1970). Competition, diversity, and the television group ownership rule. *Columbia Law Review, 70*, 791–835.
Levin, H. J. (1980). *Fact and fancy in television regulation: An economic study of policy alternatives*. New York: Sage.
Lowery, S. A., & DeFleur, M. L. (1995). *Milestones in mass communication research: Media effects*. White Plains, NY: Longman.
Lutheran Church-Missouri Synod v. FCC, 141 F.3d 344 (D.C. Cir. 1998).
Mason, L., Bachen, C. M., & Craft, S. L. (2001). Support for FCC minority ownership policy: How broadcast station owner race or ethnicity affects news and public affairs programming diversity. *Communication Law & Policy, 6*, 37–73.
Metro Broadcasting v. FCC, 497 U.S. 547 (1990).
Mid-Florida Television Corp. (1978). 69 FCC 2d 607.
Millon, D. (1988). The Sherman act and the balance of power. *Southern California Law Review, 61*, 1219–1292.
Napoli, P. (1999). Deconstructing the diversity principle. *Journal of Communication, 49*(4), 7–34.
National Advisory Commission on Civil Disorders. (1968). *Report of the National Advisory Commission on Civil Disorders*. New York: Dutton.
National Broadcasting Co. v. United States, 319 U.S. 190 (1943).
National Citizens Committee for Broadcasting v. FCC, 555 F.2d 938 (D.C. Cir. 1977).
Nesvold, H. P. (n.d.). *Communications breakdown: Developing an antitrust model for multimedia mergers and acquisitions*. Retrieved September 17, 2004, from http://www.vii.org/papers/peter.htm

Network Programming Inquiry. (1960). 25 Fed. Reg. 7295.
New York Times v. Sullivan, 376 U.S. 254 (1964).
Noam, E. M. (n.d.). *Media concentration in the United States: Industry trends and regulatory responses*. Retrieved September 17, 2004, from http://www.vii.org/papers/medconc.htm
Noll, R., Peck, M., & McGowan J. (1973). *Economic aspects of television regulation*. Washington, DC: Brookings Institute.
Nondiscrimination in the Employment Policies and Practices of Broadcast Licensees. (1976). 60 FCC 2d 226.
Notice of Proposed Rulemaking. (2002). In the matter of 2002 biennial regulatory review—review of the commission's broadcast ownership rules and other rules adopted pursuant to section 202 of the Telecommunications Act of 1996, cross ownership of broadcast stations and newspapers, rule and policies concerning multiple ownership of radio broadcast stations in local markets, definition of radio markets. MB Docket No. 02–227, MM Dockets 02–235, 01–317, 00–244.
Office of Communications of the United Church of Christ v. FCC, 359 F.2d 994 (D.C. Cir. 1966).
Petition for Rulemaking to Require Broadcast Licensees to Show Nondiscrimination in their Employment Practices. (1968). 13 FCC 2d 766.
Police Association v. City of New Orleans, 100 F.3d 1159 (5th Cir. 1996).
Police v. Mosley, 408 U.S. 92 (1972).
Policies and Rules Regarding Minority and Female Ownership of Cable Television Facilities. (1982). 52 Rad. Reg. 2d P&F 1469.
Policy Statement on Comparative Broadcast Hearings. (1965). 1 FCC 2d 393.
Powell, M. (1998, April 22). *Willful denial and first amendment jurisprudence*. Retrieved September 17, 2004, from http://www.fcc.gov/commissioners/powell/mkp_speeches_1998.html
Primer on Ascertainment of Community Problems by Broadcast Applicants. (1971). 27 FCC 2d 650.
Project for Excellence in Journalism (2001, November/December). Special report: Local tv news. *Columbia Journalism Review*. Supplement.
Prometheus Radio Project v. FCC, No. 03-3388, etc. US Court of Appeals, 3rd Cir. Decided September 3, 2003.
Prometheus Radio Project v. FCC, No. 03-3388, etc. US Court of Appeals, 3rd Cir. Decided August 24, 2004.
Public Service Responsibility of Broadcast Licensees. (1946). Washington, DC: Federal Communications Commission.
Red Lion Broadcasting Corp. v. FCC, 395 U.S. 367 (1969).
Regents of the University of California v. Bakke, 438 U.S. 265 (1978).
Report and Order. (1970). 23 FCC 2d 382; rescinded, Network Financial Interest and Syndication Rules. 1995. 60 Fed. Reg. 48,907.
Report and Order. (2003). In the matter of 2002 biennial regulatory review—review of the commission's broadcast ownership rules and other rules adopted pursuant to section 202 of the Telecommunications Act of 1996, cross ownership of broadcast stations and newspapers, rule and policies concerning multiple ownership of radio broadcast stations in local markets, definition of radio markets. MB Docket No. 02–227, MM Dockets 02–235, 01–317, 00–244.
Report on Chain Broadcasting. (1941). Pursuant to Commission Order No. 37, Docket No. 5060. Washington, DC: Federal Communications Commission.
Review of the Commission's Regulations Governing Television Broadcasting: Further Notice of Proposed Rulemaking. (1995). 10 FCC Rcd. 3524.
Rosen, P. T. (1980). *The modern stentors: Radio broadcasters and the federal government, 1920–1934*. Westport, CT: Greenwood.

Schurz Communications v. FCC, 982 F.2d 1043 (7th Cir. 1992).
Schwartz, B. (1959). Comparative television and the chancellor's foot. *Georgetown Law Journal, 47,* 655–699.
Second Report and Order. (1974). 50 FCC 2d 1046.
Seiter, E. (1999). *Television and new media audiences*. New York: Oxford University Press.
Shurberg Broadcasting, Inc. v. FCC, 876 F.2d 902 (D.C. Cir. 1989).
Siebert, F. S., Peterson, T., & Schramm, W. (1956). *Four theories of the press: Authoritarian, libertarian, social responsibility and Soviet communist concepts of what the press should be and do*. Urbana: University of Illinois Press.
Sinclair Broadcast Group v. FCC, 284 F.3d 148 (DC Cir. 2002).
Spitzer, M. L. (1991). Justifying minority preferences in broadcasting. *Southern California Law Review, 64,* 293–361.
Stahlman v. FCC, 126 F.2d 124 (D.C. Cir. 1942).
Statement of Policy on Minority Ownership of Broadcasting Facilities. (1978). 68 FCC 2d 979.
Steele v. FCC, 770 F.2d 1192 (D.C. Cir. 1985).
Steiner, P. O. (1952). Program patterns and preferences, and the workability of competition in radio broadcasting. *Quarterly Journal of Economics, 66,* 194–223.
Sunstein, C. (1993). *Democracy and the problem of free speech*. New York: Free Press.
Telecommunications Act of 1996. Pub. L. No. 104–104, 110 Stat. 56 (1996).
The U.S. Commission on Civil Rights. (1977). *Window dressing on the set: Women and minorities in television*. Washington, DC: The Commission on Civil Rights.
Tifft, S. E., & Jones, A. (1999). *The trust: The private and powerful family behind the New York Times*. Boston: Little, Brown.
Time Warner v. FCC, 240 F.3d 1126 (D.C. Cir. 2001).
Tunstall, J., & Machin D. (1999). *The Anglo-American media connection*. New York: Oxford University Press.
Turner Broadcasting System, Inc. v. FCC, 512 U.S. 622 (1994).
Turner Broadcasting System, Inc. v. FCC, 520 U.S. 180 (1997).
TV9, Inc. v. FCC, 495 F.2d 929 (D.C. Cir. 1973).
U.S. v. Syufy Enterprises, 712 F. Supp. 1386 (N.D. Cal. 1989); *aff'd* 903 F2d 659 (9th Cir. 1990).
United States v. O'Brien, 391 U.S. 367 (1968).
United States v. Paramount Pictures, 334 U.S. 131 (1948).
United States v. Storer Broadcasting Co., 351 U.S. 192 (1956).
U.S. Department of Justice and the Federal Trade Commission. (1992). *Horizontal merger guidelines*. Retrieved September 17, 2004, from http://www.usdoj.gov/atr/public/guidelines/horiz_book/hmg1.html
Waklshlag, J., & Adams, W. J. (1985). Trends in program variety and the prime time access rule. *Journal of Broadcasting & Electronic Media, 29,* 23–34.
Waldfogel, J., & Siegelman, P. (1999). *Race and radio: Preference externalities, minority ownership, and the provision of programming to minorities*. Philadelphia: The Wharton School.
Waterman, D. (1992). 'Narrowcasting' and 'broadcasting' on non-broadcast media: A program choice model. *Communication Research, 19,* 3–28.
Waterman, D. (2000). CBS-Viacom and the effects of media mergers: An economic perspective. *Federal Communications Law Journal, 53,* 531–550.
West Michigan Broadcasting Co. v. FCC, 735 F.2d 601 (D.C. Cir. 1984), cert. denied, 470 U.S. 1027 (1985).
Winerip, M. (1998, January 11). Looking for an 11 o'clock fix. *The New York Times Magazine*, pp. 30–63.
Winter Park Communications, Inc. v. FCC, 873 F.2d 347 (D.C. Cir. 1989).

Wittmer v. Peters, 87 F.3d 916 (7th Cir. 1996).

Wysocki, Jr., B. (2000, January 31). Cyberspace Inc.: More companies cut risk by collaborating with their 'enemies': Many Internet operations co-invest in bid to insure at least a slice of success. *The Wall Street Journal*, pp. A1, A10.

3

Employment and Wage Effects of Radio Consolidation

Peter DiCola
University of Michigan

A typical headline laments: "Local Radio Loses a Distinctive Voice" (Feran, 1999). Another reports: "Radio News Facing Cutbacks: Consolidation in the Industry Brings Leaner Staffing" (Knoll, 1996). A more pointed article offers a metaphor: "Localism Vanishing as N[ew] H[ampshire] Radio Is 'McDonald-ized'" (Kenny, 1998). Such accounts often tell the story of a single veteran disk jockey, ousted from his or her longtime on-air slot, often at the decision of large companies like Clear Channel, Viacom, Radio One, or their premerger predecessors. Many commentators point to the brisk pace of ownership consolidation—the phenomenon of mergers and acquisitions leading to a more concentrated market structure in the industry—as the primary cause of local radio employees losing their jobs. One article quotes an estimate that "10,000 radio-related jobs" disappeared between 1996 and 2002 (Spencer, 2002). The Telecommunications Act of 1996 eliminated the national ownership limit for owners of radio stations while relaxing the limits on local radio ownership (Federal Communications Commission [FCC], 1996). In this chapter, I examine how increased concentration of radio station ownership relates to employment and wages in three radio-industry occupations by analyzing data from the 7 years following the Telecommunications Act of 1996.

Although the employment effects of consolidation have economic importance in their own right, they also fall under the purview of the FCC's major policy goals[1] of ensuring localism and fostering diversity. One journalist in

Detroit, where four firms garner over 80% market share (Media Access Pro, 2002), argues that "radio programming leaves little room to showcase local musicians, and there has been an invasion of syndicated shows and on-air personalities spliced in from distant cities via computer" and observes that "[s]yndicated hosts ... threaten local jobs" (Whitall, 2002). The author concludes, under the heading 'Loss of Jobs,' that '[r]adio analysts are convinced that many practices the big chains are responsible for—the de-emphasis on local content—save[] money, but will ultimately kill local radio' (Whitall, 2002). A radio station's choice to carry remotely produced programming, although it may satisfy some listeners' preferences, may simultaneously detract from localism and reduce employment. To the extent that consolidated firms have a stronger tendency to rely on syndication, voice tracking technology, or national programming than smaller firms, larger job losses (or smaller job gains) will accompany greater ownership concentration. Furthermore, if media mergers lead to job losses on a local level, then media outlets could become less familiar with and less responsive to the local communities in which they are based. And thinner ranks of disk jockeys and news reporters may mean less diverse choices of music and news stories. I argue later that job losses (and indirectly, wage reductions) represent a detriment to localism and diversity that the FCC can and should consider carefully, perhaps through further quantitative studies.

Common sense—as well as much anecdotal and qualitative evidence in the public debate over media regulation—holds that media mergers have led to downsizing. After all, the proponents of relaxed ownership rules argued that more restrictive rules prevented media firms from exploiting economies of scale. That is to say, commentators on all sides expected consolidators to centralize some functions that previously existed separately in separately owned stations. But studies using aggregate data can test these theories and verify anecdotal claims, like those quoted earlier from post-Telecommunications Act newspaper accounts. Quantitative analysis allows one to ask more formally whether ownership consolidation has led to job losses or wage reductions. Furthermore, it allows one to estimate the magnitude of those relationships and to determine whether different occupations within the radio industry have experienced different levels of employment decreases and wage decreases.

Using data from the Occupational Employment Survey of the U.S. Bureau of Labor Statistics, I estimate the effects of radio consolidation on employment and wages for three occupations: announcers, news reporters, and broadcast technicians. I find that, comparing figures across metropolitan areas, an increase in the number of stations per owner within a metropolitan area was associated with both lower employment levels and lower wages during the years 1996 to 2003. Whether this represents a causal effect of radio consolidation, in the sense that increasing the concentration of ownership within a particular market over time would in fact lead to job losses and lower wages, is a more difficult question. I conclude that the relationship between greater consolidation and lower levels of employment and wages probably pre-dates the Telecommunications Act of 1996; the data studied in this chapter do not answer definitively whether consolidation "causes" job loss or wage reductions in the sense described earlier. Yet the strong correlation between radio consolidation, job losses, and lower wages for common radio occupations remains an important fact for policymakers at the FCC as they seek to promote localism and diversity in radio programming.

INDUSTRY CONTEXT

Beginning in the 1980s, Congress and the FCC passed statutes and adopted regulations to relax the limits on national and local radio ownership.[2] But the most dramatic changes to ownership policy in radio arrived with the Telecommunications Act of 1996. In that legislation, Congress repealed the national radio ownership limit, which previously capped a firm's holdings at 40 stations. Moreover, Congress raised the local radio ownership limit from a sliding scale of three to four stations, depending on the total number of stations in a market, to a sliding scale of five to eight stations. As a result, many stations changed hands and many firms merged. The national radio market became much more concentrated; by spring 2002, the 10 largest firms had two-thirds market share and the two largest (Clear Channel and Viacom) combined for over 40% market share (DiCola & Thomson, 2002, p. 18). Local radio markets became highly concentrated—in almost every metropolitan area, the four largest firms together had over 70% market share (DiCola & Thomson, 2002, p. 31). That figure generally exceeded 90% in smaller markets (that is, in all but the 50 largest U.S. cities; DiCola & Thomson, 2002, p. 33). This chapter focuses on local radio markets to study the corresponding local labor markets for radio industry occupations.

While advocating the relaxation or elimination of various media ownership rules, both before the passage of the Telecommunications Act and later in debate over the FCC's recent biennial review of its media ownership rules, (FCC, 2003), media companies and some commentators often argued that media companies were poised to benefit from economies of scale if allowed to grow bigger and to centralize some operations.[3] In other words, two stations that each required 10 employees when separately owned could, in theory, be staffed by fewer than 20 employees when jointly owned. Implicit in the economies-of-scale theory is a promise to shareholders to reduce the number of employees needed to support the same number of broadcast outlets. If media companies made good on their stated intentions, then one should observe lower employment levels in more consolidated markets.

Theoretical predictions of the effect of radio consolidation on wages in particular occupations are more ambiguous. Decreased demand for labor resulting from economies of scale could depress wages, based on a simple supply-and-demand diagram. But surely such a model is too simple. Technological developments facilitated by economies of scale could enhance productivity per worker. Macroeconomic trends could exert pressure on industry-wide wages. Perhaps most importantly, layoffs might target employees with above-average or below-average wages compared to the industry as a whole. The wage effects of firms' layoff choices will depend on many factors that are difficult to observe, especially at the aggregate level, such as the particular organizational structure of firms and the wage profile of the particular employees that are laid off.

New technologies and organizational strategies have indeed arisen in the wake of the Telecommunications Act. First, large radio companies can now adopt "voice tracking" technology. Voice tracking is the practice of broadcasting the show of a radio announcer (or DJ) nationwide while trying to make the show seem local.[4] Radio companies can enjoy the cost savings that accompany syndication while seeming local. Second, radio companies now plan much of their programming centrally. DJs have less choice; market testing of 10-sec song snippets has become prevalent; and payola-like practices allegedly have affected programming decisions. To the extent that more programming decisions occur centrally, fewer DJs and program directors are needed (DiCola & Thomson, 2002, pp. 61–67). Third, large radio firms appear to take advantage of their size to hire fewer broadcast technicians. Consider the now-infamous incident in Minot, North Dakota, which arose when a train carrying ammonia fertilizer derailed, releasing deadly ammonia gas (Burcum, 2002). When local officials sought to broadcast warnings on the radio, no one at the designated emergency broadcast station (KCJB, owned by Clear Channel) was available to answer the phone (Lee, 2003). The allocation of labor across radio stations delayed an emergency response team's attempts to alert the local community. These three examples show that firms in the radio industry have attempted to exploit economies of scale.

Consolidation of operations like the engineering tasks performed by broadcast technicians represents centralization within a local market. What used to be two jobs in a particular city becomes one job. Some centralization of programming occurs on a local level as well. If two stations previously had separate radio newsrooms but become jointly owned, the consolidator will probably close one of the newsrooms. The phenomenon of "simulcasting" functions similarly. An owner of multiple stations within a market might choose to rebroadcast all or part of one station's programming on one of the jointly owned stations within the same local market. One reason a firm might do this is to increase signal reach; its broadcast towers could stand on either side of a large city, both considered part of the same market. A decision to simulcast by a consolidating firm, like other strategies of local centralization, will cause job losses.

Centralization on a national scale also shrinks radio industry employment, but in a more complicated fashion because of the interplay between the national and local levels of organization. It is unclear whether the more consolidated local markets will experience relatively more job loss as a result of nationally centralized programming. Syndication and voice tracking have developed within larger firms, which tend to have holdings in larger markets,[5] which in turn have less concentrated ownership on average. Together these facts suggest that less consolidated markets might experience more of the job loss caused by national centralization. On the other hand, if a consolidating firm happens to locate some of its centralized operations in a particular market, that city might retain (or even gain) radio jobs. Syndicated shows and voice-tracked programs employ at least a few people and have to locate somewhere. Radio firms may choose to centralize operations in larger metropolitan areas, resulting in greater job losses within small markets, which generally have more concentrated ownership. In general, the location of jobs after a firm implements more nationally centralized programming will depend on the firm's particular strategy, its existing employment allocations across stations, and other hard-to-measure factors. Thus, national centralization may influence the correlation between local-market consolidation and job loss positively or negatively. Overall, however, based on the impact of the various forms of local centralization discussed earlier, one would predict that greater consolidation in a local market should lead to lower employment levels in that market.

REGULATORY FRAMEWORK

Labor markets are not explicitly contemplated in standard descriptions of the FCC's three overarching policy goals of competition, diversity, and localism. So where does analysis of radio consolidation, employment, and wages fit into the FCC's regulatory framework? I argue that the employment levels and wages of those in radio-industry occupations are highly relevant to whether broadcasters adequately serve local communities. The notion that employing local residents may contribute to community responsiveness runs through many of the public debates over issues like syndication and nationalization. Lower wages could indirectly decrease the quality of local radio programming by providing talented media employees with less incentive to work in radio. Labor market issues also affect diversity, particularly viewpoint diversity, because job losses mean fewer participants in media production and fewer participants means fewer viewpoints. But employment issues relate most closely to localism.

Phillip Napoli (2001) has identified two major strains within policymakers' and scholars' thinking about the goal of localism. Both can accommodate a concern for what occurs in the labor markets for radio occupations. The first theory conceives of localism geographically. As Napoli (2001) explains, under this theory "any program produced and presented within a local community would be seen as contributing to the fulfillment of the localism ideal" (p. 210). This geographic conception depends on local production and thus on local employees. In this way, local labor markets become highly relevant to the localism goal, with job losses thwarting its achievement. The second theory focuses more on content; in this conception, "the localism principle is only fulfilled if the programming addresses the unique needs and interests of the local community" (Napoli, 2001, p. 217). Whether radio employees are local to a geography (such as a city, town, or metropolitan area) will relate to the second conception of localism under two conditions: (a) if one decides that geographic definitions of "community" remain important despite mass media technology, perhaps in light of state and local politics; and (b) if one thinks that radio employees' physical presence in a community will promote responsiveness to community needs. This chapter does not address whether those two conditions hold. But if those conditions did hold true, then the employment effects of radio consolidation would matter a great deal for localism.

Historically, the FCC has scrutinized the organization and location of work in media industries. So labor market issues have always been part of the localism goal, whether directly or indirectly. Section 307(b) of the Communications Act, which the Senate has recently called the "pole star" of telecommunications regulation, directs as follows:

> In considering applications for licenses, and modifications and renewals thereof, when and insofar as there is demand for the same, the Commission shall make such distribution of licenses, frequencies, hours of operation,

and of power among the several States and communities as to provide a fair, efficient, and equitable distribution of radio service to each of the same. (S.1046, 2003)

By directing the FCC to consider "communities" and the distribution of licenses among them, the statute created a foundation for considering whether stations serve local communities well. Back when the FCC still conducted initial assignment hearings, two of the seven factors required applicants to show that "there is a need for the proposed broadcast station in the community" and that they "will be responsive to local community needs."[6] These factors related to employment issues only indirectly. But in comparative hearings, the FCC would consider the "full-time participation in station operation by owners" and explained that "[w]hile ... integration of ownership and management is important per se, its value is increased if the participating owners are local residents" (Federal Communications Commission, 1965). The FCC argued that local residents could respond to changing community needs better than nonlocals. Thus, in the days of licensing hearings, FCC policy connected the localism goal to the geographic location of station employees, specifically the day-to-day managers.

The U.S. Court of Appeals for the D.C. Circuit struck down the integration criterion for ownership and management in 1993 in *Bechtel v. FCC,* and Congress and the FCC have done away with comparative licensing hearings (Benjamin, Lichtman, & Shelanski, 2001). But those facts do not imply that the FCC may not consider labor-market issues in the course of regulating broadcast. The norms behind the former integration preference survive in the two theories described earlier, not to mention the ideals still reflected in Section 307(b). If eliminating the national radio ownership limit and relaxing local radio ownership limits led to detrimental effects on localism and diversity, then the FCC can and should examine them. The court in Bechtel had a multipronged rationale for overturning the integration preference, including concerns about the particular implementation of the FCC's policy and the ease of circumventing it (*Bechtel v. FCC,* 1993, pp. 885–886). Most importantly, the court wanted to see some kind of empirical evidence to support the FCC's policy,[7] a common theme in recent administrative-law reviews of FCC policy.[8] Suppose, for example, that the FCC collected empirical evidence linking consolidation to job loss, and coupled it with evidence associating local employees with responsiveness to their geographic community. Then, in accordance with its localism goal, the FCC could take action (such as maintaining or even reducing ownership caps) and have a strong argument that a reviewing court should show deference to in its decision.

Recently the FCC launched a Localism Task Force "to gather empirical data on broadcast localism, and to advise the Commission on concrete steps to promote this significant policy goal" (FCC, 2004). The commission announced its intentions to investigate some of the issues discussed earlier, such as voice tracking, national playlists, diminished political news coverage, and disaster warnings. In this chapter, I examine the labor markets for the very occupations involved in these policy debates: on-air announcers (including disk jockeys), broadcast news reporters, and broadcast technicians. Thus the study of the employment effects of radio consolidation provides the FCC with another angle from which to study the issues it has recently deemed most important for achieving the ideal of localism.

LABOR MARKET TRENDS

General labor market trends in employment and wages in radio provide context for analyzing the labor market effects of radio consolidation. The Current Employment Statistics survey (CES), conducted and published by the Bureau of Labor Statistics (BLS), can provide a broad overview. Figure 3.1 shows industry-wide employment levels over time for the radio industry as well as the television industry, for comparison (Bureau of Labor Statistics). (The dotted line marks the passage of the Telecommunications Act of 1996.) From this chart, it appears that radio employment has stagnated, whereas from 1992 onward, television employment has increased. This may reflect factors beyond

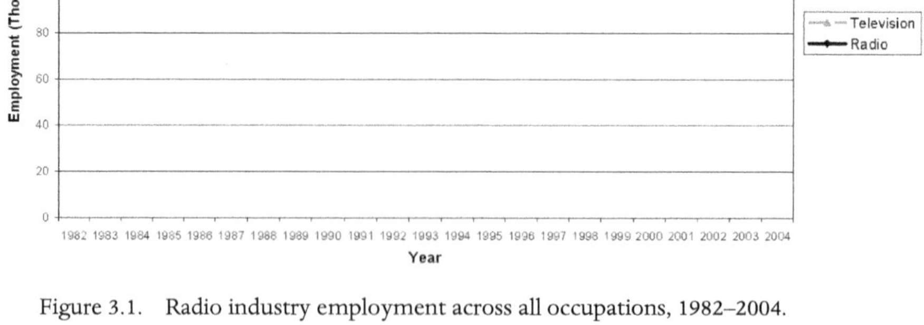

Figure 3.1. Radio industry employment across all occupations, 1982–2004.

radio deregulation, such as the upsurge of cable television along with cable music channels.

Figure 3.2 adjusts the aggregate radio employment figures for the number of stations in the United States (Bureau of Labor Statistics, 2005; Media Access Pro, 2002). It appears that the late 1980s and early 1990s actually brought about the most significant decrease in employment per station over the past two decades. From 1988 to 1995, employment per station dropped from 11.65 to 9.54, an 18.1% decrease. In the period following the Telecommunications Act of 1996, employment per station has continued to drop (from 9.54 to 8.70), but by only 8.8%. The decline between 1988 and 1995 might be explained by the incremental steps of deregulation that occurred in 1984 and 1992, that is, the gradual relaxation of both the national and local radio ownership limits. The precipitous decline may also signify a period of sagging financial outcomes for radio firms; the Telecommunications Act was pitched as a way to rescue ailing radio firms (Aufderheide, 1999).

Real wages in the radio industry show a steady upward trend over the past two decades, as illustrated in Fig. 3.3 (Bureau of Labor Statistics, 2005). Over the period from 1995 to 2004, real wages increased 38.7%; this compares to 3.3% increase from 1988 to 1995. Macroeconomic trends have no doubt influenced these figures, perhaps in unpredictable ways, but it appears from the aggregate statistics that since the Telecommunications Act of 1996, employment per station in the radio industry has declined a total of about 9% whereas real wages have risen by almost 39%.

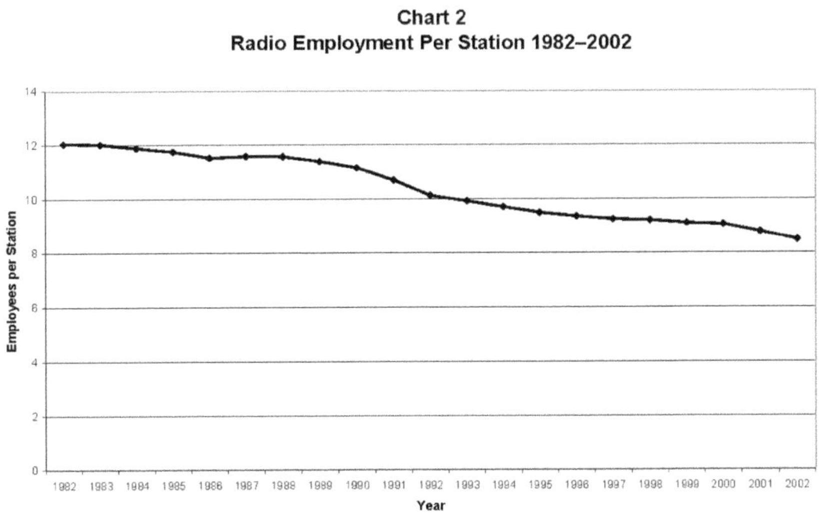

Figure 3.2. Radio industry employment per licensed station (across all occupations), 1982–2002.

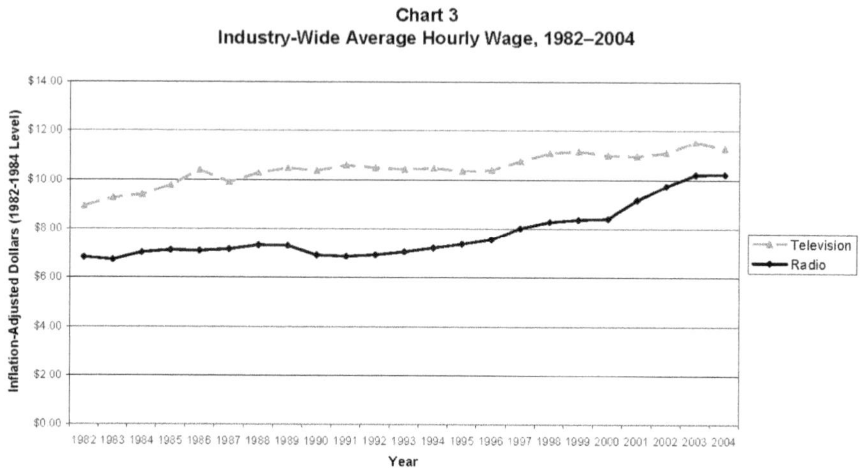

Figure 3.3. Average hourly wage in the radio industry across all occupations, 1982–2004.

In sum, total employment in the radio industry has been steady. But this, together with the growth in the number of licensed stations, means that employment per station has declined in each of the past two decades. The regulatory changes of 1996 came at a time when job losses already occurred fairly frequently; this accords with anecdotal accounts. Real wages, in contrast, have increased sharply in the years following the Telecommunications Act.

METHODOLOGY AND DATA SOURCES

Consolidation rarely occurs in a quick, coordinated way. This makes it difficult, in general, to isolate the effects of consolidation on labor market outcomes. But in the radio industry, the removal of certain regulations directly limiting the size of firms resulted in an industry-wide wave of consolidation within a relatively short period of time. Fast-paced change has occurred in radio since the passage of the Telecommunications Act of 1996, as shown by the time series of ownership changes displayed in Fig. 3.4 (Media Access Pro, 2002).

The brisk pace of consolidation provides a source of variation. Different markets started from different levels of concentration and experienced consolidation at different rates over time. Using this variation in consolidation, I use ownership concentration as an explanatory variable in a series of panel regressions with employment and wages as the outcomes. Figure 3.4 shows that the pace of consolidation peaked in 1996 and 1997 and slowed by 2001 to 2002.

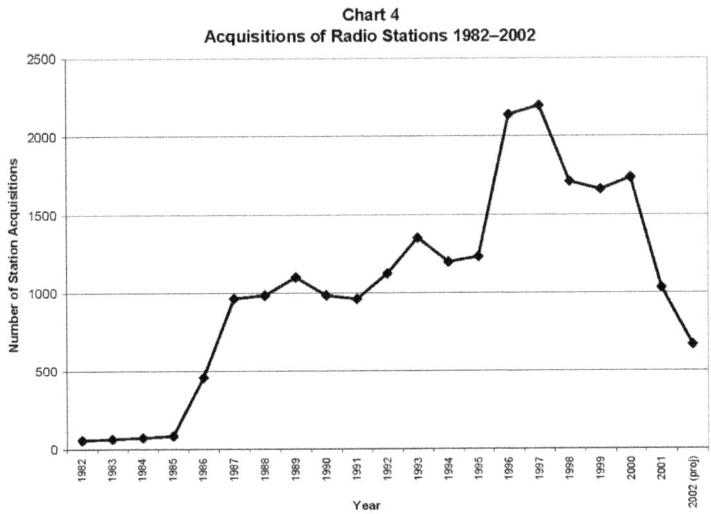

Figure 3.4. Number of radio stations changing ownership, 1982–2002.

Because the change in consolidation occurred over a relatively brief span of time, one can hope that fewer unobserved, confounding factors have influenced consolidation, employment and wages, or their relationship.

The Occupational Employment Survey (OES), conducted by the BLS, contains data on employment and wages, broken down by occupation and by metropolitan statistical area (MSA), in nonagricultural industries. In 1998, the BLS began conducting the OES on a yearly basis, rather than once every 3 years.[9] In 2003, the OES shifted again, to a twice-yearly format. Each release of the OES contains data looking back on 3 years. In this analysis, I use OES data from the 1998 release through the November 2003 release; thus, I have employment and wage data from 1996 to late 2003. The advantage of the OES data for studying the radio industry is that three occupations of interest can be studied: (1) announcers; (2) news analysts, reporters, and correspondents ("news reporters"); and (3) broadcast technicians. Table 3.1 displays some summary statistics on the OES occupational data; note that until recently the OES aggregated radio and television into one industry group (Bureau of Labor Statistics, 2004).

I merged the OES data with information from BIA Financial Networks' Media Access Pro (Radio Version) database, which contains information about every radio station in the United States, including ownership history, ratings, and estimated revenue. The database classifies stations by "Arbitron

TABLE 3.1

Occupation Employment Survey Summary Statistics, Radio and Television Industries

Occupation	*Year*	*Employment in Radio and TV*	*Percentage Radio and TV*	*Percentage Just Radio*	*Mean Hourly Real Wage*	*Median Hourly Real Wage*	*Mean and Median*
Announcers	1998	46,100	93.8%	—	$11.44	$8.51	1.34
	1999	45,010	89.3%	—	$11.98	$8.68	1.38
	2000	42,220	84.8%	—	$12.44	$9.03	1.38
	2001	40,990	81.3%	—	$12.22	$8.90	1.37
	2002	40,280	80.9%	73.6%	$12.70	$8.93	1.42
	2003 (May)	38,990	79.0%	71.4%	$12.43	$8.86	1.40
	2003 (Nov.)	38,350	78.7%	70.8%	$12.64	$9.03	1.40
News Reporters	1998	11,320	21.6%	—	$18.65	$13.35	1.40
	1999	17,530	27.1%	—	$19.39	$14.16	1.37
	2000	19,900	30.2%	—	$20.64	$15.27	1.35
	2001	19,020	29.7%	—	$20.12	$15.02	1.34
	2002	16,890	27.6%	6.8%	$20.15	$14.52	1.39
	2003 (May)	16,350	27.1%	6.3%	$20.69	$14.81	1.40
	2003 (Nov.)	17,480	28.6%	6.9%	$21.21	$15.47	1.37
Broadcast Technicians	1998	22,990	61.7%	—	$13.72	$10.70	1.28
	1999	19,820	77.5%	—	$12.57	$10.15	1.24
	2000	24,610	73.3%	—	$14.57	$10.80	1.35
	2001	21,960	70.6%	—	$14.37	$10.98	1.31
	2002	21,210	67.3%	20.1%	$13.94	$10.63	1.31
	2003 (May)	21,820	66.6%	21.2%	$13.72	$10.52	1.30
	2003 (Nov.)	21,230	68.6%	22.8%	$13.58	$10.8	21.25

markets," geographical areas that roughly correspond to MSAs and are used by the Arbitron Company.[10] I matched MSAs with Arbitron markets wherever possible to produce a panel data set with 246 markets and seven time periods (1998 through 2002, plus May 2003 and November 2003). Because the OES does not survey firms in every market about every occupation in every year, several of the potential observations in the panel are missing.

The panel data set I constructed has four main drawbacks. First, although the OES surveys about 400,000 establishments each year, the sample sizes for an individual occupation in a particular market-year combination can be tiny (or zero, when the market-year observation is missing). Second, to use the occupational data in the OES, one must look at all individuals in a given occupation, not just the individuals in one industry-occupation combination. In other words, the outcome variables I use include some employees from nonradio industries, potentially confounding the effects of radio consolidation on radio employment, especially in the "news reporters" occupation. Third, the OES reports data only at the market level—so one cannot disaggregate the data to study issues like the employment effects of two previously independent stations coming under common ownership. Fourth, both the OES and Media Access Pro data sets begin in 1996, eliminating the potential for pre- and post-analysis of the Telecommunications Act.[11] Despite these disadvantages, the panel data provide a number of interesting insights.

REGRESSION ANALYSIS

The unit of observation in my analysis is a market-year combination. As described earlier, the data set includes 246 markets and seven time periods, with many market-year observations missing due to the nature of the OES. The labor-market outcome variables I analyze come in three groups of three: the number of employees, the mean hourly wage, and the median wage for announcers, news reporters, and broadcast technicians. Sample sizes vary by both occupation and the particular outcome in question, again as a result of the OES survey methodology.

I study three explanatory variables for each market-year combination: number of stations, stations per owner, and the variance of stations owned. First, the number of radio stations in a market should affect employment simply because, all else equal, more stations will require more employees. I include both commercial and noncommercial stations, because both for-profit and nonprofit employees can show up in the OES data. Second, the number of stations in a market divided by the number of firms owning stations provides a measure of consolidation. I refer to this variable as "stations per owner," but it is important to remember that the variable is measured locally; stations owned in other markets are not taken into account. Third, the variance of stations owned by each firm within a market measures a second-order effect of consolidation that may relate to labor-market outcomes in the presence of economies of scale. Consider two markets, A and B, each with 20 total stations and each with 5 stations per owner. The holdings of the four owners in these hypothetical markets could differ considerably. For instance, in market A, each owner might have five stations, whereas in market B, two owners have nine stations and two owners have just one station. The variance of stations owned captures such differences in ownership structure within markets.

Table 3.2 reports summary statistics for the panel data set (Bureau of Labor Statistics, 2004; Media Access Pro, 2002). Because the OES employment data include a greater number of missing values than the OES wage data, the sample sizes vary. Thus, Table 3.2 contains two sets of summary statistics for the outcome variables, one corresponding to the employment regressions and one corresponding to the wage regressions.

Because the data set is a panel, I can estimate multiple types of models to measure the effect of consolidation on employment and wages. I start with a pair of pooled regressions, which treat each market-year observation as independent, essentially ignoring the panel nature of the data set (Johnston &

TABLE 3.2

Means, Standard Deviations, and Sample Sizes for Variables Used in Panel Regressions

Category	*Variable*	*Occupation*			*Total*
		Announcers	*News Reporters*	*Broadcast Technicians*	
Outcome variables	Employment	183 (215) [1,067]	275 (426) [966]	196 (360) [811]	—
	Mean hourly wage ($)	13.08 (3.77) [1,278]	17.47 (4.35) [1,114]	13.80 (3.50) [891]	—
	Median wage ($)	10.24 (2.58) [1,278]	15.13 (3.90) [1114]	12.37 (3.56) [891]	—
For employment regressions	Total stations in market	32.7 (17.9) [1,067]	35.0 (18.6) [966]	37.8 (18.3) [811]	27.0 (16.6) [2,023]
	Stations per owner	1.81 (0.356) [1,067]	1.83 (0.356) [966]	1.83 (0.342) [811]	1.82 (0.395) [2,023]
	Variance of stations owned	2.11 (1.44) [1,067]	2.28 (1.53) [966]	2.29 (1.51) [811]	2.10 (1.70) [2,022]
For wage regressions	Total stations in market	32.0 (17.5) [1,278]	34.1 (18.1) [1,114]	37.4 (18.2) [891]	27.0 (16.6) [2,023]
	Stations per owner	1.81 (0.360) [1,278]	1.82 (0.358) [1,114]	1.83 (0.345) [891]	1.82 (0.395) [2,023]
	Variance of stations owned	2.09 (1.45) [1,278]	2.23 (1.56) [1,114]	2.33 (1.57) [891]	2.10 (1.70) [2,022]

Note. Standard deviations in parentheses, sample sizes in brackets.

DiNardo, 1997, p. 390). The first of the pooled regressions uses only two explanatory variables (the number of stations and stations per owner); the second adds the variance of stations owned. Next, I estimate a similar model, using all three explanatory variables, but control for year-specific effects. Finally, I estimate a fixed effects model by adding a full set of market-specific indicators. Stated more formally, for each of the three outcome variables, I estimate four types of models:

$$\mathbf{y}_{mt} = \mathbf{w'}_{mt}\gamma + \varepsilon_{mt} \quad (1)$$

$$\mathbf{y}_{mt} = \mathbf{x'}_{mt}\beta + \varepsilon_{mt} \quad (2)$$

$$\mathbf{y}_{mt} = \mathbf{x'}_{mt}\beta + \mathbf{d'}_{t}\lambda_{t} + \varepsilon_{mt} \quad (3)$$

$$\mathbf{y}_{mt} = \mathbf{x'}_{mt}\beta + \mathbf{d'}_{m}\alpha_{m} + \mathbf{d'}_{t}\lambda_{t} + \varepsilon_{mt} \quad (4)$$

where **y** denotes the outcome variable in question (employment, mean hourly wage, or median hourly wage), **w** denotes a shortened vector of explanatory variables (just number of stations and stations per owner); **x** denotes the full vector of explanatory variables (number of stations, stations per owner, and variance of stations owned), ε denotes the error term, $\mathbf{d'}_t$ denotes a vector of year indicators, λ_t denotes year-specific fixed effects, $\mathbf{d'}_m$ denotes a vector of market indicators, and α_m denotes market-specific fixed effects.

The pooled regressions serve as a sort of baseline for comparison. Their coefficient estimates are based on both cross-sectional variation and variation over time. Including year-specific effects, which control for industry-wide time trends, allows one to focus on cross-sectional variation as well as deviations from time trends within particular local markets. The fixed-effects model, which also controls time-specific effects, has the advantage of allowing one to ignore any omitted variables that do not change over time (but do vary across individuals) as well as any omitted variables that do not vary across individuals (but do change over time) (Ruud, 2000, p. 625). This approach, in other words, attempts to avoid the common problem of omitted variable bias (Johnston & DiNardo, 1997, p. 395). Because many unobservable factors influence radio firms' employment decisions, as discussed earlier, I try to address the omitted-variable-bias issue by using a fixed-effects approach.

Striking results emerge from the pooled regressions and the regressions including year-specific effects in Tables 3.3-A, 3.3-B, and 3.3-C (Bureau of Labor Statistics, 2004; Media Access Pro, 2002). Estimates from the pooled regressions and the regressions including year-specific effects are broadly similar. The total number of stations variable has a positive correlation with employment, as expected. Markets with more stations also had higher hourly wages (both mean and median), perhaps reflecting the higher cost of living in larger markets.

Greater consolidation, as measured by stations per owner, has a negative and statistically significant association with employment of both news reporters and broadcast technicians. (The coefficient on stations per owner in column (3) of Table 3.3-A for announcers is negative but not statistically significant.) The relationship between employment and consolidation is also economically meaningful: a 1% increase in consolidation was associated with a 1.5% decline in employment of news reporters and a 0.8% decline in employment of broadcast technicians. Suppose that model (3), with year-specific effects, is the correct model of a radio market, allowing one to estimate the true causal effect of consolidation on employment. In the average Arbitron market, stations per owner increased by about 36% between 1996 and 2003 (Media Access Pro, 2002). So the isolated effect of consolidation, according to the estimates in column (3) of Table 3.1, would be that employment of news reporters declined by 56% and employment of broadcast technicians by 30% over this time period, in an average market.

Consolidation also has a negative and statistically significant correlation with mean hourly wages, for both news reporters and announcers, and with median hourly wages for news reporters. In the context of large wage increases industry-wide, as shown in Fig. 3.3 earlier, this means that markets with more ownership consolidation experienced smaller wage increases. Stations per owner has an estimated coefficient of –0.33 for announcers and –0.28 for news reporters, as shown in column (3) of Table 3.3-B. Using these estimates and making the same assumption as earlier about the veracity of model (3), it appears that wages for announcers and news reporters in an average market are 12% and 10% lower, respectively, as a result of radio consolidation.

The fixed-effects estimates in column (4) of Tables 3.3-A, 3.3-B, and 3.3-C complicate this picture. Only one of the estimates for the coefficients on stations per owner remains statistically significant after including market-specific indicator variables. (The negative association between consolidation and median hourly wages for news reporters remains statistically significant at the 5% level.) This shows that cross-sectional variation provided most of the identification in the regressions with only year-specific effects. In other words, differences across markets, rather than within markets, appear to have generated the negative correlations between consolidation and employment and between consolidation and wages. The fixed-effects regressions do not support the causal inference that if consolidation increased over time (for some reason exogenous to the workings of the market) in a particular local market, job loss and lower wages would result in that particular market. Rather, the shift in the results from the year-specific-effects model to the fixed-effects model only demonstrates a cross-sectional relationship between consolidation and job loss and between consolidation and lower wages.

On the other hand, the fixed-effects estimates have some potential problems. The OES data may be too incomplete (that is, they may contain too many missing values) to generate statistically significant estimates based solely on within-market variation over time. Because it uses a full set of indicator variables for markets and years, the fixed-effects model may ask too much of the

TABLE 3.3-A

Regression Results—Outcome Variable = Employment; All Variables in Natural Logarithms

		Model			
Occupation	*Explanatory Variable*	*(1)*	*(2)*	*(3)*	*(4)*
Announcers ($N = 1{,}067$)	Total stations in market	1.25**	1.26**	1.25**	−0.280
		(0.077)	(0.082)	(0.082)	(0.416)
	Stations per owner	−0.401**	−0.307	−0.268	−0.112
		(0.143)	(0.294)	(0.296)	(0.212)
	Variance of stations owned	—	−0.027	−0.033	−0.012
			(0.070)	(0.076)	(0.045)
	Year effects	No	No	Yes	Yes
	Market effects	No	No	No	Yes
	R^2	0.560	0.560	0.567	0.905
News Reporters ($N = 966$)	Total Stations in Market	1.39**	1.33**	1.36**	−0.124
		(0.098)	(0.100)	(0.097)	(0.402)
	Stations per owner	−1.04**	−1.58**	−1.56**	0.026
		(0.212)	(0.336)	(0.337)	(0.191)
	Variance of stations owned	—	0.162*	0.062	0.042
			(0.075)	(0.081)	(0.040)
	Year effects	No	No	Yes	Yes
	Market effects	No	No	No	Yes
	R^2	0.590	0.595	0.614	0.947
Broadcast technicians ($N = 811$)	Total stations in market	1.42**	1.39**	1.38**	0.104
		(0.111)	(0.119)	(0.119)	(0.541)
	Stations per owner	−0.582**	−0.855*	−0.838*	−0.172
		(0.181)	(0.332)	(0.337)	(0.252)
	Variance of stations owned	—	0.082	0.117	0.039
			(0.083)	(0.095)	(0.050)
	Year effects	No	No	Yes	Yes
	Market effects	No	No	No	Yes
	R^2	0.555	0.556	0.560	0.927

Note. Standard errors in parentheses.
**Denotes significance at the 1% level; *Denotes significance at the 5% level.

TABLE 3.3-B

Regression Results—Outcome Variable = Mean Hourly Wages; All Variables in Natural Logarithms

		Model			
Occupation	*Explanatory Variable*	*(1)*	*(2)*	*(3)*	*(4)*
Announcers (*N* = 1,278)	Total stations in market	0.225** (0.030)	0.192** (0.031)	0.210** (0.030)	0.075 (0.170)
	Stations per owner	–0.037 (0.073)	–0.302* (0.118)	–0.334** (0.116)	0.021 (0.092)
	Variance of stations owned	—	0.078** (0.029)	0.027 (0.031)	–0.008 (0.019)
	Year effects	No	No	Yes	Yes
	Market effects	No	No	No	Yes
	R^2	0.173	0.186	0.262	0.757
News Reporters (*N* = 1114)	Total stations in market	0.192** (0.029)	0.149** (0.030)	0.165** (0.031)	0.327 (0.180)
	Stations per owner	0.083 (0.061)	–0.285** (0.108)	–0.277* (0.108)	–0.145 (0.089)
	Variance of stations owned	—	0.110** (0.026)	0.061** (0.027)	–0.002 (0.018)
	Year effects	No	No	Yes	Yes
	Market effects	No	No	No	Yes
	R^2	0.169	0.204	0.270	0.773
Broadcast technicians (*N* = 891)	Total stations in market	0.196** (0.041)	0.178** (0.045)	0.189** (0.043)	0.408 (0.242)
	Stations per owner	–0.001 (0.074)	–0.149 (0.161)	–0.143 (0.159)	0.056 (0.114)
	Variance of stations owned	—	0.045 (0.035)	–0.011 (0.35)	–0.034 (0.023)
	Year effects	No	No	Yes	Yes
	Market effects	No	No	No	Yes
	R^2	0.140	0.145	0.197	0.763

Note. Standard errors in parentheses.
**Denotes significant at the 1% level; *Denotes significant at the 5% level.

OES data. Furthermore, fixed-effects models in general are highly sensitive to measurement error in the explanatory variable (Johnston & DiNardo, 1997). Although the data on station ownership histories from Media Access Pro are fairly reliable, they may not be perfect. More importantly, the combination of Media Access Pro and OES may introduce something akin to measurement error. Because the OES only surveys a subset of firms in a market in a given year, it may be that the most appropriate **x** variables would reflect the number of stations owned by those particular firms, the stations per owner actually surveyed by

OES, and so on. Instead, the **x** variables include market-wide measures that may not correspond properly to the **y** variables in a particular market-year, because the identities of the firms surveyed by OES are unavailable. This kind of measurement error might even attenuate (bias toward zero) the estimates somewhat in the pooled and year-specific-effects models, but would introduce stronger attenuation bias in the fixed-effects model.

Even taking the fixed-effects estimates as accurate, the pooled regressions and the regressions with only year-specific effects suggest a strong cross-sectional correlation between greater consolidation and lower employment and

TABLE 3.3-C

Regression Results—Outcome Variable = Median Hourly Wages; All Variables in Natural Logarithms

		Model			
Occupation	*Explanatory Variable*	*(1)*	*(2)*	*(3)*	*(4)*
Announcers (N = 1,278)	Total stations in market	0.115** (0.026)	0.091** (0.027)	0.106** (0.026)	0.060 (0.168)
	Stations per owner	0.031 (0.066)	−0.166 (0.106)	−0.189 (0.105)	0.135 (0.091)
	Variance of stations owned	—	0.058* (0.025)	0.013 (0.027)	−0.024 (0.019)
	Year effects	No	No	Yes	Yes
	Market effects	No	No	No	Yes
	R^2	0.062	0.072	0.147	0.681
News reporters (N = 1,114)	Total stations in market	0.155** (0.030)	0.107** (0.030)	0.122** (0.031)	0.186 (0.197)
	Stations per owner	0.040 (0.059)	−0.360** (0.104)	−0.355** (0.104)	−0.246* (0.098)
	Variance of stations owned	—	0.120** (0.026)	0.076** (0.027)	0.039 (0.020)
	Year effects	No	No	Yes	Yes
	Market effects	No	No	No	Yes
	R^2	0.107	0.148	0.201	0.729
Broadcast technicians (N = 891)	Total stations in market	0.207** (0.040)	0.199** (0.043)	0.208** (0.042)	0.369 (0.299)
	Stations per owner	−0.027 (0.073)	−0.095 (0.154)	−0.084 (0.152)	0.184 (0.142)
	Variance of stations owned	—	0.021 (0.035)	−0.034 (0.037)	−0.059* (0.028)
	Year effects	No	No	Yes	Yes
	Market effects	No	No	No	Yes
	R^2	0.133	0.134	0.173	0.695

Note. Standard errors in parentheses.
**Denotes significant at the 1% level; *Denotes significant at the 5% level.

wages. This may reflect economic relationships between the variables that pre-date the 1996 to 2003 period of study. Radio ownership limits, both national and local, began to increase gradually in the 1980s. So a causal relationship between consolidation and employment (and between consolidation and wages) may exist, but it may have commenced operating more than a decade before the time period I have been able to study using the OES and Media Access Pro. One can conclude from the regressions that more consolidated markets, controlling for the number of stations as well as year-specific effects, have lower employment levels and lower wages than do less consolidated markets.

CONCLUSION

Labor-market outcomes have not often, if ever, received explicit empirical scrutiny in discussions of broadcast media regulation. Yet many radio industry issues important to legislators, scholars, activists, and FCC regulators—syndication, voice tracking, emergency broadcast warnings, nationalized music programming, and local news coverage—have important labor-economic aspects. Under the rubric of localism, especially, but also in the context of promoting viewpoint diversity, the FCC can and should monitor job losses and wage reductions in radio industry occupations. The empirical analysis in this article, controlling for the number of stations and industry-wide time trends, demonstrates that more consolidated markets have fewer radio announcers, news reporters, and broadcast technicians. Job losses in these professions indicate that fewer local residents make decisions now about what music to play and what stories to report. The employment effects of radio consolidation thus represent a threat to both localism and diversity.

NOTES

[1]The Federal Communications Commission has cited three major, long-standing goals in its broadcast media policy: competition, diversity, and localism. See, for example, Federal Communications Commission (2002).

[2]For a fuller description of radio's regulatory history, see Peter DiCola and Kristin Thomson, Radio Deregulation: Has It Served Citizens and Musicians? 5–16 (2002), available at http://www.futureofmusic.org/research/radiostudy.cfm (last visited April 3, 2005).

[3]"Scott Ginsburg, Evergreen Media chairman/CEO, says that signing the bill into law 'will lead to a tide of radio ownership consolidation and improved economies of scale for radio broadcasters'" (Holland, 1996, p. 107).

[4]See, for example, Mathews (2002).

[5]This observation stems from a series of cross-tabulations of indicator variables for holdings of large firms versus concentration ratios in local markets (Media Access Pro, 2002).

[6]The seven-factor test grew out of the Federal Communications Commission's interpretation of Section 308 of the Communications Act, which "requires that applicants demonstrate 'citizenship, character, and financial, technical, and other qualifications'" (Communications Act of 1934). The catch-all phrase "other qualifications" permitted the Federal Communications Commission to consider localism (Benjamin, Lichtman, & Shelanski, 2001).

[7]"Despite its twenty-eight years of experience with the policy, the Commission has accumulated no evidence to indicate that it achieves even one of the benefits that the Commission attributes to it" (*Bechtel v. FCC*, 1990, p. 880).

[8]See, for example, *Fox Television Stations, Inc. v. FCC* (2002).

[9]Starting in 1998, each year the Bureau of Labor Statistics surveyed at least some establishments; some of the smaller individual establishments were surveyed on a rotating basis once every 3 years.

[10]The Arbitron Company identifies over 280 markets (cities and metropolitan areas) in which it conducts surveys on radio listenership. These markets are ranked according to population, from New York City (no. 1) to Casper, Wyoming (no. 285). I use and refer to these 280-plus "Arbitron markets" throughout my analysis. Arbitron markets differ from metropolitan statistical areas because of some adjustments based on industry practice and marketing considerations.

[11]This drawback is less important than one might initially suspect. Although it was a major policy change, the Telecommunications Act followed 12 years of gradual relaxation of ownership limits in radio. That regulatory changes occurred frequently starting in the 1980s would confound attempts to conduct pre- and postanalysis of the act.

REFERENCES

Aufderheide, P. (1999). *Communication policy and the public interest: The telecommunications act of 1996*. New York: Guilford.

Bechtel v. FCC, 10 F. 3d 875 (D.C. Cir. 1993).

Benjamin, S. M., Lichtman, D. G., & Shelanski, H. A. (2001). *Telecommunications law and policy*. Durham, NC: Carolina Academic Press.

Burcum, J. (2002, January 19). Ammonia cloud engulfs Minot. *Minneapolis Star Tribune*, p. 1A.

Bureau of Labor Statistics. (2004). *Occupational employment survey, 1998 through November 2003* [Data file]. Retrieved March 1, 2005, from http://www.bls.gov/oes/home.htm

Bureau of Labor Statistics. (2005). *Current employment statistics survey. Data from 1982–2004* [Data file]. Retrieved March 1, 2005, from http://www.bls.gov/ces

Communications Act of 1934 § 308(b), 47 U.S.C. § 308(b) (2000).

DiCola, P., & Thomson, K. (2002). *Radio deregulation: Has it served citizens and musicians? Future of Music Coalition*. Retrieved April 3, 2005, from http://www.futureofmusic.org/research/radiostudy.cfm

Federal Communications Commission, Notice of proposed rulemaking, No. 02–249, ¶ 2 (September 12, 2002).

Federal Communications Commission, Policy statement on comparative broadcast hearings, 1 F.C.C. 2d 393 (1965).
Federal Communications Commission, Report and order in the matter of the 2002 biennial regulatory review, No. 03–127 (June 2, 2003).
Federal Communications Commission, Notice of inquiry, No. 04–129, 6 (June 7, 2004).
Feran, T. (1999, June 3). Local radio loses a distinctive voice. *Cleveland Plain Dealer*, p. 1E.
Fox Television Stations v. FCC, 280 F.3d 1027 (D.C. Cir. 2002).
Holland, B. (1996, February 17). Telecommunications act signed: Legislation to revamp media climate. *Billboard, 108*(6), 107.
Johnston, J., & DiNardo, J. (1997). *Econometric methods* (4th ed.). New York: McGraw-Hill / Irwin.
Kenny, J. (1998, October 23). Localism vanishing as N.H. radio is 'McDonaldized.' *New Hampshire Business Review*, p. 1.
Knoll, S. (1996, December 31). Radio news facing cutbacks: Consolidation in the industry brings leaner staffing. *Cleveland Plain Dealer*, p. 3C. (Reprinted from *The New York Times*, December 30, 1996)
Lee, J. B. (2003, March 31). On Minot, N.D. radio, a single corporate voice. *The New York Times*, p. C7.
Mathews, A. W. (2002, February 25). From a distance: A giant radio chain is perfecting the art of seeming local. *The Wall Street Journal*, p. A1.
Media Access Pro. (2002). Version 3.1 [Computer software]. Chantilly, VA: BIA Financial Networks.
Napoli, P. M. (2001). *Foundations of communication policy: Principles and process in the regulation of electronic media*. Cresskill, NJ: Hampton.
Preservation of localism, program diversity, and competition in television broadcast service act, S. 1046, 108th Cong. (2003).
Ruud, P. (2000). *An introduction to classical econometric theory*. New York: Oxford University Press.
Spencer, T. (2002, October 1). Radio killed the radio star. *Salon* [Online]. Retrieved April 2, 2005, from http://www.salon.com/tech/feature/2002/10/01/nab/
Telecommunications Act of 1996, Pub. L. No. 104–104, 110 Stat. 56 (1996).
Whitall, S. (2002, November 10). Once distinctive sound fades into predictability: Media giants control what music played. *Detroit News*, p. 1.

4

Public and Private Decision Making: The Value of Diversity in News

Peter J. Alexander
Federal Communications Commission

Brendan M. Cunningham[1]
United States Naval Academy

The Federal Communications Commission (FCC) has a statutory obligation to pursue the public interest through its regulation of broadcast media. The FCC's interpretation of the public interest in broadcasting has led it to pursue three policy objectives: competition, localism, and diversity.[2] This policy triad reflects both efficiency and antitrust considerations and concerns about the social, political, and cultural effects of media. Therefore, in addition to pursuing competition in broadcast markets through quasi-antitrust analysis, the FCC considers the additional elements of diversity and localism. These elements can add considerable nuance and complexity, especially in light of possible interactions between competition and media content.[3]

The FCC limits the number of national viewers that a single television broadcaster can reach via station ownership across state lines.[4] From 1954 to 1984, the FCC limited national ownership to seven stations, where each station was in a separate geographic market. In 1984, the FCC expanded ownership limits to 12 stations, provided that the total number of stations owned did not reach over 25% of the national market. The 1996 Telecommunications Act raised the broadcast television ownership limit to 35% of the national market and eliminated the station ownership limit. Subsequently, the FCC's decision in 2000 to retain a national broadcast television ownership limit was challenged by Fox Television Stations in the U.S. Court of Appeals, D.C. Circuit, and the Court reversed the FCC's decision, sending the rule back to the FCC for further consideration. In 2003, the FCC increased the ownership limit to 45% of the national market. This decision proved controversial, and the United States Congress set a statutory limit of 39% in 2004.

As a result of these regulatory decisions, ownership concentration in the broadcast media has increased, most markedly since the Telecommunications Act of 1996. Although broadcast networks have argued that ownership consolidation generates efficiencies that rationalize increased ownership concentration from a purely economic standpoint, the Federal Appeals Court for the District of Columbia noted that

> Congress may, in the regulation of broadcasting, constitutionally pursue values other than efficiency—including in particular diversity in programming, for which diversity of ownership is perhaps an aspirational but surely not irrational proxy. Simply put, it is not unreasonable—and therefore not unconstitutional—for the Congress to prefer having in the aggregate more voices heard. (*Fox Television Stations v. Federal Communications Commission*, 2002, p. 104)

Thus, the Court concluded that Congress (and by proxy the FCC), might reasonably desire and pursue ownership goals other than those presumed to promote simple economic efficiency, in this case diversity.[5]

In what follows, we explore the nature of diversity in broadcast television and examine a large database of actual television news stories. We suggest that diversity in broadcast output, in particular news, may be an essential input into a healthy democratic process, although the provision of diverse news is not sufficient to guarantee the robustness of a democratic system. Moreover, we suggest that broadcast television news, as well as other types and sources of information, may have a substantial private value to viewers. For example, news regarding changes in subsidy or social security programs may help individuals recalibrate and optimally reallocate private resources devoted to such programs.

If market structure affects the production and output of privately and socially valuable news, it would be useful to have empirical evidence relating to the direction and magnitude of these changes, because theory provides competing predictions. For example, Steiner's (1952) simple model predicts monopolists would provide greater diversity. However, recent work, including that of Alexander and Cunningham (2004), suggests that a competitive market structure might be more conducive to the production of more diverse content and output.

In what follows, we examine the actual content of local broadcast news and relate our diversity measures back to structural and demographic variables. We find that competition, broadly defined, may be a significant factor in promoting broadcast news content diversity. Our results suggest that competition is not exclusively the result of intramodal competition, but also the result of intermodal competition, in particular from cable television. Thus, if media are (becoming more) substitutable, then increasing concentration within any particular media type may not generate potentially negative welfare consequences. This is simply a corollary of the so-called digital convergence argument, broadly stated.[6]

WHAT IS DIVERSITY?

Diversity for the FCC appears to refer to one of three somewhat elastic concepts—product, source, and viewpoint. Product diversity refers to the number of different program types. Source diversity refers to the number of firms, ownership structure, and the availability of substitutes. Viewpoint diversity refers to the variety of perspectives on important issues.

Standard product differentiation models demonstrate a trade-off between price competition and product diversity (i.e., greater product diversity implies softer price competition).[7] Because product differentiation models examine the welfare effects of both price competition and product diversity, empirical implementation of these models enables estimation of the market structure that maximizes welfare while accounting for both price competition and product diversity. Importantly, different types of product differentiation models generate different welfare effects from product diversity. The representative consumer model, for instance, generates much greater welfare increases from increases in product variety than the Salop (1979) model.[8]

As we noted, in addition to program diversity, there are other "types" of diversity, which include source (i.e., the number of firms, ownership structure, and availability of substitutes) and viewpoint (i.e., a variety of perspectives on important issues). Source and viewpoint diversity appear to have their roots in political-economic concerns about limiting the power of any single media owner to influence voters' beliefs. The debates between different political factions about talk radio and media bias illustrate the importance of viewpoint diversity to political discourse.

One might conclude that in two-sided markets with product differentiation, availability of substitutes provides obvious welfare benefits.[9] However, if the availability of substitutes also affects citizens' abilities to make informed votes within the political marketplace, consideration of these effects should also factor in the calculation of the optimal media market structure.[10] The additional consideration of viewpoint diversity could mitigate either for or against concentration. If, for example, firms treat viewpoint as a product characteristic, and concentration increases product differentiation, then the extra political-economic benefits of increased viewpoint diversity actually favor greater concentration.

Note that, by definition, increasing concentration reduces source diversity. Thus, viewpoint diversity and source diversity might be complements or substitutes, depending on the relationship between concentration and viewpoint diversity: if concentration increases viewpoint diversity, then viewpoint diversity and source diversity are substitutes; however, if concentration decreases viewpoint diversity, then viewpoint diversity and source diversity are complements.

Moreover, if "viewpoint" is an important product characteristic in a broadcaster's product differentiation decision, then product diversity is viewpoint diversity. In this context, it might be appropriate to utilize a product differentiation model that heavily weights product diversity, because increased viewpoint diversity may generate more voter-relevant information. For example, a regulator could employ a Hotelling model of viewpoint differentiation and assume a strongly convex consumer "transportation cost" to reflect the public good of viewpoint diversity.[11]

Along these lines, Djankov, McLiesh, Nenova, and Shleifer (2003) suggest that government ownership of media sources correlates with less political and economic freedom for citizens, a finding that does not contradict the idea that viewpoint diversity allows the citizenry to more effectively exert control over their government. Moreover, Mullainathan and Schleifer (2002) contend that competition generates a distribution of viewpoints that roughly mirrors the viewpoint distribution among media consumers.

Because source diversity does not necessarily imply more product or viewpoint diversity, the concept of source diversity suffers serious problems. If one defines source diversity as simply the number of media firms, then one confronts the following tautology: more owners increase source diversity because source diversity is defined as the number of owners—a line of reasoning that may not prove particularly helpful, especially from a consumer's perspective. However, one might rescue the idea of source diversity with a more nuanced definition. Source diversity could refer to media owners with additional political-economic interests that lead them to cover (or not cover) news events in a particular way. For example, a media owner with extramedia business interests bidding for a contract with a municipality may face incentives to avoid negative coverage of that municipality's officials. If media owners have extra-media interests that may affect their news coverage, then regulatory authorities may have an interest in guaranteeing sufficient competition from other sources. This would be an instance where viewpoint and source diversity would have a complementary relationship. This possibility may loom larger at the local level than the national level, as consumers may tend to access fewer sources for their local news coverage.

DOES SUBSTITUTABILITY AMELIORATE INCREASING CONCENTRATION?

Does media substitutability and digital convergence diminish the importance of broadcast media ownership concentration? Some observers argue that substitutability and convergence diminish the effects of concentration within any given medium by increasing the overall size of the relevant market. By this argument, if radio substitutes for television which substitutes for newspapers which substitutes for Internet content, then concentration within radio, television, newspapers, or Internet content does not necessarily confer any market power or diminish the diversity of viewpoints. Of course, because the majority of these media have simultaneously existed for long periods of time, it is really increasing substitutability (through convergence in a digital dimension) which might diminish the importance of concentration. In short, any potential welfare losses due to intramodal concentration will be off-set by gains from intermodal competition. Clearly, the extent of the market and degree of substitutability are important issues, which may render moot many of the arguments against broadcast media ownership concentration.

Perhaps surprisingly, empirical evidence regarding substitutability between various media (e.g., television, radio, Internet, newspaper) for media consumers is scant. Waldfogel's (2002) comprehensive study finds very modest evidence of substitutability between just a few different media. Using a number of detailed data sets exploring a wide variety of different media, Waldfogel estimates six regressions and reports four tables of correlations.[12] Waldfogel finds statistically significant positive relationships, implying complementarities, in his data, noting that people who use media of one type tend to use more total media in general.

The significant coefficients from Waldfogel's (2002) six regressions of media substitutability yield the following results: (a) 1 hr of Internet use subtracts, on average, approximately 4 min of broadcast television viewing; (b) for each instance of Internet news use, broadcast television news use is reduced by approximately 2½ min; (c) for every 1% increase in the cable penetration rate, the rate of increase in daily newspaper circulation per capita decreased by 18%; and (d) if daily newspapers increase in number by 1, weekly newspapers decrease in number by 8.

The strongest results from Waldfogel's (2002) effort suggest that consumers may substitute between broadcast television and Internet use, although the magnitudes of substitution appear to be modest. Importantly, there appears to be little other significant substitutability among other media.[13] Instead of various media readily substituting for one another and forming a single large media marketplace, (a large and growing pond, to paraphrase some observers) each medium's small pond may be completely unconnected to other media ponds or connected only by very narrow tributaries. Ownership concentration within any individual media may therefore warrant careful regulatory attention.

PRIVATE AND PUBLIC INFORMATION: A PORTFOLIO APPROACH

Local and national broadcast news is an important source of information for individuals in their dual roles as consumers and voters, and several recent studies suggest that the provision of such information can have a significant impact on social welfare. First, news information, perhaps about a subsidy program, may provide a significant value to an individual because it can be used to make private decisions. Second, information may have value to viewers in their capacity as voters.[14] Similarly, Stromberg (2004) observes that voters only can pursue their political interests if they are aware of the stated views and subsequent actions of politicians. Stromberg further notes that the nature of information supplied by media may encourage (or discourage) voter participation.

In Alexander and Cunningham (2004), we use portfolio theory as a means of formally analyzing the value of information to consumers. Under traditional portfolio theory, an optimal portfolio is constructed from many assets. Consumers hold assets to obtain the best possible expected return given the risks associated with the return. The central element in portfolio theory is that an optimal portfolio requires diversification of asset holdings. This is precisely the approach that we apply to information gathered via broadcast news by individuals.

We view the various outputs of broadcast news as uncertain in their value to viewers, and suggest that news consumers optimally diversify by constructing and consuming a combination of news "assets," which provide information. In our approach, a low covariance of media values across broadcasters allows consumers to diversify away the risk that the value of information from one outlet is redundant, given the media produced by some other outlet. In fact, our approach to the value of news information is close in spirit to those who suggest market competition is necessary but not sufficient for the emergence of accuracy in media. Instead, a consumer's taste for heterogeneity of content, within a competitive environment, produces a convergence to some average accuracy. It is this average that we suggest is valuable to consumers and voters.

We assume that consumer utility is determined by the quality, consistency, and variety of output provided by broadcast news media. Media with these characteristics are welfare-enhancing for consumers, but costly for media firms to produce. We assume broadcast stations select the attributes of their news content in a given competitive environment by balancing the positive impact of media characteristics on market share with their potential impact on costs.

We use our model to predict the level of media variety under two market structures—a two-firm competitive market and a monopolist who owns both outlets. We find that the quality of news output is a strategic complement under competition; in essence, this is a business stealing effect of the type first described by Steiner—an increase in quality by one station will induce an equivalent increase in quality by its competitor. An increase in quality by the firms is assumed utility-enhancing for consumers, *ceteris paribus*. Because we do not model the price consumers pay for quality enhancement—in the case of over-the-air broadcasting the price is implicitly determined by the amount of commercial time—we cannot make direct welfare assessments.

In addition, the variance of news output is a strategic substitute for competitive firms. Thus, as a station increases the variance of its content quality (and hence the uncertainty over quality to consumers), consumers shift their focus to its competitor, which then optimally decreases its variance. In contrast, a monopolist who controls two stations is not subject to these same competitive pressures and may have no incentive to increase quality or to maintain low uncertainty over such quality.

Finally, in our model, diversity is not fundamentally determined by strategic considerations, but rather is driven largely by the marginal cost of providing unique content. We find that relative to a monopoly market structure, duopoly is characterized by a higher average quality of media content, lower uncertainty over that quality, and more diverse content. We now turn to the empirical evidence surrounding the role of market structure in determining media variety.

EMPIRICAL SOURCES AND MEASURING DIVERSITY

Diversity implies difference, but as our earlier discussion makes clear, diversity is difficult to define with any precision, let alone measure. However, assuming we have a plausible measure of diversity (which assumes we have an adequate definition of diversity), it may be enlightening to relate this measure back to media market structure, as well as various demographic variables.

In this section, we describe a technique we have used in our research for measuring diversity in the content of broadcast news. We have applied this technique to a database of local news content and related the resulting diversity measure back to market structure and market level characteristics. The broadcast news archive (10,600 individual news stories from 20 designated market areas [DMAs] across 60 Big Three affiliate stations from 1998 local broadcasts) is publicly available via the University of Delaware, and was originally gathered by the Project for Excellence in Journalism (hereafter PEJ).[15] In Table 4.1, we list the sampled designated market areas covered by the PEJ and their market size ranking.

From Table 4.1, it is clear that our database samples media content from a broad variety of markets.

Two Measures of Diversity

We have employed two distinct, but related, measures of diversity in our research. First, for all local broadcast content within a particular DMA, we count the total seconds of local news coverage that are unique to the three major broadcasters (CBS, ABC, and NBC affiliates) within the DMA as contributing

TABLE 4.1

Markets and Designated Market Area Rank

DMA	*Rank*	*DMA*	*Rank*
New York	1	Buffalo	44
Los Angeles	2	Louisville	48
Chicago	3	Albuquerque	49
Boston	6	Jacksonville	52
Washington, DC	8	Wichita	65
Atlanta	10	Tucson	72
Seattle	12	Burlington	91
Minneapolis-St. Paul	14	Evansville	98
Pittsburgh	20	Lansing	107
St. Louis	21	Tallahassee	109

to diversity. We refer to this measure as *relative* or *marginal station-level diversity,* because this measure captures each network's incremental contribution to the total amount of coverage of unique stories. In this measure, if any two or more local news broadcasts cover the same story on the same day, only the seconds beyond the collective average of the respective overlapping broadcasts are counted as adding to diversity.[16]

Our marginal station-level diversity measure may not adequately capture the collective output of diverse content by the broadcasters in a DMA since it is measured on a relative basis. To investigate the robustness of our findings, we employ a second measure of diversity that counts the total time devoted to all unique stories covered by the three networks. This variable, which measures each network's contribution to the total amount of news coverage, is referred to as *total DMA diversity*. We find that the raw correlation between these two measures is 0.18, implying that the distinction between relative and total diversity is more than conceptual.

Empirical Results

In contrast to prior analyses of media industry behavior, which either place media output into broad format categories or measure the allocation of inputs, our data capture the precise nature of the output produced by the broadcast industry. We then relate our measures of diversity back to a number of potential explanatory variables, including cable penetration, total market revenues, average income, and market structure. We employ two structural measures because it can be difficult to measure the overall level of competition within a given market. Ideally, one would adjust the number of firms in the market for reach, but we do not have the data to make this transformation. Before discussing our specification and results, we give a brief discussion of our expectations for the signs of the regression coefficients.

Structure. Because market structure often is difficult to measure, we employ two measures of structure, the revenue Herfindahl-Hirshman Index (HHI) and the number of broadcast stations in the market. Loosely, one can think of the HHI as reflecting the state of actual competition within a market, whereas the number of firms reflects potential competition.[17]

It is possible that the (increasing) relative cost of producing diverse output may lead to a reduction in diversity as the market becomes more concentrated; moreover, ownership structure may influence diversity if the within-market stations are owned and operated by large broadcast networks. In this case, given the scale economies inherent in national program distribution, diverse output may become relatively more costly (although the output within any given DMA might still be "diverse" in one sense). Thus, we might expect that increasing concentration might lead to lower diversity. On the other hand, actual, emergent, or potential competition might promote greater diversity in content (such as the type found by Goettler & Shacher, 2001).

Total Industry Revenue. The total revenue of all stations is meant to capture the size of the television market. A large DMA may experience greater or lesser diversity; we do not have a strong prior expectation for the sign of the coefficient.

Cable Penetration Rate. The cable penetration rate measures the extent to which consumers within-DMA have access to cable television in addition to over-the-air signals. Ex-ante, we expect that as consumers have access to a broader set of television choices, broadcast firms may have incentives to diversify their respective outputs to counter new entry.

Average Household Income. As average household income increases, consumers tend to diversify the items they purchase, generally speaking. Simply, rising income allows consumers to indulge their underlying "taste for diversity." Thus, we anticipate that as incomes grow, broadcast content may also become more diverse. Note the possible endogeneity problem inherent in this measure (Stromberg, 2004, emphasizes that diversity in media content can improve voter, and economic, outcomes).

Computer Ownership Rate. The computer ownership rate serves as a proxy for access to additional sources of news content. If consumers can access broad news content via the Internet, local broadcast stations may have an incentive to produce news that is more local in content (i.e., they become more locally specialized), especially if Internet news is broadly substitutable for local broadcast news. Or, possibly, the content accessed by consumers via the Internet complements the output of broadcast news stations, leading to a greater overall content diversity. Thus, we do not have an expectation regarding sign for the coefficient on this variable, ex-ante.

Population Density. If population density implies heterogeneity among consumers, we expect that the output of broadcast news will become more diverse. On the other hand, a large population which is concentrated in a small "footprint" may encounter a uniformity of events, thereby leading to uniformity in news coverage. For example, there is not much room for diverse perspectives on the weather in Manhattan. The same may not be true of an equally sized population spread across a broader area, such as the greater Los Angeles metropolitan area.

Population Over 65. Given that the population over 65 years old tends to be more homogeneous than a cross-section of the entire population, we expect that this cohort might reflect a "mass point" that induces greater homogeneity and hence less diversity in local broadcast news content. Thus, we expect the sign of the coefficient to be negative.

In light of the earlier discussion, we estimate two Ordinary Least Squares (OLS) regressions given by the following:

$$\textit{Diversity} = \alpha_0 + \alpha_1 \ln \textit{HHI} + \alpha_2 \ln \textit{IndustryRevenue} + \alpha_3 \textit{Cable Penetration} + \alpha_4 \ln \textit{Income} + \alpha_5 \textit{ComputerOwnership} + \alpha_6 \ln \textit{PopulationDensity} + \alpha_7 \textit{FractionOver65} + \varepsilon \quad (1)$$

and

$$\textit{Diversity} = \alpha_0 + \alpha_1 \textit{NumberofFirms} + \alpha_2 \ln \textit{IndustryRevenue} + \alpha_3 \textit{CablePenetration} + \alpha_4 \ln \textit{Income} + \alpha_5 \textit{ComputerOwnership} + \alpha_6 \ln \textit{PopulationDensity} + \alpha_7 \textit{FractionOver65} + \varepsilon \quad (2)$$

In Table 4.2, we list the results from OLS estimation of specifications of Equations 1 and 2.

In Table 4.2, columns (1) and (4) report OLS results using the relative station-level diversity measure as a dependent variable (giving us 60 observations). Columns (2) and (3) report OLS results using the total diversity measure as a dependent variable (giving us 20 observations). The only difference between columns (1) and (4) is that (4) substitutes the number of firms for HHI. All of the independent variables for the OLS regression in columns (1) and (4) using the firm-level measure are significant at the 5% level.

Note that in column (3), average household income has been dropped from the regression. In column (2), this variable is not significantly related to the total diversity measure (*p* value .97). When we use the total diversity measure as a dependent variable, we have a small sample of only 20 observations. Note that after dropping average household income (and hence gaining a degree of freedom), the signs of all the coefficients in (2) and (3) are identical and the magnitudes of the coefficients are nearly identical. However, the additional degree of freedom allows us to obtain more precise estimates of the coeffi-

TABLE 4.2

OLS Results, Local News Data

Variable	*(1)*	*(2)*	*(3)*	*(4)*
HHI (log)	−16.81	−56.45	−56.82	—
	(.047)	(.135)	(.074)	—
Number of Stations	—	—	—	0.66
	—	—	—	(.013)
Total Industry Revenue (log)	−6.76	−12.533	−12.69	−5.81
	(.002)	(.212)	(.087)	(.000)
Cable Penetration Rate	0.47	−0.62	−0.62	.367
	(.000)	(.211)	(.200)	(.001)
Average Household Income (log)	31.58	−1.20	—	31.92
	(.002)	(.974)	—	(.000)
Computer Ownership Rate	−0.33	−0.53	−0.54	−0.41
	(.046)	(.381)	(.283)	(.005)
Population Density (log)	−3.91	4.74	4.68	−3.41
	(.000)	(.142)	(.109)	(.000)
Constant	−27.45	692.45	684.94	−164.76
	(.786)	(.057)	(.049)	(.032)

Note. *p* values in parentheses. In columns (1) and (4), the dependent variable is the average number of seconds devoted to unique stories by a given station. In columns (2) and (3), the dependent variable is the average number of seconds devoted to unique stories by all stations within a designated market area. The Findahl-Hirshman Index (HHI) is the sum of the firms' market shares.

cients on the remaining variables. Importantly, we observe statistical significance on two of the variables, HHI and Total Industry Revenue, in column (3).

Market Structure. Looking at the data in Table 4.2, there is a prima facie case to be made that market structure influences the total and relative diversity of the product offerings in local broadcast news. More precisely, according to these OLS results, HHI is significantly negatively related to firm-level diversity in column (1) and total diversity in column (3). This result is robust to redefining our measure of market structure: in column (4), the number of firms exhibits a significant positive impact on relative firm-level diversity.

Total Industry Revenue. Total industry revenue has a significant negative effect on relative news diversity, implying that as industry revenue increases, relative diversity in the content of local broadcast news diminishes. The result in (3) using total news diversity also is significant.

Cable Penetration Rate. In specifications (1) and (4) the cable penetration rate has a strong positive relationship with diversity. More generally, the presence of an outside viewing option (by which we mean alternative programming of a variety of types) is associated with increased diversity in the offerings of broadcast news outlets at the firm level. This might imply that firm-level broadcast news is responsive to the presence of alternative programming choices available to potential viewers. Thus, diversification of content may be one means by which local news broadcasts fight for viewers. Although the sign is reversed for specifications (2) and (3), the results are not significant.

As can be seen in Table 4.2, various demographic variables, including age, population density, average household income, and computer ownership, also are significantly related to firm-level, but not DMA-level diversity.

Income. Average household income is positively related to diversity, implying that as incomes within a DMA increase, diversity increases. This does not contradict the idea that consumers' "taste for diversity" increases with income growth.

Computer Ownership. Computer ownership exhibits a small but significant negative relationship with local news broadcast diversity, which implies that the Internet may be more complementary than substitutable for local broadcast news.

Population Density.

Population density also is negatively associated with diversity. This implies that the greater the population density, the lower the overall level of diversity.

Age. The fraction of the population over 65 is negatively related to diversity, possibly the result of a homogenizing cohort or "mass point" effect.

DISCUSSION OF RESULTS

To assess the relative importance of these market and demographic factors in determining broadcast diversity, we must consider both the statistical significance of the coefficients along with the underlying variance of each explanatory variable. We focus on the coefficients reported in columns (1) and (3) of Table 4.2, and we multiply the statistically significant coefficients in these columns by the standard deviation of each independent variable. This provides us with an estimate of the impact of each independent variable on the fraction of broadcast time devoted to unique content; for example, if we obtain a value of .05 then the percentage of broadcast time which is unique will go from .6 to .65 when an explanatory variable increases by a "normal" amount. We multiply this value by 20 min to get a sense of the number of broadcast minutes of unique content which will be gained or lost for a representative change in an explanatory variable.[18] The results of these calculations are presented in Table 4.3.

When we use the marginal station diversity measure as a dependent variable, we find that total industry revenue has the largest negative impact on the time devoted to unique content, which will decrease by 1.7 min in response to a representative increase in market size. Market concentration exhibits the next largest negative relationship with diversity in that a representative increase in the log of the HHI will decrease diversity by .9 min. Although these quantities seem small, they respectively represent 8.5% and 4.5% of a 20-min broadcast. The strongest positive relationship is between diversity and income. When total market diversity is our dependent variable, we find a much larger impact of market size and concentration on diversity. In particular, a representative increase in the log of the HHI will cause diversity to decline by almost 3 min (14.7% of a 20-min broadcast). From these results, we conclude that market concentration is meaningful in determining diversity, in both a statistical and economic sense.

ROBUSTNESS OF EMPIRICAL FINDINGS

There is a possibility that the results reported in Table 4.2 are not reliable because, in all likelihood, the level of broadcast news variety has an impact on industry structure and cable penetration. In other words, it is likely that uniformity in news coverage may induce lower concentration and higher cable penetration rates due to viewer response. In the presence of such "reverse causality," standard OLS estimation can lead to biased coefficients. We employ an Instrumental Variables technique to reduce this bias, using lagged values of the HHI and Cable Penetration variables as instruments for market structure and the availability of outside media options. These results are given in Table 4.4. Column (1) reports lagged values of HHI and cable penetration using the

TABLE 4.3

Determinants of Broadcast Time Diversity

Variable	*(1)*	*(2)*
HHI (log)	–0.85	–2.93
Total Industry Revenue (log)	–1.66	–3.18
Cable Penetration Rate	0.69	—
Average Household Income (log)	0.87	—
Computer Ownership Rate	–0.32	—
Population Density (log)	–0.80	0.97*
Percentage of Population Over 65	–0.39	—

Note. Results are obtained by multiplying the statistically significant coefficients from Table 4.2, columns (1) and (3), by the standard deviation of the relevant explanatory variable and 30.

TABLE 4.4

Instrumental Variables, Local News Data (Lagged Values of HHI, Cable Penetration as Instruments)

Variable	*(1)*	*(2)*	*(3)*
HHI (log)	−5.04 (.610)	−55.92 (.162)	−56.54 (.094)
Total Industry Revenue (log)	−4.06 (.098)	−12.41 (.232)	−12.64 (.108)
Cable Penetration Rate	0.50 (.000)	−0.63 (.220)	−0.62 (.208)
Average Household Income (log)	25.75 (.022)	−1.51 (.966)	——
Computer Ownership Rate	−0.27 (.100)	−0.53 (.355)	−0.54 (.274)
Population Density (log)	−3.86 (.000)	4.76 (.135)	4.69 (.116)
Percentage of Population Over 65	−1.39 (.012)	0.60 (.793)	0.61 (.785)
Constant	−90.10 (.400)	690.20 (.074)	682.35 (.059)

Note. HHI = Herfindahl-Hirshman Index. *p* values are in parentheses. In column (1), the dependent variable is the average number of seconds devoted to unique stories by a given station. In columns (2) and (3), the dependent variable is the average number of seconds devoted to unique stories by all stations within a designated market area. The Herfindahl-Hirshman Index is the sum of the firms' squared market shares.

relative diversity measure, whereas columns (2) and (3) report the total diversity measure. Note that in column (3), we have dropped average household income in response to the small sample associated with the total diversity measure.

In this specification, nearly all of the independent variables for the relative diversity measure [column (1)] are significant at the 10% level—however, the HHI is insignificant. This finding suggests that endogeniety has an impact on the OLS results given earlier, or, indicates weakness in the chosen instrument.[19] For this reason, caution should be used in interpreting the previous findings pertaining to market structure. However, when the total diversity measure is employed as a dependent variable in column (3), the lagged value of HHI is significant at the 10% level. This finding is consistent with the earlier OLS results and suggests robustness in the negative relationship between market concentration and diversity in local television news broadcasts.

CONCLUSION

There is a growing body of research which suggests that the content of media, and news in particular, has important real effects on political processes as well as the behavior of elected officials. Publicly funded media (such as radio and television) can, in part, bridge any gap between the social impact of media and the incentives confronting private media outlets. Moreover, regulatory policy encouraging diversity of media can further guarantee that consumers have access to a wide variety of information. Our theoretical research suggests that media variety allows consumers to insure against the idiosyncratic nature of information from particular sources. Moreover, the empirical evidence we have assembled suggests that concentrated media markets exhibit more homogeneity in the information conveyed to consumers. Such concentration can, therefore, inhibit the ability of individuals to derive a more stable payoff from media consumption.

This finding implies that regulatory policy designed to protect and encourage competition simultaneously helps satisfy a second policy objective: diversity. Our findings beg a question for future research: does competition policy completely or partially satisfy diversity goals? How much weight should policy place on each of these goals when they may not be independent? Our empirical results also suggest that changes in the technology of content delivery (such as cable) can stimulate greater diversity in media content. For this reason, technology policy is yet another channel by which regulators exert an indirect influence on media variety.

NOTES

[1]The opinions expressed in this chapter are those of the authors and do not necessarily represent the views of the Federal Communications Commission or the United States Government. We are indebted to Keith Brown for his many useful comments and contributions. Some of the material contained herein was originally published in "Diversity in Broadcast Television: An Empirical Study of Broadcast News," *The International Journal on Media Management*, Volume 6, 2004, Lawrence Erlbaum Associates, Inc.

[2]Napoli (2001) provides an excellent overview of the broadcast history of the Federal Communications Commission, and the policy nexus of competition, diversity, and localism.

[3]One important thread throughout this work, often implicit in the analysis of media industries, is whether diversity in civic discourse is fundamentally distinct from entertainment diversity in commercial media markets.

[4]Affiliate agreements with independent stations provide networks with national reach.

[5]As we explore later in this chapter, the argument for diversity in ownership has been linked to the robustness of broader democratic processes, and some recent research suggests that ownership diversity in broadcast media may be a necessary (although not sufficient) condition for a healthy democratic process.

[6]However, the form of media consumption appears to have an age-related component. If so, then intermodal concentration may have substantial implications for certain demographic groups.

[7]Because broadcasters do not typically charge consumers for their content, the level of advertising is typically used as a proxy for price competition.

[8]The Salop model, for example, finds parameters where introducing a tax increases economic welfare within the market because the scale effects from having fewer firms outweigh the lost welfare from decreased product variety.

[9]Two-sided markets exist when a firm interacts with two distinct types of costumers simultaneously. Broadcasters fall into this category by selling media time to both advertisers and consumers.

[10]One may want to consider the relative size of this effect if voters choose some degree of rational ignorance.

[11]In the Hotelling and other location-type models, the consumer transportation cost reflects the disutility that consumers suffer from moving away from their preferred product type. A high transportation cost therefore creates a strong social benefit from product diversity.

[12]Waldfogel (2002) takes the unusual step of reporting coefficients with a *t* statistic of 1 (significance at the 68% level), see, for example, Table 18. We do not report these results, rather only those with a significance level of 5%.

[13]The state contingent nature of media consumption (e.g., it is difficult for one to watch television or read the newspaper while driving, but it is much easier to listen to the radio) may be an important element regarding substitutability not accounted for in current research. Moreover, changes in the number of commuters, commuting time, and commuting technique are important and as yet unexplored factors in determining consumption patterns. In addition, one way substitution patterns may also be important (e.g., one cannot easily watch television while driving, but can while cooking).

[14]This line of reasoning assumes away rational ignorance arguments. Rational ignorance suggests that voters may not wish to gather much information, because absent being pivotal, an individual's vote makes no difference, and information gathering is costly.

[15]For more information on this database, visit http://www.localtvnews.org

[16]We do not explore intrastory diversity given the highly subjective nature of this task.

[17]HHI refers to the sum of squared market shares of all firms in the market, and is calculated on a revenue basis.

[18]We use a value of 20 min because the typical news broadcast in our sample is 30 min long, with 10 min devoted to advertising.

[19]There are two reasons to believe this is an unlikely, but feasible, explanation for the findings in Table 4.3. First, a variable is a poor instrument when it is not tightly related to endogenous, or caused, variables. We have found that lagged values of the HHI are very highly correlated with current values of the HHI. In addition, lags of variables have been viewed as inappropriate instruments when a variable is, by its nature, forward-looking and caused by future values of the dependent variable (so that the lag is not truly exogenous). Although this often is the case in financial markets, we believe it is a very remote possibility in broadcast media markets. For example, it is hard to believe that a viewer in Atlanta decides to subscribe to cable because he or she expects that next year local broadcast news will be less diverse.

REFERENCES

Alexander, P. J., & Cunningham, B. M. (2004). *Same story, different channel: Broadcast news and information* (working paper). Retrieved April 25, 2006, from http://papers.ssrn.com/sol3/papers.cfm?abstract_id=635662

Djankov, S., McLiesh, C., Nenova, T., & Shleifer, A. (2003). Who owns the media? *The Journal of Law and Economics, 46,* 341–382.

Fox Television Stations v. Federal Communications Commission, 280 F.3d. 1027 (D.C. Cir. 2002).

Goettler, R. L., & Shacher, R. (2001). Spatial competition in the network television industry. *RAND Journal of Economics, 32,* 624–656.

Mullainathan, S., & Shleifer, A. (2002). *Media bias* (working paper).

Napoli, P. (2001). *Foundations of communications policy: Principles and process in the regulation of electronic media.* Cresskill, NJ: Hampton.

Salop, S. (1979). Monopolistic competition with outside goods. *Bell Journal of Economics, 10,* 141–156.

Steiner, P. (1952). Program patterns and preferences, and the workability of competition in radio broadcasting. *Quarterly Journal of Economics, 66,* 194–223.

Stromberg, D. (2004). Radio's impact of public spending. *Quarterly Journal of Economics, 119,* 189–221.

Telecommunications Act of 1996, Pub. L. No. 104–104, Stat. 56 (1996), (Codified in scattered sections of 47 U.S.C.).

Waldfogel, J. (2002). Consumer substitution among media. (Media Ownership Working Group Studies). Retrieved April 25, 206, from http://hraunfoss.fcc.gov/edocs_public/attachmatch/DOC-226838A8.pdf

5

Convergence of Newspaper Election Coverage: 1992 to 2000

Alexander Halavais
University of Buffalo (State University of New York)

The problem of measuring and reporting the convergence of media content seems to be easily lost in a sea of gray, despite efforts of activists, media producers, and regulators to describe it in black and white. The need for such metrics is clear: without some way of demonstrating a problem, and an indication of whether current regulation is affecting that problem, it is impossible to craft good policy. Healthy democracy requires that the population reach consensus through informed discussion of the issues. It has long been realized that a monolithic view of the outside world does not foster an atmosphere of deliberation. It is therefore vital that we understand the degree to which the media are meeting these democratic needs by providing a multifaceted view of the world that corresponds to the variety of values and cultures in the society.

The only thing we can know with certainty is that the media are neither absolutely monolithic, nor are they presenting the broadest range of facts and opinions possible; in practice, they are somewhere between these extremes. The question of how many perspectives are enough is one that is very difficult on which to agree. The work presented in this chapter aims to answer a slightly different question: how is the breadth of content changing over time?

CONVERGENCE OF INDUSTRY AND OF CONTENT

As a whole, media industries are changing. When it comes to the mass media—publishing of books and newspapers, film, television, and radio—there is ample evidence that a smaller and smaller number of companies produce a growing proportion of information available to the public. Although new networked media were once considered a possible antidote to this process, particularly when it comes to the news media, large corporations remain the dominant source of news online as well as off. Many argue that despite such convergence of ownership, it is not reasonable to infer that the content is growing increasingly similar; that large conglomerates must still be responsive to niche audiences, and therefore produce a broad variety of content (Gameson & Latteier, 2004). Such arguments tend to be built on anecdote and conjecture. Attempts that have been made, for example, to discover broader empirical evidence of a relationship between source diversity and ownership have been unsuccessful (Entman, 1985).

There are other factors that potentially influence the creation of news and entertainment content. Greater diversity among those who produce the news, for example, might produce a greater variety of perspectives. Naturally, this is particularly true of editorial content, which more readily bears the mark of its maker. However, "hard news" is also influenced by the values and processes of the newsroom and the reporter. A news organization that embraces the diversity of its staff, many argue, may produce news that is diversely framed—although this relationship also remains unclear (Gross, Craft, Glen, & Antecol, 2002).

In other chapters in this volume, you find arguments which suggest that some of the best ways of measuring convergence and localism are through the structures of ownership, the makeup of the newsroom, the policies of news organizations, or the distribution of entertainment and news formats. Although these all may provide some indication of diversity and local interests within media institutions, they do not speak directly to content. Ben Bagdikian (2000), for example, connects ownership to content in a variety of ways, mostly focusing on the tendency of large conglomerates to concentrate on the bottom line, and relying on anecdotal evidence of corporate tampering with news coverage, backroom deals, and courting advertisers. Bagdikian's critics have suggested that such evidence is inconclusive, that the cases he cites are anomalous, and that the economic motive of a conglomerate, although it may disrupt fair coverage of public events in particular instances, leads to generally less biased news than does independent ownership (Shafer, 2000).

Some continue to see corporate ownership of media in the context of the propaganda model: the corporate media aims to bend public opinion in support of its own interests. A softer model of media effects goes hand-in-hand with a softer model of the effects of corporate ownership. Such an approach suggests that biases always exist in the production of news, and that the exigencies of corporate ownership, the culture from which the journalist observes, the structure of news production, and the nature of the medium itself all affect the content that is conveyed. They do this by presenting observed facts in news "frames" (Pan & Kosicki, 1993), and by acting as "gatekeepers": selecting what news is important enough to be observed and conveyed to an audience (McCombs & Shaw, 1972).

Given that what is of particular interest is the effects on media content, it is perhaps surprising that more has not been done to demonstrate the diversity of content available. Although it is possible to establish connections between ownership and content, establishing a snapshot of content as a whole is more challenging. An ideal measure would provide a clear indication of the degree to which media cover and frame the widest range of possible issues. Unfortunately, this often requires significant interpretation by the analyst, or time-consuming analysis of content by human coders.

Presented later is a metric that provides some indication of how one mass medium, large-circulation newspapers, may be changing over time. Given that most of the work addressed in this volume is related to the broadcast industries and the new networked media, the choice of newspapers may seem anachronistic. Newspapers have traditionally been considered to be at the heart of informing the public, and held out to be a beacon of localism. Nonetheless, the total number of newspapers has fallen precipitously over the last several decades, just as the number of chain-owned papers has increased. With relaxed ownership rules, newspapers have become the target of larger media conglomerates. In some ways, newspapers may be the bellwether for diversity within the larger media environment.

Ever since newspapers came to be a mass medium, they have served a dual role. The ability to quickly print and distribute similar news to a geographically dispersed populace helped bind together national culture. At the same time, that national culture thrives only when there is the possibility of discussing more geographically local concerns and concerns of communities of interest. By carefully measuring how a number of large newspapers have changed in their coverage over an 8-year period, we are able to better observe whether that balance has changed, and with it the role of newspapers.

DETERMINING DIFFERENCES IN CONTENT

The media famously tell us not what to think, but what to think about. Those topics that are placed prominently in the media come to be viewed as the most salient areas of concern by audiences. Likewise, choices of particular words, phrases, and themes to make sense of, or "frame," a particular story tend, once again, to influence what an audience considers important in their own environment. In studying the effects of agenda setting and framing, researchers often compare the presence of news items or particular perspectives in a story with the attitudes held by the audience. Generally, analysis of the content in these cases has been limited to determining topic categories or key phrases and terms, and counting the appearance of these terms within the coverage.

Other research examines coverage of a particular topic to determine whether reporting has cast an issue or candidate in a positive or a negative light. Gilens and Hertzman (2000) examined the coverage of the 1996 Telecommunications Act to determine whether those newspapers owned by conglomerates that would benefit from the legislation covered the story differently from those that were independently owned. As part of Domke et al.'s research on the 1996 election coverage (1997), attitudes toward candidates in newspaper content were coded. Both examples relied on a determination of whether there was bias presented in the manifest content of the newspapers that could cast an issue or candidate in a negative or positive light.

There are several ways we might attempt to measure the breadth of coverage. We could, for example, gather information about events and decide how well newspapers have covered these events. Generally, this means examining the coverage of newspapers in comparison with one another, because an objective measure of the events without relying on the work of newspapers would be very difficult. By recording all of the events covered by newspapers, and then looking for which of these events are covered by any given newspaper, it would be possible to judge how well newspapers are doing in comparison with one another.

To determine the events or stories being covered would require a great deal of interpretive work. Although we could conceivably create a coding schema that would link coverage to particular events, this makes for a process that allows for some degree of subjective judgment on the part of coders. Better than classifying the events or topics being covered would be to somehow allow these topics to emerge from the texts. That is, if we had some kind of "fingerprint" of a text that indicated the amount of space a given text devoted to a number of issues, and how they were being described, we would be able to compare these fingerprints to determine the similarity among newspapers.

Fingerprinting documents has been the chief problem of information science for the last few decades. Although it is possible to simply establish key words and search for them, it is more valuable to know which words are particularly important to a document, which terms clearly differentiate one article or book from another. Although there are a number of ways in which this is done, one of the earliest and simplest was to compare the appearance of terms (or counts of number of terms) that appeared in each document. Individual words, or pairs of words, are often used as the distinguishing features. Letters are too common across documents (the letter "e" will appear with similar frequency in any two texts of sufficient size in the same language) and identical sentences are unlikely to appear in two documents. Words, however, tend to be shared among some, but not all, documents, providing some basis for comparison.

There is a long history of using word frequencies to determine authorship. Researchers have computed various frequency scores ("stylometrics") to help determine the author of *The Imitation of Christ* (Yule, 1944), the *Federalist Papers* (Mosteller & Wallace, 1964), and *Hamlet* (Gerbner & Annenberg School of Communications, 1978). More recently, these approaches have been improved on to allow for the identification of e-mail and other electronic communications (de Vel, Anderson, Corney, & Mohay, 2001; Khmelev & Tweedie, 2001; Rao & Rohatgi, 2000). Using word frequencies alone to determine the similarity between two texts has been criticized as too inexact, and more sophisticated approaches have since been developed to help cluster documents and find similarities. In particular, relying simply on frequency information fails to account for the semantic structure of a text; it treats "dog bites man" and "man bites dog" as identical expressions. Although there remain criticisms of stylistic "fingerprinting," there are indications that it can be an effective way of determining the number, if not identity, of authors. Because the aim here is to identify the perspectives taken, this appears to be a reasonable approach.

In pairwise comparisons of each newspaper considered later, the degree to which the texts of two collections of articles are dissimilar is presented. This approach can compare the text of newspapers, showing, for example, that *The Washington Post* and *The New York Times* tend to be more similar to one another than either is to the *San Francisco Chronicle*. However, even this is of limited value alone; we can think of any number of reasons that a newspaper in the western part of the country would have different kinds of coverage than one on the east coast. But by looking at how these differences vary over time, we are provided with some evidence of whether newspaper content is converging across newspapers.

PRESIDENTIAL COVERAGE

To investigate whether large-circulation newspapers are converging in content, some subset of articles needs to be observed over a long period. Although maintaining multiple perspectives in any form of news or entertainment content is valuable, perhaps the area in which such diversity is most vital is in the coverage of political campaigns. For this reason, newspaper articles that addressed the presidential campaigns of 1992, 1996, and 2000 were analyzed to see whether the nature of coverage changed during this 8-year period.

An initial set of eight newspapers was selected for analysis: those with the highest circulations available in full text on Lexis–Nexis for the years 1992 to 2000. Articles were retrieved that contained the surnames of both the Republican and Democratic Party candidates for president somewhere in the full text, and appeared from May through the end of October of each election year.[1] These newspapers include *The Atlanta Journal-Constitution* (2,786 total articles for all 3 years), *The Boston Globe* (3,248 articles), the *Chicago Sun-Times* (2,458 articles), the *Houston Chronicle* (2,941 articles), *The New York Times* (6,006 articles), the *San Francisco Chronicle* (1,459 articles), *USA Today* (3,071 articles), and *The Washington Post* (5,158 articles). Stories that included content attributed to wire services were excluded, and news articles were separated from those that were clearly indicated as being editorials, letters, or opinion pieces.

The totality of the texts of these articles, stripped of headlines and bylines, was compared across newspapers for each of the 3 years studied. The comparison was accomplished by contrasting the appearance of words within the two texts such that a numeric measurement of dissimilarity (the inverse of the cosine similarity of raw word vectors; see Manning & Schütze, 1999) was computed, ranging from 1 for collections of word frequencies that were entirely dissimilar (orthogonal) to 0 for two texts with identical distributions of words. Because of the large size of the texts, most of these appeared to be very similar. In many information retrieval tasks, cosine similarity is used in tandem with a method of weighting terms that are out of the ordinary. Given that the aim is to measure the degree of uniqueness, rather than seek out unique identifying terms, the terms have not been weighted. As a result, similarity among the texts is very high, but we remain able to discern changes in that similarity over time.

CONVERGENCE OF COVERAGE

The results of the analysis are complicated. First, to see whether newspapers are converging toward the mean, the texts of the news articles in each newspaper are compared to the texts of the news articles in all newspapers. If we look at the average distance from the mean, even excluding *USA Today*, the breadth of coverage shrinks significantly from 1992 to 1996, and widens very slightly from 1996 to 2000. *USA Today* is very much an outlier in this process, existing far outside of the norm in 1992, and quickly moving toward the mainstream; a reflection of the newspaper's editorial strategy, bringing it from its "McPaper" origins into the proximity of America's "prestige press."

This overall view, however, misses some important differences among the newspapers. Figure 5.1 charts the changes over the 8-year period. Three of the newspapers, *The New York Times, The Washington Post,* and *USA Today,* each move significantly toward the mean. The other papers exhibit changes from year to year in both directions. In other words, the papers that might be considered more nationally oriented start out closer to the mean, and tend to converge toward that mean during the period under consideration. This pattern is largely repeated among the editorials of the newspapers under consideration (Fig. 5.2). The breadth of content is greater across the board for editorial content, as we might expect. However, the changes observed in the relationships among news stories are repeated. The major national newspapers tend to come together when it comes to the content of their editorials.

Figures 5.1 and 5.2 do not tell the whole story. Because the approach compares each newspaper to the mean for all newspapers, changes in one affect every other measurement. Also, although it may appear, for example, that the *Houston Chronicle* and the *San Francisco Chronicle* are similar in content, this is not the case. In fact, they are merely of similar distance from the mean. To better account for the multiple dimensions, distances may be compared pairwise between each of the newspapers. When looking at the differences in all dimensions for news stories in 2000 (Table 5.1), for example, it is clear that the least similar newspapers were the *San Francisco Chronicle* and the *Chicago Sun-Times.*

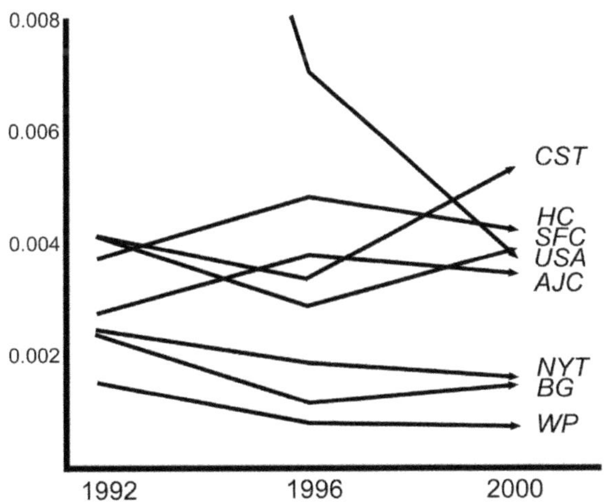

Figure 5.1. Dissimilarity of each collection of news articles from the mean news articles from all newspapers. A newspaper that exactly represented the mean would have a score of zero.

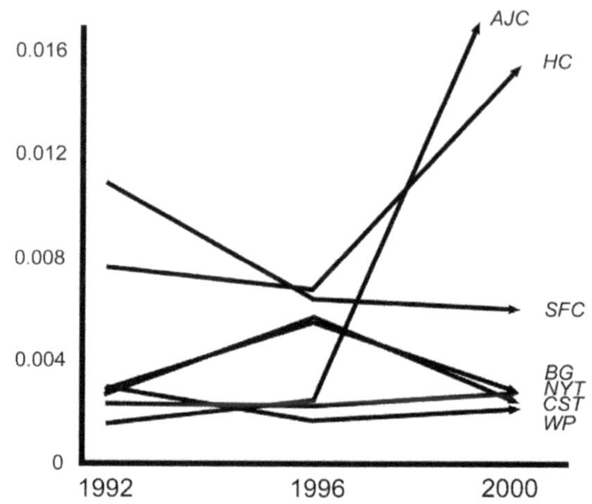

Figure 5.2. Dissimilarity of each collection of opinion articles from the mean of opinion articles from all newspapers. Because of differences in publishing format, *USA Today* is not represented. A newspaper that exactly represented the mean would have a score of zero.

TABLE 5.1

Dissimilarity Scores for News Articles for Each Newspaper in the Sample from the Year 2000 (Numbers Are in Thousandths)

	SFC	*NYT*	*USA*	*WP*	*CST*	*AJC*	*BG*
NYT	6.30						
USA	8.60	7.92					
WP	4.60	2.67	4.88				
CST	9.66	9.61	7.67	6.76			
AJC	5.79	7.06	6.72	4.96	6.03		
BG	5.30	4.12	6.14	2.57	6.22	4.32	
HC	8.80	7.76	7.36	6.37	7.16	6.31	5.15

Note. SFC = *San Francisco Chronicle;* NYT = *The New York Times;* USA = *USA Today;* WP = *The Washington Post;* CST = *Chicago Sun-Times;* AJC = *The Atlanta Journal-Constitution;* BG = *The Boston Globe.*

We are left with a clear, if contradictory, picture. Although the de facto national newspapers in the United States have similar content, and that content appears to be growing more similar over time, large newspapers with somewhat more local circulations remain relatively unusual in terms of their content. This powerful quantitative abstraction demonstrates the usefulness of such a measure, but it does leave us with a question: how are they different?

Or, to put it another way, what were the differences in content that made a difference?

WHY THEY ARE DIFFERENT

As noted earlier, one of the ways the approach taken here has been used in the past is as a way of detecting authorship. The frequency differences among newspapers may be the result of any number of systematic biases. It may have to do, for example, with regional differences in dialect. Or perhaps it is the result of selection of news of local relevance or other values inherent to the local context (Galtung & Ruge, 1965; Gans, 1979). Or it may reflect a difference of agendas, a focus on different issues. The raw measure of difference raises the question of the source of these differences.

A complete answer to these questions would require a careful and thorough reading of the newspapers in question to determine possible biases in framing and agenda. We may be able to provide some initial direction, however—some indication of what appear to be the most influential differences in the coverage. Because what we are measuring is the differences between the frequencies of words, one approach would be to compare some frequencies among particularly salient terms: the words "Bush" and "Gore" in the 2000 election, for example. Such comparisons of particular word frequencies are often used to infer differences in meaning, but are constrained by what the researcher feels are the most telling differences. Rather than framing the question through the use of an a priori set of terms, we might instead make note of those terms that are most different between the two sets of articles.

For example, when comparing the *Chicago Sun-Times* articles to those in the *San Francisco Chronicle* during 2000, a number of terms show up as being significantly more frequent in each. The *San Francisco Chronicle* uses "California," "Latino," "percent," "voters," "mail," "San Francisco," "state," "Nader," "yesterday," and "will" far more often, whereas the *Chicago Sun-Times* uses "Clinton," "Gore," "Washington," "Bush," "defense," and "was" more often. Some of the reasons for the differences in frequency are obvious; we would expect, for example, a newspaper in California to use that state's name with more frequency. Other terms, like the differences in frequency between "was" and "will," require better contextualization to explain.

One way to see how these words are being used is to list them within their original context. Unfortunately, given the number of articles under consideration, any such listing would be nearly as difficult to interpret as the original articles. Another possibility is to score each sentence in the articles and determine which of these sentences contains the highest mean difference among its words. For example, given the high-difference terms listed earlier, the sentence reading "Vice President Al Gore will make his 68th visit to California beginning today, a two-day trip for a series of campaign events and a flurry of political fund-raisers in Southern California," garners an especially high score.

Given that the *San Francisco Chronicle* seems to be an example of the more localized newspapers in this study, and *The Washington Post* appears to be particularly close to the mean and representative of the "national" newspapers, the top 200 sentences were taken from the former that most clearly differentiated the two newspapers. Because the algorithm used to parse out sentences was unsophisticated, several sentence fragments had to be excluded by hand. Most of the remaining sentences were brief and would require yet further context to understand what impact they have. See the following, for example:

> **Their bats thawed.**
>
> **It is Russian for "underwater boat," or submarine.**
>
> **Hey, at least Pants Man isn't out stealing flowers.**

Many of the sentences included polling data. Some of this may be an artifact of the approach, because numbers are likely to be unique (although the high comparative frequency of the word "percent" suggests that this isn't the only factor):

> **Green Party candidate Ralph Nader was favored by 5 percent, while Reform Party candidate Pat Buchanan had 2 percent.**
>
> **On Proposition 38, the school vouchers initiative, likely voters are still overwhelmingly against, 55 to 36 percent, with 9 percent still undecided.**
>
> **California women are backing Gore over Bush, 54 percent to 34 percent, while the Republican's lead among men has fallen to two percentage points, 44 percent to 42 percent.**

A large number clearly have to do with campaigning visits to the state of California, or with issues related to the strategic position of California in the national election:

> **"The big mistake we made in 1996 was giving up California," McCain told the California delegates.**
>
> **California voters won't be able to make their own decision on which side has the better case.**

"Gray Davis is Al Gore's go-to guy in California," Miller said.

"The race in California is a race we can win," said Gerry Parsky, who co-chairs the Bush campaign in California.

"You don't have the big left wing population, like you have on either coast ..."

Note that the last quotation is from an article on campaigning in the Midwest states, but the quote picked clearly frames the issue in comparison to California. Ralph Nader and third parties figure prominently, in comparison with *The Washington Post:*

No one doubts consumer activist Ralph Nader will beat out Jello Biafra this weekend for the Green Party's presidential nomination.

Nader's overall image rating is more negative than positive—with 29 percent viewing him favorably, 43 percent unfavorably.

"Bush is not going to win, so what should you do with your vote? Why don't you build a new conservative third party? Make your vote count."

Finally, there are a number of phrases that suggest local issues and concerns:

[Cheney] Supports drilling in Arctic wildlife area, but opposes drilling off California coast.

Issues are the key to victory in California for Democrat Al Gore, but if personality takes center stage, that's good news for Republican George W. Bush, according to a Field Poll released yesterday.

They accuse Democrats of pushing the other immigration measures purely as a political ploy to cast them as anti-Latino in an election year when their presidential candidate, Texas Gov. George W. Bush, is reaching out to Latino voters.

Two-term Rep. Jim Rogan probably would be the Democrat's top target in California even if it wasn't for the revenge factor.

If we were to begin to identify some of the features that help to explain the convergence we can see in general terms among "national" newspapers, we would see that an absence of news that is of concern at the state level is part of the difference. Equally important are the kinds of items a given newspaper thinks are important, and the kinds of sources they feel are worthy of seeking. In some cases, this may mean closely following polls or press releases.

Perhaps the clearest reason for differences among newspaper coverage can be attributed to the quotations that newspapers gather. Nearly half the "sentences that make a difference" in this case contained quotations from sources. One of the ways journalists construct a frame is by selecting quotations that provide perspectives on the news, and many have decried the shrinking number and quality of sources used by the mass media (Blevins, 2002). Not surprisingly, diverse content seems to reflect the inclusion of diverse voices, in a very literal sense.

TOWARD POLICY

Due to the selection process, the only co-owned newspapers in the sample were the *Boston Globe* and *The New York Times,* although almost all are held by media conglomerates. Hearst, owner of the *Houston Chronicle,* acquired the *San Francisco Chronicle,* after a hard-fought court battle, at the very tail end of the period studied here. It is therefore unfortunately difficult to demonstrate, using these newspapers, whether there is a strong correlation between co-ownership and convergence. The coverage in *The Boston Globe* and *The New York Times* was consistently similar, but there was no significant change in similarity over the 8-year period. What these data can provide is evidence that there is decreasing diversity among the newspapers with the greatest national reach, whereas large local newspapers appear to maintain their local character.

The approach taken here presents a clear metric of whether and to what degree newspapers are becoming more similar. If the ultimate aim of ownership policy is to maintain a healthy information environment, one that provides for a diversity of ideas and perspectives, it makes sense to measure this as proximally as possible; that is, to measure the content. Naturally, such quantitative measures need not and should not be used to the exclusion of more interpretive approaches. However, they may provide a way to gauge content over time, and prove to be one more way to ensure the continued diversity of our newspapers—as well as, with some adaptation, television and radio content. They also provide a mapping or structure through which the most fruitful sources of differences among coverage may be identified. It is clear from the earlier exploration, for example, the degree to which the selection of sources colors the nature of a newspaper's coverage.

One of the advantages to the approach described here is that it is amenable to automation. With some work, and increasingly accessible electronic sources of texts, it may be possible to construct a kind of ongoing news weather report, an indication from week-to-week of the homogeneity of the news environment national or global publics are receiving. Although no replacement for interpretive work, such a content barometer would represent a metric that would help gauge the quality and diversity of our news environment.

NOTE

[1]Stories that contained only one name tended to extend heavily into other news domains in which sitting presidents were involved. Although strong third-party candidates were involved in each election, limiting coverage to articles that mentioned all three candidates by name provided too small a sample.

REFERENCES

Bagdikian, B. H. (2000). *The media monopoly* (6th ed.). Boston: Beacon.

Blevins, J. L. (2002). Source diversity after the Telecommunications Act of 1996: Media oligarchs begin to colonize cyberspace. *Television & New Media, 3*, 95–112.

de Vel, O., Anderson, A., Corney, M., & Mohay, G. M. (2001). Mining email content for author identification forensics. *SIGMOD Record, 30*, 55–64.

Domke, D., Fan, D. P., Fibison, M., Shah, D. V., Smith, S. S., & Watts, M. D. (1997). News media, candidates and issues, and public opinion in the 1996 presidential campaign. *Journalism and Mass Communication Quarterly, 74*, 718–737.

Entman, R. M. (1985). Newspaper competition and First Amendment ideals: does monopoly matter? *Journal of Communications, 35*(3), 147–165.

Galtung, J., & Ruge, M. (1965). The structure of foreign news: The presentation of the Congo, Cuba, and Cyprus crises in Norwegian newspapers. *Journal of International Peace Research, 1*, 64–91.

Gameson, J., & Latteier, P. (2004). Do media monsters devour diversity? *Contexts, 3*, 26–32.

Gans, H. (1979). *Deciding what's news*. New York: Pantheon.

Gerbner, G., & Annenberg School of Communications (University of Pennsylvania). (1978). *The analysis of communication content: Developments in scientific theories and computer techniques* (Reprint ed.). Huntington, NY: R. E. Krieger Pub. Co.

Gilens, M., & Hertzman, C. (2000). Corporate ownership and news bias: Newspaper coverage of the 1996 Telecommunications Act. *Journal of Politics, 62*, 369–386.

Gross, R., Craft, S., Glen, C., & Antecol, M. (2002). Diversity efforts at the Los Angeles Times: Are journalists and the community on the same page? *Mass Communication & Society, 5*, 263–277.

Khmelev, D. V., & Tweedie, F. J. (2001). Using Markhov chains for identification of writers. *Literary and Linguistic Computing, 16*, 299–307.

Manning, C. D., & Schütze, H. (1999). *Foundations of statistical natural language processing*. Cambridge, MA: MIT Press.

McCombs, M. E., & Shaw, D. L. (1972). The agenda setting function of mass media. *Public Opinion Quarterly, 36*, 176–184.

Mosteller, F., & Wallace, D. L. (1964). *Inference and disputed authorship: The Federalist*. Reading, MA: Addison-Wesley.

Pan, Z., & Kosicki, G. M. (1993). Framing analysis: An approach to news discourse. *Political Communication, 10,* 55–75.

Rao, J. R., & Rohatgi, P. (2000, August). *Can pseudonymity really guarantee privacy?* In Proceedings of the Ninth USENIX Security Symposium, Denver.

Shafer, J. (2000, Jan 13). *Big is beautiful.* Retrieved March 31, 2005, from http://slate.msn.com/id/1004374/

Yule, G. U. (1944). *The statistical study of literary vocabulary.* London: Cambridge University Press.

II

Conceptual and Methodological Issues in Assessing Media Diversity and Localism

6

Mediation, Mediators, and New Intermediaries: Implications for the Design of New Communications Policies

Stefaan G. Verhulst

It is a truism today to say that we live in a period of unprecedented technological upheaval. The rise of the Internet, the emergence of wireless technologies, the arrival of digital convergence, the proliferation of iPods and other portable devices: these are but some of the technological changes sweeping through our economic, social, and political landscape. As with any such period of innovation, the changes we are witnessing present both opportunities and challenges. The line between "creative destruction"[1] (McKnight, Vaaler, & Katz, 2002; Schumpeter, 1975) and "disruption"[2] (Christensen, 1997) is often a fine one.

Media policymakers are not, of course, the only ones grappling with these changes. But in many respects, they are on the frontlines: more than many other sectors, the mass media has been utterly (perhaps unrecognizably) transformed by technological innovation (Currie, 2004). Finding the right framework to manage that transformation poses a genuine difficulty for communications policymakers and regulators. How should the communications industry be governed? Must we discard our existing communications policy toolbox, which is often technologically specific (Longstaff, 2002), or does it continue to have validity in a new landscape where the lines between television, telecommunications, and information technologies are increasingly blurred? Around the world, policymakers confront the very real difficulty of "translating" (Goldberg, Prosser, & Verhulst, 1998; Hitchens, 1997) existing principles and lessons for a drastically new technological and market environment.

This chapter presents ideas and options on how to conduct such translation. It offers a different lens for looking at existing media policy, and suggests analytical continuities between today's rationales for policy intervention and the new methods required to adapt to technological change and innovation. We argue that many of the rationales behind current media and communications policy are based indirectly (and often without acknowledgment) on a concept of "mediation."[3] "Mediation," we suggest, can (and should) be used as an analytical tool to better understand how to update our current communications policy toolbox. Furthermore, we show, technology-led challenges to existing policies can be seen, in large part, as arising from changes to the nature and functioning of media intermediaries or "mediators." We therefore suggest that any attempt to design communications policies in a new information environment could benefit from a closer look at the concept of mediation.

In the next section, we explain the concept and importance of mediation, showing how it applies across a range of sectors in society and to a range of different intermediaries. The following section discusses media intermediaries in particular: we explain why mediation is such a powerful force in the mass media, especially when combined with scarcity, and show how it provides a conceptual rationale for our existing policy toolbox. The next section shows how technological change is transforming existing notions of mediation, altering both the nature and the functioning of media intermediaries. The precise nature of these changes is sometimes unexpected—the widely touted process of disintermediation, for example, has led instead to a process of reintermediation. Nonetheless, the changes have been real enough to suggest that we need a new approach to mediation, and in the last section, we begin outlining a "new mediation ecology" for policymakers.

Here, we only sketch the outlines of this new mediating ecology. Much further and ongoing analysis will be required to develop specific policy mechanisms, and these mechanisms, moreover, will vary depending on the particular context and application. The main purpose of this chapter, however, is not to develop an elaborate new framework for policymaking but rather to show some potential continuity between existing policy rationales and new policies. The concept of mediation, we suggest, can serve as an organizing principle for policymaking: it can help link the old to the new, and it can help us apply principles across hitherto separate sectors.

CONCEPT OF MEDIATION

Before turning specifically to the media, it is helpful to begin by considering the notion of mediation more generally. Mediation, according to Silverstone (2005), is a "fundamentally dialectical notion, which requires us to address the processes of communication as both institutionally and technologically driven and embedded" (p. 3). Yet what does a mediator or an intermediary do? In fact, multiple functions can be associated with mediation, and the concept will vary depending on the context and who (or what) is doing the mediation.

In one of the most common interpretations, we can say that an intermediary filters our perceptions of the world, acting as a *gatekeeper* (Lewin, 1947; White, 1950) and sifting through the masses of information that help us determine reality. Intermediaries can also play the somewhat more passive role of a *mirror or even a hologram* (Baudrillard, 1983), presenting some "reflective" version of reality. Various other functions can be attributed to intermediaries. According to McQuail (2000), mediators can also act as a guide or provide a forum or platform; or, in the case of journalism, operate as an interlocutor and informed interpreter (p. 66).

One particularly useful way of understanding the role of intermediaries is to consider the concept of "framing" (Entman, 1993). "Frame analysis," of course, has a long pedigree in media studies, going back to the classic work of Erving Goffman (1974). In his widely quoted definition (which built on Goffman's work), Todd Gitlin (1980) defined a frame as follows: "Frames are principles of selection, emphasis and presentation composed of little tacit theories about what exists, what happens, and what matters" (p. 6).

Frames, in other words, determine which parts of reality we notice; at a more fundamental level, they shape our perceptions of reality. They provide a way to "understand" events, building on existing "frames of reference" or embedded knowledge (Cappella & Jamieson, 1997, p. 46).[4] This is precisely one of the important functions performed by intermediaries in society, especially if one acknowledges that our perceptions of reality or our "frames of mind" ultimately directly or indirectly determine how we respond and behave in any given situation (Gladwell, 2005).

It is, however, important to understand, at the outset, that the media are not the only intermediary in society. Educational, religious, and political establishments, for example, frame reality in much the same way as do traditional media. Librarians filter and navigate information; school textbooks offer a particular (and often biased) view of reality[5] (FitzGerald, 1979; Ravitch, 2003), artists represent humankind in a mediated fashion, and religious leaders offer a particular interpretation on our world (and beyond).[6] Indeed, the influence of religion, and the profusion of religious rhetoric in U.S. policymaking is a powerful example of the way in which a nonmedia intermediary determines and shapes our world.[7]

The framing function performed by the media (and other intermediaries) is essential to understand because of another characteristic shared by all intermediaries: they are inherently subjective. In framing the world, they are also presenting a particular version of the world. In truth, intermediaries are never value-neutral or objective; they always present a certain perspective of the world. As we shall see, this property, which is common to all intermediaries, is particularly important when it comes to the mass media: it is one of the underlying reasons, in fact, that much policymaking is based (albeit often with acknowledgment) on a concept of mediation.

MEDIA AND MEDIATION

To understand why and how this is so, however, we first need to understand some features that distinguish the media from the various other intermediaries discussed earlier. These features, three of which are discussed in this section, help us see how much current media policy is based on the media's role as an intermediary.

The first reason the media are unique (or at any rate special) is because they combine all the various functions that can be assumed by an intermediary. Although literature from the field of media studies (Severin & Tankard, 1992) generally emphasizes the media's role as "gatekeeper," in fact, the media perform many of the other functions discussed earlier. For example, newspapers do not only sift through information (i.e., act as gatekeepers), but also offer a window or mirror onto reality. Likewise, with the rise of 24 hr news programs, the media increasingly perform the role of interlocutor or informed discussion partner. The point is simply that different kinds of media, on different occasions, mediate differently; as we see later, the precise manner of mediation can have an effect on communications policymaking.

A second, and perhaps more important, differentiating factor is the media's pervasiveness in society. Although mediation is performed by multiple mediators in society and has been going on for centuries, the arrival of mass media, with its unparalleled reach, provided for steep increase in the variety and the intensity of mediation (De Zengotita, 2005, p. 47). Given its wide diffusion, the media have the power to shape the public imagination and to determine the terms of discourse in what Jurgen Habermas (who himself drew attention to the role of the media) has famously called "the public sphere" (1962). Indeed, in *Imagined Communities: Reflections on the Origin and Spread of Nationalism,*

Benedict Anderson's (1991) classic work on nationalism, he shows how the modern nation-state and national identity was itself brought into existence by what Anderson calls "print capitalism." Today, as Cass Sunstein (2001) and others have shown, notions of citizenhood and nationalism are in much the same way sustained by the modern media.

Mediation and Power

This unique potency begins to show why the media's role as an intermediary is relevant to policymakers. But it is when this potency is combined with a third distinguishing feature of the media that we truly begin to understand how much of our current communication policy toolbox is based on a concept of mediation. This third characteristic is the inherent scarcity in the media marketplace—the fact that (traditionally at least) there existed only a limited number of media intermediaries.[8]

This scarcity can arise from many sources. It can be a result of (perceived) technical limitations, for example in the electromagnetic spectrum, where (until recently) shortages and the threat for interference have constrained the number of broadcasters. Or it can be economic, for example in the form of high barriers to entry or costs of content production, or limited market size. Scarcity can also be imposed artificially through government regulation—license requirements can limit the number of television broadcasters or telephone operators; ownership caps or other restrictions can have a similar effect, making the state itself a mediator in affecting (and selecting) other mediators. In addition, scarcity can result from the de facto adoption of proprietary standards.[9] It is, for instance, now well understood and documented (Laven, 2004) that the development of TV in Europe, in the 1950s and 1960s, was hampered by arguments over proprietary standards. Each member state considered it a sovereign right to choose technical standards that were different from its neighbors, resulting in a confused mixture of incompatible TV standards (e.g. 405, 819, and 625 lines, PAL and SECAM, analogue stereo and digital stereo). In many ways, this can also be seen as a form of market- or even state-induced scarcity.

Whatever the source, and whatever the layer—the physical, logical, or content layer[10]—the important point is that the fact of scarcity imposes power. Because of scarcity, those intermediaries that do enter the market are in a privileged position, freer to disseminate their mediated views or capture market share. This is potentially problematic for a healthy public sphere, and thus has led to policymakers' attention, for at least two reasons: first, because scarcity can lead to anticompetitive practices, facilitating dominance by certain players and making it impossible for others to compete (Singh, 1999). The most powerful cable operators, for example, are in a privileged position to display content produced by themselves or affiliated companies (Cooper, 2002). Likewise, dominant telecom companies (e.g., incumbents) can limit interconnection or colocation facilities to competitors (Bauer, 1999).

In addition, and perhaps more importantly, scarcity and power are problematic because of the inherent bias of media intermediaries. Recall the earlier statement that intermediaries are never neutral, that they always present a particular view of the world. The ability of certain intermediaries to exploit scarcity and dominate the marketplace thus means that certain subjective worldviews come to determine the way we consume information and content (De Zengotita, 2005). The reality consumers perceive, in other words, is often simply the framed reality as presented by a dominant group of content producers amidst a situation of scarcity (Cohen, 2005).

Scarcity of Mediation as a Basis for Policymaking

These potential problems help us understand how much of our current policy toolkit depends on the concept of mediation, and more particularly on the scarcity of intermediaries. Indeed, as the earlier discussion shows, at least two broad strands of policy are directly related to the nature and functioning of intermediaries: general competition laws, and laws relating specifically to (access to) content. In the remainder of this section, we examine these two categories of policymaking addressing the scarcity of mediation.

Consider, first, general competition rules. These rules, which include broad principles of nondiscrimination and transparency requirements, are designed specifically to prevent abuses of power arising from the scarcity of intermediaries (Price, 1994). For example, interconnection policies, which prevent dominant operators from shutting off access to their networks, are necessary in a situation of bandwidth (and resource) scarcity, where smaller operators may not possess the backbone to serve all customers.

One of the limitations of competition policy in addressing scarcity of "mediation" involves its primary focus on the "abuse" of dominant position (Goldberg, Prosser, & Verhulst, 1996). Because dominance in mediation may already be harmful, communications regulators have therefore established ownership caps on newspapers or television and radio stations, with limited success, that can be used to ensure that the respective audience is exposed to a diversity of mediated viewpoints.

In addition to general competition rules and media ownership rules, much of our existing media policy toolbox consists of laws and regulations designed specifically to prevent abuse of dominance in the content layer. Policies to support public broadcasting to "entertain, inform, and educate" (Holtz-Bacha & Norris, 2001) are a good example: they are designed to overcome some of the inherent biases of content intermediaries,[11] and to present instead a somewhat "neutral," "noncommercial,"[12] or "multiviewpoint" content platform (Dahlgreen, 1999). Must-carry obligations perform a similar function: as noted earlier, they prevent larger operators from blocking access to the limited number of TV channels available.

A number of other access provisions can be cited: program prescriptions, fairness of reporting,[13] public service subsidies, and a host of more general support mechanisms for smaller and third-party producers and mediators. The important point, however, is not to present a comprehensive list of specific rules, but to show how much current media policy can be understood through the analytical concept of mediation, and particularly through the scarcity of available intermediaries (Streeter, 1990). This concept, as we have suggested, is often unacknowledged in the media studies and public policy literature. Yet it is a critical underpinning of our existing toolbox. In the following section, we shall see how the nature and functioning of intermediaries is being transformed by technological change. This transformation is at the root of many questions and challenges confronting communications policy today; the final section offers some possible responses.

NEW MEDIA AND NEW INTERMEDIARIES?

Many of the examples discussed thus far have been drawn from what we might call the "traditional" (or pre-Internet) media: print publications, telecommunications, and broadcasting. With the takeoff of the Internet in the mid-1990s, however, the media landscape has been transformed. In particular, three technological developments that have accompanied the Internet have driven these transformations: digitalization, convergence, and the rise of networking technology (Dennis, 2003). Together, these forces have conspired to alter old habits and shake old assumptions. The way we produce and consume information, the way information is bought and sold, and the way policymakers regulate (or can regulate) media—all of these appear very different today than just a decade ago.

This is not the place to list all the multiple changes ushered in by technology. What is important for our purposes is to understand the way these forces have changed the nature of mediation. If, as we have been arguing, mediation has been the underlying, albeit often unacknowledged, principle for media policymaking, then changes in patterns of mediation are simply changes in the way policies are (and should be) formulated and applied.

Changing Mediation: Original Assumptions

From the start, with the arrival of the personal computer and before the Internet became the mass phenomenon it is today, it was clear that new technologies would have a dramatic impact on the nature of mediation (Johnson, 2005). In the 1980s, for instance, various unique characteristics were attributed to the so-called "computer mediated communications" or CMCs (Kerr & Hiltz, 1982). CMCs, it was argued, facilitate communication among people who may be dispersed in space or time (Hiltz & Johnson, 1990). CMCs, it was further suggested, are asynchronous (Rice & Bair, 1984) and interactive (Thurlow, Lengel, & Tomic, 2004). They are faster than traditional media, no matter the distance crossed, and ultimately less expensive (Quarterman, 1990).

More important for the relevance of mediation in policymaking is the widely believed assumption that new communications technologies would lead to some kind of "disintermediation." Michael Hammer, writing in 2000, pointed out the following:

> Today, disintermediation is supposedly dooming distributors, retailers, wholesalers, and all other intermediaries between manufacturers (or service providers) and the ultimate customer. Because the Internet lets customers connect to and order from the primary source of a product, there's presumably no need for traditional distribution channels and their costs and delays. (p. 2)

But, as Hammer (2000) goes on to suggest, this assumption was perhaps the greatest "myth" surrounding the arrival of the Internet. Although the conventional wisdom was correct in its general belief that new media would mean new intermediaries, it was somewhat off the mark in its specific predictions about how that process would take place.

Two predictions, in particular, are interesting to consider. The first of these was the assumption that new technologies would mark an end to scarcity and herald a new era of abundance in which, as George Gilder (2000) optimistically put it, bandwidth would become "infinite." Digitalization and convergence, in particular, were assumed to be at the forefront of this revolution. Although digitalization would dramatically increase the amount of available information, convergence, it was argued, would radically increase the amount of available bandwidth (because resources could now be pooled). Together, these forces, combined with networking technologies, would ensure that the old paradigm with a limited number of producers (i.e., intermediaries) would be a thing of the past.

Perhaps more dramatically, it was predicted that the Internet would not simply change the nature of mediation, but, as Hammer's (2000) earlier quote suggests, would even put an end to the very existence of mediation. For many early media commentators, *disintermediation* (a term borrowed from the finance industry) was the leitmotif of the Internet age (Hammer, 2000). In the new era of abundance, it was believed, receivers and senders of information would have entirely different, and far more direct, channels of communication. P2P technologies, blogs, Wikis, and various forms of personalization using identity management would diminish the power of the intermediary, and empower the user or edges (who would also be a producer; Alberts & Hayes, 2003). As Dan Gillmor memorably put it in his volume *We the Media: Grassroots Journalism by the People, for the People,* with the arrival of such personalized technologies, "the former audience joins the party" (p. 136).

This frictionless marketplace, it was believed, would extend not just to the economic realm, but even to social and political life. As Harold Rheingold (1998) wrote in *The Virtual Community,* "[t]he combination of free expression, lack of central control, many-to-many communication access, and volunteer effort has created a new kind of social organization." In this "populist vision" of the Internet, citizens would bypass existing bureaucratic structures and create policy directly in an infinitely democratic process that would include, for example, a series of referendums. Much as the Internet would usher in the ideal of a free marketplace, so it would also create a frictionless marketplace of ideas.

Reintermediation and New Intermediaries

Predictably, many of these assumptions have failed to materialize or are only partially embedded in reality. Although new technology has certainly altered mediation,[14] it has done so in an often-unexpected fashion, and with results not always as salubrious as predicted. Perhaps most importantly, as we see in this section, changes in the media have led not to disintermediation but to reintermediation (Shapiro, 1998). Likewise, instead of the much-heralded end of scarcity that was supposed to accompany digital convergence, we are finding that new "mediating" technologies simply introduce new (and often artificial) forms of scarcity. Such technologies include, for instance, content and identity management systems, digital rights management and filter, search and navigation tools. It is important to understand the nature and causes of this process of reintermediation because they will provide a basis for formulating new policies (a task we take up in the next section).

Among the chief causes of reintermediation has been the emergence of what may be called "information pollution" (Nielsen, 2003). If the original assumption held that the Internet would usher in a frictionless marketplace of ideas, actual developments have proven very different. In fact, when the number of intermediaries multiplies, consumers suffer from information overload[15]—there is simply too much information to go around. Moreover, the death of traditional intermediaries means that consumers lose their existing information filters. The end result is that there is often no way to differentiate quality information, no way to isolate the signal from the noise. Far from a perfect marketplace, we end up in a marketplace where the surfeit of information chokes the system (van Zandt, 2001).

This information overload translates, in effect, to a scarcity of intermediaries: with only information, consumers no longer have a "frame," and they do not have the attention span to consume all the information.[16] The result, perhaps surprisingly, is a situation in which consumers themselves demand mediation, limit their choice and information intake,[17] and opt for new intermediaries—new technologies and forms of media that can help them sift through the information. In addition, new business models within the communications sector are aimed at restructuring the "attention economy" (Davenport & Beck, 2001) by applying access controls and price discrimination,[18] generating new and artificial scarcities (Goldhaber, 1997). To be sure, the new intermediaries, and the way in which they navigate or filter information, are very different from what came before. Rather than traditional gatekeepers like newspapers or TV broadcasters, for example, today our information is filtered by search engines and electronic program guides, personal video recorders and various other digital "editors." Similarly, the links, browsers, or search engines we use and the operating system on which they depends, are likely to be as important in determining the way we read the news as our old set-top boxes (Walker, 2002).

One particularly important distinguishing feature of the new intermediaries is that they frequently operate at the code layer. Much like the editors and producers of old, metadata, context-sensitive tags and algorithms now determine what we see, read, and hear. Today, it is code that determines our frame of reference and shapes the way we see the world. Search engines are perhaps the most important of these new digital gatekeepers (Hargittai, 2000; Introna & Nissenbaum, 2000). Algorithms for news aggregation (such as those that drive Really Simple Syndication [RSS] feeds or Google's news site) play a similarly important role. In addition, as a whole set of Digital Rights Movement (DRM) and identity management features (including methods for verification, authentication, and authorization), combined with federation and Web services (Zuboff & Maxim, 2002), become prevalent, they too act as filters to determine what types of information consumers can access. Inevitably, these code-based intermediaries become commercialized, with the result that "framing" also becomes commercialized. One important example is the increasing use of commercial search results like Google's Adwords program or Yahoo's use of Overture; although separated from traditional (non-fee-based) results, these paid placements nonetheless direct traffic in important ways, and as such represent an important form of mediation (Sheu & Carley, 2001).

Consequences of Reintermediation: New Challenges for Policymakers

This reliance on code has important implications for the nature of reintermediation—and ultimately, for media policymaking in the digital age. In changing the nature of mediation, it changes the underlying (mechanistic) approach for policymaking. Indeed, as we see in this section, reintermediation introduces a host of new challenges (and perhaps, opportunities) for policymaking. It forces us to rethink our policy toolbox.

Old Challenges Repackaged. Some of these challenges are, in fact, familiar, and simply represent repackaged versions of the challenges we have already seen with traditional intermediaries. These include, for example, the creation of new scarcities and gatekeepers which (against predictions) have accompanied reintermediation. Indeed, as some of the new intermediaries become increasingly dominant and visible, they begin controlling the flow of information much like old intermediaries. If in the past prominent newspaper editors and TV producers squeezed less prominent intermediaries out of the market, today it is a select group of search engines and software programs (including spyware) that are similarly dominating the "battle for eyeballs." Contra original assumptions, there is not an abundance (much less an infinity) of intermediaries today, but a segmented and fragmented market where the concentration of ownership and patterns of access appear very similar to the old market. This consolidation of the new media space has been statistically documented by Eli Noam (2003), who concludes that, given current trends, the Internet might "move from an entrepreneurial and libertarian model to one of market power ... resembling or even exceeding that of other electronic media" (p. 13).

Unlike the old scarcities—which were largely the result of technological limitations—the new scarcities are often artificially imposed, but their effects are in many respects similar. For one thing, the new scarcities confer power: Google or Yahoo or Microsoft today determine our access to information in much the same way as *The New York Times* or the BBC once did (and still do, if to a lesser extent). In addition, scarcity and limitation in access is becoming dependent on the growing relationship between identity and mediation. Access to information and the framing of reality is increasingly being determined (some may call this customized) by a verification procedure of identity and a subsequent authorization process, creating new power positions among those who design and determine the identity management systems.[19] Much as with the old intermediaries, this power is problematic in large part because the new digital intermediaries often lack neutrality. Indeed, as Nissenbaum, Friedman, and others linked with the "Values in Design" project have illustrated, "computers and information systems promote and obscure the values to which we, individually and as societies are committed, values such as freedom, privacy, justice and autonomy."[20]

This challenge—a lack of neutrality—is, of course, familiar from our discussion of traditional intermediaries. But it is a particularly important point to understand with regard to the new intermediaries because their reliance on technology and algorithms is often assumed to confer a greater degree of objectivity. In fact, however, science and technology almost always themselves contain certain biases and subjectivities (Mowshowitz, 1982). The problem is simply that those biases, cloaked beneath a veneer of scientific objectivity, are often less apparent.

Lack of Transparency. This brings us to a second consequence of, and new challenge posed by, reintermediation: the lack of transparency. With so much mediation now done at the level of code, it becomes very difficult to track (or regulate) the biases of intermediaries. This is in large part because the code is complex (or because regulators lack the requisite technical knowledge to decipher algorithms). It is also because code writers include nonobjective methods alongside more objective ones. Consider, for example, the inclusion of paid placements on leading search engines. Combined with the difficulty of deciphering Google's or Yahoo's algorithms, this code-driven process of automated advertising simply makes it very difficult to apply old standards of objectivity or balanced programming to the new media.

Commercialization. The reference to paid placements points to perhaps the most significant (and difficult) challenge posed by reintermediation: the steady commercialization of the Internet. Inherent in the original assumption of disintermediation was a belief that communication could be liberated from the commercial dictates of the traditional media. In fact, however, the creation of new scarcities and the emergence of new intermediaries have simply brought new commercial concerns to the fore. As eloquently demonstrated by its recent Initial Public Offering (IPO), intermediaries like Google are, of course, also businesses. In much the same way, the Microsoft Windows operating system—which for the vast majority of computer users represents the gatekeeper to the Internet—is very much designed to accord with commercial imperatives. In fact, despite early predictions, virtually every intermediary on the Internet is today driven by such imperatives. This commercialization has also major implications for so-called nonprofit mediated content. Hargittai (2003) observed as follows:

> Commercial interests underlie the most popular Web sites and those to which users turn to find their way to online content. Non-profits lack many of the resources that nowadays seem essential to obtaining the necessary exposure for reaching users. The implications of this for diversity of content online is that sites presented by nonprofits and individuals lacking resources will have less of a chance to reach audiences and users may not find the most relevant information in response to their needs. (p. 74)

This commercialization of the new intermediaries poses several challenges to communications policymakers. First, there is the problem of transparency discussed earlier: the nature and results of commercialization may be dramatic, but they are not always evident. Second, commercialized intermediaries can challenge important public interest goals like privacy and security: the prevalence of cookies and spyware on our computers is ample evidence. And finally, the commercialization of information on the Internet makes it imperative to come up with new ways of achieving quality and diversity. Today, as noted previously, legitimate search results are placed alongside—or even below—paid placements; information submitted to an online petition may be resold to mass marketers and data-brokers (O'Harrow, 2005); and credit card and other personal data submitted at one site may be sold to another.

Personalization and Polarization. Finally, a significant impact of new intermediaries and the increasing personalization of information services involves audience fragmentation, leading to what Christine Rosen (2005) calls "egocasting":

> With the advent of TiVo and iPod, however, we have moved beyond narrowcasting into "egocasting"—a world where we exercise an unparalleled degree of control over what we watch and what we hear. We can consciously avoid ideas, sounds, and images that we don't agree with or don't enjoy. As sociologists Walker and Bellamy have noted, "media audiences are seen as frequently selecting material that confirms their beliefs, values, and attitudes, while rejecting media content that conflicts with these cognitions." Technologies like TiVo and iPod enable unprecedented degrees of selective

> avoidance. The more control we can exercise over what we see and hear, the less prepared we are to be surprised. It is no coincidence that we impute God-like powers to our technologies of personalization (TiVo, iPod) that we would never impute to gate-keeping technologies. (p. 51)

Similarly, Sunstein has argued in *Republic.com* (2001) that increased mediation and personalization may lead to "group polarization," which occurs when individuals in a group tend to gravitate toward the most extreme views of the members of the group.[21] Not only do we see the decline of "general interest intermediaries," special interest intermediaries (such as blogs) drive like-minded groups closer together and farther from all other groups. Adamic and Glance (2005), for instance, provided empirical evidence of this polarization in their study on the Political Blogosphere and the 2004 U.S. Election, where they found that liberals and conservatives were linking primarily within their separate communities, with far fewer cross-links exchanged between them. In addition, this division extended into their discussions with liberal and conservative blogs focusing on different news articles.

Each of these challenges and examples is ample evidence that we need to rethink our notions and our ways of ensuring access to public interest content—and more generally, to communications policymaking. We take up that task in the next section.

TOWARD A SOLUTION: A "NEW MEDIATION ECOLOGY"

The preceding discussion has highlighted two key facts: far from disintermediation, we have new and very pronounced patterns of mediation. In addition, disintermediation, much like traditional mediation, cries out for some accountability. Indeed, if the old policy toolbox is in many ways based on the behavior of traditional intermediaries, then a new design needs to adapt to the presence and role of new and interdependent intermediaries, a phenomenon still largely ignored by scholars[22] and policymakers. This is a central argument of this chapter, and in this final section we begin outlining some of the ideas and options of the new methodology. Needless to say, we cannot present every component of this approach. In fact, as we suggest at the end of this section, what is required is a policy strategy that adapts to an entirely new ecology of mediation; here, we only begin to give shape to that new ecology.

Borrow From Old Toolbox

At the outset, it should be clear that at least part of the new toolbox would borrow significantly from the old. Although we cannot entirely reuse the existing toolbox, there exist enough similarities between the function of old and new intermediaries to provide at least some analytical continuity between the present and the future.

For example, although the specific nature of general competition laws and content access laws (the two components of our old toolbox) will doubtless change, these nonetheless remain important principles. Indeed, the continuing role of scarcity and power in the new environment makes these principles critical. The task, then, is to adapt these principles to new circumstances. Cass Sunstein (2001), for example, has proposed that existing public-interest content regulations applied to broadcasters can be "translated" to the Internet through a system of mandated links to quality content and highly opposing viewpoints so as to create "deliberative domains." Similarly, it should be possible to apply the spirit of existing must-carry provisions to new wireless and third-generation networks. In a final example, it is imperative to similarly adapt and expand existing universal service obligations (USOs) to the converged network: in most countries, USOs continue to apply only to the Public Switched Telephone Network (PSTN), with cable and wireless operators remaining free of such obligations.

Increase Transparency and Mediation Literacy

One key requirement in adapting the old toolbox to new times will be to increase the level of transparency. As we have seen, new intermediaries pose a challenge to policymakers because they frequently operate under the radar, at the level of code or at the logical layer. If policymakers are to apply their standards of public interest content and accountability to a new age, then it is essential to increase the transparency of new intermediaries. Consumers and policymakers alike need a better understanding of the processes and effects of new forms of mediation.

Similarly, users need to acquire a mediation literacy as to identify and mitigate mediation strategies that may determine their "frame of mind." In particular, Hargittai (2003) suggests the following:

> Given the current state of online content organization and presentation, users must be educated about the myriad of commercial incentives that influence search result listings and directory placements. They have to be conscious of the fact that the most prominent results are not necessarily the most—or the only—possible sources online in response to their query. Users also have to learn how to do more refined searches and how to turn to a more diverse set of resources online in order to avoid the sidetracks that result from commercial interests. Although the Web does offer all users the

ability to contribute to online content, all content is not created equal when it comes to reaching users. (p. 74)

Toward a New Mediating Ecology: Learning From Complex Adaptive Systems

Ultimately, these steps are but specific techniques in a more general process that requires us to develop a new approach toward a new "mediating ecology." This approach would represent a comprehensive adaptation and rethink for new times; it would rest on existing principles and ideals, but translate them so as to make them effective in the new technical landscape. In particular, it would require considering the converged information and communications environment as a complex adaptive system (CAS)[23] or ecology.[24] Systems are said to become "complex" and "adaptive" when they are made up of several parts that are interdependent on each other to function (Longstaff, 2004). CAS theories have successfully been used in immunology, ecology, epidemiology, demography, finance, and meteorology. More recently, some scholars have examined the relevance and the application of complex theory in networked communications environments,[25] albeit the discipline is still in its infancy.

It is impossible to consider here all the lessons from complex theory (Wolfram, 1988) for policymaking in a converged mediated environment.[26] Yet, at least four CAS characteristics are relevant when considering the design of a "mediating ecology" approach (Eoyang & Berkas, 1999). Each element has consequences for how we structure policymaking (Sanderson, 2000).

Dynamic. First, ecologies (or any CAS for that matter) are in a state of dynamic flux. Because of the number of agents, their interdependence, and their openness to external influences, a CAS changes constantly and discontinuously. This change does not always follow a smooth, predictable pattern. Change happens at every point in time, but it may bring surprising or disruptive innovations and outcomes, such as with the introduction of blogs or personal video recorders.

These temporal and dynamic characteristics challenge many of the assumptions of the traditional policymaker. The policymaker cannot expect a smooth, linear path between policy intervention and outcome. At the very least the approach needs to be flexible and synthetic, and capable of adapting rapidly to the dynamics of the ecology and the arrival of new technologies. Thus far, policymakers have largely been reactive, changing tactics and approaches in response to technical developments. But such a technology-led approach to policymaking is insufficient in an era of constant flux. The new approach should be sufficiently flexible and accommodating to assimilate new mediating technologies as they emerge. Policy plans must adjust to the perpetual but unpredictable dynamic behavior of the "mediating ecology." The changing patterns within the system must be captured and described, without depending on natural endpoints of behavior or extrapolation or interpolation from timed samples.

Interdependent. Second, relationships in ecologies are complicated and highly interdependent. Many CASs are driven by a large number of interdependent variables and their behavior is influenced by a wide variety of factors. In addition to being numerous, variables can be nonlinear and discontinuous. Some variables may lie dormant for long periods until a trigger sparks them into action.

One way to respond to these multiple and unruly variables is to develop a risk management approach and look for those "differences that make a difference" in the system. The number of potential differences is quite large and virtually unknowable in mediating systems. In addition, over time, the relevance, power, or interrelationships among differences may change. Such a complex interaction of variables makes it unrealistic to expect that the ecology can be represented with a finite number of independent and dependent variables. Most traditional policymaking systems seek to identify a small number of key variables, such as ownership and audience share, that affect change and to establish the relationships among those variables. Unfortunately, these strategies are insufficient to represent the complicated interdependencies in a "mediating ecology." New indicators need to be developed based upon an emerging model of causal and interdependent relationships determining mediation in society.

This also requires a multilayered approach. As we have seen, new intermediaries operate at multiple levels: at the layer of content, of course, but also at the logical and physical layers. It is essential that a new policy approach address the interdependencies among all three layers. The relationship between the last two layers, in particular, is important because mediation at their level frequently goes unnoticed (cf. our discussion of transparency, earlier).

Self-organizing.[27] Third, ecologies exhibit emergent, or self-organizing, behavior. New patterns are generated by the interaction of the agents. New structures are established, and old ones disappear. More importantly, CAS is sensitive to small changes in initial conditions. An apparently trivial difference in the beginning state of the system can result in enormously different outcomes. This phenomenon is sometimes called the "butterfly effect."[28] Because of the butterfly effect, the future of a CAS is unpredictable, but not all of the future is equally uncertain. The near-term future can be relatively knowable; midterm will be less predictable; and far-term future will be uncertain at best. As time passes, uncertainty increases because there will be more opportunities for various conditions and more time for those variations to raise uncertainty. Because of this dynamic, a "mediating ecology" approach must have distinct strategies for assessing a range of possible short-, medium-, and long-term goals.

The implications of the butterfly effect for policymaking are indeed many. Traditional policymaking tools assume the effectiveness of an intervention, such as ownership caps, to be a direct result of the intervention itself. In a mediating ecology, however, the results of the same intervention may vary widely because of small variations in initial conditions. One of the implications is a need for a shift in thinking about the outcome of policymaking. Instead, policymaking should focus on developmental and emergent patterns of mediating behavior that can and should track patterns and pattern changes over time, such as the increasing personalization and polarization, rather than focusing exclusively on the impact of specific technologies. Although it may be unreasonable to expect a particular path of development or a predetermined outcome from a mediating ecology, emergent patterns can be expected outcomes. An effective policy approach must be able to capture and report on these evolving patterns.

Transformational and Open Systems. Finally, the interdependent agents of an ecology are transformed and transforming in their interactions. Because ecologies are open systems, transformation occurs across the system's external boundaries. Feedback loops generate both change and stability in the system. As such, in an ecology, dominant agents, closing down the "open system" and limiting feedback, have the potential to destabilize the system and undermine the transformational potential.

To develop an approach to sustain open systems and limit dominance in a mediating ecology, we need a better understanding and definition of the mediating environment as an open system. We need to understand patterns of dominance and scarcity, and we need to understand who are the determining intermediaries (including mediators outside the realm of communications). This chapter has only begun the process by offering an analytical (and theoretical) understanding of the concept of mediation in a complex system. Now, we need a more detailed mapping of the specific players and their roles.

CONCLUSION

Such a detailed understanding is essential not just because it could help us formulate a new policy toolbox in the abstract. A better understanding of mediation and intermediaries is also critical because the approach it could help develop could ultimately address some of the key challenges and issues confronting policymakers, producers, and consumers. As we have argued throughout this chapter, mediation should be understood as the analytical construct underlying an entire range of policy and regulatory issues: everything from the debate over diversity and media concentration, to notions of universality and universal access, to strategies for bridging the digital divide—we believe that the seeds of solutions to these and many other problems lie in a better understanding of mediation and intermediaries. Ultimately, in designing a communications policy suited to a "new mediation ecology" as a complex adaptive system, we can work toward overcoming some of the most intractable regulatory and policy issues of our time.

NOTES

[1]Joseph Schumpeter stated that processes intrinsic to a capitalist society produce a "creative destruction," whereby innovations destroy obsolete technologies, only to be assaulted in turn by newer and more efficient rivals.

[2]Clayton Christensen's (1997) research explains why established companies have difficulties countering or embracing disruptive innovations such as those discussed in this chapter. His theory is that organizations customarily develop mind-sets and processes that revolve around doing what they already know. Once that pattern becomes established, managers have great difficulty justifying to others the need to change their processes to respond to a barely emergent market change. Similar challenges can be seen among policymakers when confronted with so-called "disruptive innovation."

[3]The study of "mediation" is a well-established, albeit relatively recent, area of focus among media scholars, yet has so far received little attention within the communications policy field (Silverstone, 2005).

[4]Cappella and Jamieson (1997) list, however, two problems with the concept of framing: "First, it has been used in different ways in several different disciplines to mean different things. A general definition of framing seems to reduce to 'the way the story is written or produced,' including the orienting headlines, the specific word choices, the rhetorical devices employed, the narrative form and so on. Any production feature of the verbal or visual text would seem to qualify at least as candidate for framing the news. This view is clearly too broad. Second, differences in framing have been assumed to yield differences in outcome" (p. 39).

[5]Ravitch (2003) has, for instance, described how both those concerned with political correctness and morality have clamped down on the education system, where more and more subjects, words, and ideas have become taboo.

[6]And even within one religion, various realities can be mediated as is exemplified in the ongoing debate and reinterpretation of the so-called Scripture and the various different "Bible" versions determining various Christian "beliefs" (see, e.g., Pelikan, 2005).

[7]Bill Moyers (2005) has, for instance, described in detail how the coupling of political ideology and religion affects the ability to respond in an evidence-based fashion to the various ecological crises.

[8]Perhaps the best-known discussion of scarcity as a basis for regulation took place in the famous *Red Lion* case in the United States (*Red Lion Broadcasting Co. v. FCC, 395* US 367, 1969).

[9]For a debate whether code is law or law is code, see, for instance, Burke (2005).

[10]Professor Benkler (2000), for instance, organizes the Internet into three "layers": the "physical infrastructure" layer underlying the Internet and through which applications operate and information travels, the "code" or "logical" layer that controls the infrastructure and the information, and the "content" layer, which is the information that runs through the network. Each of those layers faces different challenges for mediation and policymaking, and each may require a different solution.

[11]Historically, however, the concept of public service broadcasting was less around countering commercial mediation than it is today, partly because it previously exclusively had to do with radio and television monopolies, but also because most of the electronic media concerned had the formal status of institutions in the public domain. When these monopolies were dissolved in the course of the 1980s, public broadcasting became more seen as a "public service" (Søndergaard, 1999).

[12]In the United States, for instance, the positioning of public broadcasting or PBS as a "noncommercial" is in itself part of a commercial strategy aimed at leveraging the PBS brand to create new revenue streams by licensing the PBS logo, selling new forms of advertising, and developing several PBS brand-name product lines (Hoynes, 2003).

[13]The "Fairness Doctrine," developed in the United States by the Federal Communications Commission (FCC), is an excellent example of the role of scarcity of mediation in media policy. The Fairness Doctrine was an attempt to ensure that all coverage of controversial issues by a broadcast station be balanced and fair. It grew out of a concern that because of the large number of applications for radio stations being submitted and the scarcity of the number of frequencies available, broadcasters—as mediators—should make sure they did not use their stations simply as advocates with a singular perspective. The FCC took the view, in 1949, that station licensees were "public trustees," and as such had an obligation to afford reasonable opportunity for discussion of contrasting points of view on controversial issues of public importance (Simmons, 1978). The FCC later also mandated stations to actively seek out issues of importance to their local community. The Fairness Doctrine was, however, dissolved in the 1980s (Aufderheide, 1990).

[14]Charlie Firestone (1997), in an early article on the New Intermediaries, lists a set of envisaged benefits behind the new intermediaries: they would not only filter information, but also integrate systems and audiences, serve as agents for users, help navigate the vast worlds of information resources, analyze and contextualize information to facilitate its conversion to knowledge in the minds of the user, and authenticate the value of the information.

[15]For an estimate on how much information gets created each year, see Varian and Lyman (2003).

[16]According to Davenport and Beck (2001), the scarcest resource in today's economy is no longer just land, capital, or human labor, or information: attention is in short supply.

[17]Research by Lada Adamic and Bernardo Huberman (2000), for instance, shows that the distribution of visitors per site follows a universal power law, characteristic of winner-take-all markets. In other words, a small number of sites have tens of millions of visitors each month—Google, Yahoo, MSN, and so forth—whereas millions of sites attract only a handful each. Counterintuitively, the more choices there are, the more extreme the curve becomes, which exemplifies in part the need for mediation within society as to cope with abundance.

[18]Especially by using intellectual property rights (Gordon, 1998).

[19]For a rare, more public interest oriented view on how identity and reputations of management systems may determine access in society, see Jordan, Hauser, and Foster (2003).

[20]For more information about the "Values in Design" Project, see http://www.nyu.edu/projects/valuesindesign/

[21]For an interesting critique of Sunstein's theories, see Ulen (2001).

[22]For a rare discussion of new intermediary liability, see Mann and Belzley (2005).

[23]Overall, a complex adaptive system consists of interdependent agents. The behavior of each agent conforms to a short list of simple rules, and the group of agents exhibits emergent, system-wide patterns of behavior.

[24]For the purpose of explaining the relevance of a complex adaptive system (CAS) to mediating ecology, I use CAS and ecology as interchangeable.

[25]See, for instance, The Workshop on "Complexity and ICT," at http://quello.msu.edu/complexity/main.htm

[26]For a more extensive discussion on how complex theory can inform communications policy, see, for instance, Bauer (2004); Cherry (2004); and Longstaff (2004).

[27]Luhmann's (1986) theory on autopoiesis and its application to communication is especially relevant when considering a mediating ecology.

[28]It was meteorologist Edward Lorenz who developed the butterfly theory, which ultimately became a crucial concept in the development of chaos theory. When considering weather forecasting, he found that with a minute change in the initial conditions, weather patterns could diverge dramatically. Since then, the phenomenon became reduced to the phrase "sensitive dependence on initial conditions" and known in terms of the "butterfly effect"—that, for instance, a butterfly flapping its wings over Cuba in August could influence the course of a hurricane headed inland in September (Stites, 1994).

REFERENCES

Adamic, L., & Glance, N. (2005). *The political blogosphere and the 2004 U.S. election: Divided they blog*. Retrieved January 22, 2005, from http://www.blogpulse.com/papers/2005/AdamicGlanceBlogWWW.pdf

Adamic, L., & Huberman, B. (2000). Power law distribution of the World Wide Web (comment). *Science, 287,* 2115.
Alberts, D. S., & Hayes, R. (2003). *Power to the edge. Command and control in the information age. CCRP.* Retrieved March 26, 2005, from http://www.dodccrp.org/publications/pdf/Alberts_Power.pdf
Anderson, B. (1991). *Imagined communities: Reflections on the origin and spread of nationalism.* (Rev. ed.). London: Verso.
Aufderheide, P. (1990). After the fairness doctrine: controversial broadcast programming and the public interest. *Journal of Communication, 40*(3), 47–72.
Baudrillard, J. (1983). *Simulations.* New York: Semiotext(e).
Bauer, J. M. (1999, September 25). *Competition as a turbulent process: Lessons for telecommunications regulatory reform.* (Paper presented at the 27th Telecommunications Policy Research Conference. Abstract retrieved December 1, 2004, from http://www.tprc.org/ABSTRACTS99/bauerpap.PDF
Bauer, J. M. (2004). Harnessing the swarm: Communications policy in an era of ubiquitous networks and disruptive technologies. *Communications and Strategies, 54,* 19–43.
Benkler, Y. (2000). *From consumers to users: shifting the deeper structures of regulation towards sustainable commons and user access.* 52 Fed. Comm. L.J. 561, 561–79. Retrieved April 7, 2005, from http://www.law.indiana.edu/fclj/pubs/v52/no3/benkler1.pdf
Burke, D. (2005). Law as networked standard. Retrieved January 31, 2005, from http://islandia.law.yale.edu/isp/GlobalFlow/paper/Burk.pdf
Cappella, J., & Jamieson, K. (1997). *Spiral of cynicism: The press and the public good.* Oxford, England: Oxford University Press.
Cherry, B. A. (2004, October 2). *The telecommunications economy and regulation as coevolving complex adaptive systems: implications for federalism.* Paper presented at the 32nd Research Conference on Communications, Internet and Information Policy, Arlington, VA.
Christensen, C. (1997). *The innovator's dilemma: When new technologies cause great firms to fail.* Cambridge, MA: Harvard Business School Press.
Cohen, E. (Ed.). (2005). *News incorporated: Corporate media ownership and its threat to democracy.* New York: Prometheus Books.
Cooper, M. (2002). *The failure of 'intermodal' competition in cable markets.* Oxford, England: Consumer Federation of America.
Currie, D. (2004). *RTS Fleming memorial lecture 2004: Television and the digital future.* Oxford, England: Ofcom.
Dahlgreen, P. (1999). Public service media, old and new: Vitalizing a civic culture? [Electronic version]. *Canadian Journal of Communication, 24.*
Davenport, T., & Beck, J. (2001). *The attention economy: Understanding the new currency of business.* Cambridge, MA: Harvard Business School Press.
Dennis, E. E. (2003). Prospects for a big idea: Is there a future for convergence? *The International Journal on Media Management, 5,* 7–11.
De Zengotita, T. (2005). *Mediated: How the media shapes your world and the way you live in it.* New York: Bloomsbury.
Entman, R. (1993). Framing: Toward clarification of a fractured paradigm. *Journal of Communication, 43*(4), 51–58.
Eoyang, G., & Berkas, T. (1999). Evaluating performance in a complex adaptive system. In M. Lissack & H. Gunz (Eds.), *Managing complexity in organizations* (pp. 313–335). Westport, CT: Quorum Books.
Firestone, C. (1997). *The new intermediaries.* Washington, DC: Aspen Institute.
FitzGerald, F. (1979). *America revised: History schoolbooks in the 20th century.* New York: Vintage.

Gilder, G. (2000). *Telecosm: How infinite bandwidth will revolutionize our world.* New York: Free Press.

Gillmor, D (2004). *We the media: grassroots journalism by the people, for the people.* Retrieved November 24, 2004, from http://www.oreilly.com/catalog/wemedia/book/

Gitlin, T. (1980). *The whole world is watching: Mass media in the making and unmaking of the new left.* Berkeley: University of California Press.

Gladwell, M. (2005). *Blink: The power of thinking without thinking.* New York: Little, Brown.

Goffman, E. (1974). *Frame analysis: An essay on the organization of experience.* New York: Harper & Row.

Goldberg, D., Prosser, T., & Verhulst, S. (1996). *Consultant study on the impact of new communications technologies on media concentrations and pluralism.* Strasbourg, France: Council of Europe.

Goldberg, D., Prosser, T., & Verhulst, S. (1998). *Legal responses to the changing media.* Oxford, England: Oxford University Press.

Goldhaber, M. H. (1997). What's the right economy for cyberspace? *First Monday, 2.* Retrieved May 7, 2005, from http://www.firstmonday.org/issues/issue2_7/goldhaber/

Gordon, W. J. (1998) Intellectual property as price discrimination: Implications for contract. *Kent Law Review, 73,* 1367–1390.

Habermas, J. (1962). *Struktarwandel der Öffentlichkeit; Untersuchungen einer kategorie der bürgerlichen Gesellschaft* [The structural transformation of the public sphere: An inquiry into a category of bourgeois society]. (T. Burger, Trans.). Cambridge: Polity.

Hammer, M. (2000). The myth of disintermediation. *Information Week Online.* Retrieved October 30, 2004, from http://www.informationweek.com/794/94uwmh.htm

Hargittai E. (2000). Open portals or closed gates? Channeling content on the World Wide Web. *Poetics, 27,* 233–253.

Hargittai, E. (2003). The changing online landscape: From free-for-all to commercial fatekeeping. In P. Day & D. Schuler (Eds.), *Community practice in the network society: Local actions/global interaction* (pp. 66–76). New York: Routledge.

Hiltz, S. R., & Johnson, K. (1990). User satisfaction with computer-mediated communication systems. *Management Science, 36,* 739–764.

Hitchens, L. (1997). Introduction to the special feature on communications regulation: New patterns and problems. *The Journal of Information, Law and Technology* (JILT), 1997 (3). Retrieved June 24, 2005, from http://elj.warwick.ac.uk/jilt/issue/1997_3/hitchen.htm

Holtz-Bacha, C., & Norris, P. (2001). "To entertain, inform, and educate:" Still the role of public television. *Political Communication, 18,* 123–140.

Hoynes, W. (2003). Branding public service: The "new PBS" and the privatization of public television. *Television & New Media, 4,* 117–130.

Introna, L., & Nissenbaum, H. (2000). Shaping the web: Why the politics of search engines matters. *The Information Society, 16,* 1–17.

Johnson, S. (2005). *Interface culture: How new technology transforms the way we create and communicate.* San Francisco: Harper San Francisco.

Jordan, K., Hauser, J., & Foster, S. (2003). The augmented social network: Building identity and trust into the next-generation Internet. *First Monday, 8.* Retrieved May 1, 2005, from http://firstmonday.org/issues/issue8_8/jordan/index.html

Kerr, E. B., & Hiltz, S. R. (1982). *Computer mediated communication systems: Status and evaluation.* New York: Academic.

Laven, P. (2004). *Standards, who needs them? Diffusion 2004/20.* Geneva, Switzerland: European Broadcasting Union.

Lewin, K. (1947). Frontiers in group dynamics: 11 channels of group life: Social planning and action research. *Human Relations, 1,* 145–146.

Longstaff, P. H. (2002). *The communications toolkit how to build and regulate any communications business*. Cambridge, MA: MIT Press.

Longstaff, P. H. (2004). *The puzzle of competition in the communications sector: can complex systems be regulated or managed?* Cambridge, MA: Harvard University Press.

Luhmann, N. (1986). The autopoiesis of social systems. In F. Geyer & J. van der Zouwen (Eds.), *Sociocybernetic paradoxes* (pp. 172–192). London: Sage.

Mann, R. J., & Belzley, S. R., (2005). The promise of internet intermediary liability. *William and Mary Law Review, 47*, 239–308.

McKnight, L. W., Vaaler, P. M., & Katz, R. L. (2002). *Creative destruction: Business survival strategies in the global internet economy*. Cambridge, MA: MIT Press.

McQuail, D. (2000). *McQuail's mass communication theory*. Thousand Oaks, CA: Sage.

Mowshowitz, A. (1982). The bias of computer technology. In W. M. Hoffman & J. M. Moore (Eds.), *Ethics and the management of computer technology*. Boston: Oelgeschlager, Gunn & Hain.

Moyers, B. (2005, March 25). Welcome to doomsday. *The New York Review of Books, 52*(5), 8–10.

Nielsen, J. (2003). IM, not IP (information pollution). *ACM Queue, 1*. Retrieved April 4, 2006, from www.acmqueue.com/modules.php?name=contentepa=showpage&pid=96

Noam, E. (2003). *The Internet: Still wide open and competitive?* Retrieved February 22, 2005, from http://tprc.org/papers/2003/200/noam_TPRC2003.pdf

O'Harrow, R., Jr. (2005). *No place to hide: Behind the scenes of our emerging surveillance society*. New York: Free Press.

Price, M. E. (1994). The market for loyalties: Electronic media and the global competition for allegiances. *Yale Law Journal, 104*, 667–705.

Pelikan, J. (2005). *Whose Bible is it?* London: Viking.

Quarterman, J. S. (1990). *The matrix: Computer networks and conferencing systems worldwide*. Bedford, MA: Digital.

Ravitch, D. (2003). *The language police: How pressure groups restrict what students learn*. New York: Knopf.

Rheingold, H. (1998). *The virtual community*. Retrieved March 29, 2005, from http://www.rheingold.com/vc/book/

Rice, R. E., & Bair, J. H. (1984). New organizational media and productivity. In R. E. Rice (Ed.), *The new media: Communication, research, and technology* (pp. 185–215). Beverly Hills, CA: Sage.

Rosen, C. (2004–2005). The age of egocasting. *The New Atlantis, 7*, 51–72.

Sanderson, I. (2000). Evaluation in complex policy systems. *Evaluation, 6*, 433–454.

Schumpeter, J. A. (1975). *Capitalism, socialism and democracy*. New York: Harper & Row.

Severin, W. J., & Tankard, J. W. (1992). *Communication theories: Origins, methods, and uses in the mass media* (3rd ed.). White Plains, NY: Longman.

Shapiro, A. (1998). Digital middlemen and the architecture of electronic commerce. *Ohio Northern Law Review, 24*, 795–812.

Sheu, T. R., & Carley, K. (2001, October 27). *Monopoly power on the web: A preliminary investigation of search engines*. Paper presented at the 29th Telecommunications Policy Research Conference. Retrieved June 7, 2005 from http://arxiv.org/ftp/cs/papers/0109/0109054.pdf

Silverstone, R., (2005). Mediation and communication. In C. Calhoun, C. Rojek, & B. Turner (Eds.), *The Sage handbook of sociology*. London: Sage. Also available at www.lse.uc.uk/collections/medialse/pdf/mediation.pdf

Simmons, S. J. (1978). *The fairness doctrine and the media*. Berkeley: University of California Press.

Singh, J. P. (1999). Universal service: Competition, interconnection, and monopoly in the making of the American telephone system, and telecommunications competition: The last ten miles. *Technology and Culture, 40*, 450–452.

Søndergaard, H. (1999). Some reflections on public service broadcasting. *Nordicom Review 1*. Retrieved May 7, 2005, from http://www.nordicom.gu.se/common/publ_pdf/33_sondergaard.pdf
Stites, J. (1994, May). Complexity: Research on complex systems and complex adaptive systems. *Omni Magazine*. Retrieved April 6, 2006, from www.findarticles.com/p/articles/mi_m1430/is_n8_v16/ai_15347893
Streeter, T. (1990). Beyond freedom of speech and the public interest: The relevance of critical legal studies to communications policy. *Journal of Communication, 40*(2), 43–63.
Sunstein, C. (2001). *Republic.com*. Princeton, NJ: Princeton University Press.
Thurlow, C., Lengel, L., & Tomic, A. (2004). *Computer mediated communication: Social interaction and the Internet*. London: Sage.
Ulen, T. S. (2001). Democracy and the Internet. [Review of the book *Republic.com*]. *Journal of Law, Technology and Policy, 2*, 224.
van Zandt, T. (2001). Information overload in a network of targeted communication (CEPR Discussion Paper, No. 2836). London: Centre for Economic Policy Research.
Varian, H., & Lyman, P. (2003). *How much information?* Retrieved June 5, 2005, from http://www.sims.berkeley.edu/research/projects/how-much-info-2003/
Walker, J. (2002). Links and power: The political economy of linking on the Web. *Proceedings of hypertext 2002* (pp. 78–79). Baltimore: ACM Press.
White, D. M. (1950). The "gate keeper": A case study in the selection of news. *Journalism Quarterly, 27*, 383–390.
Wolfram, S. (1988). Emerging syntheses in science. In *Proceedings of the founding workshops of the Santa Fe Institute* (pp. 183–189). Boston: Addison-Wesley.
Zuboff, S., & Maxim, J. (2002). *The support economy*. London: Allen Lane.

7

The Limits of Diversity

Sandra Braman
University of Wisconsin—Milwaukee

It seems on the face of it to be inherently a good thing: More ideas are better ideas. As translated into media policy, this becomes the principle of "diversity." Media content diversity is still a good thing, but in operationalization matters become more complex. Questions about just what it is that is "diverse" and how the extent of diversity can be measured are the subjects of the rest of the chapters of this volume and are not further addressed here. There is a deep contradiction in arguments for content diversity grounded in the concept of the "marketplace of ideas" by authors who otherwise insist that neoclassical economic analyses of media effects are insufficient. This essay addresses a third type of problem: the fetishization of diversity as a policy principle underestimates its limits.

The word "fetish" is used here deliberately. The concept was born in anthropological efforts to describe the role of spiritually animated inanimate objects in "primitive" religions. As early as 1837 Ralph Waldo Emerson, however, used the word fetish to describe certain widespread attitudes toward governance. The meaning of the word for Emerson is "something irrationally reverenced" (Oxford English Dictionary, n.d.). Sigmund Freud (1928), presumably not thinking about governance, used the word to refer to things that act as a substitute for what is not there. William Pietz (1985, 1988), whose analyses of the concept of the fetish across disciplines and time are considered the most comprehensive and masterful of such explorations available, points out that one enduring theme in conceptualizations of the fetish that endures is the way in which it subverts the ideal of the autonomously determined self.

As used in contemporary media policy discourse, diversity has become a fetish in the Emersonian and Freudian senses when it is believed that the mere accomplishment of diversity, however measured, is sufficient to ensure an ideal type of participatory governance. The consequences of that fetishization are political for the reasons suggested by Pietz. Although the importance of content diversity to the quality of public decision making about shared matters of public concern is not disputed, there are limits to its value as both a policy principle and policy tool that have implications for those who make and those who critique laws and regulations.

There are two caveats: Although the principle of diversity is constitutionally based in the United States and thus applies across media, it has been most explicitly operationalized as applied to broadcasting and it is broadcasting that is the focus of the discussion here. And although the Federal Communications Commission (FCC) has replaced content with ownership when it evaluates compliance with diversity-related regulations, the diversity of concern remains in the actual information, language, and ideas communicated through the medium—not the technologies used, the ways in which those technologies are used, who is using those technologies, or who owns the technologies.

The limits of diversity as a regulatory principle and tool are worth exploring not only for the purpose of enriching public debate and regulatory practice, but for what it tells us regarding what may also be limits to the possible efficacy of the contemporary "media reform" movement, which seeks to reduce the extent of broadcast ownership concentration on the basis of its consequences for diversity. Although this movement has certainly expanded the range and number of people actively engaged in thinking about important media policy matters, the singular focus of this movement may ultimately undercut not only its attempts to achieve the target goal as identified, but also the larger goal of improving the quality of participatory democracy, because it ignores the consequences of the limits of diversity.

This problem was highlighted by what was touted as a media reform movement success in the fall of 2003. When a rider to a budget bill dealing with military matters (and thus not the subject of much public discussion) would have raised the cap on the percentage of the national audience one broadcaster could serve, those in the media reform movement generated so much of a public response that Republicans dropped this increase to achieve sufficient Democratic support to pass the bill. This was touted publicly as a major movement success.

There was, however, a second rider in that bill. This was the piece of legislation that expanded the Federal Bureau of Investigation's (FBI) ability to request financial information from any entity on anyone of interest without even the requirement of any judicial scrutiny of the grounds claimed to justify such surveillance that remained in the USA PATRIOT Act (2001). (All that was required by way of justification was that the FBI write a letter to itself saying that the surveillance to be undertaken was of interest.) This extraordinary expansion of FBI surveillance powers included a gag on those entities from whom information was requested, generating a condition in which anyone could be surveilled at any time for any type of activity that involved an economic transaction, without knowledge.

It is not difficult to argue that this issue is at least of the same political importance as a drop in the broadcast audience cap; many would argue that the privacy issue was of greater importance because it marked a watershed in the history of U.S. surveillance. Yet that rider was accepted by those in the media reform movement and by Congress without question because all attention was on the media concentration question. Whatever the claims of the media reform movement—itself driven by self-proclaimed interests in civil liberties—regarding its "success" on the matter, it is difficult to interpret the expansion of surveillance powers to which the media reform movement efforts contributed as a positive development from the privacy perspective.

At least one leader of the media reform movement responded to a question regarding the fact that the bill claimed to be such a success included this extraordinary change in our privacy environment by saying that it was "not their issue." Of course it is. Fragmentation of the policy environment in this way by those who seek change offers great opportunities to those who prefer the status quo, or who seek change in the opposite direction, and appreciate much more fully than do media activists and advocates the interrelationships among diverse policy matters.

Indeed, even meaningfully achieving diversity requires attention to many other policy principles and tools. We can identify limits to diversity on the way "in," at the point of content production; in the "middle," in the course of the sense-making that is sometimes referred to as reception; and at the "end," in the relationship between media content and actual decision-making processes. Each of these is discussed here in turn, including a look at their policy and research implications.

THE LIMITS TO DIVERSITY IN CONTENT PRODUCTION

On the way in, there are limits to diversity that derive from constraints on the types of information available from which content can be built, differences in the availability of information and other content across media, and the importance of taking into account the extent to which the "hypermedia chain" of content flows has been ignited.[1]

The Limits of Informational Input

Essentially all of the discussion about media diversity, from both those who are critical of its extent and those who design and implement pertinent policy tools likely to further limit the range of content, focuses on elements of the production process itself that come into play after information has been gathered. These typically include lack of diversity among the personnel in the newsroom, conformity of content imposed by common ownership across broadcasting entities, and the impact of either direct imposition of mandates regarding content or indirect "chilling" of speech in response to political and/or economic pressure. There is one more all-critical input into media content, however—the information on which stories are based. It is from this information that ideas, opinions, arguments, stories, and "facts" all derive.

There is no politically meaningful diversity of content if we do not have available information about what the government is actually doing, the local conditions of our daily lives, or the results of scientific research. This is an enduring problem that has become particularly acute in recent years through expansions of exemptions to the Freedom of Information Act (FOIA) and increased ease in using those exemptions, the removal of vast swathes of scientific and technical information from public access under the rubric of national security concerns, deletion of the results of scientific research from government and government-funded Web sites that do not support particular policy positions of the current Administration, demands that public libraries destroy databases long in public hands, and even—though these efforts have so far failed—attempts to prevent public access to federal statutes and regulations.[2]

Policymakers and politicians tend to look across types of law and sources of law when they are seeking to achieve particular goals, but policy analysts typically focus on individual laws or regulations in isolation. Thus those who are concerned about content diversity in the media because they are interested in the type of rich public conversation about public issues believed to be fundamental to participatory democracy must attend not only to regulation of broadcasting but also to the variety of factors that influence access to pertinent information. On the research side, it would be valuable to see analyses of content diversity that relate the relative extent of diversity to the relative availability of information needed to produce stories on specific topics.

The Limits of Medium Specificity

Although content diversity is generally understood to apply to all media, it has been directly translated into an explicit regulatory tool only in the area of broadcasting as managed by the FCC. This has been justified by what we might call the "oomph" factor—the belief that the relative impact of broadcasting in terms of shaping perceptions, beliefs, and understanding of audience members is greater than that of print. Various versions of the oomph factor were put forward when it became necessary to justify licensing and other regulation of broadcasting within a First Amendment environment that had historically forbidden licensing of media because of the opportunities licensing inherently offers for those who would censor or otherwise punish content producers. (The other two justifications were the need for a "traffic cop," and relative scarcity of access to the spectrum compared to the widespread availability of print; the last of these is no longer defensible, and the first of these remains.) Some research—particularly on the effects of television violence on children—tends to support belief in the oomph factor, but not all research does; despite this, belief in the relative importance of the need to regulate broadcasting continues to be strong.

Of course, since the question of the relative impact of various media was first raised, the range of media has expanded significantly. The Internet, with genres ranging from classical modern newspaper content to electronic games involving global participation in the hundreds of thousands, is demonstrably drawing audiences away from television. There is renewed appreciation for very traditional media, such as church sermons experienced in a synchronous and often face to face environment, as religious groups raise their profile in the U.S. political world. Content is now distributed in mobile formats, for the cellphone is now a mass medium as well as a narrowcast and interpersonal medium. And content is increasingly delivered as a feature of the architectural and urban environment. Of course face-to-face interpersonal communication, and the distribution of content and information via interpersonal networks, remain important.

This expansion of the range of media that feed into the diversity of content available in each of our personal information ecologies[3] revives the research question. And what we have learned about the psychological as well as sociological effects of media use suggests additional dimensions of importance. What is the relative impact of content as delivered through each of the media—and how should we be defining "impact" today? How does the content of one medium affect how we perceive content received through another medium? Does the relative extent of active content pull, as opposed to the long familiar passive reception of content push, affect impact? We know from studies that compare news stories as presented via broadcast television and print that the difference in medium essentially creates two different genres although they are both referred to in the same way as news stories, for the amount of information provided in news stories in papers such as *The New York Times* and *The Washington Post* is often 800% that of broadcast news stories, and the narrative structure differs between the two media as well. How do genre differences affect the relative impact of various media? Finally, given that people born after 1970 cognitively process information differently from those who were born before—because of the predominance of information presented to them in visual as opposed to verbal form in their lives—how do shifts in the nature of cognitive information processing within and across groups, and across time, affect the relative impact of various media?

The research questions point to the policy questions: If the impact of television content relative to the impact of content received through other media is relatively unimportant, does diversity matter as a regulatory tool? Conversely, if other media are actually more important—at least for the political purposes at the heart of media diversity goals—different types of regulatory tools are suggested. One that immediately comes to mind would be regulatory and statutory support for community-wide free access to wi-fi (wireless local networking), so that everyone in a community can have access to the Internet and its capacities for distributing political information, serving as a forum for public discourse, and mobilizing political action. Another, just to be provocative, might be forbidding discussion of political issues within the church for those churches that seek to retain their tax exemption status. These research questions also draw attention to means of restricting content diversity that are not touched by FCC regulations attempting to operationalize the basic principle.

The Limits of the Hypermedia Chain

Blogs are currently receiving so much attention precisely because they introduce information, stories, and perspectives not made available by the mainstream media. In this way, they are significantly adding to the diversity of content available to the over two thirds of the U.S. population who use the Internet as well as television and print media (Pew Internet and American Life Project, 2005). The question of whether or not bloggers, too, should be considered "journalists" has received its first legal attention around the issue of whether or not they should be forced to provide information about confidential sources. This type of information is protected by "shield laws" in many jurisdictions (if certain conditions are met), but that protection applies only to journalists and not, for example, to non-journalists who may be relying on information in sources claimed by the subjects of public comments to be libelous. At the time of writing, the decision has been that bloggers are journalists for this particular legal purpose, but the possibility of further denials of the journalistic value of bloggers and other news content that does not come from media organizations recognized as such prior to the introduction of the Internet remains. (It is, of course, difficult to describe any news organization as "traditional," because *The New York Times*-style journalism that predominated during the 20th century only came into being in the middle of the 19th century, and the large broadcast organizations now treated as "traditional" only appeared in the middle of the 20th century.)

It is well documented that mainstream news organizations, including television broadcasters, rely almost exclusively on official sources for their news (see, e.g., Ericson, Baranek, & Chan, 1989). The ability of independent media groups and of bloggers to introduce stories and information that then find their way into mainstream news reports is therefore absolutely critical to meaningful content diversity in the broadcast outlets regulated by the FCC. Drawing a line between such news outlets and "journalists" undermines the credibility of the information the former offer and puts pressure on mainstream news outlets not to use that information, again decreasing opportunities for diversity.

One means of operationalizing a firm distinction between journalists and non-journalists as a means of restricting the diversity of media content is via the criteria for participating in press pools. Press pools limit the number of reporters in attendance at official press conferences and in unofficial environments such as a president's travel entourage by selecting specific individuals from among those nominated by news organizations who accept the responsibility along with a commitment to then share information received with those who are not in the pool. Although press pool information is shared, the makeup of the press pool affects which information all media outlets receive; members of alternative news organizations, who might be expected on the basis of experience to ask more difficult and probing questions, are kept out of press pools because their organizations are not classified as legitimate news organizations and thus, in essence, they are not journalists. This distinction in practice between journalists and nonjournalists received quasi-legal status in the 1990s, when rules for press pools in war zones were put in place. (Described by the Department of Defense as a set of rules agreed on consensually by the journalism and military communities, journalists' organizations claim these rules—which require such things as prepublication approval of stories by the military and the presence of members of the military at all interviews—were imposed on them.)

It is one thing to have many media available, but quite another to appreciate—and make use of—the ways in which what happens in one stimulates, feeds into, or changes the way we use others. The use of blogs to introduce information and stories that will then be taken up by the mainstream media is a self-aware use of relationships among media that ignite the hypermedia chain. Current policies regarding treatment of bloggers as non-journalists and alternative media as not legitimate for purposes of official news conferences are among the techniques being used to reduce diversity of media content by trying to limit the cross-medium information exchanges that can be so valuable in an hypermedia environment.

THE LIMITS TO DIVERSITY IN CONTENT SENSE-MAKING

At the point of content distribution—the moment in which messages are typically analyzed—there are also limits to effective content diversity that derive from the ability of those who receive the content to perceive, process, and make use of whatever range of views of information and perspective is made available. What has long been called the "audience" in television studies, suggesting passive reception of whatever content is delivered, is now more valuably understood through the lenses of "reception" and "sense-making," approaches that acknowledge the very active role played by those who receive content. Studies within and across societies demonstrating the wide range of interpretations of both entertainment and news programming depending on demographics, culture, and socioeconomic context make clear that the actual meaning conveyed by content is only partially determined by those who produce it. From the point of view of those who do research on content, this shift in perspective suggests that evaluations of relative diversity must take into account differences in interpretation as shaped by communal context and individual context and capacities—not by content alone. Information about a change in prime rate may be useless to many U.S. citizens because they would not understand what the consequences will mean for them, but to others (and in communities heavily populated by such individuals) it would be a story complete in itself and replete with implications. A story about the injury of a Black suspect during the course of being taken into police custody may be read as yet another typical story in some communities, but as a politically explosive piece of information in others, and so on.

The suggestion to map analyses of content diversity onto an actual understanding of the social, cultural, economic, and political characteristics of the community within which that content is received would seem to be suggested by now-attenuated FCC requirements that local broadcasters ascertain the nature of their communities, but has not been borne out in research practice with the full panoply of research tools developed by those who do in-depth work on sense-making and reception. The changes in the nature of cognitive information processing mentioned earlier suggest that analysis of differences in reception at the individual level must go beyond demographics to include psychological factors as well. Existing research on psycho-physiological responses to various dimensions of news stories that has led to specific recommendations about how to communicate news via broadcasting most effectively[4] could valuably both be extended to other media (so that comparisons are possible) and be linked with group- and community-level analyses.

THE LIMITS TO DIVERSITY IN POLICY USE OF CONTENT

The underlying assumption of those involved in discussing media diversity and trying to design and implement regulatory tools to enhance it is that making a range of types of information and perspectives available through the media will inevitably and effectively affect the nature of political debate, ensuring that the views of all are seriously taken into account at the point of decision making. It is here that the most serious limits to diversity arise. They come in two flavors: use of content diversity by the public, and the use of public opinion by policymakers.

Content Diversity and Public Opinion

There is an assumption in most of the discourse about content diversity that members of the public will know what to do with it when they find it. The 2004 U.S. presidential election raises some questions about that assumption. Both popular and scholarly discourse about news before the election took the position that only one side of the story was being told in the mainstream media, so that one had to turn to alternative media sources to receive additional, or other, information and analysis. Was this true?

A study of stories presented on the Web site of Truthout.org offers an opportunity to answer this question. Truthout.org is a news aggregator that collects and presents news from the self-admitted perspective of some discomfort with present U.S. leadership and political directions. If the perception that only one side of most stories was presented by the mainstream media were correct, the news sources on which Truthout.org relies would be those of alternative media. However, a study of the original sources of Truthout.org stories about the politically fraught issue of the 9/11 Commission proceedings revealed that 90% to 95% of the stories presented come from mainstream media such as *The New York Times, The Los Angeles Times, ABC News,* Associated Press, and Reuters. In other words, in this suggestive case dealing with U.S. political affairs prior to the 2004 presidential election, the mainstream media were the alternative media!

This raises an important question for those who promote media diversity. In the last section, we asked whether there is meaningful content diversity if people receive information but cannot make sense out of it, and/or cannot discern differences in positions. The problem goes further: Can we say there is meaningful content diversity if people receive information and make sense out of it, but cannot connect that information with their political behaviors and decision making?

There are policy as well as research implications from the insight that the actual extent of content diversity differs according to the communal and individual contexts of reception, primarily in the area of education. Raising the political salience of and financial support for media literacy in primary and secondary as well as tertiary schools would be one piece. Another would be treating education in "civics," political affairs, as important enough to be taught by specialists rather than, as is too often the case, the football coach in his extra time.

On the research side, this phenomenon has received little attention. Perhaps the link between information and political mobilization has been broken. Perhaps the link remains but, for this generation and current modes of cognitive information processing, information must be presented in ways not familiar to practicing journalists. Perhaps the link remains but the directions of causality are no longer those that might be predicted by either political scientists or sociologists. Or perhaps citizens still are politically mobilized by information they receive, continue to be able to make sense of information being broadcast, and act on their political beliefs—but find that familiar types of activity have no traction in the contemporary political environment.

Public Opinion and Policymaking

The extent to which public opinion as measured statistically is used by policymakers goes up and down (as does the relative political sophistication of those doing the measuring). In the early 21st century, however, the explicit White House position is that public opinion does not matter. Behavioral manifestations of that position are visible: the lack of availability to journalists, the strict constraints on press conferences and manipulation of the press conference and news formats, and the willingness to act even in the face of widespread opposition to particular policies and positions.

There are, of course, other ways in which the opinions, preferences, and knowledge of U.S. citizens can inform policymaking. The postal provision was included in the U.S. Constitution because it was understood that participatory democracy only works if representatives can communicate with their constituencies, and vice versa. Yet since 9/11 there have been long stretches of time in which paper-based mail didn't reach those to whom it was addressed in Washington, DC, for months (if ever), as it was side-tracked for evaluation of possible traces of dangerous substances; telephone calls were not being received; and e-mail messages were ignored because they were viewed as having no substance. There are numerous ways in which scientific and technical expertise as well as citizen preferences can be inserted into federal agency decision-making processes, but no guarantee that that information will actually be used once it arrives in the appropriate venue; indeed, recent FCC decisions regarding possible mergers so egregiously ignored empirical data that the Chief Economist resigned. Ever since the last decades of the 19th century at the very least, the U.S. government has relied on the results of research as inputs into policymaking, but toward the close of the 20th century, the Office of Management and Budget (OMB) put in place a series of strictures on the use of research results by federal agencies that have minimized and/or made ineffectual such practices.

LOOKING BEYOND THE LIMITS

On the face of it, diversity is still a good thing—surely maximizing the breadth of perspectives, information, and ideas available to U.S. citizens is a goal toward which we should strive. But if news stories are based on conjecture or prescripted content rather than information independently evaluated, the value of diversity goes down. If those who receive the news are unable to make political sense out of the information, the value of diversity further declines. If those who receive the news are able to translate information received into political decisions, and then action, but those to whom their words and actions are addressed decline to listen or treat them as worthy of attention, the value of diversity declines yet again.

It is likely to be a long time before we fully understand what happened in the 2004 presidential election. The 2003 budget bill was likely to have passed whether or not the privacy, as well as media concentration, issue had been raised. But fetishization of content diversity as if its achievement, alone, would turn around the quality of contemporary democratic practice and process is, as Freud would say, to focus on something that simply is not there. Those who are battling to increase media diversity need also to attend to policy issues such as access to information, education, integrity of the voting process, and the ability of citizens to meaningfully participate in decision-making processes—as well as the impact of their actions on other important policy areas such as privacy—before the winning of any single battle can be called a success.

NOTES

[1]The term "hypermedia" was coined by Bolter and Grusin (1998); Kraidy (2005) expanded on the notion with his discussion of ways in which interactions among diverse media increase the effectiveness of each.

[2]A number of nonprofit organizations, such as OMBWatch, the Electronic Frontier Foundation, and the American Civil Liberties Union, are tracking these efforts to restrict our access to information.

[3]Nardi and O'Day (1999) use the phrase "information ecology" to distinguish the informational world we each create for ourselves through choices we make in hardware, software, and content selection from the "information environment" defined as all of the information potentially available in a given context.

[4]For an application-oriented synthesis of dozens of studies in this area, see Lang, Potter, and Grabe (2003).

REFERENCES

Bolter, J. D., & Grusin, R. (1998). *Remediation: Understanding new media*. Cambridge, MA: MIT Press.

Ericson, R. V., Baranek, P. M., & Chan, J. B. (1989). *Negotiating control: A study of news*. Milton Keynes, England: Open University Press.

Freud, S. (1928). Fetishism. In J. Strachey (Ed.), *The standard edition of the complete works of Sigmund Freud* (Vol. 21, pp. 152–157). New York: Norton.

Kraidy, M. (2005). Hypermedia and governance in Saudi Arabia. Presented to the conference Command Lines: The emergence of governance in global cyberspace, Milwaukee, WI.

Lang, A., Potter, D., & Grabe, M. E. (2003). Making news memorable: Applying theory to the production of local television news. *Journal of Broadcast and Electronic Media, 47,* 113–124.

Nardi, B. A., & O'Day, V. (1999). *Information ecologies: Using technology with heart*. Cambridge, MA: MIT Press.

Oxford English Dictionary. (n.d.). *OED Online*. Retrieved February 2, 2005, from http://dictionary.oed.com/entrance.dtl

Pew Internet and American Life Project. (2005). Retrieved July 2, 2005, from www.pewinternet.org

Pietz, W. (1985). The problem of the fetish, I. *Res, 9,* 5–15.

Pietz, W. (1988). The problem of the fetish, IIIa. *Res, 16,* 103–123.

8

Indexing Diversity

Steven S. Wildman
Michigan State University

Media have always presented a special challenge to policymakers. As commercial enterprises, they raise the usual economic policy concerns regarding the efficiency with which they respond to consumer demands. At the same time, the media are conduits for the debate and exchange of viewpoints on public issues that are vital to the functioning of a democratic society. They are also intimately bound up in the creation of cultural products and the dissemination of cultural values. Ideally, all of these concerns would be addressed in the design of media policy, but there are unavoidable trade-offs among goals and how that might best be accomplished is by no means obvious.

Although research and debate over specific applications continue, the basic analytical framework for addressing efficiency concerns has been established and widely employed for quite some time. One of the more visible manifestations of this approach is the Herfindahl-Hirschmann Index (HHI) of market concentration that is used by the U.S. antitrust authorities as a starting point for assessing the likelihood that a merger between two firms already serving a market will increase market power sufficiently to permit a sustainable increase in the prices charged for their products. In its June 2, 2003, Report and Order on media ownership (hereafter Report and Order), the Federal Communications Commission (FCC) introduced a diversity index (DI), which was to play a role in assessments of the effect of ownership structure on the performance of local media markets with respect to certain noneconomic policy goals analogous to that played by the HHI in antitrust enforcement. The FCC's DI (hereafter FCC-DI) immediately became the focus of an intense and very public debate over media ownership policy. Challenged in court along with other elements of the Report and Order, it was rejected on a 2-to-1 vote by the Third Circuit Court of Appeals on June 24, 2004, as one component of the Report and Order's cross-media ownership limits the Court remanded to the FCC.

The FCC-DI is just one of a potentially infinite number of DIs that might be constructed. Because DIs may differ substantially in their usefulness as policy instruments, the choices made in selecting an official DI (should there be one) is a matter of some importance. This chapter takes a close look at the FCC-DI as part of a broader examination of certain unavoidable choices that must be made and the trade-offs involved in the construction of any DI. The chapter is organized as follows. The first section describes the FCC-DI, compares it to the HHI after which it was modeled, and briefly reviews the Court's reasons for rejecting it. The second section takes a broader look at the problem of index construction by posing a set of questions that must be answered, whether consciously or not, in the construction of a DI that is theoretically sound, internally consistent, and able to withstand legal challenge. The concluding section offers a few observations on the process of DI construction.

THE FCC-DI

The FCC-DI was inspired by the HHI (Federal Communications Commission, 2003) and was designed to have similar mathematical properties. In discussing the FCC-DI, it is therefore helpful to begin with a brief description of the HHI, including how it is constructed and applied.[1]

The HHI

The HHI is a measure of ownership concentration within an economic market for a specific good or service. Before a HHI can be calculated, a relevant product market must first be identified. A product market is defined in terms of two types of substitution relationships—one characterizing the degree of substitutability among different sellers' products and the other the geographic extent of the market. Two or more sellers' products may be in the same economic market if buyers view them as sufficiently close substitutes that a small but nontrivial increase in the price of one seller's product would cause a sufficient number of its customers to switch to the other sellers' products to render the price increase unprofitable. This substitutability relationship defines the product dimension of an economic market. Because for most products the cost to a seller of serving a buyer increases with the distance between them, distant sellers may not be able to effectively compete with local sellers to serve local customers. Two sellers of products that satisfy the product test for inclusion in a common market actually are in the same market if the distance between them is not so great as to preclude one from profitably serving customers of the other should the second raise its price by a nontrivial amount.

The first step in calculating the HHI for a market identified in this way is to determine the market share of each firm serving the market. It is common to calculate a firm's share of a market as its percentage of the total revenue generated by all firms serving the market. However, shares may also be measured in other ways, including units sold and production capacity available to serve the market. Once individual firms' shares are determined, each firm's share is squared. The sum of the squared shares for all firms in a market is the market's HHI. For example, a market served by two firms, one with a 40% share and the other with a 60% share, would have a HHI of 5,200 ($40^2 + 60^2$). Less concentrated markets have lower HHIs and the maximum value for the HHI is 10,000, which occurs when a single firm serves a market ($10{,}000 = 100^2$). The squaring of shares in the index means that large firms contribute substantially more per share point to the value of the index than do small firms. Similarly, the merger of a small firm with a large firm increases the HHI by more than the merger of two small firms. Markets with HHIs less than 1,000 are classified as unconcentrated, which means a market is structurally predisposed to perform competitively. Markets with HHIs above 1,800 are classified as highly concentrated, which implies a much higher likelihood that firms in the market will be able to profit from the exercise of market power. The presumption regarding the anticompetitive effect of a merger shifts from no effect to increasingly likely as the postmerger HHI increases from 1,000 to 1,800 and beyond.

The FCC-DI

Like the HHI, the FCC-DI is a measure of structure rather than a direct measure of performance with respect to a policy goal, reflecting, as with the HHI, a belief that ownership structure influences performance. For a DI, it is performance in a marketplace of ideas that matters, rather than a product market for which a HHI might be calculated. Although ownership shares in FCC ideas markets are determined differently than for antitrust markets, the algebraic formulations for the two indexes are identical once shares are known.

The methodology employed by the FCC to determine which media to include in its DI differs considerably from the two criteria employed by the antitrust authorities to identify antitrust markets. The FCC started with the results of a media use survey it commissioned from A. C. Nielsen (Nielsen

Media Research, 2002). Survey participants were asked to rate different media in terms of how much they relied on them for coverage of local news and public affairs. Responses to this question, combined with additional evidence in the case of cable television, determined which media were included in the index. Respondents indicated meaningful levels of reliance on newspapers, local television and radio stations, the Internet, and cable television. However, the FCC excluded cable television from the index because it believed that respondents frequently mistook the newscasts of local broadcast stations retransmitted by cable systems for cable-originated programming. The fact that the cable systems serving a majority of cable subscribers did not offer local or regional news channels also influenced this decision (Federal Communications Commission, 2003).

Once media owners' shares of an ideas market are known, calculating the market's FCC-DI is the same as calculating an antitrust market's HHI. However, the FCC's rather complex procedure for determining individual outlets' shares of a market makes calculating a FCC-DI much more complicated. For a local ideas market, within-medium outlet shares (measured in percentages that sum to 100) are first calculated for each medium included in the index, then medium-specific weights (which sum to one) are applied to these shares to determine each outlet's share of the larger ideas market. Each medium's weight in the FCC-DI can be interpreted as its share of the local ideas market. For radio stations, television stations, and daily newspapers, within medium outlet shares are determined by giving all of a medium's outlets equal shares of the medium's portion of the ideas market. Thus, for example, a market with 10 television stations, 25 radio stations, and 2 daily newspapers would assign a within-medium share of 10 to each television station, 4 to each radio station, and 50 to each daily newspaper. Each resident of a local ideas market was assumed to have access to one weekly newspaper and the Internet share of the index was divided between cable companies and telephone companies in proportion to the numbers of Internet subscribers served by each. The weights assigned the five media included in the index were broadcast television 0.338, radio 0.249, daily newspapers 0.202, weekly newspapers 0.86, and Internet 0.125 (Federal Communications Commission, 2003).

The Court's Critique of the FCC-DI

The Third Circuit Court pointed to two critical flaws in remanding the FCC-DI to the FCC. First, the "commission did not justify its choice and weight of specific media outlets" (*Prometheus Radio Project v. Federal Communications Commission* [Prometheus], 2004, p. 60). In essence, the Court found that the FCC did not have a consistently applied methodology for determining the weights assigned to different media in its index. In particular, the majority on the Court argued that the FCC-DI gave "too much weight to the Internet as a media outlet," relative to what would have made sense had it applied to the Internet the principles the Commission cited as justification for excluding cable television from the index (Prometheus, 2004, p. 61). Second, the FCC-DI "irrationally assigned outlets of the same media type equal market shares," (Prometheus, 2004, p. 56), which the Court found to be inconsistent with the "Commission's decision to assign relative weights to the different media types themselves" (Prometheus, 2004, p. 67).

The Court's criticism of the FCC's media weights for lack of sound analytical grounding is absolutely correct. The media weights employed in the FCC-DI were derived from respondents' answers to a question asking them to identify media they used in the previous 7 days for local news and current affairs.[2] From this type of question, however, it is not possible to determine whether the responses don't mask a more fundamental variation in importance among outlets of all types. Consider as an example, a hypothetical local ideas market with 5 television stations and 10 radio stations. Three of the television stations cover local news and public affairs as does the only all-news radio station. No other TV and radio stations provide news programming. Two thirds of the market's residents get their broadcast news in the evening after dinner, watching a local news program on television. The other third get their local news from the all-news radio station while commuting to and from work. Citizens are asked which media they relied on during the previous week for coverage of local news and current affairs. Two thirds of respondents would list television and one third would list radio. A two-media DI similar to that developed by the FCC would assign weights to the two media that preserved the proportionality of the average scores and summed to one, so that television would have a weight of 0.667 and radio would have a weight of 0.333—half that of television. By the FCC methodology, each television station would be credited with an ideas market share of 0.133 and each radio station's share would be 0.033.

Clearly this approach underrepresents the contributions of stations (of both types) with news relative to those without news. It is also likely to misrepresent the relative importance of radio and television outlets with news. Suppose each of the three television stations providing news gets one third of the television audience and survey respondents are asked to identify the outlets, rather than media, they rely on for local news and public affairs. Each of the three TV stations with news would be listed by one third of the respondents that get their news from television, which is two ninths of all respondents, and the all-news radio station would be listed by one third of all respondents. No other TV and radio stations would be listed. Applying the FCC weighting approach to outlets, the radio station with news would be 50% more important than any of the television stations offering news, and outlets with no news would not count at all.

The Court was also correct in criticizing on consistency grounds the FCC's decision to include the Internet in its diversity index while excluding cable television. As described earlier, an important reason why cable was not included in the FCC-DI was that the FCC believed that much of the importance respondents attributed to cable for coverage of local news and public affairs was that cable subscribers mistook local broadcast services retransmitted over cable for cable-originated programming. The Court pointed out that most of the Web sites providing local news were owned by local television stations and newspapers (Prometheus, 2004). They could therefore not be considered independent sources for local news and coverage of public events any more than local newscasts on retransmitted broadcast stations could be counted as cable-provided news.

The simplest response to the Court's observation that the FCC's reasons for excluding cable TV from the FCC-DI apply with equal force to the Internet would be to drop the Internet from the FCC-DI, as recommended by the Court (Prometheus, 2004), and scale up the weights of the remaining media accordingly. It would seem more reasonable, however, to assign some portion of the importance survey respondents attributed to the Internet to the newspapers and television stations whose Web sites they turned to for local news. Similarly, some of the importance survey respondents attributed to cable news programming should be assigned to the retransmitted television stations. To see the logic of this suggestion, suppose that there are several, popular, independently owned Internet sources for local news, that these Internet news services are important enough to be included in a FCC-DI, and that the FCC is asked to rule on the merits of an attempt by a radio or TV station owner to acquire one of them. The agency would certainly see the acquisition as increasing ownership concentration in the marketplace of ideas. A straightforward application of the FCC-DI approach to evaluating ownership combinations would require that the market shares of the Internet news source and the broadcast station be added together and then squared, giving the two sources a greater weight under common ownership than their summed weights when independently owned. The Internet services currently owned by television stations and newspapers should be treated the same way. The same logic suggests the FCC erred in totally eliminating cable from its DI. Instead the FCC should have increased the media weight of local television by some portion of the importance survey participants attributed to cable television.

The Court criticized the FCC's decision to assign different outlets from the same medium equal shares on several grounds: (a) It was inconsistent with one of the rationales the FCC advanced on behalf of its DI, which was to measure actual contributions to diversity rather than simply counting voices; (b) "[A]ssigning equal market shares to outlets that provide no local news almost certainly represents an understated view of concentration in several markets" (Prometheus, 2004, p. 68); and (c) the Court claimed that "there is no dispute that the assignment of equal shares generates absurd results" (Prometheus, 2004, p. 68). As evidence of the irrationality of assigning all outlets from the same medium equal shares, the Court observed that in the New York City ideas market, the FCC-DI would give the same weight to the Dutchess Community College television station as to a station owned by ABC, and that this college television station would have a greater weight in the index than that assigned to the combination of *The New York Times* and its co-owned radio station.

The claim that the assignment of equal shares within a medium is inconsistent with the FCC's stated desire to reflect actual contributions to diversity and avoid simply counting voices is perhaps a bit unfair, because the different weights applied to outlets in different media means that outlets from different media are weighted differently in the index. It is true, however, that the FCC offered no convincing argument for assigning equal shares to all outlets from the same medium in the face of data (discussed later) reported in the Report and Order showing that many television stations in the larger markets do not produce local news programs. The same observation supports the Court's claim that concentration in markets (in terms of contributions to diversity) is understated when all outlets are assigned equal shares. The hypothetical market example shown earlier with five television stations and ten radio stations also illustrates this point. Only three television stations and one radio station covered news and current affairs.

Although the comparison of a college television station to ABC's New York affiliate or to the radio and newspaper properties of *The New York Times* is intuitively compelling, it is important to note that the Court (like the FCC) made reference to no clearly defined standard for measuring diversity or assessing media outlets' contributions to it in support of its claim that these comparisons are absurd.

TOWARD A MORE SYSTEMATIC APPROACH TO INDEX CONSTRUCTION

As the preceding discussion of the Third Circuit Court's response to the FCC-DI makes clear, this index is plagued by problems of both internal consistency and external validity. If a DI is to be added to the arsenal of communication policy tools in the future, we need to develop a set of analytically defensible principles to guide index construction if we are to avoid a recurrence of the types of problems identified by the Court. This section responds to this challenge by posing 11 questions, the answers to which should aid in the construction of a more defensible DI.

Question 1: What Ultimate Policy Goal Is to Be Served by the Index?

The term *diversity* has been employed with a variety of meanings in the ongoing debate over media policy (Napoli, 1999, 2001). The Report and Order specifically identifies and defines five distinct types of diversity: outlet diversity, program diversity, viewpoint diversity, source diversity, and minority and gender ownership diversity. Although outlet diversity (defined as the number of independently owned media firms in a market; Federal Communications Commission, 2003, ¶ 38) was described as a policy instrument that might be employed to promote more primary policy goals, the other four types of diversity are media policy goals, the achievement of which contributes toward the attainment of one or more of three more fundamental goals of public policy: a more effective and representative democratic process, economic efficiency, and greater participation of women and ethnic minorities in economic and political affairs.

The Report and Order defines viewpoint diversity as "the availability of media content reflecting a variety of perspectives" (Federal Communications Commission, 2003, ¶ 19). That greater viewpoint diversity contributes to the fundamental policy goal of an improved democratic process is generally accepted as obvious. Program diversity is an application of the more general economic concept of product variety—the range of differentiated products a market makes available to consumers—to media markets. Other things equal, greater product variety is better because a broader range of consumer preferences are satisfied.[3] A measure of program diversity could be used as one component of an assessment of the economic efficiency of media markets. The Report and Order defines source diversity as "the availability of content from a variety of content producers" (Federal Communications Commission, 2003, ¶ 42). Diversity in the ethnic and gender composition of media ownership is self-explanatory. The FCC dismissed content diversity as a matter of concern for the ownership proceeding, saying it was "best achieved by reliance on competition among delivery systems" (Federal Communications Commission, 2003, ¶ 37). Concerns with source diversity were also rather summarily dismissed for lack of evidence of a problem (Federal Communications

Commission, 2003), and consideration of gender and ethnic ownership diversity was set aside for a subsequent proceeding. Given the decision to focus solely on viewpoint diversity, we can say that enhancing the democratic process by contributing to a better-informed citizenry was the fundamental policy goal the various elements of the Report and Order, including the FCC-DI, were intended to serve. For the remainder of this chapter, I assume that this is the only goal motivating index construction and that a DI is to be used to assess the implications of the ownership structures of local media markets for viewpoint diversity.

Question 2: What Types of Diversity Contribute to a More Effective Democratic Process?

The FCC's decision to focus on viewpoint diversity does not mean that other types of diversity should not be considered in a fresh start analysis. With the possible exception of program diversity as defined by the FCC, which, to avoid definitional overlap might be interpreted as content untainted by viewpoints, it would be difficult to argue that the other types of diversity mentioned in the Report and Order are not themselves connected to viewpoint diversity and thereby to the effectiveness of the democratic process. Napoli (1999, 2001) provides a typology of diversity definitions employed in the formulation and analysis of media policy that makes these links quite clear. He points out that the FCC's categories of program diversity (which Napoli calls "program-format diversity") and viewpoint diversity refer to two ways in which the content of media products may be diverse, whereas policy concern with source diversity and gender and ethnic ownership diversity has to a substantial degree focused on their impact on the two types of content diversity.[4] If we accept the FCC's position that gender and ethnic ownership policy raises issues that should be addressed in a separate proceeding, then source diversity still remains to be considered.

Furthermore, the fact that program diversity can be defined as diversity of content other than viewpoints does not in itself justify ignoring program diversity in an ownership proceeding. Even programs selected by networks and stations solely for their entertainment value convey viewpoints. How else can we explain the oft-voiced concerns over the portrayals of women and minorities in popular entertainment? Or concerns that entertainment programs promote more liberal or more conservative views than various public commentators feel is appropriate? Or that violence is glorified? When Vice President Dan Quayle publicly criticized the popular television program "Murphy Brown" for its positive portrayal of the lead character's decision to become a single mother, he was criticizing the program's creators for promoting a viewpoint he found objectionable and presumably harmful to some greater public good if widely adopted.

Finally, we must also ask whether there are types of diversity not identified by the FCC that should be considered as part of an ownership proceeding. Napoli (1997, 1999, 2001) points out that viewpoint diversity is treated as a matter for policy concern because the supply of a diverse set of viewpoints is implicitly equated with citizens' being exposed to diverse viewpoints. His review of the relevant, although sparse, research shows that the connection between viewpoint diversity and exposure diversity is not so straightforward.

I would add what I will call *coverage diversity* as another type of diversity that was not addressed with much clarity in the Report and Order. Viewpoints are conceptual frameworks and belief structures relied on by citizens in passing judgment on the performance of public officials and the proposals of policy advocates. However, these frameworks and perspectives are neither formed nor applied in a vacuum. They are employed to assess the implications for political choices of relevant facts and policy officials' and advocates' claims of facts. Conversely, facts and claims of fact are used to assess the relative merits of different viewpoints. As the facts regarding any politically charged situation are almost always somewhat in dispute, the public interest would appear to be best served if claims of fact were investigated and reported by a diverse set of independent media vehicles. Although presentations of viewpoints will often be combined with claims of fact, the checking and reporting on factual issues is an activity that is both conceptually and operationally distinct from the reporting of viewpoints. The fact that the Report and Order sometimes pairs "information" with viewpoint diversity in its discussion of the logic underlying the FCC-DI suggests that the FCC may have been sensitive to the importance of coverage and intended that it be subsumed in the definition of viewpoint diversity.[5] There is no reason to believe, however, that the impact of local media market structure on coverage diversity is coincident with its effect on viewpoint diversity. Nevertheless, to avoid frequent use of the rather cumbersome combination "viewpoint and coverage diversity," for the most part I use "viewpoint diversity" to refer to both for the remainder of this chapter.

Question 3: Which of the Relevant Types of Diversity Are Meaningfully Influenced by the Ownership Structure of Local Media Markets?

Although there is no general agreement on the nature of the relationship, and relevant empirical evidence is scarce (Napoli, 2001), it is widely accepted that ownership structure does influence viewpoint diversity and policy has generally reflected a presumption that viewpoint diversity increases with outlet diversity.[6] We would similarly expect coverage diversity to be influenced by a market's ownership structure, although again, the nature of the relationship is not obvious. However, to the extent we are willing to accept the amount of news and public affairs programming as a proxy for viewpoint and coverage diversity, a recent study by Yan and Napoli (2005) suggests this is largely unaffected by market structure. Although the FCC cited a lack of evidence of inadequate source diversity as justification for focusing on viewpoint diversity, failure to demonstrate poor performance is not equivalent to evidence that a change in local ownership patterns would not improve performance. If more independently produced programming is better, then policy analysts should be asking whether the number of independent sources of content increases or decreases as media markets become more concentrated. In the end, the knowledge required to determine whether any of these relationships can be ignored in the crafting of ownership policy must be generated through empirical investigation.

Question 4. What Types of Media Content Should Be Reflected in the Design of a DI?

The FCC's answer to this question was that it was sufficient to focus entirely on media coverage of local news and current affairs. The focus on news was justified by the claim that "it relates most directly to the Commission's core policy objective of facilitating robust democratic discourse in the media" (Federal Communications Commission, 2003, ¶ 32) and the FCC argued that it was reasonable to focus on the effects of local ownership structure on sources of local news and current affairs programming because there is already an abundance of sources of information on national news and current affairs (Federal Communications Commission, 2003, ¶ 35, ¶ 406).

Neither of these justifications is persuasive. The claim that viewpoints are most likely to be found in news and public affairs programming is backed by no empirical evidence. The content analysis required to compare the frequency with which viewpoints of various types are presented in news and other types of programs has not been done. However, even if there were compelling empirical support for such a relative frequency claim, it still would say nothing about the effectiveness with which viewpoints are represented in different types of programs, and thus which are more important to democratic decision making.

But even if we knew with certainty that news and public affairs programs were more important to the supply of viewpoints than other types of programs, this would still not justify focusing solely on news and public affairs, let alone local news and public affairs, in deciding what constraints on ownership best serve the public interest in promoting viewpoint diversity. Economic efficiencies constitute the primary justification for allowing media ownership consolidation, and it is the opportunity cost of lost efficiencies that must be balanced against whatever prospective benefits might be claimed for limiting consolidation. The optimal balance of these contending societal interests occurs where the marginal opportunity cost of further limiting concentration just equals the marginal benefits of whatever increase in diversity arises from doing so. However, the appropriate marginal benefits schedule is the sum of the marginal diversity benefits for all types of programming influenced by local ownership structure. If ownership policy is determined by comparing benefits to opportunity costs for only one type of diversity, then all types of diversity will be undersupplied relative to the policy optimum.

This point is illustrated in Figure 8.1. Restrictions on local market concentration imposed to meet diversity objectives are measured on the horizontal axis. The origin is the level of market concentration that would be observed if concentration were determined solely by market forces subject to antitrust constraints and restrictions on ownership consolidation increase with rightward movement along this axis. The marginal benefits and opportunity costs associated with ownership restrictions are measured on the vertical axis. Hypothetical marginal viewpoint diversity benefits schedules for three types of programming—local news and public affairs, national news and public affairs, and entertainment—are shown. The marginal benefits schedules all slope downward from left to right, reflecting an assumption that the marginal benefits realized from an increase in viewpoint diversity produced by more stringent controls on ownership diminish as ownership policy becomes more restrictive. As drawn, the marginal benefits of increased restrictions are always highest for local news and public affairs programs and lowest for entertainment programs, although, as was argued earlier, there is no compelling theory or empirical evidence to support this ordering. The marginal total benefits schedule is the sum of the marginal benefits for the three types of programs and reflects the total benefit to society at the margin of an increase in restrictions on ownership.

The marginal opportunity cost of the restrictions rises from left to right starting at the origin, reflecting an assumption that the marginal economic efficiency gains from increased concentration diminish as concentration approaches the maximum level of concentration a market subject to antitrust law will generate. The socially optimal level of restrictions is R_S, the level at which the marginal opportunity cost curve intersects the sum of marginal

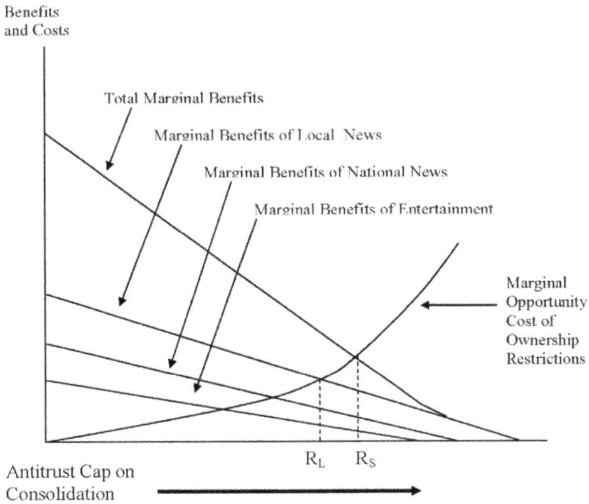

Figure 8.1. Balancing diversity benefits and costs.

benefits from the diversity curve. A policy based on the benefits of increased diversity in local news and public affairs programming alone would set the level of ownership restrictions at the lower level of R_L. Only if the marginal benefits associated with entertainment and national and international news programming were close to zero, which could be the case, for example, if the content of national and international news programming and of entertainment programming was largely unaffected by changes in local media ownership concentration, would R_L be a reasonable approximation to R_S. This last observation is restated as Question 5.

Question 5: For Which Types of Programming of Concern for Diversity Policy Is the Supply Meaningfully Influenced by Local Ownership Structure?

Clearly the answer to Question 5 can only be determined empirically.

Question 6: Do Different Outlets From the Same Medium Make Different Contributions to Diversity?

Implicit in the construction of the FCC-DI is a belief that for radio, television, and daily newspapers, all outlets in a market make equal contributions to diversity. Unfortunately, no empirical support was offered on behalf of this assumption and it also seems inconsistent with the FCC's decision to focus on local news and public affairs programs as the carriers of viewpoint diversity. In particular, the Report and Order cites data showing that in markets with more than four stations, only 19% of stations not ranked among the top four in audience size offer local news programs, whereas 85% of top four stations provide news (Federal Communications Commission, 2003). This basic pattern is confirmed in studies by academic researchers (Yan & Napoli, 2005; Singleton & Rockwell, 2003). It is also generally understood that many radio stations in larger markets also do not provide news. If local news and public affairs programs contribute more to viewpoint diversity than other types of programs, then stations that program news must make larger contributions toward viewpoint diversity goals than those that don't. On the other hand, to claim that stations that don't cover local news and public affairs make contributions to viewpoint diversity equal to those that do would completely undermine the FCC's justifications for focusing on local news and public affairs in constructing its index and for excluding cable television for lack of such programming.

If we accept that different outlets from the same medium may make different contributions to diversity, then some measure of outlet performance with respect to diversity goals should be employed in either the construction or the interpretation of a diversity index—ideally both. Whether an outlet does or does not provide programs of a type deemed important for achieving diversity goals is perhaps the most basic of such measures. It is also the standard the FCC claimed justified eliminating cable television from the FCC-DI. Suppose, for example, that local news and public affairs programs are all that matter for local ownership policy. If we want to take advantage of the administrative economies of a structural index in lieu of assessing performance on a market-by-market basis, then we need to know the relationship between the number of TV (or radio) stations in a market and the number of stations that offer local news. For television, a rather loose interpretation of the FCC's statistics on which types of stations are likely to offer news is that in markets with four or fewer stations, the number of television stations programming local news will closely approximate the number of stations in the market, but as the number of stations increases beyond four, the likelihood that the incremental station will offer news is quite low.

The nonlinearity of the relationship between the number of television stations and the number covering news and public affairs means that although the television portion of the FCC-DI may be interpreted as a measure of ownership concentration in a local economic market that coordinates the supply of programs to viewers and audiences to advertisers, it cannot be interpreted as a measure of concentration in the associated marketplace of ideas. Needed is a formula, presumably based on observed statistical regularities, relating concentration in the economic market to some measure of performance in the corresponding ideas market. For a DI based on a single medium, constructing such a simple formula might not be too difficult. For an index with multiple media, this task will be considerably more complicated, and, if the relationship between the number of outlets and the number of outlets with content contributing to viewpoint diversity differs by medium, it may be difficult to construct an index that involves more than a simple adding up of individual outlet contributions for which individual index numbers are not associated with multiple levels of actual media contributions to diversity.

To illustrate this point, suppose there are only two local media: medium 1 and medium 2. The two media differ in the fractions of their outlets that provide content that contributes to viewpoint diversity (viewpoint-laden content). Although half of medium 1 outlets provide viewpoint-laden content on average, the expectation is that only a fourth of medium 2 outlets will do so. Finally, assume that every outlet that provides viewpoint-laden content makes the same contribution to a market's viewpoint diversity, regardless of the medium to which it belongs. Now consider a market with four outlets for each medium in which three of the eight total outlets provide viewpoint-laden content as would be expected if the statistical averages for the two media held true for this market. If we use the number of contributing outlets as our measure of performance, the value of the measure would be three. We would also predict a performance measure of three for markets with two medium 1 outlets and eight medium 2 outlets, for markets with six medium 1 outlets and zero medium 2 outlets, and for markets with zero medium 1 outlets and twelve medium 2 outlets. These four ways of generating a performance level of three are captured in a formula that simply adds the number of outlets for the two media after assigning weights of 0.05 and 0.25, respectively, to medium 1 and medium 2 outlets.

Now consider a FCC-type DI for these two-media markets with each medium assigned a weight of 0.5 as would be expected if the typical market had twice as many medium 2 as medium 1 outlets, and, following FCC methodology, audience members were asked to rate the two media in terms of how much they relied on each for coverage of local news and public affairs. Applying these weights would produce a FCC-type DI of 1,250 for the market with four outlets for each medium we have been considering. A market with eight medium 1 outlets and no medium 2 outlets would also have an index value of 1,250, as would a market with no medium 1 outlets and eight medium 2 outlets. However, we would expect the medium 1-only market to have four outlets with viewpoint-laden content and the market with only medium 2 outlets to have just two outlets with viewpoint-laden content. The same value of this FCC-type DI is associated with three quite different levels of predicted performance. Having multiple performance levels associated with each index value is likely to be a problem for FCC-type DIs in general, and is a matter that should be investigated when considering any index much more complicated than a simple weighted sum of individual outlets' contributions.

Question 7: Do Outlets From Different Media Make Systematically Different Contributions to Diversity?

The different weights assigned to the several media included in the FCC-DI reflect assumptions or beliefs about the relative importance of their contributions to a local marketplace of ideas. However, as the example of the local market with 5 television stations and 10 radio stations presented in the previous section demonstrated, the consumer survey relied on by the FCC in assigning weights to media did not provide information that could be used to distinguish variation in outlets' contributions to viewpoint diversity within the various media from differences that are innate to the media. Suppose there is significant variation among the outlets of a given medium in their contributions to viewpoint diversity, as is clearly the case for broadcast media if outlets with no news and public affairs programming are treated as making zero contributions. Then at an absolute minimum, any cross-media comparison must be restricted to those outlets from each medium that make positive contributions.

There are at least two fundamental ways in which outlets' (positive) contributions to viewpoint and coverage diversity might differ by medium: (a) Content presented by outlets of one medium may reach larger audiences than content from another medium's outlets. I will refer to differences of this type as *reach differences*. (b) Independent of the size of the audience reached, the exposure to a viewpoint in one medium may affect audience members' political choices differently than exposure to the same viewpoint in another medium because the technical characteristics of different media impose different constraints on the presentation and/or processing of information related to viewpoints. I will refer to differences of this sort as *impact differences*. These two potential sources of cross-media variation in outlets' contributions to viewpoint and coverage diversity can have profoundly different implications for media policy and the design of a DI.

That differences in size of audience reached should matter for diversity policy is not obvious. News and public affairs programs attract audiences in part for the information conveyed, but also due to esthetic factors such as the personal appeal of on-air talent and the literary quality of writing. If audience members actively seek different sources of ideas, all should eventually encounter all relevant ideas even if they spend more time-consuming viewpoint-laden content from one source than another. On the other hand, if audience members do not actively seek out contending ideas from multiple sources, and esthetic considerations dominate their selection of sources of news and public affairs coverage, there is a danger that a substantial fraction of the citizenry will be exposed to a limited range of ideas delivered by the same few outlets whose content appeals to the majority of the audience. In this case, it may be appropriate for ownership policy to be less tolerant of ownership of multiple outlets for media that attract larger audiences.

Media-specific impact differences have different implications for diversity policy and DI construction. Suppose one medium has a substantial advantage over another for the presentation of all, or at least many, types of viewpoint-related information. For example, certain types of information may be most easily understood if presented with the aid of visual images. In this case, television would have a basic information processing advantage over radio. Other things (such as medium penetration in the general population) equal, policy presumably should be more concerned with ownership concentration in the processing-advantaged medium. If some media do have substantial processing advantages over others, this raises serious questions about the merits of DIs like the FCC-DI for which an increase in ownership concentration in one medium may be offset by a reduction in ownership concentration in another medium. It simply may not be possible to offset the impact on the quality of citizen decision making of a reduction in the number of voices in the more effective medium by increasing the number of independent voices in a less effective medium.

Different media may also have comparative advantages for the presentation of different types of information. The fact that a reader can process information at his or her own pace and return to an information source repeatedly if the information is presented in print may be an advantage relative to broadcast media for presenting complex information.[7] On the other hand, broadcast media can report breaking news as it happens, and there may be some types of information (such as emotion and subtle clues to character conveyed by a political candidate speaking live) that are conveyed much more effectively by broadcast media. As both types of information are relevant to political choices, media may play complementary roles in the presentation of viewpoints (see, e.g., Chaffee & Kanihan, 1997). If such is the case, viewpoints may be most effectively presented if done in a coordinated fashion across media, which may be reason to favor cross-media ownership combinations over within-medium combinations.

Question 8: Are Number of Independent Voices and Ownership Concentration in Voices Distinct Concerns That Should Be Addressed in an Index?

If audience members actively and effectively seek contending viewpoints, policy should be concerned primarily with the number of independent sources of viewpoints rather than the degree to which outlet ownership is concentrated. Thus, assuming all outlets carry viewpoint-laden programs, a market with 10 independently owned outlets and another 10 outlets owned by a single firm would represent a one voice improvement over a market with just the 10 independently owned outlets. The FCC-DI does not work this way because outlets are assigned shares which are squared and the shares of co-owned outlets are added together before squaring. As a result, the entry of a new voice opening up new outlets can increase the value of the FCC-DI rather than reduce it if the entrant adds too many outlets to the market. This point is illustrated by Table 8.1, which calculates the television contribution to the FCC-DI for a market with two independently owned stations and a variable number of stations introduced by a third owner entering the market, assuming no cross-ownership with other index media. Adding an owner with a single station reduces television's contribution to the market's FCC-DI from its initial two-owner, two-station level of 573.9 by a third, which, as the FCC-DI is interpreted, represents an improvement with respect to promoting the public's interest in greater viewpoint diversity. Entry by an owner with two or three stations will also lower the FCC-DI, but by successively smaller amounts, and, according to the FCC-DI, the market is back to its original state diversity-wise if the new owner adds four stations, which would give it control of two thirds of the market's total. An entrant with more than four stations makes things decidedly worse.

TABLE 8.1

Effect of Entry on Television Portion of the Federal Communications Commission's Diversity Index (FCC-DI)

Number of Stations Added by Third Owner	*Television Portion of FCC-DI*
0	573.9
1	382.6
2	430.4
3	505.1
4	573.9
5	632.5
6	681.5
7	722.7
8	757.6

Because the mathematical properties just illustrated for the television component of the FCC-DI apply to daily newspapers and to radio stations as well, a clear implication of the formula employed to calculate a market's FCC-DI is that markets with more independent voices in any of these three media are not necessarily better served than markets with fewer voices. Of course, current government controls over spectrum allocated to broadcasting and the licenses to use it preclude the possibility of multistation entry by a broadcaster just illustrated. However, the number of channels offered by cable and satellite services dwarf the number of over-the-air television channels. Shifting even a small portion of these channels to local news programming would produce exactly the situation illustrated by Table 8.1. Consider also a future in which Internet content services grow to the point where they cannot reasonably be excluded from a DI. One owner could easily provide a number of Internet-based local news and public affairs services, just as most webcasting services currently offer many channels of music programming.

If we accept the proposition that only the number of independent media voices matters if audience members actively seek and find divergent viewpoints, then justification for a DI that can interpret an added voice as reducing viewpoint diversity must be grounded in either a belief that some substantial fraction of the aggregate audience does not actively seek contending viewpoints or that a desire for exposure to different viewpoints is often thwarted by difficulty finding the outlets that present them. If we accept the passive audience justification for a DI with properties like those of the FCC-DI, then we must also ask whether the addition of a new owner with a single station could make the market worse off if the new station was popular enough to dramatically increase ownership concentration in audiences even as concentration in outlets declined. Similarly, would a market's performance with respect to diversity goals decline if the owner of an existing station managed to dramatically increase its share of audience? What if the outlet attracting such a large fraction of the audience did so because it did a superior job of presenting a diverse selection of viewpoints? Perhaps it would make sense to penalize audience share acquired through the acquisition of outlets (which could be measured as predicted share assuming all outlets perform equally well), as the FCC-DI does, while ignoring share acquired through programming prowess, although the belief in audience passivity or search limitations that is required to justify a focus on audience share would dictate concern in either case.

Another troubling implication of the pattern illustrated in Table 8.1 is that an entrant adding two or more new outlets is always credited with a smaller contribution to a market's viewpoint diversity than an entrant introducing one outlet. If this is the case, policy interests in viewpoint diversity are always better served by letting failing outlets exit a market than by allowing them to be purchased or operated by a competitor, because the failing outlet can be thought of as a second outlet introduced by its potential acquirer or joint operating partner. It can be shown that this is a general algebraic property of the radio, television, and daily newspaper components of the FCC-DI. We must ask whether this property, which is not discussed in the Report and Order, reflects a principle that should be applied systematically in crafting media ownership policy. The FCC that wrote the Report and Order apparently did not believe this to be the case because the FCC explicitly stated that waivers allowing mergers that violated its rules restricting co-ownership of stations might be granted if the merging parties committed to significantly increasing news and local programming on one or both stations (Federal Communications Commission, 2003, ¶ 230). Clearly the relative importance of number of voices versus concentration in voices should be explicitly addressed in constructing the next DI.

Question 9: Is There an Empirical Measure of Performance With Respect to the Fundamental Policy Goal Served by Viewpoint Diversity to Which a DI Might Be Calibrated?

Because it chose to model the FCC-DI on the HHI, the FCC was careful in the Report and Order to document support for the HHI in the scholarly literature, including empirical evidence that market competitiveness varies in accordance with changes in markets' HHIs as predicted (Federal Communications Commission, 2003, fn 609). No comparable empirical evidence was offered linking performance with respect to diversity goals to changes in the FCC-DI. This is a critical, if not fatal, flaw in the FCC's approach to DI construction. Without a measure of performance with which a DI might be paired, there is no way of knowing if there is a systematic relationship between the DI's measure of changes in a market's ownership structure and the diversity of viewpoints available to and consumed by its citizens.

Ideally, a theoretically sound and empirically reliable measure of the health of democratic institutions in local markets could be employed to calibrate an index. Lacking such a measure, less direct measures of democratic health might still be used to good effect, however. Rates of participation by eligible voters in local elections is one possibility. George and Waldfogel (2002) and Oberholzer-Gee and Waldfogel (2001) provide evidence that this measure of political participation is influenced by the structure of local media markets and Scheufele (2002) links use of different media with differential rates of political participation. Knowledge of political issues relevant to electoral choices is another possibility. Mondak (1995a, 1995b) provides evidence that media coverage of elections does influence voter knowledge. Even less direct would be measures based on content analyses of the amount of information related to viewpoints or relevant to the evaluation of viewpoints carried in local media. Perhaps the simplest, although least direct, measure of performance would be a count of media outlets providing the type(s) of content deemed relevant to a diversity assessment.

Question 10: Is There a Theoretically Natural Form for a DI?

If a DI can be calibrated according to an accepted measure of performance, a variety of indexes might be employed. There would be interpretational advantages, however, to an index that mirrors in its algebraic form an observed relationship between a measure of media ownership structure and a chosen measure of performance. The advantages would be greater still if the index's mathematical properties mirrored a theoretical understanding of the relationship between ownership concentration and performance. Even without an empirical measure of performance to calibrate an index, there would be interpretational benefits from having a DI that mirrored our understanding of this relationship, in which case changes in index values might provide some information about relative, if not absolute, changes in performance. One of the principle advantages claimed for the HHI over the four-firm and eight-firm concentration ratios it replaced for antitrust analysis was that its mathematical properties mirrored theoretical predictions for the relationship between a market's ownership structure and the prices charged by the firms serving it.

The theoretical relationship between media ownership concentration and the health of democratic institutions depends crucially on assumptions made (or beliefs held) regarding citizens' desire to seek out contending viewpoints and their effectiveness in doing so. If most audience members actively and effectively seek exposure to alternative viewpoints, and their ability to evaluate a viewpoint is largely independent of the medium in which it is presented, then an index based on numbers of owners with outlets that qualify in terms of the type of content provided has a lot to recommend it. Such an index could still take a variety of forms, however, depending on how it is believed that ideas are likely to be distributed among owners and how policymakers choose to measure performance. Here I describe two versions of what I call a *better viewpoint index* (BVI) to illustrate how theory might guide index construction. For the BVI, "better" is used to describe a viewpoint for which the implied policy response to one or more critical policy issues is superior to the policy responses implicit in other viewpoints generally known to the public. Each version of the BVI describes the likelihood that a new owner will introduce a better viewpoint, one, BVI_a, for an active audience, the other, BVI_p, for a passive audience. Both assume outlets from different media to be good substitutes for the consumption of viewpoints.

Consider a market with m media owners and $n \geq m$ outlets. Each owner presents a single viewpoint (its own) through the outlets it controls. Suppose that for any two viewpoints, there is always a third viewpoint between them on a viewpoint quality spectrum, so that the likelihood that two owners will have the exact same viewpoint is close to zero. Then for each of the m owners, the probability that its viewpoint is the best is $1/m$ and the likelihood that a new owner added to a market that previously had m owners will offer a viewpoint superior to those of the initial m is $1/(m+1)$. If audience members actively and effectively seek out the best viewpoint, then $BVI_a \equiv 1/(m+1)$ is one measure, both simple and intuitive, of the incremental benefit of adding an extra owner, whether by adding a new outlet via an owner new to the market, or by forcing a multi-outlet owner already in the market to sell an outlet to someone currently not in the market.

A similar index for a passive audience would be the joint probability that a new owner will introduce a better idea to the market and a representative audience member will be exposed to it. Suppose media consumers determine the number of outlets whose contents they consume on the basis of considerations entirely unrelated to viewpoint diversity and let r be the maximum number of media outlets that an audience member will sample. For $n \leq r$, each audience member will be exposed to all n outlets, and when $n > r$, each audience member is exposed to r outlets. Clearly when $m < n$ and $n < r$, increasing the number of owners by one results in a $1/(m+1)$ probability that each audience member will be exposed to an idea better than the best offered by the initial m owners. So $BVI_p = 1/(m+1)$ when $n < r$, which is the same as for an active audience.

Now suppose $n > r$ and each audience member's r outlets are selected randomly from those available. If a new owner enters by introducing a new outlet, the likelihood that the new owner's viewpoint will be superior to the incumbent owners' viewpoints is $1/(m+1)$, as before, and the probability that a representative audience member will be exposed to this viewpoint is $r/(n+1)$. In this situation, $BVI_p = r/[n+1)(m+1)]$. If $n > m$ and the new owner enters by purchasing an outlet from an owner with multiple outlets, we have $BVI_p = r/[n(m+1)]$.

Question 11: How Should the Internet Be Incorporated in a DI?

The Internet differs from traditional media in that there is no single technology of distribution with which it is uniquely associated. Rather it is a set of capabilities defined by protocols for data exchange that may be employed with a variety of very different transmission media. This distinction raises a number of significant questions for diversity policy in general, and for DI construction in particular. Here I address three, the first of which concerns the treatment of the phone companies and cable companies that supply the physical network connections by which users access the Internet. This is a matter that cannot be ignored simply because the FCC treated cable companies and telephone companies as Internet gatekeepers in the construction of the FCC-DI and it is reasonable to expect an explanation for departures from the FCC approach. I see no logic in the way cable companies and telephone companies are incorporated in the FCC-DI. The Internet serves as a vehicle by which users gain access to suppliers of various types of content, the overwhelming majority of which are not affiliated with a cable company or telephone company. Although cable and telephone company suppliers of broadband access services often do limit subscribers' ability to access a select few service providers, such restrictions are commonly justified by concerns with network and or service integrity and it is hard to discern a content basis for these restrictions related to the goals of diversity policy. Although such restrictions deserve scrutiny, the fact remains that the overwhelming bulk of content on the Internet is available to anyone with a browser and a willingness to pay subscription fees to the minority of services that charge. If any Internet-related entity is to be treated as similar to traditional media outlets, it should be the content providers users access, not the companies supplying the access lines. It would make just as much sense to treat news vendors as gatekeepers for purposes of developing media policy rather than the publishers of the magazines and newspapers on their shelves.

If we accept that it is the content providers accessed via the Internet that are most similar to traditional media outlets, then it must be asked which qualify for inclusion in a DI. The answer is not nearly so obvious as it is for traditional media. Radio stations, television stations, and newspapers all must generate revenues sufficient to cover the fairly sizeable fixed costs associated with the production or acquisition of content and distribution just to stay in business. The need to cover these costs limits the number of outlets for each of these media within any given geographic market. As a consequence, the opportunity cost of the audience lost should listeners, viewers, or readers not find an outlet's programming attractive in a competitive environment ensures that not insubstantial resources will be committed to the creation and acquisition of content. In contrast, anyone with a personal computer and a broadband connection can offer content on the Internet, even if the audience attracted is close to zero.

If all Internet-based content providers are to be treated as the equivalents of traditional media outlets for purposes of diversity policy, then all policy concerns about an adequate supply of diverse viewpoints should cease once the Internet is available to the vast majority of people. Access for those unable to pay could be dealt with as a universal service issue. Such a policy approach would represent a break with current thinking on diversity matters. The audiences for most Internet content suppliers are tiny in comparison to those for traditional media outlets, largely because they do not supply content with broad appeal. If all content suppliers are to be counted regardless of the size of the audience reached, then purveyors of viewpoints via handbills distributed on street corners should have been counted in the past. To avoid trivializing diversity policy, some cutoff, whether based on audience reach or resources committed to generating or acquiring content, will be required to determine which Internet-based content suppliers are to be counted in a DI.

Finally, it must be asked how the Internet operations of traditional media outlets should be treated in a DI. For the reasons given in the second section of this chapter, I believe that if the Internet operation of a traditional media outlet attracts an audience large enough to qualify for inclusion in a DI if it were operated on a stand-alone basis, it should be treated as a separate outlet owned in common with one or more traditional media outlets in whatever DI is developed.

CONCLUDING THOUGHTS

The 11 questions posed in this chapter all speak to fundamental issues of theory and fact that must be addressed in constructing a DI. The theoretical component is of critical importance because if the theory guiding index construction is not thoroughly worked out in advance, there is a strong likelihood that the next DI will be rejected by the courts for the same types of internal inconsistencies that plagued the FCC-DI. Robert Horwitz (2005) recently characterized the concept of diversity as undertheorized, and it should be apparent from the preceding discussion that the theoretical and empirical inputs to DI development are still in need of substantial development. Nevertheless, even with what we know now, a more defensible index can be constructed if we do not shy away from questions like those raised in this chapter that need to be addressed. As the quality of the answers to these questions improves in the future, better indexes can be devised as well.

NOTES

[1]Much of discussion of the Herfindahl-Hirschmann (HHI) and its use in merger analysis that follows draws on the description of the HHI and its applications to merger review in the U.S. Department of Justice and the Federal Trade Commission's Merger Guidelines (U.S. Department of Justice, 1992).

[2]The question and the distribution of responses are reported in Table 97 of Nielsen Media Research (2002).

[3]Of course other things are not always equal. At some point higher costs must be incurred to provide greater variety. A large economics literature examines this trade-off. See Spence and Owen (1977) and Owen and Wildman (1992) for applications to television.

[4]Gender and ethnic ownership diversity may also be pursued to ensure broader participation by women and minorities in the ownership-side of the economy as a goal unto itself.

[5]For example, at one point the Report and Order states that "viewpoint diversity refers to the availability of a wide range of information and political perspectives on important issues" (Federal Communications Commission, 2002, ¶ 393).

[6]Yim (2003) finds that as the number of outlets for any medium increases, audience members limit their attention to a smaller fraction of available outlets. But a higher percentage of concentration of sources consulted is not the same as consulting fewer sources.

[7]This is consistent with Scheufele's (2002) finding that newspapers cover news events in more depth than broadcast media and have a larger effect on political participation.

REFERENCES

Chafee, S. H., & Kanihan, S. F. (1997). Learning about politics from the mass media. *Political Communication, 14,* 421–430.

Federal Communications Commission. (2003). Report and Order and Notice of Proposed Rulemaking, in the Matter of 2002 Biennial Regulatory Review—Review of the Commission's Broadcast Ownership Rules and Other Rules Adopted Pursuant to Section 202 of the Telecommunications Act of 1996, MM Docket 02–277, Cross-Ownership of Broadcast Stations and Newspapers, MM Docket 01–235, Rules and Policies Concerning Multiple Ownership of Radio Broadcast Stations in Local Markets, MM Docket 01–317, Definition of Radio Markets, MM Docket 00–244, Definition of Radio Markets for Areas Not Located in an Arbitron Survey Area, MM Docket 03–130.

George, L., & Waldfogel, J. (2002, July 5). *Does the* New York Times *spread ignorance and apathy?* East Lansing, MI: Michigan State University Department of Economics. Philadelphia: University of Pennsylvania, the Wharton School.

Horwitz, R. B. (2005). On media concentration and the diversity question. *The Information Society, 21,* 189–204.

Mondak, J. J. (1995a). Media exposure and political discussion in U.S. elections. *Journal of Politics, 57,* 62–85.

Mondak, J. J. (1995b). Newspapers and political awareness. *American Journal of Political Science, 39,* 513–527.

Napoli, P. M. (1997). Rethinking program diversity assessment: An audience-centered approach. *Journal of Media Economics, 10,* 59–74.

Napoli, P. M. (1999). Deconstructing the diversity principle. *Journal of Communication, 49*(4), 7–34.

Napoli, P. M. (2001). *Foundations of communications policy: Principles and process in the regulation of electronic media.* Cresskill, NJ: Hampton.

Nielsen Media Research. (2002). Consumer survey on media usage (Media Ownership Working Group Working Paper No. 8). Washington, DC: Federal Communications Commission.

Oberholzer-Gee, F., & Waldfogel, J. (2001). Electoral acceleration: The effect of minority population on minority voter turnout (NBER Working Paper No. W8252). Retrieved August 1, 2005, from http://ssrn.com;/abstract+268390

Owen, B. M., & Wildman, S. S. (1992). *Video economics.* Cambridge, MA: Harvard University Press.

Prometheus Radio Project v. Federal Communications Commission. On Petition for Review of an Order of the Federal Communications Commission (FCC No. 03-127), June 24, 2004.

Schuefele, D. A. (2002). Examining differential gains from mass media and their implications for participatory behavior. *Communication Research, 29,* 46–65.

Singleton, L. A., & Rockwell, S. C. (2003). Silent voices: Analyzing the FCC 'media voices' criteria limiting local radio–television cross-ownership. *Communication Law and Policy, 8,* 385–403.

Spence, A. M., & Owen, B. M. (1977). Television programming, monopolistic competition and welfare. *Quarterly Journal of Economics, 91,* 103–126.

U.S. Department of Justice & Federal Trade Commission. (1992). *Horizontal merger guidelines.* Retrieved March 11, 2005, from http;//usdoj.gov/atr/public/guidelines/horiz_book/hmg1.html

Yan, M., & Napoli, P. M. (2005). Market competition, station ownership, and local news & public affairs programming on local broadcast television (The Donald McGannon Communication Research Center Working Paper). Bronx, NY: Fordham University.

Yim, J. (2003). Audience concentration in the media: Cross-media comparisons and the introduction of the uncertainty measure. *Communication Monographs, 70,* 114–128.

9

Tracking "Localism" in Television Broadcasting: Utilizing and Structuring Public Information

Stephen D. McDowell & Jenghoon Lee
Florida State University

Localism is one of three primary goals, along with diversity and competition, that the Federal Communications Commission (FCC) listed when, in June 2003, the agency announced its new rules regarding media ownership. In that announcement, the FCC articulated some indicators of localism, which included local selection of the programs and local news quality and quantity (FCC, 2003b, 2003c).

Although many different actors in the ownership debate are trying to promote localism in local media outlets, those parties have expressed widely varying views about the best ways to achieve these goals. The National Association of Broadcasters, representing most strongly the perspectives and concerns of chain-owned affiliates of broadcast networks, has supported the removal of some of the caps while maintaining cross-ownership limitations in other instances (Fritts, 2003a, 2003b), and has emphasized the role of stations affiliated with—but not owned by—broadcasting networks, in making local programming decisions. As James Goodman (2003) noted in testimony to the FCC Task Force on Localism in October 2003, a "Public Interest Programming Community Service Certification Form," was proposed in 1999 by the Presidential Commission on Public Interest Obligations for Digital Television Broadcasting (see also FCC, 1999b; 1999c). A "Voluntary Public Interest Code of Conduct" was also proposed by Paxson Communications in response to MM Docket 99–360 (Paxson, 1999). This intervention emphasized that localism was an important part of the obligations of broadcast license holders.

The difficult task for policymakers is to conceptualize localism in ways that also are compatible with—and provide for—healthy competition and diversity in small local markets. To preserve the local voices in local media markets, the clear definition and identification of local voices is important. The difficulty of definition results from not only the ambiguity of the concept of localism but also from uncertainty regarding the voices to be encouraged. Any attempt to develop indicators of localism must recognize that it is a complex policy goal. Methodologies to track and assess the achievement of this goal must therefore include a number of dimensions, and go beyond program content. Although program content is the most prominent focus of debates about localism, policy approaches to assess localism should examine the broader context, including the processes whereby programming is produced, the ways in which programming decisions are made, and the characteristics of station operation and management.

This chapter examines the applicability of an adapted "points" system, similar to that employed in Canada, as a way to measure "localism" in television program production in the United States. It suggests practical guidelines to identify various forms of local participation in media markets and clarify the elements of localism. These guidelines, it is argued, should include criteria such as local involvement, local outreach, and locally oriented programming. Much of this information is already available in the public inspection file, but this information needs to be more clearly structured and organized around a self-reporting mechanism.

THE CANADIAN CONTENT POLICY AND THE POINTS SYSTEM

The program production points system in Canada provides one public policy example that focuses on support for certain groups in media production, and makes programming with Canadian participation available. It has been part of Canadian broadcasting policy since the 1970s. Since then, the government of Canada has used various mechanisms to promote the production of Canadian audiovisual programming and its distribution on television channels. One of these mechanisms has been to designate programs as "Canadian content" using a points system. The points system does not make reference to programming content, but rather to roles in the process of producing a program. These roles include the following: director, screenwriter, lead performer, second lead performer, art director, director of photography, music composer, and picture editor. The Canadian points system is designed to identify live action or animation programming (not news, current affairs, sports, etc.), that would be eligible for public support through tax credits, and also for broadcaster license holders to certify they have met their promises of performance.

The development of localism indexes or measures along these lines would serve to more clearly track local participation in broadcasting. However, with the exception of the promotion of children's television, in the United States, policies shaping broadcasting content have been concerned more with limiting certain types of programming, such as obscene or indecent programming, than with promoting specific program types. Limitations have been implemented through mechanisms such as direct prohibitions, responses to public complaints, safe harbor rules, and most recently, the V-Chip and television ratings that required a measure of industry self-regulation. Content controls that can withstand court review are undertaken in the face of a clear and compelling public interest, with a narrowly defined scope of implementation.

In contrast, the concept of "Canadian Content" has been used by communications policymakers and regulators in Canada since the 1970s as a vehicle to promote the availability of Canadian programming to Canadian audiences. Apart from political and rhetorical uses of the term in official policy planning and implementation, labeling a program as "Canadian Content" serves two distinct purposes. First, if the program production meets the Canadian content criteria, parts of the program production costs may be eligible for public subsidies to support Canadian program production, or these costs may also be eligible for tax credits. Second, a radio or television broadcaster may have certain license obligations that require it to broadcast Canadian programming for a certain part of the day, and the Canadian Content program label will ensure that it fulfills its obligation.

In one of the main support programs, the Canadian Film or Video Production Tax Credit (CPTC), producers provide documentation about employment in the production process to the Canadian Audio-Visual Certification Office (CAVCO), which certifies eligibility for tax credits. The CPTC is designed to support the production of Canadian dramatic (live action) or animation programs. It is not used to support news, sports, or other such types of programming, which are excluded from eligibility. According to the CAVCO (2003), the tax credit program has several objectives:

> In general, the three main objectives of the CPTC program are economic, industrial and cultural.
>
> 1. There is an economic objective that aims to develop and strengthen the Canadian film and television industry through stable sources of financing;

2. The industrial objective of the program is to encourage the growth of a strong Canadian-owned production sector and foster long-term corporate growth;
3. The cultural objective is to encourage the production of film and television programs that will be seen by Canadians, and ensure that Canadian producers maintain a real beneficial interest and a strong position of control over their productions.

A certified production would be eligible for a tax credit of 25% of qualified labor expenditures under the CPTC. Because these labor costs cannot exceed 48% of the cost of the production, the maximum tax credit available under the program would be 12% of total production costs. These conditions were modified slightly in an announcement by the Department of Finance in November of 2003 (Canada, Department of Finance, 2003).

To qualify for the certification, a program must meet several criteria or obtain a requisite number of points, as outlined in Table 9.1. Certification is available to both Canadian program producers as well as Canadians engaged in international ventures covered under coproduction agreements.

The Canadian Radio-Television and Telecommunications Commission (CRTC) is the federal regulatory agency that monitors the performance requirements of broadcast licensees. Licensees are currently required to broadcast Canadian content during 60% of the broadcast day, and 50% of the prime-time hours from 6 p.m. to midnight (CRTC, 2003). During 1 week, 8 hr of "priority programming" should be broadcast within the 7 p.m. to 11 p.m. prime-time peak hours. Priority programming is Canadian content drawn from the genres of "drama, music and dance, variety, long-form documentary, regional programming, and entertainment magazines" (CRTC, 2003). If a dramatic program has all 10 Canadian content points, then the broadcaster receives a credit for 150% of program time (or 1½ hr of Canadian content for 1 hr of programming). Although the CRTC recognizes all CAVCO certified programming as "Canadian content," for its purposes, it also recognizes news, sports, and other forms of programming that are not eligible for the tax credit as Canadian content for the purposes of broadcasters' fulfillment of their broadcast time requirements.

APPLICABILITY TO TRACKING LOCALISM?

How useful is this example as an illustration of the types of considerations that might go into the design of localism indicators in United States broadcasting? The points system achieves several things that are useful for conceptualiz-

TABLE 9.1

Points System for Eligibility for Canadian Audiovisual or Film Production Tax Credit (Source: Canadian Audiovisual Certification Office)

Live Action		*Animation*	
Director	2 points	Director	1 point
Screenwriter	2 points	Scriptwriter and storyboard supervisor	1 point
Lead performer	1 point	First or second voice	1 point
Second lead performer	1 point	Design supervisor	1 point
Art director	1 point	Music composer	1 point
Director of photography	1 point	Picture editor	1 point
Music composer	1 point	Layout and background	1 point
Picture editor	1 point	Key animation	1 point
		Assistant animation and in-betweening	1 point
		Camera operator and operation	1 point
Notwithstanding this list, at least one of the directors or screenwriters, and either the lead performer or second lead performer, must be Canadian. As well, points for screenwriters may be obtained only if all screenwriters are Canadian, or if both the principal screenwriter and the author of the work o n which the production is based are Canadian and the work is published in Canada.		Notwithstanding this list, at least one of the directors or scriptwriters and storyboard supervisors, and at least one of the first or second voice performers, must be Canadian. The key animation must be done in Canada.	
At least 75% of the total costs for services provided must be paid to Canadians except the following: (a) remuneration paid to the producer, (b) remuneration paid to key creative personnel listed earlier, (c) legal, (d) accounting, (e) insurance, and (f) financing costs. Also, at least 75% of postproduction processing and final preparation (lab) costs must be paid for services provided in Canada.		At least 75% of all production costs must be paid to Canadians except the following: (a) Remuneration paid to the producer, (b) remuneration paid to key creative personnel listed earlier, (c) legal, (d) accounting, (e) insurance, and (f) financing costs. Also, at least 75% of postproduction processing and final preparation (lab) costs must be paid for services provided in Canada.	

ing localism and developing indexes for use in policy analysis. Although any simple transfer of an index is not proposed here, several elements that may serve as guides can be identified

First, like the idea of "Canadian Content," the concept of localism as discussed in United States broadcasting policy is diffuse and ambiguous. A single measure, therefore, is unlikely to capture all the important components of localism. A "points" system allows for the inclusion of a number of different types of criteria. It also allows for the recognition of the existence of some components of localism, even if all of the elements are not present in a specific program or production process. Although the Canadian content points system focuses primarily on labor participation, a localism index or checklist could also consider a number of elements of local participation.

Second, it is notable that the points system has not been applied ambitiously to try to address all public policy objectives in broadcasting. The CPTC program is narrowly focused to provide support through tax credits for a portion of labor costs of certified production. It deals with individual productions, rather than with companies, geographic markets, or industries as a whole. Through this narrow focus, however, it has leveraged a limited amount of tax credit support (a maximum of 12% of total production costs) to encourage private actors to assist in the achievement of a public objective. Similarly, the CRTC program deals with stations that hold broadcast licenses.

Third, it should also be noted that both of the applications of the point system apply to a relatively small portion of the total hours of television and motion picture distribution in Canada, and a small proportion of the total number of broadcast hours in the overall Canadian broadcasting system. The limited objectives of these programs contribute to their acceptability. One lesson that might be drawn is that any localism index used on the United States should be phrased with clear, precise, and narrow objectives.

Fourth, it is notable that the Canadian content points system does not refer centrally to message content, although the inclusion of themes of interest to Canadian audiences is mentioned. Rather, CAVCO addresses participation in the production process by various types of creative and production personnel. This approach avoids one of the major pitfalls that might face localism policy objectives in the United States, that is attempting to promote local participation and local content in broadcasting while not invading the First Amendment rights of broadcasters.

Fifth, the points system is used as a way to encourage the implementation of a specific public program (the tax credit), and this program is only one mechanism to achieve an important public policy goal. It is not primarily an index used to track Canadian audiovisual production overall, because any firm or individual may choose not to seek the tax credit, nor to inform policy analysts and decision makers about industry health or fortunes. In this way, tracking participation in a points system does not serve to collect data in the ways that other industry or audience surveys would.

Sixth, the points system ties into a number of other institutions and cultural norms in communications policy and public policy more broadly. A CAVCO certification makes programs eligible for tax credits for a portion of labor costs. Hence the burden of information collection and completion of application forms is tied to a clear incentive. The CRTC approval is tied to a central public policy goal for broadcast license holders, and is a core condition for license renewal. These are both national level institutions. Hence, the significance of the points system in Canada, and the willingness of industry participants to complete the requisite forms, is premised on the role of other institutions, including the income tax system and the broadcast license renewal system, that also make use of this index. A points system may not be transferable to a different institutional context, especially if there are significant data-collection burdens required of program producers or broadcasters.

Although there are no doubt many others factors that have contributed to the strength or weakness of the Canadian content points system, in the next section we propose that these institutional factors provide some basic criteria that can help guide the development of ways to measure and assess localism in broadcasting in the United States.

DEVELOPING A LOCALISM INDEX

Given the considerations mentioned in the earlier discussion of the Canadian example, we argue that several premises should guide the development of a checklist of elements to measure and track localism in broadcasting:

1. Multiple criteria—Because localism is a complex concept, multiple elements or criteria should be included in any index.
2. Narrowly focused objectives—Rather than addressing a wide range of concerns about localism, diversity, and competition in national broadcasting or designated market areas, focus should be placed on individual broadcasting stations that hold local broadcast licenses, and the application of various criteria as they relate to the local broadcast license holder.
3. Application to small portion of total broadcasting schedule—Rather than trying to track the whole broadcast schedule, by identifying specific criteria relevant to localism and a smaller subset of programming, tracking and data collection efforts can be limited and focused.
4. Participation in the production process—Similarly, we sought to make use of an approach that focused primarily on the local characteristics of broadcast program production, rather than being concerned solely with the content of programs. Our search objectives focused initially on ownership and employment information, but as noted later, changed somewhat to make use of publicly available information and to include community consultation.
5. Broader institutional and cultural context—Because the goal of localism cannot at this time be tied to any clear legislative obligation or any in-

centive for extensive data collection by broadcasters in the United States, any data collection burden should be limited. We sought to make use of information and data that were already available from public and nonproprietary sources. This approach would recognize these institutional characteristics, as well as the resource constraints of public interest advocates. Hence, we sought to limit as much as possible any additional reporting requirements, whether for industry participants or for public interest and advocacy organizations.

DATA SOURCES: THE PUBLIC INSPECTION FILE

Our search for information sources of relevance to the identification and tracking of localism criteria initially considered industry and audience research data. However, we began to explore the possibilities of using the information in the "Public Inspection File." This is a collection of data that all broadcast license holders are required to maintain and make accessible to the public.

The FCC requires each station to maintain specific items in the public inspection file. These items include the license, applications and related materials, citizen agreements, contour maps, material relating to an FCC investigation or a complaint, ownership reports and related material, lists of contracts required to be filed with the FCC, the political file, annual employment reports and related material, copies of the station manual, letters and e-mail from the public, issues and programs list, children's television programming reports, records regarding children's programming commercial limits, radio time brokerage agreements, a list of donors, local public notice announcements, and must-carry or retransmission consent election (FCC, 1999a). Of special interest here are the overall purposes of the file, which emphasize the role of the local public in monitoring "programming and possible rule violations." The FCC (1999a) stated the following:

> ... stations have an obligation to serve their local community's needs and interests and to comply with certain programming and other rules. Because we do not monitor a station's programming, viewers and listeners are a vital source of information about the programming and possible rule violations. The documents in each station's public inspection file have information about the station that can assist the public in this important role.
>
> ... all stations have an obligation to cover important issues facing their communities, to comply with requirements governing use of their facilities by candidates for public office, and to refrain from airing indecent program-

ming during times children are likely to be in the audience. In addition, TV stations must air educational programming for children and limit the amount of advertising in children's programs. We encourage a continuing dialogue between broadcasters and members of the public to ensure that stations meet their obligations and remain responsive to the needs of the local community.

Several different types of information that stations are required to include in their public inspection file relate to criteria of relevance for tracking localism, including citizen agreements, ownership reports, the political file, annual employment reports, letters and e-mail from the public, an issues and programs list, and children's television reports. The FCC (1999a) describes these various requirements as follows:

Citizen Agreements. Stations must keep a copy of any written agreements they make with local viewers or listeners. These "citizen agreements" deal with programming, employment, or other issues of community concern. The station must keep these agreements in the public file for as long as they are in effect.

Ownership Reports and Related Material. The public file must contain a copy of the most recent, complete Ownership Report filed for the station. This report has the names of the owners of the station and their ownership interests, lists any contracts related to the station that are required to be filed with the FCC, and identifies any interest held by the station licensee in other broadcast stations.

Political File. Stations must keep a file containing records of all requests for broadcast time made by or for a candidate for public office. The file must identify how the station responded to such requests and (if the request was granted) the charges made, a schedule of the time purchased, the times the spots actually aired, the rates charged, and the classes of time purchased. The file must also reflect any free time provided to a candidate. The station must keep the political records for two years after the spot airs.

Annual Employment Reports and Related Material. We require all radio and TV stations to afford equal opportunity in employment. We also prohibit employment discrimination on the basis of race, color, religion, national origin, or sex. We require stations to file reports annually describing how they have complied with these policies ....

Letters and E-Mail from the Public. Commercial stations must keep written comments and suggestions received from the public regarding their operation for at least *three years*. Noncommercial stations are not subject to this requirement.

Issues/Programs List. Every three months, all stations must prepare and place in their file a list of programs that have provided their most significant treatment of community issues during the *preceding three months*. The list must briefly describe both the issue and the programming where the issue was discussed. The stations must keep these lists for the entire license term.

Children's Television Programming Reports. The Children's Television Act of 1990 and our rules require all TV stations to air programming that serves the educational and informational needs of children 16 and under, including programming that is specifically designed to serve such needs. In addition, commercial TV stations must make and retain Children's Television Programming Reports identifying the educational and informational programming for children aired by the station. (Noncommercial stations are not required to prepare these reports.)

How useful can the public inspection file be as a source of information for constructing a localism index? The documents in each station's public inspection file contain information to assist the public in monitoring the extent to which various public service and public interest obligations have been met. Initially, the public inspection file was not intended solely for public examination (ShawPittman Limited Partnership including Professional Corporations, 2003). Instead, the public inspection file functioned as a collection of general documents regarding a station's operation. Although the current public inspection file is designed to help the public in monitoring the local stations, some limitations in the filing system have created difficulties for stations, the public, and regulators. Most importantly, the amount of information and its lack of structure limit its usefulness for this purpose, unless modified.

Lacking clear guidelines for the public inspection file, each station has developed its files in different ways. To solve this problem, it would be useful for the FCC to articulate more clearly the specific data collection purposes of the public inspection file, and to outline standardized procedures for the filing system. Clear guidelines also would limit the costs of maintaining files for local stations with insufficient financial resources.

Given the public's lack of expertise and financial resources, the public file should be organized in such a way as to be useful to evaluate stations' performance in achieving localism objectives. A better organized filing and reporting system might help the public to monitor local stations and also encourage the public to interact more fully with the local stations. It is important to make information available to the public in a form that is practical and useful.

With appropriate items in the public inspection file, the file also can be used to provide information to station managers to better respond to local needs. For the management team of local stations, accurate measures regarding stations' performance could identify stations and management teams that are meeting localism objectives, and help them to obtain community recognition and support.

SUGGESTED OUTLINE FOR THE SELF CERTIFICATION REPORT ON LOCALISM

Three major goals are salient in this effort. The first is to provide a tool measuring stations' performance in advancing localism. The second is to encourage members of the public to make use of the file, and hence serve to build local links and accountability relationships that will advance this policy objective. The third objective is to include reporting on elements in the file that highlight the emphasis on localism, potentially leading stations to emphasize certain activities in local markets and institutionalizing local programming objectives in their decision making. The information available in the public inspection file, we argue, needs to be organized and structured more clearly. Some items may need to be added to achieve these three major goals. Possible elements of a checklist follow, as illustrations of the types of categories and items that might be derived from existing sources.

1. Geographic Location: Assumption—Broadcast stations, owned, managed, or located in the local communities, may serve communities better than the stations without these connections.
   a. Ownership: Check point—Location of owner in broadcast area; Information—Ownership reports in public inspection file, List of Contracts in public inspection file
   b. Management integration with workplace: Check point—Location of management team in broadcast area; Information: May be part of citizen agreement, may be part of annual employment reports in public inspection file.
   c. Location of main studio: Check point—Location in broadcast area, access to public inspection file; Information: License in public inspection file.
2. Local Outreach: Assumption—Broadcast stations with procedures for consultation and interaction with the local public may respond to local needs more effectively or understand the local communities more completely.
   a. Dialogue between stations and the public: Check point—The existence of communication channels with the local community; Information: Citizen agreements in public inspection file, new information.

   b. Community nonprogramming services: Check point—The direct public services by the stations for the local community; for example, organizing or promoting local community events; Information—Not included in public access file.
3. Locally Oriented Programming: Assumption—Stations broadcasting local-oriented programming or locally originating views better serve local needs.
   a. Policy Statement on Localism in Broadcast Programming: Check point—Certify policy on localism exists, with assessment methodologies and reporting mechanism; Information—May be part of citizen agreement.
   b. Local Public Affairs and Politics: Check point—Coverage of local elections and local politics; Information—Political file in public inspection file.
   c. Represent Diverse Voices in Local Audience: Check point—Promotion of diverse voices in the programming; Information—Contour maps of signal coverage in public inspection file, audience research for designated market area.
   d. Local Issues: Check point—Promotion of local community's voices; Information: Letters in public inspection file, issues and program list, local public notice announcement.

DISCUSSION AND CONCLUSIONS

This checklist is presented as a way to focus discussion of what is meant by localism, but also to move that discussion forward by asking about specific criteria that make up localism, as well as the available forms of information that are relevant to this question. We seek to present one way to place the assessment of localism on the public agenda and to build a self-sustaining way for data collection and review to take place. To conclude, we discuss the proposed checklist by returning to the five institutional features mentioned earlier that contributed to the Canadian content points system.

Multiple Criteria

Because localism, like most important policy goals, is a complex concept, we have included a number of factors or criteria arising from the data included in the public inspection file. A points system allows stations to demonstrate some elements of localism, even if they do not meet all the criteria.

To consider the question more broadly than the list proposed earlier, it would be useful to conceptualize the possibility of using different procedures or elements to promote localism, or a list that is not standardized. Each station might face unique market situations that shape its performance as a local station. This approach would run parallel to the quality improvement plans used in many organizational contexts, and recognized by the federal Department of Commerce in the Baldridge Awards. In this approach, stations would be asked to identify what they would identify as the key components of localism, ways that they will track their performance, and how they will report to the public. The inclusion of a policy statement on local broadcasting in checkpoint 3a allows for this flexibility already. However, to save on time and effort, industry groups might develop their own best practices. A strategy of self-certification limits direct regulatory involvement, but parallels the practices of professional groups (accountants, architects) in the preparation of public statements or annual reports that can be audited.

Narrowly Focused Objectives

This checklist focuses on the broadcast station holding a public license, and refers to its operations, relations with the public, and coverage of local issues in programming. This provides a set of criteria relevant to the decision making and responsibilities of the local management team, and serves to develop a tracking mechanism that can be used in decision making. Although the ownership of television broadcasting is concentrated in networks and groups, broadcast licenses are still held on a station-by-station basis, and the local station provides a nexus of accountability. It is recognized that this does not create a centralized database of localism achievements in broadcast performance, but it does provide a basis for this type of data collection by civil society groups and public agencies.

Application to Small Portion of Total Broadcasting Schedule

The reporting required here would be drawn from materials already in the public inspection file. Only one of the groups of criteria refers to programming, and then only to very specific subsets of programming such as public affairs or children's programming.

Participation in the Production Process

Rather than focus solely on program content, the criteria we propose relate to the location of ownership, management, and operations, and putting processes in place for community outreach and consultation.

Broader Institutional Context

We would propose working within the broader institutional context in several ways. This proposal would make use of information and data that already are available from the public inspection file, and augment this information by structuring it more usefully, and by completing annual reports of the achievement of various localism criteria. However, we do not propose any changes in the broader regulatory or policy context at this time, or address the question of whether self-certification should be a regulatory requirement or a recommendation for industry self-regulation. Should data derived from the public inspection file system be used as requirement to renew or obtain the broadcast station's license? Or, could information from the file be used as the criteria to grant financial incentives or rewards by public or private sector agencies?

A more important role in the broader institutional context would fall to local groups to find the time and resources to engage in consultations with broadcasters and make use of the available information. The Center for Media Education proposed the use of the Public Inspection File by members of the public in their relations with local stations. A self-reporting approach would require continued vigilance on the part of the members of the public.

REFERENCES

Canada, Department of Finance. (2003, November 14). *Government announces changes to the Canadian film or video production tax credit* (Press Release). Retrieved April 7, 2005, from http://www.fin.gc.ca/news03/03-058e.html

Canadian Audio-Visual Certification Office. (2003). *Programs*. Retrieved November 2, 2004, from http://www.canadianheritage.gc.ca/progs/ac-ca/progs/bcpac-cavco/pubs/2001-02/ra-ar/prog_e.cfm

Canadian Radio-Television and Telecommunications Commission. (2003, September). Evaluation of the 'Dramatic Choices' report: Economic considerations of certain audience-based incentives (Report prepared for the CRTC by Nordicity Group Ltd.). Retrieved January 3, 2005, from http://www.crtc.gc.ca/eng/publications/reports/drama/nordicity2003.htm

Federal Communications Commission. (1999a, June). *The Public and broadcasting*. Retrieved May 7, 2005, from http://www.fcc.gov/mb/audio/decdoc/public_and_broadcasting.html#PIF

Federal Communications Commission. (1999b, December 15). *FCC begins proceedings to seek comment on public interest obligations of television broadcasters as they transition to digital transmission technology* (News Release). Retrieved April 21, 2006, from http://www.fcc.gov/bureaus/mass_media/news-releases/1999/nrmm9030.html

Federal Communications Commission. (1999c). In the matter of public interest obligations of tv broadcast licensees, MM Docket No. 99–360, *Notice of Inquiry*. Retrieved April 21, 2006, from http://www.fcc.gov/bureaus/mass_media/notices/1999/fcc99390.doc

Federal Communications Commission. (2003b, July 2). In the matter of 2002 biennial regulatory review—Review of the commission's broadcast ownership rules and other rules adopted pursuant to section 202 of the Telecommunications Act of 1996, MB Docket 02–277), *Report and Order and Notice of Proposed Rulemaking, FCC 03–127*. Retrieved April 21, 2006, from http://hraunfoss.fcc.gov/edocs_public/attachmatch/fcc-03-172A1.doc

Federal Communications Commission. (2003c, June 2). *FCC sets limits on media concentration: Unprecedented public record results in enforceable and balanced broadcast ownership rules* (Press Release). Retrieved April 21, 2006, from http://hraunfoss.fcc.gov/edocs_public/attachmatch/doc-235047A1.doc

Fritts, E. O. (2003a, April 23). *Speech to the media institute*. Retrieved March 8, 2005, from http://www.nab.org/Newsroom/PressRel/speeches/042303.htm

Fritts, E. O. (2003b, October 28). *Broadcasting deregulation: Positive or negative? Speech at Temple University*. Retrieved March 8, 2005, from http://www.nab.org/Newsroom/PressRel/speeches/102803.htm

Goodman, J. F. (2003, October 22). *Testimony of James F. Goodman before the Federal Communications Commission hearing on localism in broadcasting*. Retrieved March 1, 2005, from http://www.fcc.gov/localism/hearing-charlotte102203.html

Paxson Communication Corporation. (1999). In the matter of public interest obligations of tv broadcast licensees, MM Docket No. 99–360, comments of Paxson Communication Corp. Retrieved February 27, 2005, from http://ftp.fcc.gov/cgb/dro/comments/99360.html

ShawPittman Limited Partnership including Professional Corporations. (2003, July). Commercial radio and television station public inspection file advisory. Retrieved April 21, 2006, from www.pillsburylaw.com

10

When Law and Social Science Go Hand in Glove: Usage and Importance of Local and National News Sources—Critical Questions and Answers for Media Market Analysis

Mark Cooper
Consumer Federation of America

Social scientists in the media and communications fields should view the recent Appeals Court (*Prometheus Radio Project v. FCC,* 2004) ruling that overturned the Federal Communications Commission's (2003) proposed media ownership rules as a huge victory and a golden opportunity. Following up on the ruling by the D.C. Circuit Court of appeals in *Sinclair Broadcasting Inc. v. FCC* (2002), which demanded that the Federal Communications Commission (FCC) close an empirical gap in its analysis of media markets, the Third Circuit Court of Appeals embraced social science analysis wholeheartedly.

Opponents of the FCC rules, who had used traditional analytic tools and data from the fields of communications and media analysis to show that "the agency spent two years misreading the record, misinterpreting the law and mangling the analysis," (Cooper, 2003, p. 6) predicted the outcome. What was less predictable was the depth and clarity of the analysis provided by the Court. Perhaps because this was the second rejection of FCC efforts to rewrite several of the rules on the grounds that the FCC had failed to provide a reasoned, empirical basis for key decisions, the Court felt compelled to lay out a detailed framework for rigorous market structure analysis. It instructed the FCC to carefully measure media audiences, assess media usage, and apply a rigorous understanding of the functions of media in democracy.

This chapter shows that, contrary to Former FCC Chairman Michael Powell's claim that the Court decision "sets near impossible standards for justifying bright-line ownership limits," (Powell, 2004, p. 1) the Court has presented a highly refined road map for charting the media landscape. It presents the results of a survey conducted about 6 months prior to the Court ruling that was intended to highlight the methodological and conceptual flaws in the FCC analysis, the very flaws that the Court ultimately noted.

With the Court decision, however, the focus should shift from what the FCC did wrong to what the Court recommends is the right way to conduct the analysis. Therefore, this chapter proposes a framework for identifying and integrating the necessary data to build a media market analysis that will pass court scrutiny and applies it to the 10 cities for which the FCC did detailed analysis.

Five methodological and substantive issues are highlighted in this chapter:

- Distinguishing news and public affairs programming from entertainment or distribution of personal opinions.
- Focusing on local rather than national news sources.
- Assessing the importance of various media.
- Consistent identification of media sources.
- Estimation of the audience of various media.

The chapter is divided in two parts. Part 1 describes how the FCC went astray. The second section presents the legal context for the critique of the FCC analysis. It examines both the substantive goals of media ownership policy and the standard of evidence that an FCC rule must meet. The third section discusses the methodological flaws in the FCC analysis as described by the Court.

Part 2 presents the approach to solving the problem. The fourth section describes how the survey and market data were designed to address the critical mistakes made by the FCC in evaluating the importance of media as sources of news and information. It identifies the data sources and methods used to estimate the size of local news media markets, a critical step in market structure analysis completely ignored by the FCC. The fifth section demonstrates why the FCC approach went astray and proposes a direction for future analysis. It shows that the use of improper media weights and the failure to estimate audience size led the FCC to underestimate the concentration of local news markets and therefore accept mergers in many more markets than was justified. The chapter concludes with survey evidence that shows that the public perceives local markets very differently than does the FCC.

PART 1: DISMANTLING THE DIVERSITY INDEX

The Legal Context

Although the chapter focuses on methodological and substantive issues, a quick review of the law is critical for two reasons. Substantively, the law establishes the public policy objectives that set the context for analysis. Procedurally, the law establishes the nature of the evidentiary and analytic support rules require to pass judicial scrutiny.

First Amendment Principles

For over 60 years, since the landmark ruling in *Associated Press v. United States* (1945), the Supreme Court has expressed a bold aspiration for the First Amendment in the electronic age. The Court declared that "the widest possible dissemination of information from diverse and antagonistic sources is essential to the welfare of the public"(*Associated Press v. United States,* 1945). Although *Associated Press* was an antitrust, newspaper case, the Court has applied this concept to every form of electronic media involving regulatory law.

In its ruling, the Third Circuit Court chose the most aggressive starting point for evaluating media ownership from a 1978 case in which ownership limits were upheld (*FCC v. Nat'l Citizens Committee For Broadcasting,* 1978). "In setting its licensing policies, the Commission has long acted on the theory that diversification of mass media ownership serves the public interest by promoting diversity of program and service viewpoints, as well as by preventing undue concentration of economic power" (*Prometheus Radio Project v. FCC,* 2004, p. 6). This picked up the line of reasoning that the D.C. Circuit had adopted in *Sinclair,* where it declared "the greater the diversity of ownership in a particular area, the less chance there is that a single person or group can have an inordinate effect, in a political, editorial, or similar programming sense, on public opinion at the regional level" (*Sinclair,* 2002, p. 160).

That this line of cases remains the font of First Amendment jurisprudence was affirmed recently when the Supreme Court cited *Red Lion v. FCC* (1968a) favorably in upholding campaign finance reform (*McConnell v. Federal Election*

Commission, 2003). *Red Lion* is cited as the seminal case for broadcast television doctrine. It asserts that "it is the purpose of the First Amendment to preserve an uninhibited marketplace of ideas in which truth will ultimately prevail, rather than to countenance monopolization of that market, whether it be by the government itself or a private licensee" (*Red Lion Broadcasting v. FCC*, 1969, p. 390). In *Red Lion*, the court elaborated that "the 'public interest' in broadcasting clearly encompasses the presentation of vigorous debate of controversial issues of importance and concern to the public" (*Red Lion Broadcasting v. FCC*, 1969, p. 390) and "the right of the public to receive suitable access to social, political, esthetic, moral and other ideas and experiences" (*Red Lion Broadcasting v. FCC*, 1969, p. 390). A similar sentiment was expressed for cable in *Turner Broadcasting Systems, Inc. v. FCC* (1994), where the court declared that "[a] diverse and robust marketplace of ideas is the foundation of our democracy" (pp. 663–664).

Further, although the FCC Media Ownership Order repeatedly applauded the abundance of choices consumers have as listeners, the Third Circuit Court emphasized that the primary concern of the First Amendment is the ability of citizens to speak. "In NCCB, the Court referred to the 'physical scarcity' of the spectrum—the fact that many more people would like access to it than can be accommodated. The abundance of non-broadcast media does not render the broadcast spectrum any less scarce" (*Prometheus Radio Project v. FCC*, 2004, p. 56).

Although not precise, the direction of the bold aspiration expressed by the Supreme Court is clear. Democracy requires wide dissemination and vigorous debate in which no speaker has undue influence.

Writing Reasonable Rules

The legal standard for reviewing rules is important because it establishes the quality of the analysis that must be conducted in support of a rule. At the most basic level, Congressional intent is important and a Court "may find an agency rule is arbitrary and capricious where the agency has relied on factors which Congress has not intended it to consider ... [or] an abuse of discretion, or otherwise not in accordance with the law" (*Prometheus Radio Project v. FCC*, 2004, p. 31). The Court asks whether "the agency examined the relevant data and articulated a satisfactory explanation for its action, including a 'rational' connection between the facts found and the choice made or the agency made a clear error in judgment" (*Prometheus Radio Project v. FCC*, 2004, p. 31).

At a more complex level, although an expert agency like the FCC is given discretion in writing rules, the Courts will overturn rules if the agency "entirely failed to consider an important aspect of the problem, offered an explanation for its decisions that runs counter to the evidence before the agency, or is so implausible that it could not be ascribed to a difference in view or the product of agency expertise" (*Prometheus Radio Project v. FCC*, 2004, p. 31). In the case of an exercise such as identifying thresholds for merger review under the Administrative Procedures Act (APA)

> the traditional APA standard of review is even more deferential "where the issues involve 'elusive' and 'not easily defined,' areas such as program diversity in broadcasting." Yet ... a "rationality" standard is appropriate ... when an agency has engaged in line-drawing determinations ... its decisions may not be "patently unreasonable" or run counter to the evidence before the agency. (*Prometheus Radio Project v. FCC*, 2004, p. 31)

Thus, legal practice does not demand (and social science cannot produce) perfection or even great precision in the analysis, but evidence must be substantial, reasoning consistent, choices reasonable, and results rational.

The FCC's Narrow View of the First Amendment Led to Absurd Analysis

Unfortunately, the FCC has turned its back on this First Amendment jurisprudence. Instead of accepting the challenge of the Supreme Court's bold aspiration for the First Amendment, the FCC has adopted the narrowest vision imaginable.[1] The FCC has adopted the broadcasters' "leak out" view of the public interest under the First Amendment that the Supreme Court has consistently rejected:

> What really matters with ideas from a political point of view is whether they can be suppressed. But given the importance of interpersonal communications, it is extremely difficult to suppress ideas—they can "leak out" even through small or economically minor media outlets. (Owen, 2003, p. 10)

For the broadcasters, the First Amendment is reduced to simple economics. They reject the notion that Congress can pursue public policies that the courts have upheld. The only expert proffered by the broadcasters asks, "Why should the government seek to promote local content as opposed to, and especially at the expense of, any other category of idea?" (Owen, 2003, p. 13). Citizens engaging in political debate disappear, having been devoured by consumers enjoying entertainment: "[T]he commission's sometime preoccupation with news and public affairs, as distinct from entertainment programming ... makes even less sense than localism. First, broadcast news is entertainment—it has to be, at least in part, in order to attract audiences that can be sold to advertisers" (Owen, 2003, p. 11). The Communications Act disappears and the Commission becomes superfluous, having been devoured by economics interests.

The FCC's embrace of the narrow view is explicit and fundamental. It has declared that it is concerned only with ensuring that ideas can leak out: "In the context of evaluating viewpoint diversity, this approach reflects a measure of the likelihood that some particular viewpoint might be censored or foreclosed, i.e. blocked from transmission to the public" (FCC, 2003, ¶ 420). The "leak out" view of the First Amendment leads to a discourse that looks nothing like the bold aspiration expressed by the Supreme Court. The ideas of the network's owners are likely to be broadcast much more widely than those that leak out. The FCC shrugs this off. If the distribution of media ownership undermines a robust exchange of views, the FCC is unconcerned, declaring the following:

> Nor is it particularly troubling that media properties do not always, or even frequently, avail themselves to others who may hold contrary opinions. Nothing requires them to do so, nor is it necessarily healthy for public debate to pretend as though all ideas are of equal value entitled to equal airing. (FCC, 2003, ¶ 353)

The "leak out" view of the First Amendment led the FCC to assume that all outlets of a particular medium should be given an equal weight. If all that matters is whether an idea can leak out, the size of the audience does not matter. Whispers and shouts are equal in the "leak out" view. As the Court noted, the impact on empirical analysis is disastrous:

> The assumption of equal market shares is inconsistent with the Commission's overall approach to its Diversity Index and also makes unrealistic assumptions about media outlets' relative contributions to viewpoint diversity in local markets.
>
> The Commission's decision to assign equal market shares to outlets within a media type does not jibe with the Commission's decision to assign relative weights to the different media types themselves, about which it said "we have no reason to believe that all media are of equal importance ...." It also negates the Commission's proffered rationale ... to allow it to measure the actual loss of diversity from consolidation by taking into account the actual "diversity importance" of merging parties, something it could not do with a simple "voices" test ...
>
> Additionally, there is no dispute that the assignment of equal market shares generates absurd results ... A Diversity Index that requires us to accept that

> a community college television station makes a greater contribution to viewpoint diversity than a conglomerate that includes the third-largest newspaper in America also requires us to abandon both logic and reality. (*Prometheus Radio Project v. FCC*, 2004, pp. 69–70)

Even if the Court had found that the Diversity Index was reasonable, it would still have overturned the rule. The Court found that "the commission did not rationally derive its Cross-Media Limits from the Diversity Index results" (*Prometheus Radio Project v. FCC*, 2004, p. 72). It found that "the Cross-Media Limits allow some combinations where the increases in Diversity Index scores were generally higher than for other combinations that were not allowed" (*Prometheus Radio Project v. FCC*, 2004, pp. 73–75).

As blunt as the Court was in its criticism of the Diversity Index, we should not forget that the Court also pointed out that "the Commission's decision not to retain a ban on newspaper/broadcast cross-ownership is justified ... and is supported by record evidence" (*Prometheus Radio Project v. FCC*, 2004, p. 48). The Court found evidence in the record that "Newspaper/broadcast combinations can promote localism" and "a blanket prohibition on newspaper/broadcast combinations is not necessary to protect diversity" (*Prometheus Radio Project v. FCC*, 2004, p. 49). The Court felt that "[g]iven the Commission's goal of balancing the public's interest in competition, localism, and diversity, it reasonably concluded that repealing the cross-ownership ban was necessary to promote competition and localism, while retaining some limits was necessary to ensure diversity" (*Prometheus Radio Project v. FCC*, 2004, p. 54). It brushed aside complaints that continuing to regulate cross-media ownership violated the First and Fifth Amendment rights of the media owners (*Prometheus Radio Project v. FCC*, 2004, pp. 48–55).

In other words, limits on media ownership are permissible but they must reflect empirical facts and sound analysis.

ANALYTIC AND METHODOLOGICAL FLAWS IN THE FCC ORDER

In *Sinclair Broadcasting Inc. v. FCC* (2002), the D.C. Circuit Court had criticized the FCC's rule limiting the ownership of multiple TV stations within a single market because it had counted media "voices" in the same market differently for each of its rules. At the same time, in reviewing the rule that prevented the holder of a television station license from owning a newspaper in the same market, the FCC had to confront the challenge of combining media in one framework.

The FCC responded by adopting a modification of a standard antitrust approach to create a consistent empirical framework for evaluating media outlets in a local area. Where different types of media had to be considered together—for example, in the question of mergers between newspapers and television stations—the FCC attempted to create a single Diversity Index.

The Court accepted the general antitrust framework and even the idea that a single index could be created, but found the FCC's implementation faulty. "But for all of its efforts, the Commission's Cross-Media Limits employ several irrational assumptions and inconsistencies" (*Prometheus Radio Project v. FCC*, 2004, p. 58). The Court identified three primary problems in the implementation of the Diversity Index:

- The FCC refused to analyze the actual audience of a media outlet, assuming instead that all outlets within a media type are equal.
- Its weights for each type of media were inconsistent and not based on sound empirical measures.
- The link between the index and the merger approval was tenuous at best.

The Antitrust Approach to Market Structure Analysis

For the purpose of merger analysis, antitrust officials define markets by the substitutability of products (U.S. Department of Justice & Federal Trade Commission, 1997). Products have to be good substitutes and readily available in a given geographic area to be included in the market.

After the product and geographic market is defined, the analyst looks at the size of the firms in the market as a first screen in assessing the likely impact of a merger. When the number of firms in a market is small, or a single firm is very large, there is a concern that market power can be exercised. Prices can be raised or quality reduced to increase profits by coordinated or parallel actions among a small number of firms, or the unilateral acts of a single dominant firm.

The level of concentration is calculated by taking the market share of each firm, squaring it, and then summing the result for all firms.[2] Known as the Herfindahl-Hirschmann Index (HHI), this index has an easy interpretation.[3] A market that is made up of 10 equal-sized firms will have an HHI of 1,000. Each firm has a 10% market share. Squaring the share yields 100 points for each firm, times 10 firms ($10 \times 10 \times 10$). A market with 5 equal-sized firms will have an HHI of 2,000 ($20 \times 20 = 400 \times 5$).

The Department of Justice considers a market with fewer than 10 equal-sized firms to be concentrated (see Fig. 10.1). It considers a market with fewer than the equivalent of approximately 5.5-equal sized firms (HHI = 1,800) to be highly concentrated. Markets with an HHI between 1,000 and 1,800 are considered moderately concentrated. A highly concentrated market is called a tight oligopoly (Shepherd, 1985). A moderately concentrated market is called a loose oligopoly.

It should be noted that the HHI is just one statistical measure of dispersion and there are many others. The HHI has become infused with significance in antitrust because a direct conceptual link between this measure of market structure and the performance of the market can be defined (Viscusi, Vernan, & Harrington, 2001). The theoretical link is supported by empirical evidence (FCC, 2003, p. 120).

The judicial language on the relationship between ownership and viewpoint diversity and the desire to prevent excessive economic concentration

DEPARTMENT OF JUSTICE MERGER GUIDELINES	TYPE OF MARKET	EQUIVALENTS IN TERMS OF EQUAL SIZED FIRMS	TYPICAL HHI IN MEDIA MARKETS	4-FIRM SHARE
↑	MONOPOLY	1[a]	5300+	~100
	DUOPOLY	2[b]	3000 - 5000	~100
		5	2000	80
HIGHLY CONCENTRATED	TIGHT OLIGOPOLY		1800 OR MORE	
MODERATELY CONCENTRATED		6	1667	67
UNCONCENTRATED	LOOSE OLIGOPOLY	10	1000	40[c]
↓	ATOMISTIC COMPETITION	50	200	8[c]

Note:
[a] = Antitrust practice finds monopoly firms with market share in the 65% to 75% range. Thus, HHIs in "monopoly markets can be as low as 4200.
[b] = Duopolies need not be a perfect 50/50 split. Duopolies with a 60/40 split would have a higher HHI.
[c] = Value falls as the number of firms increases.
Sources: U.S. Department of Justice, Horizontal Merger Guidelines, revised April 8, 1997, for discussion of the HHI thresholds; William G. Shepherd, The Economics of Industrial Organization (Englewood Cliffs, NJ: Prentice Hall, 1985), for a discussion of four firm concentration ratios.

Figure 10.1. Describing market structures.

and undue influence is certainly broadly consistent with the rhetoric of antitrust. However, the precise analytic link between the diversity outcomes and the statistical index that has developed in the economics literature does not exist for media. Sufficient qualitative evidence was entered into the record to support the link that the Court accepted the application of the antitrust approach to media markets for purposes of diversity analysis, but this is an area in need of further study and reinforcement.

The Court's Critique of FCC Implementation

The FCC must define a market, measure concentration, and establish a principle for rejecting or accepting mergers. To define the market for the purposes of cross media mergers, the FCC endeavored to combine different media (TV, newspapers). It had to decide which media to include and how much weight they should be given.

The Court found that the FCC had not properly weighted the various media: "In converting the HHI to a measure for diversity in local markets, however, the Commission gave too much weight to the Internet as a media outlet" (*Prometheus Radio Project v. FCC,* 2004, p. 58). The Court focused on the handling of the Internet, in part, because of the extensive arguments presented by media owners to the FCC that the Internet had dramatically changed the media landscape. In fact, the mishandling of radio actually has a larger impact. However, viewing the issue through the portal of the Internet provided the Court with the opportunity to present a richly nuanced discussion of the media's output and function.

The Court drove home the critical factor that diversity comes from independent sources of information and there is very little independent news on the Internet:

> There is a critical distinction between websites that are independent sources of local news and websites of local newspapers and broadcast stations that merely republish the information already being reported by the newspaper or broadcast station counterpart. The latter do not present an "independent" viewpoint and thus should not be considered as contributing diversity to local markets. (*Prometheus Radio Project v. FCC,* 2004, p. 64)

The distinction between local and national sources was also emphasized in the Internet discussion:

> The Commission does not cite, nor does the record contain, persuasive evidence that there is a significant presence of independent local news sites on

> the Internet ... And the examples the Commission does cite—the Drudge Report and Salon.com—have a national, not local, news focus.[a/]

The unique characteristics of the "information" that is the object of First Amendment policy and the role of the media also come out here:

> Search-engine sponsored web pages such as Yahoo! Local and about.com, which were suggested by commenters as sources of local news and information, may be useful for finding restaurant reviews and concert schedules, but that is not the type of "news and public affairs programming" that the Commission said "was the clearest example of programming that can provide viewpoint diversity." ...
>
> In terms of content, "the media" provides (to different degrees, depending on the outlet) accuracy and depth in local news in a way that an individual posting in a chat room on a particular issue of local concern does not. But more importantly, media outlets have an entirely different character from individual or organizations' websites and thus contribute to diversity in an entirely different way. They provide an aggregator function (bringing news / information to one place) as well as a distillation function (making a judgment as to what is interesting, important, entertaining, etc.) Individuals ... and entities ... may use the Internet to disseminate information and opinions about matters of local concern ... but ... are not, themselves ... "media outlets" for viewpoint-diversity purposes. Like many entities, they just happen to use a particular media outlet—the Internet—to disseminate information. Similarly, advertiser-driven websites such as hvnet.com ... hardly contribute to viewpoint diversity. (*Prometheus Radio Project v. FCC*, 2004, pp. 66–67)

The reach of the outlet is also important. The Court made this clear in the discussion of the way the FCC treated cable and the Internet. The Court said it chose to "affirm the Commission's reasoned decision to discount cable. But we think that the same rationale also applies to the Internet" (*Prometheus Radio Project v. FCC*, 2004, p. 62). The FCC had excluded cable from the local news and information market because it found that there was little local news available and few such channels reach the public. For example, the FCC found that for many who said they watched cable for news, "cable news channels were probably confused with broadcast network news" (*Prometheus Radio Project v. FCC*, 2004, p. 63). Moreover, "only 10 to 15% of cable systems include channels

[a/] Moreover, the Drudge Report is an "aggregator" of news stories from other news outlets' websites and, as such, is not itself normally a "source" of news, national or local. (*Prometheus Radio Project v. FCC*, 2004, pp. 64–65)

that provide local and public affairs programming" (*Prometheus Radio Project v. FCC*, 2004, p. 63).

A close look at the data showed that the Internet exhibits characteristics that are similar to cable. For example, "62 percent of Internet users get local news from newspaper websites, 39% visit television web sites" (*Prometheus Radio Project v. FCC*, 2004, p. 65). The FCC's claim that "the Internet is available everywhere," was challenged by the fact that "almost 30% of Americans do not have Internet access" (*Prometheus Radio Project v. FCC*, 2004, p. 68). The Court concluded that "on remand the Commission must either exclude the Internet from the media selected for inclusion in the Diversity Index or provide a better explanation for why it is included in light of the exclusion of cable" (*Prometheus Radio Project v. FCC*, 2004, p. 68).

The question here is one of degree.

Methodological Problems

Part of the FCC's problem was caused by weak methodology. The FCC recognized the importance of evaluating the use of the media.[4] To address the issue, it commissioned a survey. Yet, the FCC failed to ask the right questions and proceeded to make rules with admittedly faulty data: "*Unfortunately, we do not have data on this question specifically with regard to local news* and current affairs. The available 'primary source' data address local and national news together and do not show that different media have different importance, in the sense that primary usage differs across media" (FCC Report and Order Rules, pp. 410–411, emphasis added).

In its effort to identify the most important sources of news, the FCC asked a question that combined national and local news: "What single source do you use most often for local or national news and current affairs?" (Nielsen Media Research, 2002). This, of course, destroys the possibility of using this question to specifically assess the importance of local media. Therefore, the FCC fell back on a much weaker question about local sources of news: "What source, if any, have you used in the past 7 days for local news and current affairs?" (Nielsen Media Research, 2002). Obviously, this question doesn't necessarily tell us anything about what people use or rely on the most for local news and information. Note, however, that this approach is consistent with the "leak out" view; there is no difference between "any" and "the single most" in that view.

The FCC compounded the problem by mishandling the responses to its weak question. This was an open-ended question in which respondents were allowed multiple responses. Sources they mention first clearly came to their minds. One might infer that what they recall reflects the importance of the sources to them. Unfortunately, the FCC did not simply accept these responses. It followed up with a prompted question directed only at those who did not mention a source. The FCC asked those people who failed to mention a source whether they had used it. The FCC then combined the answers to the two questions, giving them equal weight. This approach was certain to overweight the less prevalent sources by asking many more people about those sources a second time with a prompted question. This methodology, which treats first and second responses equally, would, of course, be consistent with the "leak out" theory, because whispers and shouts are equal in importance in that view.

PART 2: A RIGOROUS APPROACH TO MEDIA MARKET STRUCTURE ANALYSIS DATA AND METHOD—SURVEY RESEARCH

The survey we conducted was designed to correct the analytic problems of media weights. We used identical wording to the FCC, but we asked separate questions about national and local sources of news. To distinguish the national from local object of the question, we gave referents in the question. Furthermore, because the criticism of the FCC approach stems in part from reliance on a "weak" question about the frequency of use, which failed to directly address the importance of sources, we asked a second question about each source that was intended to get at the importance of the sources in determining public opinion. To accommodate multiple sources of information, we adopted the approach used by the Pew Research Center for People and the Press (2004) so that primary and secondary sources can be distinguished:

The Interviewer reads the same list of potential sources twice:

> Now thinking about national issues, like the Presidential election or the war in Iraq, what single source do you use most often for news and information?
>
> And what do you use second most often?
>
> Which single source is most important in determining your opinion about national issues?
>
> And what source is second most important?
>
> Now thinking about local issues, like the a city council election or school, police and fire department services, what single source do you use most often for news and information?
>
> And what do you use second most often?

Which single source is most important in determining your opinion about local issues?

And what source is second most important?

These survey questions address the problems of weights by distinguishing between national and local sources of news and information. We use the survey responses to define the media weights. The "value" to a viewer, listener, or reader is defined as its influence in forming opinions.

Defining Geographic Markets

The survey questions address the issue of the "value" of each medium. They do not address their market reach. Thus the survey data must be combined with available data on media markets. To build a general model of media markets we have compiled data on the market shares of all TV stations, daily newspapers, weekly newspapers, and radio stations (see Table 10.1). Following the Court's reasoning, the exercise of estimating the size and make-up of the local news and information market is one of identifying which sources of independent local news respondents use.

We followed the FCC's (2003) general approach to geographic market definition, which seems reasonable. However, unlike the FCC, which ignored the size of the audience of each type of product, we focus on estimating the average daily output of relevant news and information for each media firm in the market. In defining the market on a city-by-city basis, with the household as the unit of analysis, we include the following:

- Households that use television during news day parts on an average daily basis.
- Listeners who tune into news and talk and information channels on a routine basis.
- Daily circulation of newspapers.
- Weekly circulation of newspapers (converted to an average daily basis).
- The percentage of the population that uses the Internet on a routine basis.

For the purpose of intensive analysis, we focus on the 10 markets that the FCC used to illustrate its index.

Weeklies

Weeklies provide a good example and starting point for how to proceed. We find that weeklies are a surprisingly influential source of local news. However,

TABLE 10.1

Constructing the Media Market Measures

Media weights

Weighted Average of first and second mentions for usage and influence (Consumer Federation/Consumers Union Survey).

Reach

Television = All channels in the DMA assumed to reach population in city. Population reached is households using television (HUT) in early evening and late evening day parts (news day parts) from BIA Financial, Television Market Reports (2003). City population from Arbitron (Market Ranks: Spring 2004)

HUT (news day parts) × City Population

Dailies = Average daily circulation (Editor and Publisher Database, 2003; Beacons Newspapers, 2003)

Weeklies = Average daily circulation (average weekly circulation divided by 7; Beacons Newspapers, 2003)

Radio = Households using news/information/talk programming (AHQ; Arbitron, Radio Today, 2004)

AHQ (News/Info/Talk in the region) × City Population

Internet = Access to the Internet is assumed to be 70%; 33% of those with Internet access assumed to have routine daily use for news gathering (Madde, 2003).

City Population .7 * .33

Concentration

Television = Local Commercial share (BIA Financial, Television Market Reports, 2003)

Dailies = Average daily circulation (Editor and Publisher Database, 2003; Beacons Newspapers, 2003)

Weeklies = Weekly circulation (Beacons Newspapers, 2003)

Radio = Revenue market share (Federal Communications Commission, Radio Industry Review 2002: Trends in Ownership, Formats, and Finance, Media Ownership Working Group Study 11, September 2002, Appendix D)

Internet = Assumed to be atomistically competitive, 100 equal-sized voices

Note. DMA = designated market area.

weeklies are a very targeted source of information. Indeed, they may be influential precisely because they are so targeted. They deal with the microlevel detail that is directly relevant to the neighborhood or community. Because they are targeted they are not widely circulated. They are not sold all over a city on newsstands. A city may have a hundred weeklies, but only a few are readily available to the average citizen. Thus, it is important to factor circulation and the geographic reach of the source. We included all the weeklies in the Designated Market Area (DMA). This overstates the reach of weeklies, because most weeklies are only available in a restricted area. However, the small circulation, particularly when the weekly circulation is converted to daily equivalents to render it comparable to the daily reach of the other media, compensates for this.

For weeklies, we used the average circulation (from the Beacons data base). It is divided by 7 to adjust to the daily basis of other media usage. Concentration ratios were calculated based on the total circulation of papers throughout the DMA.

Radio

If weeklies are the most "micro" of the local information sources, radio is likely the next most "micro." In counting radio stations, we have the added problem that the vast majority of radio stations do not do news. Many of those that do provide news simply read wire service stories. They are not independent sources of local news as defined by the Court.

To estimate the reach of radio news and information dissemination, we used the Arbitron rating for households that listen to news, talk, and information (Arbitron, 2004). Arbitron provides this data at the regional level. We multiplied by the population of the city. Concentration ratios were taken from the FCC and converted to the equivalents of equal-sized voices (Williams & Roberts, 2002, Appendix F).

Newspapers

In contrast to radio, which is the least news intensive of the media, daily newspapers are predominantly dedicated to news and cover a wider geographic area, usually a city or county (Cooper, 2003). In an earlier analysis, we found that the daily newspaper circulation in large metropolitan areas tends to be highly differentiated by county. Figure 10.2 shows the figures for the counties in the Los Angeles area, which is one of the least concentrated markets in the United States. We used average daily circulation for newspapers (the *Editor and Publisher* and Beacon data bases). The FCC defined daily newspaper markets as a city, apparently following Arbitron market areas, so we based the concentration ratio only on the newspapers included in the FCC analysis.

Broadcast Television

Because most households receive their television signals from cable or satellite and local stations have the right to be carried, they tend to be the most "macro" medium. They are available through a wider area, although not all stations are available throughout the DMA (which is the unit of analysis for the television industry).

However, only about half of all local stations provide news. All TV stations within a DMA are included because their signals are generally available. Based

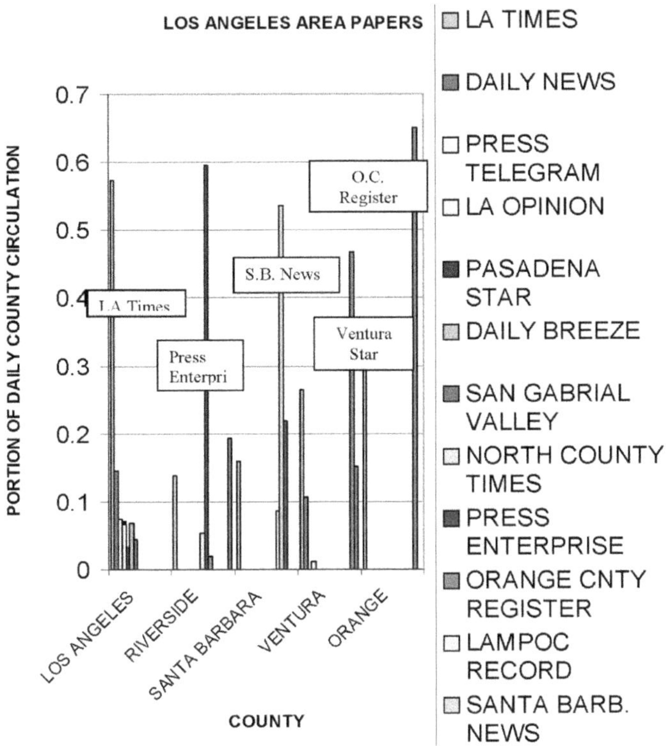

Figure 10.2. Local papers dominate home counties.

on Nielson ratings as reported in BIA Television Market Report, 2003, we used households using television (HUT) in the day parts that are usually devoted to news as the base of viewers. We use the HUT figure as the average of the early evening (e.g., 4 p.m. to 6 p.m. eastern) and late evening (e.g.. 11 p.m. to 11:30 p.m.) news day parts. Although this implicitly assumes that all local TV stations provide news, which is not the case, in earlier analysis we have shown that the simple count of broadcasters that provide local news is close to the concentration ratio based on the viewer-based HHI. The largest firms that contribute most to the HHI are likely to be represented in each city in the DMA and they provide news.

The news day part of HUT was multiplied by the city population. The HUT analysis includes noncommercial stations. However, market shares were based on the local commercial audience viewing share as calculated by BIA Financial. This overestimates concentration slightly, because noncommercial stations are excluded.

Internet

We use the 70% figure cited by the Court for penetration of the Internet. Survey evidence indicates that less than one third of those with Internet access use it for news and information on a daily basis (Madde, 2003). The Internet market was assumed to be atomistically competitive, with 100 equal-sized competitors. If ISP market share were used, the number would be closer to 10-equal sized competitors. We conducted the analysis with the Internet included and excluded, because the Court left that question up in the air.

RESULTS

Sources of Local News Differ Dramatically from Sources of National News

Because we are stressing the difference between national and local sources, we begin the analysis by comparing our approach to asking people about their most frequent sources of national news and information to the December 19, 2003, to January 4, 2004, survey results obtained by the Pew Research Center for People and The Press (Pew Research Center for People and the Press, 2004). Pew asked about national news; the results are very similar to ours (see Fig. 10.3).

The results for both the first mentions and the total mentions are very similar. For national news, television dominates in both surveys, getting the first mention over 60% of the time. Newspapers are next, with first mentions in the midteens. Radio and the Internet are 10% or slightly less.

Total mentions are similar. Throughout this analysis, whenever we show the sum of first and second mentions, we present them as a percentage of the total mentions. This is essentially what the FCC did by creating an index that summed to 100%. In both surveys, newspapers move up as a percentage of total (first plus second) mentions, whereas TV declines. Radio and the Internet remain at around 10%. In fact, these national results have been quite stable for over a decade. Over the course of the past dozen years, the Internet appears to have reduced the importance of newspapers, radio and other sources of national news by a few percentage points (see Fig. 10.4).

A careful analysis of major sources for local news and information tells a very different story. Our survey shows that the difference between sources of national and local news is quite dramatic and consistent with widely recognized patterns of media usage (see Table 10.2).

Newspapers are a much more important source of local news. Daily newspapers are the first mentions of 35% of the respondents compared to

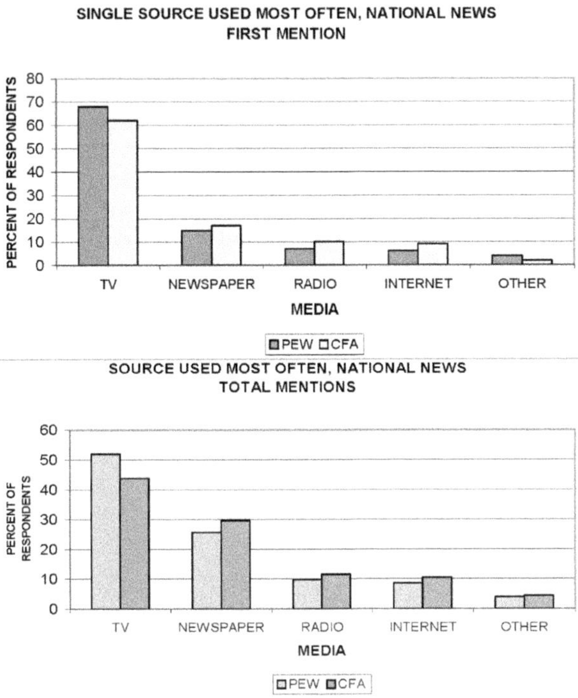

Figure 10.3. National news sources: Pew Center for People and the Press and Consumer Federation of America.

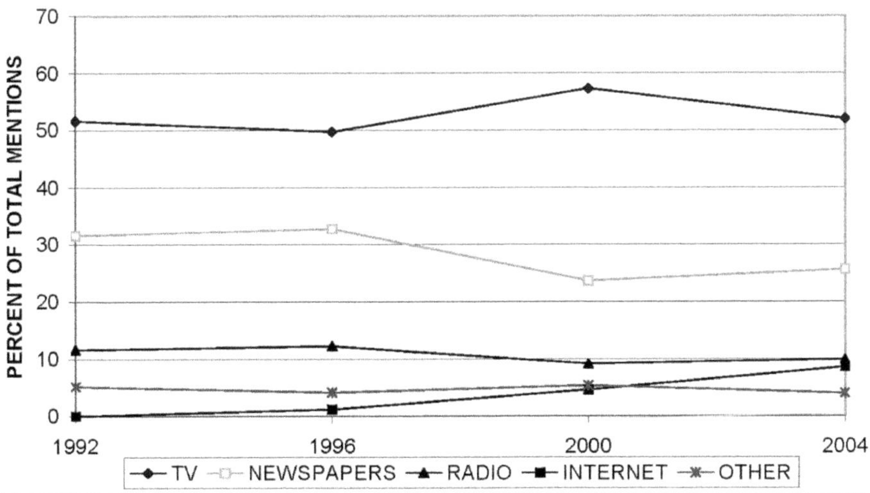

Figure 10.4. Trends of most used media: early in presidential election years.

TABLE 10.2

Frequency of Use and Importance of Local and National News and Information Sources

	First Mention		*Total Mentions*	
	Local	*National*	*Local*	*National*
Most Often Used				
Dailies	35	14	30	21
Weeklies	22	3	20	6
Broadcast	21	27	24	23
Cable	6	35	9	25
Internet	2	10	4	12
Radio	7	9	13	11
Magazines	0	1	0	2
Most Important				
Dailies	34	16	29	22
Weeklies	18	3	17	6
Broadcast	21	24	24	20
Cable	6	30	10	23
Internet	3	10	5	9
Radio	8	9	14	10
Magazines	0	2	0	1

Note. This material is used by permission of the Consumer Federation of America/Consumers Union Survey.

only 14% for national news. Weeklies are the first mention as a source of local news for 22% of respondents, compared to only 3% for national news. Television drops from 62% (for national news) to 27% (for local news). The bulk of the difference is for cable, which is the first mention for national news for 35% of the respondents, but only 6% for local news. Broadcast declines somewhat, from 27% to 21%. The Internet drops from 10% (for national news) to 2% (for local news). Radio is constant at just under 10% for both national and local news.

For total mentions we found the same pattern. Newspapers are much more frequently mentioned for local news, TV and the Internet much less so. Radio is relatively constant.

The results for responses to the question asked about "the most important news source" track the results for responses to "the most often used news source" quite closely. For national news, TV is most frequently cited, followed by newspapers, radio, and the Internet. For local, newspapers are the most important, followed by broadcast television.

These results provide strong support for the Court's lengthy discussion of the Internet. They confirm that the Internet is not a major source of local news, a fact that was repeatedly demonstrated in the FCC proceeding, but ignored by the FCC when it created its Diversity Index. We examined this in detail.

The recent Pew survey did find that the Internet was a particular source of national news for younger respondents (see Fig. 10.5). We also find that the Internet is much more likely to be cited as a source of national news by younger respondents than by the remainder of respondents—about three times as often. However, the Internet drops off dramatically as a source of local news even among this younger age group (see Fig. 10.6). The percentage of respondents age 18 to 24 who mentioned the Internet first drops from 23% for national news to 3% for local news.

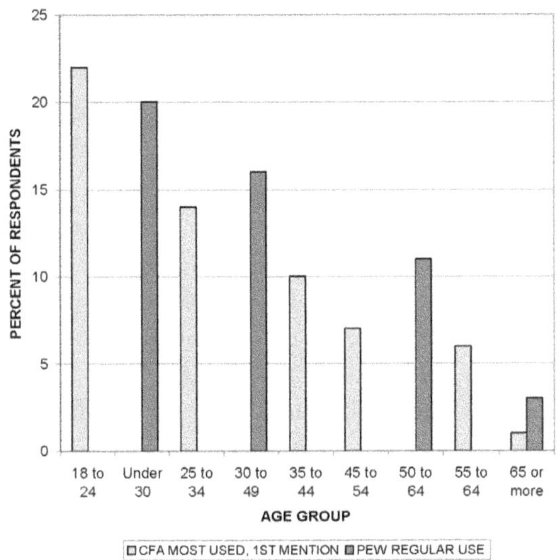

Figure 10.5. Internet use for national news varies strongly by age group.

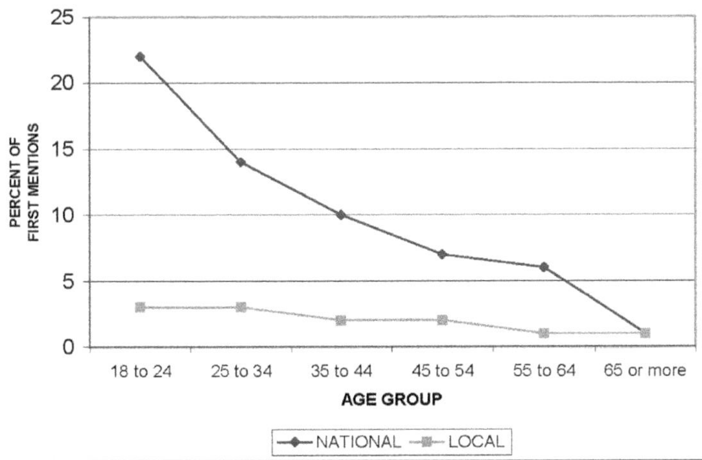

Figure 10.6. Internet use for local news is uniformly low across age groups.

The ability of respondents to distinguish between different media for different types of news is reinforced by their nuanced responses to the television question; this supports the Court's finding that upholds the FCC's decision not to include cable. Our survey question distinguished between cable and broadcast as sources of news. The FCC acknowledged that it had problems with the responses to these questions on its survey, noting that "[a]lthough the responses to one survey question ... suggest ... that cable is a significant source of local news and current affairs, other data from the study casts some doubt on this result ... Our experience suggests that the local cable news response is too high" (FCC, 2003, ¶s 413–414). The huge difference we find between cable as a source of local and national news is consistent with the evidence in the FCC's media ownership record that cable does not provide a significant independent source of local news, whereas broadcast is a very significant source of local news.

Table 10.3 presents a simple approach to combining the responses to the four questions asked about the media. A first response is given twice as much importance as a second response. This calculation is carried out separately for frequency of use and importance. We then take an average of use and importance and turn it into an index, as the FCC did.

Even on the basis of the use-influence questions, alone, the FCC's index dramatically underestimates the importance of newspapers and dramatically overestimates the importance of radio and the Internet. The Internet is given 3 to 4 times the weight it deserves, whereas radio is given 2 to 3 times the weight it deserves. Newspapers should be given 1½ to 2 times as much weight.

In theory we would like to have this type of data for each local market. The cost of such intensive surveying would be prohibitive. However, our analysis of market reach is very much influenced by individual market characteristics, which may compensate for this weakness.

TABLE 10.3

Media Importance as a Source of Local News and Information

Media	*I*	*II*	*III*	*IV*	*V*	*VI*	*VII*
	Use			*Influence*			*Overall*
	1st	*2nd*	*Weighted*	*1st*	*2nd*	*Weighted*	*Weighted*
Media			*(2 × I) + II/Total*			*(2 × IV) + V/Total*	*Avg III + VI*
Broadcast	27	32	33	25	20	28	30
Dailies	34	17	31	35	17	35	33
Weeklies	18	12	19	22	12	23	21
Radio	8	17	13	7	10	10	12
Internet	3	5	4	2	5	4	4

Note. This was calculated by the author (see text).

The Reach of the Media

The weight of the media type is one of the factors that defines its role in the market. The second factor is its reach in the market. This characteristic is specific to the market. The reach of the media varies substantially from market to market.

For example, the Arbitron estimates of listenership for news, talk, and information varies by a factor of 2, from 10% in the South Central region to over 21% in New England. Similarly, households using television varies by a factor of 2 even within the 10 markets studied, from a low of 27% in Charlottesville, VA, to a high of 53% in Birmingham, AL. Cable penetration, which was assumed to make broadcast signals available, varies from 54% to 80%.

Figure 10.7 shows the reach of each medium, which is the share of each medium in the total news and information market as described earlier. The reach of the media varies substantially from market to market.

The media share in these markets is calculated as the product of its influence and reach. An index is created which totals to 100% to parallel the Diversity Index (see Table 10.4). This detailed analysis of local sources of news demonstrates that the FCC's rules derived from the weights it used to create a

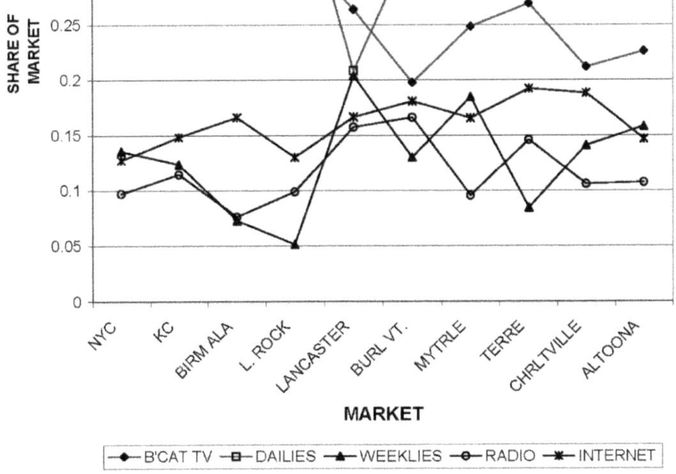

Figure 10.7. Media reach in 10 markets.

TABLE 10.4

Average Media Weights, Reach, and Final Media Share: Compared to Federal Communications Commission Diversity Index (10 Markets)

Media	*Influence*	*Reach*	*Media Share*	*FCC DI*
Broadcast TV	28	27	35	33.8
Dailies	35	32	45	20.2
Weeklies	23	13	12	8.6
Radio	10	12	6	24.8
Internet	4	16	3	12.5

Note. This was calculated by the author (see text). FCC DI = Federal Communications Commission Diversity Index.

Diversity Index are far off the mark. The combination of weight and reach increases the relative importance of newspapers substantially and television slightly, compared to the weight based on the survey. Compared to the Diversity Index, when we factor in the reach of the sources, the importance of newspapers was underestimated by a factor of 2. Weeklies were underestimated by almost 50%. Television and newspapers are the dominant sources by far, accounting for about 80% of the total market.

The underweighting of newspapers is both ironic and important. The ban on holding a television broadcast license and ownership of a newspaper in the same market was the oldest of all the rules that the FCC proposed to change. The change it proposed was more pervasive than for any other rule. The cross media limit it proposed was not much of a limit, as it would have allowed mergers to take place in over 85% of all markets in the country, where over 95% of the population resides. By underestimating the importance of newspapers, the FCC opened the door to a massive wave of cross-media mergers.

The FCC Analysis Underestimates the Concentration of Local Media Markets

Because we have estimated the total local news media market, the market concentration analysis is based on a firm's market share of the media share. For example, a daily newspaper owner with a 30% market share in a market where dailies have a 45% media share would have a 13.5% share of the media market. It would add 182 points to the HHI ($13.5 \times 13.5 = 182$).

The FCC's flawed approach to market structure analysis painted a picture of relatively unconcentrated markets (see Fig. 10.8). Nine of the ten markets for which it presented detailed data were below the concentrated level. One

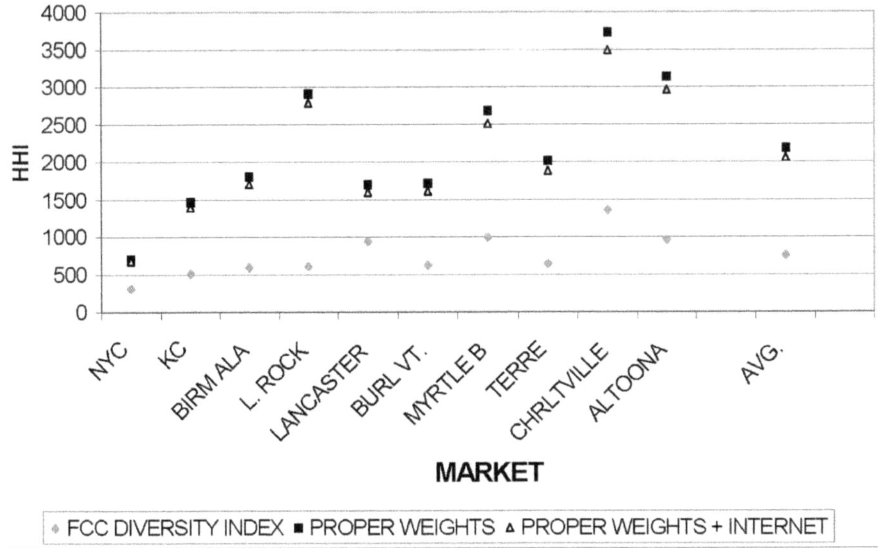

Figure 10.8. Concentration of sample media markets.

was in the moderately concentrated range. We calculated two sets of concentration ratios with the reweighted media and audience market shares of the firms—one included the Internet, one excluded it. We arrive at a very different conclusion from the FCC. Three of the ten markets are moderately concentrated; six are highly concentrated.

The public policy implications of these different conclusions are immense. The point of the analysis is to establish limits on mergers. The Department of Justice's *Merger Guidelines* (1997) indicate that mergers in moderately concentrated markets that raise the HHI by more than 100 points deserve scrutiny. Mergers in highly concentrated markets that raise the HHI more than 50 points are a special concern. The FCC adopted a much more lenient standard, noting that the Department of Justice rarely challenges a merger in court that raised the HHI by less than 400 points. We have argued that the standard should be higher for media mergers and that the FCC has drawn the wrong lesson from the 400-point behavior of the Department of Justice, but those matters can be put to the side here. As shown in Table 10.5, even by the FCC's lax standard, once careful market structure analysis is conducted, most markets would fall in the range where mergers between any major media outlets would not be allowed.

TABLE 10.5

Federal Communications Commission Analysis and Approval of Mergers (Highlighted Mergers Violate the Department of Justice Merger Guidelines; Dashed Lines Indicate Mergers That Would Not Be Allowed Under the Diversity Index)

Base Case Index		*Average Change in Diversity Resulting from Mergers*				
TV Stations in Market	*Average Diversity Index*	*Newspaper and Television*	*Newspaper, TV, and ½ Radio*	*Newspaper and TV Duopoly*	*Newspaper, Radio, and TV Duopoly*	
1	1707	**910**	**1321**	——	——	Rigorous analysis places most markets
2	1316	**731**	**1009**	——	——	
3	1027	**331**	**515**	——	——	
4	928	**242**	**408**	——	——	FCC Diversity Index places most markets here
5	911	**223**	**393**	**376**	**846**	
6	889	**200**	**340**	**357**	**688**	
7	753	121	**247**	242	**533**	
8	885	**152**	**314**	**308**	**734**	
9	705	86	207	172	**473**	
10	635	51	119	101	292	
15	595	48	145	97	302	
20	612	40	128	80	350	

Note. The source is Federal Communications Commission, "Report and Order," In the Matter of 2002 Biennial Regulatory Review—Review of the Commission's Broadcast Ownership Rules and Other Rules Adopted Pursuant to Section 202 of the Telecommunications Act of 1996, Cross Ownership of Broadcast Stations and Newspapers, Rules and Policies Concerning Multiple Ownership of Radio Broadcast Stations in Local Markets, Definition of Radio Markets, MB Docket No. 02–277, MM Dockets 02–235, 01–317, 00–244, July 2, 2003, Appendix D.

A Reality Check

The example that bothered the Court of "a community college television station mak[ing] a greater contribution to viewpoint diversity than a conglomerate that includes the third-largest newspaper in America" provides a reality check (*Prometheus Radio Project v. FCC*, p. 70). In our analysis, the conglomerate (*The New York Times*) accounts for about 9% of the New York media market, whereas the community college TV station accounts for barely a speck.

Interestingly, even that large newspaper conglomerate comes in second in its market, because it happens to reside in a market where the largest news media conglomerate in the world (News Corporation) owns one of the few TV-newspaper combinations (*New York Post,* Fox) that has been waived through the ban and one of the TV duopolies that were made possible by the Telecommunications Act of 1996. It is a close call between the two (News Corporation has just under 10% of market share). But that is the point. When one thinks about the New York media market, the fact that *The New York Times* and News

Corporation come through as the two largest players makes sense. In fact, our earlier qualitative analysis demonstrating that "ownership matters" started by recounting a battle between *The New York Times* and Fox (Cooper, 2003, pp. 45–46).

It is also reassuring to find that the Tribune Company (which also owns a TV-newspaper combination) comes in a very close third. The fourth and fifth largest firms in the market are ABC and NBC, at about half the size of the top three because they do not own newspapers. These are the entities that influence public opinion. The Court demanded that the analysis must get the major features of the media landscape right. Our approach does.

Inconsistencies in the Nine Station Limit

The FCC's lax standard provided the media companies with the opportunity to try an end run around the Court's decision. The Tribune Company asked the Court to lift the stay on mergers in markets with more than 9 TV stations, arguing that the Court had not challenged the threshold and there could be no harm to allowing mergers in such markets.[5] The argument misses the point for two reasons.

First, the nine station standard does not lead to consistent results. The Court remanded the cross media limit for a very precise reason:

> Although the Commission is entitled to deference in deciding where to draw the line between acceptable and unacceptable increases in markets' diversity scores, we do not affirm the seemingly inconsistent manner in which the line was drawn. As the chart above illustrates, the Cross-Media Limits allow some combinations where the increases in Diversity Index scores were generally higher than for other combinations allowed. (*Prometheus Radio Project v. FCC,* 2004, pp. 74–75)

The Court chose as an example a look at midsize markets to demonstrate the inconsistency in the FCC's line drawing:

> Consider the mid-sized markets (four to eight stations), where the Commission found that a combination of a newspaper, a television station, and half the radio stations allowed under the local radio rule would increase the average Diversity index scores in those markets by 408 (four stations) 393 (five), 340 (six), 247 (seven) and 314 (eight) points respectively. These permitted increases seem to belong on the other side of the Commission's line. They are considerably higher than the Diversity Index score increases resulting from other combinations that the Commission permitted, such as the newspaper television combination, 242 (four stations), 223 (five), 200 (six), 121 (seven) and 152 (eight). They are even higher than those resulting

> from the combination of a newspaper and television duopoly—376 (five stations), 357 (six), 242 (seven), and 308 (eight)—which the Commission did not permit. The Commission's failure to provide any explanation for this glaring inconsistency is without doubt arbitrary and capricious, and so provides further basis for remand of the Cross-Media limits. (*Prometheus Radio Project v. FCC*, 2004, p. 75)

As Table 10.6 shows, the nine TV station threshold that the Tribune Company proposes is afflicted with the same inconsistency problem. The mergers it would allow result in much larger increases in Diversity Index scores than some it would prohibit. They would appear to belong even farther on the other side of the line than the ones the Court singled out.

Second, the problem is that even if one accepts the threshold, the flawed analysis mischaracterizes the nature of markets. The FCC has miscounted the voices in the markets.

Because the Diversity Index is irrational, these numbers actually tell us little about how a newspaper-TV-radio merger would actually affect the concentration of the market. Because the assumption of equal market shares is wrong, and most media markets have a small number of large firms, along with several small firms, as I have shown in several filings in the record of the proceeding on which the rule was based, the Diversity Index dramatically underestimates the actual concentration of markets.

The FCC provided detailed analysis of two markets with nine or more TV stations, New York and Little Rock. The Court has already commented on the absurdity of the results for New York, so I focus on Little Rock. The following

TABLE 10.6

Inconsistencies in the Application of the Nine Station Limit

	The Midsize Market Inconsistencies			*Tribune Proposal For Large Market*
Status	*Permitted*	*Prohibited*	*Permitted That Seems to Belong on Other Side of the Federal Communication Commission's Line*	*Permitted Under the Tribune Petition*
Combination	*Newspaper + Television*	*Newspaper + Television Duopoly*	*Newspaper + Television + ½ Radio*	*Newspaper + Television Duopoly + Radio*
4	242	n a	408	473
5	223	376	393	350
6	200	357	340	302
7	121	308	247	292
8	152	242	314	n a

Note. This source is *Prometheus Radio Project v. Federal Communications Commission*, p. 73.

table shows the impact of using actual market shares on the evaluation of the merger. I focus on the worst case scenario merger, which is how the FCC approached the issue, as in the previous discussion.

As Table 10.7 shows, the FCC attributes a 7.1% share of the TV market to the two leading stations based on its equal market shares assumption. Given the media weights, each is attributed a 2.4% share of the total media market. Each adds 5.8 points to the Diversity Index. In fact, the two leading TV stations in Little Rock that have markets shares within the TV media market are 29% and 28%. The would have a 9.8% and 9.5% share of the overall media market and contribute 96 and 90 points respectively.

The largest radio group under the FCC equal shares approach has a 22.7% market share. The FCC reports the leading radio firm has a 37% market share in Little Rock (Williams & Roberts, 2002). The *Arkansas Democrat* is attributed a 33% share of the daily newspaper market, when it actually has a 93% market share.

Individually, these four leading firms contribute only 89 points to the Diversity Index under the FCC assumptions of equal market shares. If they merged, they would contribute 283.9 points to the Diversity Index. This would be a net increase of 194.8 points.

Using the actual market shares, I find that these four firms would contribute 622 points to the Diversity Index. A merger between them would make

TABLE 10.7

Nine Station Markets are Mischaracterized

	FCC Equal Shares			*Audience Included*			*Audience Included, Internet Excluded*	
	Market Share		*DI Points*	*Market Share*		*DI Points*	*Market Share*	*DI Points*
	Within Medium	*in Total Market*		*Within Medium*	*in Total Market*		*in Total Market*	
No. 1 TV Station	7.1	2.4	5.8	29	9.8	96	11.2	125
No. 2 TV Station	7.1	2.4	5.8	28	9.5	90	10.9	119
No. 1 Radio Group	22.7	5.7	32.0	37	9.2	85	10.5	110
No. 1 Daily Newspaper	33.3	6.7	45.5	93	18.7	350	21.4	458
Total			89.1			622		812
Merger Total		16.85	283.9		47.2	2,228	54.0	2,916
Merger Induce Increase		194.8		1,606			2,104	

Note. The source is BIA Financial, *Television Market Report: 2003;* Keith Brown and George Williams, *Consolidation and Advertising Prices in Local Radio Markets* (Federal Communications Commission, Media Bureau Staff Research Paper, September 2002). Editor and Publisher, *Database, 2003.*

FCC = Federal Communications Commission; DI = Diversity Index.

the total contribution to the Diversity Index 2,228 points, for an increase of 1,407 points.

The final column of the table adjusts the overall media market share by excluding the Internet. The Court found that the FCC had not adequately justified its inclusion. Needless to say, this raises the market shares of the leading firms and compounds the problem of assuming that the nine station limit is adequate to protect the public interest.

The order of magnitude of difference between an analysis based on market shares and one based on the unrealistic assumption of equal market shares in a nine station market is quite large. The market shares of TV and radio stations may change a little, but there is no doubt that the nine station threshold does not protect against a huge increase in concentration that far exceeds the standard that the FCC declared.

THE BEGINNING

The FCC set out to create a bright-line test to provide certainty for the industry. On one side of the line all mergers would be approved, with no questions asked, on the other side, they would be rejected. This is not the way the *Merger Guidelines* (1997) work. The Department of Justice uses merger thresholds as a screen, but deals with each merger on a case-by-case basis. The Court accepted the approach, but the FCC's narrow view of the First Amendment led to assumptions and analytic approaches that led to entirely illogical results. The Court demanded that the lines be drawn on the basis of a more realistic map of the media landscape. The information and analyses necessary to portray the media marketplace are, of necessity, social scientific in nature. Much of the data in preliminary form had been introduced in the hearing record and provided the basis for rejecting the FCC's approach.

This is the beginning of a new era in FCC media ownership rules. Although the Supreme Court has not yet spoken, the circuit courts have set off down a path in which social science analysis will play a key role. We believe that this type of analysis meets the standards the Court established. The social science analysis is certainly "messy" in terms of defining markets and finding data to fit the definitions, but the law does not require perfection. It requires a reasonable, consistent, rational fit.

NOTES

[1]As the *Washington Post* puts it in an article headlined

> It is only a matter of time before nearly all barriers to cross-ownership in the media industry are lifted ... In major metropolitan areas it may be possible, even

common, for one giant corporation to own the dominant newspaper, the cable television monopoly, a local broadcast station, several radio stations and even the dominant Internet access provider.

The decisions will give added support to FCC Chairman Michael K. Powell, who views such restrictions as anachronisms in an era of Internet, broadband and satellite technology ... Any excess concentration, Powell argues, can be handled by the Justice Department in its traditional role as enforcer of the antitrust laws.

[2]Shepherd (1985, p. 389) offers the following formula for the Herfindahl-Hirschman Index (HHI):

$$H = \sum_{i=1}^{n} S_i^2 \times 10{,}000$$

where

n = the number of firms

m = the market share of the largest firms (4 for the four firm concentration ratio)

S_i = the share of the ith firm.

The HHI is calculated based on ratios rather than percentages and the decimals are cleared by multiplying by 10,000. For ease of discussion, the Court adopts the convention of describing the calculation in percentages.

[3]The Herfindahl-Hirschman Index can be converted to equal-sized equivalents as follows: Equal-sized voice equivalents = (1/HHI) * 10,000.

[4]"If media differ in importance systematically across respondents (e.g. if television were most important to everyone, and everyone made only minor use of radio to acquire news and current affairs information), *then it would be misleading to weight all responses equally*" (FCC Ownership Rules Order 2003 ¶¶4410; emphasis added).

[5]Motion of Petition Tribune Company For a Partial Lifting of This Court's Stay of the FCC's Cross-Ownership Rules (July 22, 2004; "Mot."). The Court's July 26 Order extended the time for this response until August 13, 2004.

REFERENCES

Arbitron. (2004). *Arbitron radio today*. Retrieved April 4, 2006, from www.arbitron.com/study

Associated Press v. United States, 326 U.S.1, 20. (1945).

Cooper, M. (2003).Testimony on Media Ownership, before The Senate Commerce Committee, October 2, 2003a; Promoting The Public Interest Through Media Ownership Limits: A Critique Of The FCC's Draft Order Based On Rigorous Market Structure Analysis And First Amendment Principles (Consumer Federation of America and Consumers Union, Washington, DC: May 2004), Ex Parte, filed in Federal Communications Commission, In the Matter of 2002 Biennial Regulatory Review—Review of the Commission's Broadcast Ownership Rules and Other Rules Adopted Pursuant to Section 202 of the Telecommunications Act of 1996, Cross Ownership of Broadcast Stations and Newspapers, Rules and Policies Concerning Multiple Ownership of Radio Broadcast Stations in Local Markets, Definition of Radio Markets, MB Docket No. 02–277, MM Dockets 02–235, 01–317, 00–244 July 2, 2003a.

Cooper, M. (2003b). *Media ownership and democracy in the digital information age*. Stanford, CA: Center for Internet and Society.

Department of Justice Merger Guidelines. (1997). Retrieved April 4, 2004, from www.fbi.gov/bc/docs/horizmer.htm

Federal Communications Commission v. National Citizens Committee for Broadcasting 436 U.S. 775 (1978).

Federal Communications Commission, "Report and Order," In the Matter of 2002 Biennial Regulatory Review—Review of the Commission's Broadcast Ownership Rules and Other Rules Adopted Pursuant to Section 202 of the Telecommunications Act of 1996, Cross Ownership of Broadcast Stations and Newspapers, Rules and Policies Concerning Multiple Ownership of Radio Broadcast Stations in Local Markets, Definition of Radio Markets, MB Docket No. 02–277, MM Dockets 02–235, 01–317, 00–244 July 2, 2003, para. 420.

Madde, M. (2003). *America's online pursuits.* Washington, DC: Pew Internet and Life Project.

McCain, J. (2003, October 2). *Opening Statement of Senator John McCain.* Washington, DC: The Senate Commerce Committee, United States Senate Committee on Commerce, Science, and Transportation. Retrieved April 4, 2006, from www.commerce.senate.gov/hearings/testimony.cfm?id=905&wit_id=2360

McConnell v. Federal Election Commission (02–1674) 251 F. Supp. 2d 176, 251 F. Supp. 2d 948 (2003), affirmed in part and reversed in part.

Nielsen Media Research. (2002, September). Consumer survey on media usage (Media Ownership Working Group Study No. 8).

Owen, B. M. (2003). "Statement on Media Ownership Rules," Attachment to Comments of Fox Entertainment Group and Fox Television Stations, Inc., National Broadcasting Company, Inc. and Telemundo Group, Inc., and Viacom, In the Matter of 2002 Biennial Regulatory Review—Review of the Commission's Broadcast Ownership Rules and Other Rules Adopted Pursuant to Section 202 of the Telecommunications Act of 1996, Cross Ownership of Broadcast Stations and Newspapers, Rules and Policies Concerning Multiple Ownership of Radio Broadcast Stations in Local Markets, Definition of Radio Markets, MB Docket No. 02–277, MM Dockets 02–235, 01–317, 00–244, January 2.

Pew Research Center for People and the Press. (2004, January). *Cable and Internet loom large in fragmented political news universe.* Princeton Survey Research Associates.

Powell, M. (2004, June 24). FCC *Chairman Michael Powell Reacts to Third Circuit Media Decision.* Retrieved October 14, 2005, from http://hraunfoss.fcc.gov/edocs_public/ attachmatch/DOC-248793A1.pdf (Accessed October 14, 2005).

Prometheus Radio Project v. Federal Communications Commission (3rd Cir. 2004).

Red Lion Broadcasting v. FCC, 395 U.S. 367 (1969).

Shepherd, W. G. (1985). *The economics of industrial organization.* Englewood Cliffs, NJ: Prentice Hall.

Telecommunications Act of 1996. Pub. Law No. 104-104, 110 Stat 56 (1996).

Turner Broadcasting System, Inc. v. FCC, 512 U.S. 622 (1994).

U.S. Department of Justice & Federal Trade Commission. (1997). *Horizontal merger guidelines, 1997.* Retrieved April 5, 2006, from www.ftc.gov/bc/docs/horizmer.htm

Viscusi, W. K., Vernon, J. M., & Harrington, J. E., Jr. (2001). *Economics of regulation and antitrust.* Cambridge, MA: MIT Press.

Williams, G., & Roberts, S. (2002, September). *Radio industry review 2002: Trends in ownership, format and finance* (Media Ownership Working Group Study No. 11). Washington, DC: Federal Communications Commission.

III

Minorities, Media, and Diversity

11

White Out: The Absence and Stereotyping of People of Color by the Broadcast Networks in Prime Time Entertainment Programming

Leonard M. Baynes
The Ronald H. Brown Center for Civil Rights and Economic Development
St. John's University School of Law

> [F]or too long, women and minorities have faced barriers to working in front and behind the camera .... Our nation benefits when television better reflects the diverse market it serves.
>
> —Former Federal Communications Commission Chairman William Kennard (1999)

In the fall of 1999, the then-new television schedule was announced and "none of the twenty-six new fall programs starred an African American in a leading role, and few featured minorities in secondary roles" (Williams, 2000, p. 100). This absence caused the National Council of La Raza to organize a protest called a "National Brownout" in which they advised their members to refrain from watching television during the week of September 12, 1999 (Fletcher, 1999; Kolker, 1999). At the same time, Kweisi Mfume, the President of the National Association for the Advancement of Colored People (NAACP),[1] threatened a boycott and legal action against the networks' broadcasting licenses based on the belief that the networks were violating the 1934 Communications Act. The major networks scrambled to add actors of color to their previously all-White shows.

Ultimately the major networks and the NAACP announced an agreement in which FOX, CBS, ABC, and NBC agreed to hire more actors, producers, writers, and directors of color (NAACP, 2001). All four networks have hired a vice president of diversity to monitor their progress in hiring writers, directors, actors, and executives from diverse backgrounds (NAACP, 2001). However, ABC's vice president of diversity reports to the senior vice president of human resources, whereas at the other three networks, the vice president of diversity reports directly to the network president (NAACP, 2001). The agreements have been called "vague" because they have no specified goals or timetables.[2] In its report, *Out of Focus—Out of Sync,* the NAACP noted that FOX and CBS established diversity advisory boards that are actively involved in various stages of development, sometimes influencing casting decisions. Neither ABC nor NBC have established a comparable institutional structure to promote diversification (NAACP, 2001).

The networks do know how to program shows that draw from what they at least think is Black life. For example, those networks that emerged over the last 10 years tend to program to those members of society that are not represented by the established networks. It gives the new network an automatic market niche that is otherwise not being filled. So it was no surprise that, in the early years, the FOX network programmed several shows with mostly minority casts like *Martin, Living Single, New York Undercover,* and *In Living Color* (Lowry, Jensen, & Braxton, 1999). However, once FOX became established and won acclaim for some of its other shows like the *X-Files* and *Ally McBeal,* it abandoned this programming and demographic and its programming became as White as that of the other major networks (Patterson, 2001).

In the past, many feared that the two youngest networks, UPN and WB, would abandon their initial emphasis on the minority demographic once they became more established. Of course, the recent merger of the two networks to form the new CW Network raises similar concerns.[3] In 1999, 32% of UPN and 27% of WB viewers were African American (Dawidziak and Feran, 1999). Forty-five percent of the characters on UPN, and 23% of the characters on WB, were African American ("Minorities Are Relatively Prevalent on Television," 1999). Despite the presence of African Americans on these networks, the WB programs seemed to be targeted more toward young, White audiences (Lowry et al., 1999),[4] and the UPN Black-oriented shows were segregated to Monday nights (Long, 2002).

Although the networks and the NAACP have agreed on how to diversify the shows and their writing staffs ("NAACP Reports Little Progress in Network Diversity," 2001), in August 2001, Mfume said that he found that the major networks had made little progress in diversifying what we see on television

(Braxton, 2001a). In fact, prior to the events of September 11, 2001, he said that he would probably propose to the NAACP Board of Directors that ABC, CBS, NBC, and FOX be singled out for a "massive, targeted and sustained economic boycott" (Braxton, 2001a, p. F1). In 2002, a multi-ethnic coalition (consisting of the NAACP, National Latino Media Council, American Indians in Film & Television, and the Asian Pacific American Coalition) gave low marks to the networks for diversity in their programming. This coalition gave ABC a D-minus, CBS a D-plus, FOX earned a C-minus, and NBC received the highest grade, a C (Braxton, 2002a).

Children Now's 2001 to 2002 Prime Time Diversity Report indicated that dramas were five times more likely than comedies to feature people of color as recurring cast members. The report indicated that 39% of dramas featured mixed opening credit casts compared to 7% of situation comedies. More than two thirds of the drama series featured at least one racial minority character in a primary recurring role. The report indicated that the 2001 to 2002 season featured more programming with racially homogenous casts that were either all Black or all White. Only 25% of the season's programs featured casts that were racially mixed. Most of the diversity gains over the past 3 years have been attributable to nonrecurring and secondary characters. For example, in the 2001 to 2002 season, Latinos and Latinas comprised 4% of the entire prime time population but only 2% of the opening credit cast. Similarly, Asian Americans comprised 3% of the total prime time population but only 1% of the opening credit cast.

Several members of Congress have been concerned about the media's negative minority stereotypes. In August 2001, Congressmen Eliot Engel, Michael Makoto Honda, and Bobby Lee Rush introduced legislation to amend the Communications Act so as to direct the FCC to establish an office on victims of media bias (H.R. 2700, 107th Cong., 2001). Several other countries handle the problems of negative media stereotypes by actually regulating content of their broadcasters.[5]

The Federal government has an interest in regulating these absences and stereotypes because it owns the electronic spectrum through which the broadcast signal travels.[6] Under the Communications Act of 1934, the FCC awards licenses to broadcasters in trust for, and as fiduciaries of, the American public [see 47 U.S.C. Sections 307(a), 309(a), 2001]. Because of the electronic media's almost-omnipresence in the lives of our citizens, it has a very strong influence over the cultural, political, social, and racial attitudes of our society (Graves, 1999). Ninety-eight percent of U.S. homes have a television set; 49% have more than one set (Adler & Pittle, 1984). The average family watches over 7 hr of television a day (Gardner, 1985; Hall, 1994; Rubin, 1990).

The absence and the stereotyping of people of color by the mass media is a source of concern for all (Chandrasekaran, 1996). Because we live in a relatively segregated country, many Whites often have more electronic, rather than personal, encounters with people of color (Graves, 1999). Therefore, their attitudes and actions are likely to be shaped by what they see on television (see generally, Entman & Rojecki, 2000). Some African Americans and Latinos and Latinas may also have similarly limited encounters of Whites. Some live in hyper segregated communities with few contacts with members of other racial groups (Massey & Denton, 1993). Broadcast television and its images and representations are very important because television can be the common meeting ground for all Americans. However, because Nielsen surveys show that African Americans and Latinos and Latinas are watching different programming than White Americans (see Sterngold, 1998), broadcast television fails to play this important role as the societal meeting ground. In addition, broadcast television fails to serve the minority audiences, which comprise almost 30% of the U.S. population, by neglecting to provide these groups with programming they desire. This failure is bad business (Baynes, 2003a) and violates the broadcasters' public interest obligations under the Communications Act of 1934 (discussed later) and should be grounds for FCC disciplinary action against the broadcasters.[7]

The purpose of this chapter is not to advocate censorship or to point fingers at any single television program or network. Its purpose is to start the process of engaging in a useful and productive dialogue on the media's responsibility to portray full-bodied and realistic depictions of all people of color on television in entertainment programming. The depictions of people of color by the media should avoid the perpetuation of harmful stereotypes.

This chapter explores how the television networks currently depict racial and ethnic minorities, and explores what the Federal Communications Commission (FCC) should do, pursuant to the Federal Communications Act, to correct this situation. This chapter gives the FCC a possible way to resolve this recurring problem by evaluating network programs for discrimination, through the lens of the "ordinary viewer."

The next section of this chapter examines how stereotypes of racial minority groups are abhorrent. The next section examines how discrimination by the advertising industry affects the broadcasters' choice of programming. The following section explores how casting decisions are made. The next section examines how African Americans, Latinos and Latinas, Asian Pacific Americans, and Native Americans, respectively, are portrayed by the entertainment media. The following section considers why cable television is not a substitute for broadcasting when it comes to minority depictions. The next section analyzes the social consequences of these stereotypical character portrayals. In the following section, this chapter describes and advocates that the FCC adopt an "ordinary viewer test" to find broadcasters in violation of the Federal Communications Act when they fail to cast people of color or when they broadcast patently offensive images of them. The last section concludes that the "ordinary viewer test"[8] is the best way to remedy these media absences and stereotypes.

THE ABHORRENCE OF STEREOTYPES

Historic Governmental Concerns About Media Images of People of Color

The government has repeatedly expressed concern about the absence and stereotyping of people of color in the media. After the civil unrest in several African American communities in the 1960s, President Johnson appointed Governor Otto Kerner of Illinois to chair the National Advisory Committee on Civil Disorders (the "Kerner Commission") to investigate "what happened," "why ... it happen[ed]," and "what [could] be done to prevent it from happening again" (see Report of the National Advisory Commission on Civil Disorders [hereinafter Civil Disorders], 1968, p. 1). As part of its charge, the Kerner Commission examined the media's depiction of people of color and found that

> television and print media failed to communicate to the majority of their audience—which is white—a sense of the degradation, misery, and hopelessness of living in the ghetto. They [had also failed to] communicate to whites a feeling for the difficulties and frustrations of being a[n] [African American] in the United States. (Civil Disorders, 1968, p. 383)

Moreover, the Kerner Commission found that "[the media had] not shown understanding or appreciation of—and thus [had] not communicated—a sense of [African American] culture, thought, or history" (Civil Disorders, 1968, p. 383). The report concluded that the media must become more sensitive to the portrayal of minorities in order to prevent the persistence of stereotypical images. As if it were talking about current conditions with African Americans, Latinos and Latinas, Asian Americans, and Native Americans, the Kerner Commission noted that "most television programming ignores the fact that an appreciable part of their audience is black" (Civil Disorders, 1968, p. 383). Furthermore, the Kerner Commission stated that the media act as if African Americans do not "watch television, give birth, marry, die, and go to PTA meetings " (Civil Disorders, 1968, p. 383).

In 1977, the United States Civil Rights Commission conducted a study of the portrayal of people of color on network news and in dramatic programs ("Window Dressing on the Set," 1977). The study concluded that people of color were underrepresented on television, but when they did appear they were frequently seen in token or stereotypical roles. The study concluded that the portrayal of people of color is critically important to American society because "viewers' beliefs, attitudes, and behaviors may be affected by what they see on television" ("Window Dressing on the Set," 1977, p. 1).

Two years later the U.S. Civil Rights Commission conducted another survey of this topic and found that stereotyping of people of color by the media continued and in some instances worsened.[9]

The U.S. government has had consistent and long-term concerns over media absences and stereotyping of people of color. It has also interpreted these absences and stereotypes as having a deleterious effect on these groups. Section 151 of the Communications Act makes race discrimination illegal and the FCC has interpreted the lack of minority representations as a violation of a broadcaster's public interest mandate under section 309(k). To help the FCC analyze future cases of oversight, I suggest that the FCC use an "ordinary viewer" test to analyze these questions.

Concerns About Media Stereotypes by Prominent People of Color

Historically, prominent people of color have decried how society stereotyped them and believed that a correlation existed between media portrayals and their status in society. These commentators have analyzed how their group was depicted by the larger society and how these stereotypes can affect one's ability to succeed in society. Very often the identity of people of color is two-pronged. The first prong involves the individual's personal view of himself or herself and the second derives from society's view of the racial group to which the individual belongs.

W. E. B. DuBois (1997) described this two-pronged identity, stating the following:

> [T]he [African American] is sort of the son, born with a veil, and gifted with second sight in this American world,—a world which yields him no true self-consciousness, but only lets him see himself through the revelation of the other world. It is a peculiar sensation, this double-consciousness, this sense of always looking at one's self through the eyes of others ... One ever feels his two-ness ... The history of the [African American] is the history of this strife,—this longing to attain self-conscious manhood, to merge his double self into a better and truer self. (1997, pp. 38–39)

Over the last several years, several prominent Black entertainment figures and organizations have criticized network depictions of African Americans. Film director Spike Lee criticized the networks for airing shows that feed stereotypes about Blacks, stating "I would rather see *Amos and Andy* .... At least they were just straight-up Uncle Tommin. We've gone backwards" (Watkins & Emerson, 2000, p. 161). Bill Cosby has said that he "finds it difficult, often painful, to watch television" because he sees himself "as an African American who is exploited" (Brown, 1997, p. 6), and that he "can't believe the way African Americans are being portrayed on the small screen" (Randolph, 1994, p. 100).

Whites, on the other hand, do not have to worry about White media absences or stereotypes for several reasons (see generally Ross, 1998). First, few media genres exist where Whites are wholly absent. It is more often that the White images dominate. These all-White images "explicitly and implicitly connote whose values, points of view, and symbols are important" (Robinson, 1995, p. 74). "Dominant white images authenticated a world that did not include blacks" (Robinson, 1995, p. 75). Second, there are very few negative stereotypes against Whites as a group (see McIntosh, 1997, pp. 295–296). Whites often are seen more as individuals rather than as members of a group (see McIntosh, 1997; see Tuv, 2002). Thus, if there is a negative depiction of a White person, it would be seen as related only to that particular White individual and not ascribed to Whites as a group (see Jensen, 1998). The negative stereotypes that do refer to Whites are usually isolated to some specific group of Whites—such as those who live in trailers, those who are from Appalachia, and those who might have certain southern European origins (see generally Ignatiev, 1995; Sacks, 1997). These stereotypes do not apply to all Whites as a class or group, just to some particular subcategories. In other words, it is not the "Whiteness" of the group members that account for the stereotype against them, but some other perceived characteristic. As a consequence of being the dominant group in society, Whites are often less vulnerable to the consequences of media absences and stereotypes (see Ignatiev, 1995).

Most Whites today do not overtly espouse racist views of minority groups (see "A Conversation on Race," 2000; Gaiter, 1999). It is estimated that only 20% of Whites hold such traditional overtly racist views (Entman et al., 1998). Whites are more likely to have more ambivalent feelings about race issues and individuals of different races (see Schulman, Bobo, Krysan, & Steeh, 1997). These feelings are often conflicted, ranging from animosity at times to admiration (see Entman & Rojecki, 2000). However, many Whites still have stereotypical views of people of color. For instance, in a 1990 General Social Survey from the University of Chicago, 52.8% of respondents considered violence as a characteristic of African Americans, 42.8% considered violence as an attribute of Latinos and Latinas, 21.3% considered violence as a characteristic of Asian Americans, and only 18.8% considered violence as a characteristic of Whites (Entman et al., 1998). The same survey found that 57.1% believed African Americans prefer welfare to work, 45.6% believed the same is true of Latinos and Latinas, 19.1% believed the same for Asian Americans, and only 4.6% believed that Whites prefer welfare (Entman et al., 1998). In 1996, the survey results indicated that 27.8% of the respondents believed that African Americans were lazy, 18.1% believed that Latinos and Latinas were lazy, and 7% believed that Whites were lazy (Entman et al., 1998). These results rate Whites most favorably and African Americans least.

In an AARP (American Association of Retired Persons, 2004) survey of racial attitudes, 52% of Whites acknowledged that society treats them better than African Americans (p. 7). However, Whites responded overwhelmingly that African Americans (76%) and Latinos and Latinas (77%) were treated treated fairly (p. 17). In contrast, only 38% of African Americans and only 48% of Latinos and Latinas responded respectively that they were treated fairly (p. 17). More specifically, 61% of Whites responded that African Americans have equal job opportunities to Whites whereas only 12% of African Americans agreed (p. 47). Similarly, 51% of Whites responded that Latinos and Latinas had equal job opportunities to Whites whereas only 40% of Latinos and Latinas agreed (p. 48). Sixty-nine percent of African Americans and 52% of Latinos and Latinas reported at least one incident of unfair treatment in the past 30 days or of being discriminated at some point during their lives (p. 7). In contrast, 21% of Whites claim that they experienced at least one incident of "reverse discrimination" (p. 7).

These negative stereotypes of people of color and disagreement about how people of color are treated are of concern. The stereotypes are learned from the prejudices of friends and family members. Some of these stereotypes may be learned through limited, but bad experiences. Because we live in a fairly segregated society, however, most of these stereotypes are probably learned through electronic encounters, that is, what people see on television (see Jensen, 1998). Consequently, the absence and stereotyping of people of color by the broadcast media has an effect on the attitudes that White people have toward people of color and the attitudes that each group has about itself. These stereotypical views influence policy. The programs or issues that are more likely to be perceived to be directed at, or to effect, people of color are profoundly influenced by negative stereotypes (Entman & Rojecki, 2000). For example, if I hold the views of a majority of Whites, believing that African Americans and Latinos and Latinas prefer welfare to work, but Whites prefer work over welfare, I would support candidates who require welfare recipients to work in almost all circumstances. If I believe that African Americans and Latinos and Latinas are more violent than Whites, I would also support stiff penalties for convicted criminals in almost all circumstances. These negative stereotypes not only influence policy, but they also influence us in our everyday dealings with each other.[10] These negative stereotypes may lead to discrimination against people of color in procuring employment, in renting housing, and in everyday life.

ADVERTISING DISCRIMINATION

In the broadcast industry, profit maximization depends on the quantity and the price of the commercials sold (see Wilkerson, 1996). Advertisers often say they are looking for the right demographics and will often pay higher advertising rates for a younger, more affluent (and most likely White) audience.[11] This "search" for the "right audience demographics" is reminiscent of past advertiser practices in refusing to place spots on *The Nat "King" Cole Show, East Side West Side,* or *I Spy* because of fear of Southern boycotts of their products (see generally Baynes, 2003a). This "search" may merely be a pretext designed to avoid advertising on programs that have large minority viewership. Because advertising drives programming, and advertisers search for certain demographics, advertisers will avoid airing commercials during programs that they believe do not appeal to the desired demographic. In turn, broadcasters will air programming that appeals to the "right" demographic to win advertising. The discrimination that exists against people of color by the broadcast network is driven by the profit structure of the broadcast industry, which relies almost exclusively on advertisers for their revenues. Because the market fails to remedy advertising discrimination and its corollary effect on broadcast discrimination, it is appropriate for the government to regulate.

An FCC study on advertising practices may be illustrative of the fact that advertisers have engaged in prejudicial thinking in deciding where to place advertisements ("When Being No. 1 Is Not Enough," 2002). In terms of minority-formatted and minority-owned radio stations, some advertisers had practices, called "No Urban/Spanish Dictates," that prohibited the placement of advertisements on radio stations that air urban, Black or Spanish-language formats ("When Being No. 1 Is Not Enough," 2002). When these radio stations did receive advertising, the rates were often discounted from what other stations received. Consequently, although these minority-formatted stations in certain markets may have larger audiences[12] than other stations, the minority-formatted radio stations earn less advertising revenue per listener than other radio stations ("When Being No. 1 Is Not Enough," 2002). The study indicated that approximately 90% of the minority broadcasters encountered the "No Minority / Spanish Dictates" ("When Being No. 1 Is Not Enough," 2002). The minority broadcasters estimated that 61% of the advertisements placed on their radio stations were discounted, and they estimated the size of the minority discount to be 59% ("When Being No. 1 Is Not Enough," 2002). The No Minority / Spanish Dictates together with the minority discounts were estimated to reduce revenues for these stations by 63% (Briefing Notes on Advertising Study, 1998).

The FCC study contains anecdotal evidence that the advertisers stereotyped the minority consumer, resulting in the advertisers' lack of interest in placing advertisements on minority-formatted radio stations. Several of the most outrageous comments reported follow. In a written report to its sales force, Katz Radio Group stated the following: "Get buyers to understand that WABC is one of the most upscale select stations in New York. We must get the buying community to understand and appreciate the unique qualitative, personality, and foreground profile of WABC. Advertisers should want prospects not suspects" ("When Being No. 1 Is Not Enough," 2002, p. 43). Minority station salespeople soliciting an advertisement from the Beef Council were told that the Council was not going to buy advertising time on urban-formatted radio stations because "Black people don't eat beef" ("When Being No. 1 Is Not Enough," 2002, pp. 1–2). A major mayonnaise manufacturer refused to buy commercial time based on the perception that "Black people don't eat mayonnaise" ("When Being No. 1 Is Not Enough," 2002, pp. 1–2). One of the study respondents reported the following:

> I recall being in front of a buyer and we were discussing at the time Ivory Soap and the buyer was telling me they were not going to buy the stations. And the question was: "Why not?" And they said, "Well, we have studies that show that Hispanics don't bathe as frequently as non-Hispanics." ("When Being No. 1 Is Not Enough," 2002, p. 37; interview with Luis Alvares, Local Sales Manager, WSKQ and WPAT, Spanish Broadcasting System)

The report noted that there are categories of products in which people of color are predominant customers. For example, African Americans represent 60% to 70% of the purchasers of expensive cognacs, but advertisers almost never directly target them ("When Being No. 1 Is Not Enough," 2002; interview with Byron Lewis, Chairman and CEO of The UniWorld Group).[13]

Advertisers are sometimes concerned that advertising to customers of color will cause too many of them to actually patronize their businesses. For example, Michael Banks, Station Manager of the urban-formatted station,

WBGE-FM, was told the following by one potential advertiser: "Your station will bring too many Black people to my place of business" (Briefing Notes on Advertising Study, 1998, p. 6).

Luis Alvarez, the Sales Manager of WSKQ and WPAT, Spanish Broadcasting System, reported that he had a similar experience: "I was managing a station where the sales [representative] came back and she was practically in tears because the agency had told her that [Macy's Department Store] said that the reason they don't advertise in the Hispanic market ... was because their pilferage will increase" (Briefing Notes on Advertising Study, 1998, p. 42).

The FCC study reviewed the practices of the advertisers only with respect to minority-owned and minority-formatted radio stations. The FCC study reported that there were very few minority-owned or minority-formatted televisions stations. The FCC study did not evaluate the advertising practices on network television shows. But it seems likely that advertisers probably hold the same views toward advertising on network television shows that have minority themes.

The FCC's failure to act against the broadcast networks and their possible complicity in the discrimination by advertisers may make the FCC a passive participant in the broadcast networks' discrimination. Justice O'Connor has found discrimination as a result of passive participation sufficient grounds for establishing a race-based affirmative action program (*City of Richmond v. J. A. Croson Co.*, 1989).[14] For example, if prime contractors on a government project were discriminating against minorities and this discrimination became known to the government, the government might be deemed sufficiently complicit (a kind of joint tortfeasor, coconspirator, or aider and abettor) to allow for remedial action. This chapter advocates invoking an "ordinary viewer test" to determine whether a broadcaster is discriminating in violation of the Communications Act.

CASTING DECISIONS

As scripts develop, casting directors stay in touch with writers and producers. Specific descriptions of characters are sent to agents and posted on the Internet (see generally Breakdown Services Ltd., 2003; see also Calvo, 1999). Rene Balcer, the White executive producer of the NBC crime drama *Law & Order,* said that the story dictates "who's going to be what" (Littlefield, 1999, p. F10). Balcer indicated that "there is a phenomenon that if you don't specify race in a script, nine times out of ten a white person will be cast—that if you want a person of color you write it down and if you want a white person you don't write it" (Littlefield, 1999, p. F10). Casting decisions are not about who is best qualified for the role or who is the best actor, but instead are about fitting a certain type that the directors and writers want in the role (Williams, 2000). The personality of a television show is subtly shaped by its actors' stature, height, weight, features, skin, and hair color (see also Williams, 2000). By failing to consider people of color for these roles, it appears that the casting directors consider these factors only when it comes to White actors but not for actors of color (Williams, 2000). These casting decisions appear to eliminate actors of color almost by default. How can a television show occurring in New York City, like *Friends* or *Seinfeld,* have an all-White cast? Since New York City has a majority minority population, the casting decisions in *Seinfeld* and *Friends* are not reflective of New York's reality. Instead, it is someone's fantasy. Of course, television need not portray reality, but the absence of racial and ethnic groups from the media becomes a problem to the extent it suggests that the excluded groups do not matter or do not exist. Correspondingly, when the presented images of people of color are stereotypical, the larger society relies on these images to define the group (Roman, 2000).

This absence of minority images has an effect on the availability of acting roles for actors of color. In 1998, African American actors filled 13.4% of all roles in television series, movies, and miniseries (Diuguid & Rivers, 2000). But on the four major networks, only 10% of all characters were African American in 1998, compared with 17% in the 1992 to 1993 season (Hall, 1999). Hispanic actors filled 3.3% of the remaining roles in 1998, whereas Asian American actors filled 1.9% and Native American actors 0.2%. White actors held 78.9% of the roles in 1998 (Hall, 1999). Of the 839 writers currently employed on prime time network shows, only 55 are African American (Williams, 2000). Eighty-three percent of those African American writers are employed on Black-themed shows (Braxton, 1999). Only eleven Latino and three Asian American writers were working on prime-time series in 1999 (Braxton, 1999). There are no Native American writers employed on a prime time series (Braxton, 1999). There is also a dearth of minority directors (Braxton, 2002b). A recent Directors Guild of America study shows that, of the 40 most popular series of the 2000 to 2001 season, 80% of the drama and comedy episodes were directed by White men. African American men directed 3% of the total, Latino men 2%, Asian American men about 1%. White women directed 11% of the total. The participation of women of color as directors was limited to only two Asian American women (Braxton, 2002b).

BROADCAST MEDIA STEREOTYPES

Historically, people of color have either been absent or stereotyped by the media. In the film documentary *Ethnic Notions* (1986), producer/director Marlon

Riggs shows how African Americans were historically stereotyped by society and the media. African Americans are not the sole victims of racial stereotypes. Richard Delgado and Jean Stefanic have written about the different yet subtly common ways that members of American racial and ethnic minority groups have been stereotyped (Delgado and Stefanic, 1992). The following sections describe how each of the major minority racial groups—African Americans, Latinos and Latinas, Asian Americans, American Indians, and Arab Americans—have been portrayed by broadcast television.

Depictions of African Americans

Although there was an absence of new roles for African Americans in new shows in the 1999 to 2000 prime time season, more African Americans were featured in prime time television shows (Williams, 2000) than ever before. African Americans comprise an ever larger and growing segment of the viewing audience. Black households watch an average of 70 hr of television per week as compared to 50 hr for other households (Braxton, 1992; Williams, 2000).

Historically, the networks have had difficulties in seeing the possible audience ratings success of some previous African American themed shows, like, *I Spy*, *Julia*, *The Jeffersons*, and *Sanford and Son* (see generally Baynes, 2003a). The networks have also historically succumbed to boycotts and threats from Southern-affiliated stations and advertisers who objected to African Americans in network series (see Baynes, 2003a). In the past 15 years, a few very thoughtful, well-defined, and full-bodied depictions of Black characters appeared in several network drama series.[15] In the 1980s, *The Cosby Show* was a ratings success and eschewed the stereotypical depictions of Black families by presenting a strong and very successful black family.[16] NBC even consulted Dr. Alvin Poussaint, noted Harvard psychiatrist, to advise on the script and character development. But the network executives were initially concerned about broadcasting *The Cosby Show*. Dr. Poussaint recalled that "some of the networks shied away from [*The Cosby Show*] because they didn't think that it would appeal to the white audience" (Aucoin, 1999a, p. A1). "When it became the most popular series of the decade, the same network executives were stunned and confounded" (Aucoin, 1999a, p. A1). It has been more than 10 years since *The Cosby Show* was aired during prime time. It seems as if *The Cosby Show* was in a class by itself, as many of today's sitcoms still present very stereotypical images of African Americans. In the 1990s, the newer networks produced a lot of African American situation comedies that were panned by the critics and by the African American community. Much of the criticism was directed at the short-lived UPN show *Homeboys in Outer Space*, which was about a pair of 23rd-century "brothers" who "hung out" in the universe at large, hopping from one galaxy to another in their "Space Hoopty" (see Biddle, 1996). *My Wife and Kids* is the first major network family sitcom about an African American family to achieve wide popularity with White audiences since *The Cosby Show* (Braxton, 2001b). It is also the first Black family sitcom to succeed on one of the major networks since NBC canceled *The Fresh Prince of Bel-Air* in 1996 (Braxton, 2001b). In addition, FOX debuted *The Bernie Mac Show*, which was the number 1 ranked show for African Americans for the 2000 to 2001 season (Petrozzello, 2002).

Drama Series. The networks need to develop, encourage, and safeguard all-Black drama shows. The networks need to give these types of dramas an opportunity for the audience to grow. Several attempts have been made to create an all-Black family drama series. *Under One Roof* debuted in 1995, and starred James Earl Jones, Joe Morton, and Vanessa Bell Calloway (Braxton & Lowry, 1999). Although it was critically acclaimed, CBS canceled it for low ratings (Braxton & Lowry, 1999). In the early 1990s, NBC developed the show *I'll Fly Away*, which involved a multiracial drama during the 1950s (at the start of the Civil Rights Movement; Farhi, 2000; Jacoby, 2000). NBC canceled the show for low ratings although it was critically acclaimed (O'Connor, 1993).

In 1999, to great fanfare, CBS launched a predominately Black drama series entitled *City of Angels*, produced by Steve Bochco, the creator of such television hits as *LA Law*, *Hill Street Blues*, and *NYPD Blue* (Lowry, 1999). Unfortunately, *City of Angels* lasted for only two seasons (Johnson, 2002). At present few, if any, network programs depict "normal" everyday Black life from a noncomedic perspective.

Sitcoms. Less than one fifth of network sitcoms have racially mixed casts (Storm, 1996). This lack of racial diversity may derive from the fact that Whites and Blacks have different viewing patterns in watching sitcoms. This divergence in viewing patterns developed in the 1990s. For instance, NBC called its Thursday night "Must See TV" (Battaglio, 1997). It had some of the network's most popular shows like *Friends* and *Seinfeld*—often ranked in the top 10 by the Nielsen Ratings (Feran, 1997). But most of the viewers of these shows were White (Feran, 1997; see also Storm, 1996). Ironically, despite taking place in New York City, neither of these shows had any regular minority characters. Most of the Black viewers, in the 1996 season, were watching FOX shows—*Martin*, *Living Single*, and *New York Undercover*.[17] The divergence in viewing patterns between African American and all other viewers held true for the 1999 to 2000 season where the highest Nielsen-ranked television show for most Black viewers was UPN's *The Parkers* (Top Primetime Programs—

African American Homes, 1999–2000), whereas the highest Nielsen-ranked show for all others was ABC's *Who Wants To Be A Millionaire* (Highest-Rated Primetime Programs—All Other Homes, 1999–2000). The story line of *The Parkers* revolves around two large, loud, dark-skinned African American women who play a mother and daughter and are contemporaneously attending college. Their "signature" greeting to each other is "Heeyyy" (see generally BET Reaches Syndication Deal With Paramount TV, 2003). Director Spike Lee has harshly criticized *The Parkers,* stating that "the stereotypes in it weren't much different from those in the minstrel shows" that he lampooned in the movie *Bamboozled* (Sandell, 2002, p. E14). *The Parkers* is no longer in original production.

A similar divergence in viewer demographics also occurred in the 2001 to 2002 prime time season. Only 7 of TV's 20 top-ranked shows in African American homes made White viewers' top 20 list (Petrozzello, 2002). This demographic divergence in viewer preference was actually worse (by one show) than the previous year (Petrozzello, 2002). In the 2000 to 2001 prime time season, the number 1-ranked show for African American viewers was FOX's *The Bernie Mac Show* and for Whites it was NBC's *Friends* (Petrozzello, 2002). In contrast to *The Parkers, The Bernie Mac Show* has won critical acclaim and received a 2002 Emmy for writing in a comedy series (McKissack, 2002). Comedian Bernie Mac plays himself and is a "reluctant father figure" to "three obnoxious children" that his sister left with him while she is in drug rehabilitation (McKissack, 2002, p. 1D). Ironically, during the 2002 to 2003 season, FOX and ABC had scheduled in the same time slot the only two shows on the major networks that feature middle class African American families, *The Bernie Mac Show* and *My Wife and Kids. My Wife and Kids* stars comedian Damon Wayans as "a not-so-modern man in a modern society" (McKissack, 2002, p. 1D). *My Wife and Kids* has been described as "not as innovative in its approach as *The Bernie Mac Show*" and perhaps "a bogus representation of blackness" (McKissack, 2002, p. 1D).

My Wife and Kids and *The Bernie Mac Show* returned for the 2004 to 2005 TV season (Ryan, 2004). Unfortunately, many other all-African American television shows were cancelled. NBC's *Whoopi* and *The Tracey Morgan Show,* ABC's *The Big House,* and the WB's *Like a Family* and *All About the Andersons* did not return in the fall of 2004 (Ryan, 2004).

Depictions of Latinos and Latinas

The viewing patterns for Latinos and Latinas are also different from those of Whites. For instance, in 1996, most Latinos and Latinas were watching shows that featured Latino and Latina actors like *New York Undercover* (Dougherty, 1997) on FOX, whereas most of the White viewing audience was watching other shows ("Hispanics Now Watching More of Same Hits as Other Viewers," 1996).

When Lucille Ball proposed that her then-real-life husband Desi Arnaz play her television husband on the *I Love Lucy* show, the network initially refused (see Zoglin, 2002). The network was concerned that the viewing audience would not accept Desi Arnaz as Ms. Ball's television husband because he was Cuban American (Perigard, 1995). The network finally agreed to let Arnaz play her husband, and the show was one of the most successful in the history of television (see Anderson, 2002).[18]

Very few Latino and Latina actors have starred in nighttime dramas[19] or situation comedies (see generally Perigard, 1995). Jimmy Smits starred in *LA Law* in the 1980s and starred in *NYPD Blue* in the 1990s. More recently, Hector Elizondo starred in *Chicago Hope,* and Martin Sheen starred in the nighttime drama *The West Wing*. In each of these cases, the racial identities of the characters that the actors play are "e-raced," because they play non-Latino characters (see generally Poniewozik, 2001). The casting of Latino and Latina actors in non-Latino and non-Latina roles gives some Latino and Latina actors more opportunities[20] to work their craft in ways that African American actors are usually not able to, unless they can pass for White. As a result of this "erasure" of some Latino and Latina actors in television dramas, the audience does not have the opportunity to counter any of their negative stereotypes about Latinos and Latinas by experiencing positive modern-day images.

PBS debuted an all-Latino drama called *American Family* about a Latino family in Los Angeles. Originally the show was developed for CBS's 2000 to 2001 lineup, but the network failed to include it on its schedule (MacMillan, 2002). Unfortunately, it was not renewed for the 2004 to 2005 season (Ryan, 2004).

According to a study commissioned by the National Council of La Raza, Latino and Latina characters are either absent from television or presented in stereotypical portrayals (Ferris, 1994). For 1 month during the 1992 fall season, the researchers surveyed approximately 300 shows with 7,000 characters. Comparing the content of the 1992 season to the 1950s, the study found that the number of Latino and Latina characters on television in 1992 declined to 1% of all characters, although Latinos and Latinas, at the time, were 9% of the population. In contrast, in the 1950s, Latinos and Latinas were approximately 3% of all television characters, although they were a smaller percentage of the population. According to the study, 16% of the Latino and Latina characters committed crimes as compared to 4% of the African American and White characters. Approximately 28% of the Latino and Latina characters were poor as compared to 24% of the African American and 18% of the White characters. Only one Latino and Latina was depicted as a business executive (Ferris, 1994).

Offensive images of Latinos and Latinas declined by almost half from the 1992 to 1993 television season to the 1994 to 1995 season (Superville, 1996). However, the reality-based television shows (see Ferris, 1994)[21] disproportionately depict Latinos and Latinas and African Americans as criminal perpetrators (Superville, 1996). Latinos and Latinas are often portrayed as drug pushers, as violent, and as foreigners with no ties to the United States (Superville, 1996).

A study conducted by Professor George Gerbner of the Annenberg School for Communication found that Latino and Latina characters make up only 1% of the roles in prime time and 0.5% on children's shows, although Latinos and Latinas make up about 10% of the U.S. population (see "Out of the Picture: Hispanics in the Media," 1994). According to the Gerbner study, 60% of those portrayals of Latino men were negative stereotypes. The Latino male character was either a failure or ineffectual. In comparison, White characters were failures only 23% of the time. Negative portrayals of Latinos and Latinas and cultural insensitivity in the media contributes to many Latinos and Latinas turning to Spanish-language broadcasts (see Padilla, 1997). The Spanish-language broadcasts are perceived to be more balanced (see Padilla, 1997).

When presented as characters on sitcoms, Latinos and Latinas are sometimes shown disrespect. For example, the penultimate episode of *Seinfeld* angered many Puerto Ricans when Kramer inadvertently burned the Puerto Rican flag and stepped on it to put out the flames at the Puerto Rican Day parade in New York City (Janison, 1998; Snow, 1998). In response to the criticism, the creators of *Seinfeld* promised not to rerun the episode, although they refused to promise that it would not be rerun in syndication. Ironically, during the Hispanic Brownout in the fall of 1999, the premiere episode of the sitcom *Will & Grace* had an offensive scene in which a White character, Karen Walker, used an ethnic slur against her Salvadoran maid (Elber, 1999). In the scene, the White character notices that the Salvadoran character is engaging in conversation and has paused from working (Elber, 1999). The White character tells the Salvadoran character, "Hey, you're on the clock, *tamale*. Get to work" (Elber, 1999, p. 4E, emphasis added).

In the 2002 to 2003 season, ABC debuted *The George Lopez Show*, which is the first successful network show starring Latino characters in over 20 years (Porter, 2002). The sitcom stars Latino comedian George Lopez who plays a plant manager with a stay-at-home wife, two kids, and a difficult mother. Mr. Lopez has described the show as not trying to "represent the average Latino. But it meshes with the aspirations of many children and grandchildren of immigrants who worked hard to advance and achieve a better life for their kids" (Porter, 2002, p. A9). Although the characters on the show principally speak English without accents, they occasionally speak Spanish, like using the Mexican slang "chi-chis" to describe a woman's breasts (Porter, 2002). ABC also broadcasts the show in Spanish on its secondary audio program, hired a Latino public relations firm to market the show, and placed advertisements promoting the show on Spanish-language media (Porter, 2002).

Although approximately 20% of Latinos and Latinas in the United States have incomes below the poverty line, "the fantasy of *The George Lopez Show* is attainable in an upwardly mobile sort of way" (Porter, 2002, p. A9). Lisa Navarette, spokeswoman for the National Council of La Raza, said the following: "It's not so beyond the pale. He's not a dot-com billionaire" (Porter, 2002, p. A9). Ms. Navarette also said that "Latinos like [the show] because it's an extraordinary thing to turn on the TV and see somebody that is just like your dad, just like your uncle" (Porter, 2002, p. A9). The show generally does not pander to ethnic stereotypes (Jicha, 2002), except one episode where Lopez defends his daughter's aversion to taking swimming lessons by joking, "Why does she need to learn to swim? We're already here" (Porter, 2002, p. A9).

Among English-language programs for the 18-to-49 age Latino and Latina audience, the ratings for *The George Lopez Show* are now second only to *Friends* ("Nielson Ratings: Viewers Go Eye to Eye with CBS' 'Survivor,'" 2002). Nielsen Media Research found that *The George Lopez Show* was ranked number 45 for the general 18-to-49 demographic, but it is the top-rated show in its time slot for this particular demographic (Porter, 2002). *The George Lopez Show*'s viewers are very diverse: 11% are Latino or Latina; 63% are non-Latino White; and 18% are African American (Porter, 2002).

In its 2003 to 2004 Prime Time Diversity Report, Children Now (2003) found improvement in the number of Latino or Latina characters portrayed on television. In fact, the percentage of the prime time Latino or Latina characters rose from 4% in 2001 to 6.5% in 2003. Moreover, the percentage of Latino or Latina characters appearing in opening credits increased from 2% in 2001 to 3% in 2003. However, Latino or Latina characters were still more likely to be depicted as being of low socioeconomic status. The Latino or Latina characters were four times more likely to portray domestic workers than other racial or ethnic groups. However, for the 2004 to 2005 season, fewer scripted all-Latino or all-Latina shows were broadcast than the previous season (see 2003–2004 Prime Time Diversity Report, pp. 2, 8).

Depictions of Asian Pacific Americans

In the 1994 television season, *All American Girl* debuted as the first all-Asian-American sitcom. It starred Margaret Cho, a Korean American stand-up comic (see Graham, 1994). The Asian Pacific American community had mixed reactions to the pilot (see Braxton, 1994). Guy Aoki, head of the Media Action Network for Asian Americans, praised the sitcom (Braxton, 1994). Sumi Haru, President of the Association of Asian Pacific artists, said the following: "I'm glad television is finally doing something with Asian Americans, and the buzz is good. This is healthy stuff, to show the generational and cultural differences that all of us go through. It's very true to life and should generate a lot of stories" (Braxton, 1994, p. 1). In contrast, Jerry Yu, Executive Director of the Korean American coalition, said some members of his community group were "bothered" by the pilot for *All American Girl*. He said the following: "[A] lot of people didn't think it was funny. It showed the older people in the family not speaking English well. There was a funny confusion of various Asian cultures. Much of the stuff from the show was not from the Korean culture" (Braxton, 1994, p. 1).

Despite hiring two Asian American writers and a consultant on Korean culture, *All American Girl* received this mixed reaction from the Asian Pacific American community, and the show was canceled in its first season (Kim, 1999). In the 1997 to 1998 television season, only one network show had an Asian American as the lead character, *Mystery Files of Shelby Woo,* starring actress Irene Ng (see Lawler, 1996). The 1998 fall schedule included a new CBS program called *Marshall Law* (Michaelson, 1998), starring Sammo Hung, Kelly Hu, and African American actor Arsenio Hall (Dawidziak & Feran, 1999). The show was about an Asian American police officer who uses martial arts to apprehend criminals (Michaelson, 1998). Although the show has Asian American characters, it often portrayed them in a stereotypical setting—practicing Kung Fu (see, e.g., Sardar, 2000). In the late 1990s, Lucy Liu was one of the supporting actresses in the hit FOX series *Ally McBeal,* but she also played to stereotypes as the bitchy dragon woman (Johnson, 1999).

Very few Asian Pacific Americans star in any television series. Some television shows still use White actors to portray Asian Pacific American characters (see Aucoin, 1999b). For example, in *Kung Fu,* a show that was on in the 1970s starring a White actor, has been revised in the 1990s as *Kung Fu: The Legend Con-*

tinues with the same White actor playing the lead character (see Aucoin, 1999b). Scott M. Sassa, President of NBC West Coast and the highest ranking minority in network television, stated that "Seeing David Carradine in [*Kung Fu*] as a Chinese guy really [ticked] you off ..." (quoted in Aucoin, 1996, p. D1).

Some shows have used Asian Americans to provide comic relief. For instance, *The Tonight Show* with Jay Leno featured many appearances of the "Dancing Itos," which was a very disparaging reference to Judge Lance Ito, the presiding judge in the O. J. Simpson criminal case, but led to high ratings for *The Tonight Show* (Marder, 1995; Taylor, 1995). As a result of their appearances on *The Tonight Show,* they received commercial offers (Hevrdejs & Conklin, 1995). Some shows have ridiculed Asian Pacific Americans by having someone speak in a stereotypical, heavily accented Asian Pacific American dialect—all feeding into the stereotype that Asian Pacific Americans are foreign born (see generally Wu, 2002; see also Quan, 2002).

Children Now's (2003) Prime Diversity Report showed that the percentage of Asian and Pacific Island characters remained small and unchanged from 2001 (pp. 2, 8).

Depictions of American Indians

American Indian characters historically have been depicted as "fearsome warriors and savages" (Pattison, 1996, p. SV4), "bloodthirsty scalpers," "treacherous scouts," "inscrutable squaws," "noble primitives," "beatified victims," and "new Age-y healers" (Berson, 1994, p. F1). The current representations of American Indians still focus on the 19th century or the 1970s conflict at Wounded Knee. Very few American Indians are depicted on broadcast television, and, of those, most are not modern depictions (Berson, 1994). The depictions of American Indians focus on their "spirituality" or tend to "appropriate" Indian culture (Dowell, 1995). Some American Indian commentators believe that "Hollywood's interest in Indian spirituality redresses a movie slur of the past, the charge of heathenism ...." (Dowell, 1995, p. P6). Others believe that spiritual devotion "feminizes" or "unmans" American Indians, "thereby implicitly neutraliz[ing] him as a social or political threat" (Dowell, 1995, p. P6). As for appropriation of American Indians, some believe that the "new impulse [is] to claim indigenous tribes as the pre-Philadelphia founding fathers," showing how Whites captured the American Indians's "worshipful rustling," "land," and "woodland skills" (Dowell, 1995, p. P6).

The older portrayal of American Indians as "fearsome warriors" and the more modern stereotype "spiritual shaman" are broadcast on television. The cable networks periodically broadcast the cowboy classics. TNT cable network has a $60 million initiative to produce over 14 hr of Westerns films with American Indian themes such as *Geronimo: An American Legend, Broken Chain,* and *Lakota Woman* (Berson, 1994). These TNT features have the more modern American Indian stereotypes of "spiritual shaman." However, almost contemporaneously in 1997, TNT, with the largest library of cowboy classics, broadcast over 26 hr of classic Westerns (see generally, Berson, 1994).

Broadcast television has had very few contemporary portrayals of American Indians. One of the few was the television show *Northern Exposure,* which took place in Alaska and had American Indian characters played by Native American actors (Berson, 1994; see also Engstrom, 1991, 1993). The show was critically acclaimed (DuBrow, 1991) for its sensitive and nonstereotypical portrayal and was broadcast for 5 years, but those portrayals have most often been of the one-dimensional positive stereotype (see generally Taylor, 1993). *Northern Exposure*'s creators and producers, Joshua Brand and John Falsey, stated that they were "trying to break the [Native American] stereotypes that people have built up over all these years of television and the movies" (Schapiro, 1992, p. 5). *Dr. Quinn, Medicine Woman, Walker Texas Ranger,* and *Star Trek Voyager* also have had recurring American Indian characters. American Indian actor, D. Martin Pera, agreed that "media images of [Native Americans] are maturing" (Berson, 1994, p. F1). Currently, very few American Indian characters or actors appear on prime time television shows (see Holston, 2002b). Children Now's (2003) Prime Diversity Report showed that the percentage of American Indian characters remained virtually nonexistent and unchanged (p. 2).

Depictions of Arab Americans, Asian Indians, and Pakistani Americans

Arab American, Asian Indian, and Pakistani characters were virtually nonexistent on broadcast television. The canceled *Whoopi* situation comedy was the first television show since *Make Room for Daddy* to have a person of Middle Eastern ancestry as a major character, although Danny Thomas was "de-ethnicized" in that 1950s situation comedy (Beale, 2003). The *Whoopi* show costarred actor-comedian Omid Djalilil as an Iranian handyman who worked for hotel owner Whoopi (Beale, 2003). Some of the humor revolved around the Iranian character being mistaken for an Arab (Beale, 2003). The show received some criticism for joking about terrorism (Pierce, 2003), although the writers stated that they took great pains to stay away from some sensitive subjects (Beale, 2003).

Despite the presence of one Middle Eastern character, most Arabs were virtually nonexistent in entertainment programming. Of those that did appear, nearly one half of the Arab American characters were portrayed as criminal as compared to 15% of Latino and Latina and Asian and Pacific Islander characters, 10% of African American characters, and only 5% of White characters (Beale, 2003).

CABLE TELEVISION DOES NOT PROVIDE SUFFICIENT ALTERNATIVES FOR PROGRAMMING FOR PEOPLE OF COLOR

Cable television fails as an alternative to broadcast television's absences and stereotypes of minority characters primarily because cable is a pay service whereas broadcast is free. In addition, broadcast licenses are part of a public grant given to the licensees as trustees for the public (see generally *FCC v. League of Women Voters of California*, 1984). Therefore, although there may be some cable offerings that appeal to people of color, these offerings are insufficient and fail to provide those groups with the array of free choices that Whites have on broadcast television. People of color should not have to pay to get entertainment programming suitable to their needs and devoid of stereotypes. The broadcasters are required to operate their stations in the public interest and provide programming for all.

Cable does offer a number of options for people of color. Black Entertainment Television (BET), which used to be a Black-owned company, has primarily Black-oriented programming and has been criticized for mostly playing music videos. In some markets, it is available as part of the basic package, in other markets it is offered as a premium channel, and in some markets it is not available at all. BET's founder Robert Johnson recently sold the company for $2 billion to Viacom (Hofmeister, 2000). BET reaches 62.4 million of the nation's 76 million pay-television households (Hofmeister, 2000). BET viewership has actually increased by 20% since the purchase (Umstead, 2001a, 2001b). Nonetheless, BET is not the channel most viewed by African Americans (Schneider, 2001). Statistically, African Americans' order of preference is ABC, CBS, UPN, FOX, NBC, and WB (Schneider, 2001). Unfortunately, BET viewers have the lowest median incomes among adults 18 to 49 of any network (see Lafayette, 2000). Having viewers with such low median incomes makes it harder for BET to attract the advertising dollars that other networks get. Having fewer advertising dollars makes it harder to produce quality programming. Although BET has been Black owned and has provided largely Black entertainment programming, some in the African American community have criticized its limited offerings, which consists mostly of music videos and recycled sitcoms (see Open Letter to Robert Johnson, 2001; see also de Moraes, 2001). Aaron MacGruder, the creator of the "hip" urban comic strip *Boondocks,* has made Robert Johnson and BET's lack of original minority programming the brunt of recurring jokes in his strip (see Farhi, 1999). In one strip, Huey, one of the characters, says that he used to believe in the "economic philosophy of black nationalism," but he does not any more because "BET shot a few holes in that theory" (Farhi, 1999, p. B6). In another strip, Huey calls the cable company and says that he is watching "Black Entertainment Television, but I don't see anyone black and it is not entertaining" (Farhi, 1999, p. B6). The cable company operator says that he gets "this complaint all the time" (Farhi, 1999, p. B6).

Latinos and Latinas have more cable options than African Americans, but they are produced and often broadcast only in Spanish. They fail to give the viewer a modern view of the North American Latino or Latina experience. Moreover, with a recent merger between two industry leaders, fewer Latino voices are on air.

Latinos and Latinas have Univision, Telemundo, and Galavision. Telemundo was acquired by NBC in in 2001 (Shin, 2004). The Hispanic Television Network reaches 15% of the country and consists of 20 television stations (Grover, 2001). However, it filed for bankruptcy protection in 2002, and sold off many of its assets like its production studios and its English language television network of 35 affiliates.

Univision captures 80% of the market, and Telemundo 20% although it has an audience reach of 88% of Latino and Latina households (Berkowitz, 2001). Univision has 26 stations and 32 affiliated stations (James, 2001). In contrast, Telemundo has 10 full power stations and 40 affiliated stations (Berkowitz, 2001). Univision owns Galavision, which is available to 25 million cable subscribers (James, 2001). In addition, it owns an Internet portal and music label and plans to launch a second television broadcast network (James, 2001). In 2003, the FCC approved a merger between Univision and Hispanic Broadcasting. The deal created a Hispanic media conglomerate, which controls 63 of 65 radio stations owned by Hispanic Broadcasting, two broadcast television networks, one cable network, one record label, and 53 television stations (Dreazen & Porter, 2003).

Univision and Telemundo enter viewers' homes as a local broadcast station carried by the cable providers pursuant to the FCC's must-carry rules either as a basic or an expanded basic offering (Appelbaum, 2001).

Although Galavision sometimes has some English-language advertisements and broadcasts, most of its broadcasts are only in Spanish, not providing a benefit to those Latinos and Latinas whose primary language is English (see generally McPherson, 2001). Thus it should come as no surprise that these Spanish-language networks draw only 35% of United States Latino and Latina viewers (Poniewozik, 2001). United States Latinos and Latinas spend more time watching programs in English rather than Spanish-language shows on Telemundo, Univision, or Galavision (James, 2001).

There have also been a few other Latino-themed shows on other cable networks. For instance, Nickelodeon broadcast the Latino-themed *The Brothers Garcia* (Russakoff, 2000). In 2000, Showtime broadcast a Latino-themed television show called *Resurrection Blvd.* (Ryan, 2002). In addition, some of the other cable networks have created Spanish-language alternatives like Discovery *en Español,* CNN *en Español,* and FOX World Sports *en Español* (Romano, 2001).

Although Latinos and Latinas have more options on cable than African Americans, Native Americans, or Asian Americans, it is an illusory advantage. Cable penetration is much lower among Latino and Latina households than other American households (Romano, 2001). The lower penetration rate may also be due to lower average household income for Latinos and Latinas as compared to the national average (Romano, 2001). Thus, even if Latinos and Latinas have more choices, they may not be able to access the choices. In addition, if the goal is to disperse positive images throughout the spectrum, so that everyone, of all backgrounds, can see them, having these images on costly and specialized cable channels will not effectuate that goal.

THE SOCIAL CONSEQUENCES OF STEREOTYPICAL CHARACTER PORTRAYALS

Many more African American characters appear on television series today than at any other time in television history. Some of today's portrayals of African American characters seem fair and responsible. However, on closer examination, one realizes that certain stereotypes still exist. For instance, more Black characters appear in sitcoms than family dramas (Farhi, 1995). In sitcoms, the Black characters are more often than not portrayed as the buffoon. In sitcoms where the Black character portrays the "friend," "colleague," or in rare instances the "boss," the character is often one dimensional; we do not see the Black character's friends or family.

Some may say that the television shows that feature predominantly White characters also portray the White characters as buffoons and in stereotypical ways. However, the consequences are different; because so few Black characters appear in television, they are more likely to leave a lasting impression with the viewing audience. Because African Americans are a small minority in the United States, many non-Blacks are likely to learn about African Americans from television. Therefore, those limited impressions, especially those that reinforce negative stereotypes, are indelibly etched in many viewers' minds (see, e.g., Entman & Rojecki, 2000).

The networks have a lot of work to do with respect to the portrayal of Latinos and Latinas on television. Still too few depictions exist of America's largest minority group.[22] Ironically, Latino and Latina characters are sometimes played by Whites, as when Madonna was cast as Eva Peron in Disney Studios' 1996 film musical *Evita*. Many of the depictions are still very negative. In addition, Spanish-language cable stations are not a substitute for broadcast television shows that have wider viewership. Hardly any portrayals of Asian Pacific Americans, Native Americans, or Arab Americans are on television, and many of those have been stereotypical, as discussed earlier.

These negative portrayals, stereotypes, and invisibility can have a profound effect on children.[23] Research suggests that children devote the greatest proportion of their leisure time watching television (Worthy, 1996). Many children spend more time watching television than attending school (Worthy, 1996). Black children in the survey watched nearly twice as much television as Whites (Tagney & Feschbach, 1988). Dr. Bradley Greenberg found that Black children[24] identify with Black television characters and rate them high in handsomeness, friendliness, and strength (Tagney & Feschbach, 1988). What is the impact on our children if they see Blacks portrayed on television most often as criminals or any other negative stereotypes? Social scientists Paula Poindexter and Carolyn Stroman have concluded that these stereotypes impact negatively on the self-concept of African American children (Poindexter & Stroman, 1981). The television roles in which Blacks are cast communicate to Black children the negative value, which society places on them (Poindexter & Stroman, 1981).

For White children, these minority portrayals also have negative implications (Worthy, 1996). Dr. Greenberg's study shows that White children are more likely to learn about other races through electronic rather than through personal interaction (Greenberg, 1972). Forty percent of White children attributed to television their knowledge about how Blacks look, talk, and dress (Greenberg, 1972). Those White children who had the least opportunity to encounter Blacks were most likely to believe that television portrayals were realistic (Greenberg, 1972). Children are more vulnerable to media images because they lack real-world experience and the necessary basis for comparison. Nancy Signorielli and Susan Kahlenberg have explained that although ideas, stereotypes, and roles depicted by the television industry do not reflect the real world, young children may not "distinguish" between symbolic and social reality (Signorielli & Kahlenberg, 2001).

The negative media stereotypes of people of color impact how children perceive minority characters (see also Carmody, 1998; Children Now, 2002). Indeed, it appears that children make generalizations about race based on television characters. Children more often associate positive qualities such as financial success and intelligence with White characters and negative qualities including lawbreaking and laziness with minority characters (Children Now, 2002). Seventy-one percent of children said that the role of boss is played by Whites whereas 59% said the criminal is typically played by Blacks (Children Now, 2002).

These stereotypes play a role in shaping children's perceptions of people of color, and children may carry these stereotypes as adults. As seen earlier, a 1990 University of Chicago study found that 52.8% of Americans believe that violence is a characteristic to describe African Americans (Entman et al., 1998). Approximately 42.8% believed the same thing about Latinos and Latinas (Entman et al., 1998). If children falsely learn from television that all criminals are African American or Latino or Latina, and that members of these groups are inherently prone to violence and other bad acts, then racism and discrimination is perpetuated in our society. These absences and stereotypes may "condition the viewers' expectation of what is ordinary and normal in the larger society" and create a "schism" between Whites and people of color in this country (Civil Disorders, 1968, p. 383).

THE ORDINARY VIEWER TEST

This chapter proposes that the FCC adopt an "ordinary viewer test" to evaluate whether the networks are broadcasting television shows with no people of color or are broadcasting shows with too many stereotypical characterizations; and argues that failing this test would violate either section 151 (as is or as may be amended) or the public interest standard for license renewals under section 309(k) or the Communications Act. In 1999, Congressman Eliot Engel introduced the Ethnic and Minority Bias Clearinghouse Act requiring the FCC to establish an Office on Victims of Media Bias. This office would function as a clearinghouse for complaints, grievances, and opinions relating to television depictions of race and ethnicity. This office would collect and analyze data on media portrayals and conduct an annual conference designed to focus attention on the images of media bias. This proposed legislation is a good first step because having access to information often provides evidence of disparity. However, my proposal advocating an "ordinary viewer test" augments the proposed Act. The FCC would collect and analyze grievances, but the "ordinary viewer test" identifies two criteria the FCC could use to find broadcast content to be discriminatory in violation of section 151 of the Communications Act or the public interest standard. First, a network's failure to cast people of color would be per se discriminatory. Second, a disproportionate number of stereotypical representations of people of color would also violate section 151 of the Communications Act and the public interest standard.

Discrimination by Absence

Under the first prong, a network's failure to cast any people of color in a given television season would be a per se violation of section 151 of the Communications Act. Under this standard, the broadcaster would have the burden of proof to refute the violation. The regulation is loosely modeled after the Civil Rights Act of 1991, which codified the disparate impact theory of liability. Under this theory, an employer can refute the finding of discrimination by demonstrating that the challenged practice is job related for the position in question and consistent with business necessity (Civil Rights Act of 1991; see also Turner, 1995). The employer has the burdens of production and persuasion of establishing business necessity.

This regulation might have included a minimum percentage of minority representations as a safe harbor, similar to the Children's Television Act regulations (1990). Under the Children's Television Act, a broadcaster must broadcast a regularly scheduled weekly program of "core programming" of at least 30 min between 7 a.m. and 10 p.m.[25] These guidelines defined "core programming" as programming that is "specifically designed" to educate and inform children ("Policies and Rules Concerning Children's Television Programming," 1996).[26] To provide some certainty to the broadcasters, the FCC adopted a processing guideline that would give the broadcasters some guarantee of staff-level approval of the Children's Television Act portion of their renewal application when they air at least 3 hr of core programming per week or its equivalent ("Policies and Rules Concerning Children's Television Programming," 1996). If a broadcaster fails to broadcast the minimum amount of children's programming, its renewal application is set for hearing to determine whether its actions during the previous license term meet the public interest, convenience, and necessity ("Policies and Rules Concerning Children's Television Programming," 1996). Although the "ordinary viewer test" proposed here could have advocated such mandatory minimums of minority programming, it does not do so out of concern that some would see mandatory minimums as an affirmative action program, thus triggering strict scrutiny judicial review (see generally Baynes, 2000).[27] To avoid such a high standard in evidencing past discrimination, this author instead decided to anchor the proposed rule in current race-based discrimination jurisprudence. By not triggering the strict scrutiny analysis, the proposed regulation should survive 14th Amendment Equal Protection challenges.

Discrimination by Stereotyping

The second determination the FCC may make under the proposed regime is whether a network has presented a disproportionate number of stereotypical portrayals of characters of color as compared to the White characters. Evidence of lack of any portrayals or of stereotypical disparities in any given television season would establish a prima facie case of discrimination under the Communications Act. Such a disparity could be shown by statistical studies. The FCC would have administrative oversight and would conduct proceedings to evaluate whether, on average, the network is discriminating by the absence or by the disproportionate portrayals of negative stereotypes of people of color. If the FCC found that there is an absence or disparity, it could revoke a station license, impose a monetary forfeiture, or issue a warning to the broadcaster.

The "ordinary viewer test" may initially seem onerous because it appears as though the FCC is scrutinizing broadcast content, but it is no more onerous or burdensome than what the FCC does in evaluating indecent programming. With indecency, section 1464 prohibits the utterance of "any obscene, indecent, or profane language by means of radio communication" (Communications Act of 1934, Section 303(g)). The FCC has the administrative responsibility of enforcing the statutory provisions, which prohibit indecency. To be indecent, the material must describe or depict sexual or excretory organs or activities (see WPBN/WTOM License Subsidiary, Inc., 2000). The broadcast must be patently offensive as measured by contemporary community standards for the broadcast medium. Elaborating on the notion of community standards, the FCC has said that "the determination as to whether certain programming is patently offensive is not a local one and does not encompass any particular geographic area. Rather, the standard is that of an average broadcast viewer or listener and not the sensibilities of any individual complainant" (WPBN/WTOM License Subsidiary, Inc., 2000, pp. 1840–1841).

In determining whether the material is patently offensive, the full context in which the material appeared is critically important. Contextual determinations are highly fact specific, which would make it highly difficult to categorize the patent offensiveness of the material. No specific criteria exist to specifically categorize whether a broadcast is indecent, yet the courts have upheld the indecency statute and the related FCC rules. The courts usually justify the restrictions on indecency because of the pervasiveness of media and the difficulty of tuning out indecent speech.

Similar to the FCC indecency rules, the determination of whether programming violated the "ordinary viewer test" would be a highly fact sensitive analysis. The analysis would take into account both historical and current stereotypes, for example, that African Americans are lazy. The decision maker would then consider whether a disproportionate number of African American characters in any given season meet that stereotype. The alleged stereotype would be analyzed in the context of the story to determine whether in fact the depiction was a stereotype. If a disparity exists, the FCC has the power to impose any sanction provided for in its enabling statute. The larger the size and the more often the frequency of the disparity, the more likely that the FCC will impose a more severe penalty, such as license termination or heavy fines.

The "ordinary viewer test" proposal is fairly modest; it does not require that there be a percentage quota of programming with minority characters. Rather it requires that stark absences and disproportionate stereotypical portrayals be considered a per se violation of the Communications Act. The proposal allows for an administrative proceeding in which the broadcaster could challenge the evidence of the disparity. The "ordinary viewer test" does not require that all stereotypical programming be eliminated. It only prohibits that such programming not be disproportionate in comparison to the representation of people of color on any individual network. But again, the broadcasters are not automatically penalized for a disparity. They have an opportunity to do their own statistical analysis and to show that some of the stereotypes are not really stereotypes because of the context. Both branches of the test should withstand judicial scrutiny. It does not require that the ordinary viewer be the ordinary African American or Latino or Latina viewer (Robinson, 1995). It basically would use the standard of the average viewer who is not necessarily the most scrutinizing. It also does not make any single episode of a television show that contains all-White characters or negative minority stereotypes a violation of the test (Robinson, 1995). Instead, the "ordinary viewer" test analyzes the whole network season in determining whether there is a violation.

CONCLUSION

The depiction of people of color by the media is a very important issue. People of color—African Americans, Asian Pacific Americans, Latinos and Latinas, and Native Americans—currently comprise almost 30% of the U.S. population (see generally Overton, 2002). Many people learn about other groups from television. We need to make sure that people learn about each other in ways that provide a full-bodied depiction—not a stereotypical one. The absence and stereotyping of people of color by the media is a serious problem. This situation is akin to that in *Brown v. Board of Education* (1954) where the Court was made aware that segregation led young black children to have low self-esteem.

Studies have also shown how young children identify with television characters of their race. In addition, White children often have very little exposure to people of color except through what they see on television. What is portrayed on television is critically important to our society and the concept of group identity. This matter lies squarely within the public interest. By failing to portray a more integrated world, the broadcasters are implying that certain individuals and groups do not exist. The FCC has a mandate to regulate the communications field in a manner that comports with the public interest. The public interest should be broad enough to include everyone in media depictions.

By statute, the FCC is supposed to ensure that the carriers provide service in a nondiscriminatory manner. Failing to have any new minority programs or having a disproportionate percentage of negative minority stereotypes during a new season raises a prima facie case of discrimination (*In re Applications of Alabama Educational Television Commission,* 1975). The *United Church of Christ* case established that viewer groups have standing to challenge a license at license renewal time (*Office of Communication of the United Church of Christ v. FCC,* 1965). The challenge can be based on factors such as how well the broadcaster serves the community, including the minority community. Thus La Raza and the NAACP are more than able to bring a complaint before the FCC, which may allow a hearing to go forward provided these groups prove that they have presented a substantial material question. Whether such claims will prevail is a question of fact. In *In re Applications of Alabama Educational Television Commission* (1975), the FCC found that the absence of people of color on a broadcaster's programs, when people of color comprised a sizable part of the viewing audience, was prima facie evidence of discrimination. Moreover, the FCC held that the disparity alone was enough to find wrongdoing; an intent to discriminate need not be shown.

The issues today are much more complicated. Many networks have some people of color on their shows—although very few Latinos and Latinas, Asian Americans, American Indians, or Arab Americans. In addition, quality portrayals of underserved groups is often nonexistent. Many shows use cheap stereotypes of people of color. It seems that the FCC should move to a deeper level of analysis to help it decide these more troubling cases. This chapter suggests that the FCC analyze all such cases of underrepresentation or stereotype under an "ordinary viewer test" standard. Each case would be analyzed separately. The ordinary viewer would be the reasonable person. If it is clear that there is no representation of a particular racial and ethnic group, then clearly that would be a violation of the Communications Act. In addition, if evidence was presented that members of a certain racial or ethnic group were always being portrayed as criminals or villains, then that would also be a violation.

Some may argue that this proposed rule would require the FCC to censor content of network programming. But it is not so much censoring as it is prohibiting discrimination. Further, the FCC has a long history of defining within broad areas the type of content that is broadcast. The network shows are not in the category of commercial print advertising, which is lower down on the First Amendment hierarchy, but a parallel exists because broadcasting has less First Amendment protection than print media (see generally, *Red Lion Broadcast Company v. FCC,* 1969). This situation involves making sure that the broadcasters use the spectrum as trustees for all the American people, and they use it in a way that is nondiscriminatory. As such, the implementation of the proposed "ordinary viewer" test would make sure that the public interest is met by avoiding the broadcast of either all-White images or negative stereotypes of people of color.

NOTES

Leonard M. Baynes, Professor of Law and Director of The Ronald H. Brown Center for Civil Rights and Economic Development, St. John's University School of Law, Jamaica, NY; B.S. New York University, 1979; J.D. Columbia University, 1982; M.B.A. Columbia University 1983. I also want to acknowledge that the idea for this chapter came about while I served as a scholar-in-residence at the Federal Communications Commission. I want to thank the individuals who provided me with very helpful comments at presentations of prior drafts of this chapter at the Fifth Annual Northeast People of Color Legal Scholarship Conference at City University of New York School of Law, at St. John's University faculty forum, and at the University of Virginia Black Law Students Association and Journal of Sports and Entertainment Law Symposium. I also want to thank my former Western New England School of Law colleague, Bruce Miller, for his insights and expertise on a prior draft of this chapter. Finally, I also want to thank my research assistants Ben Darvil, Sheilagh DePeters, John DiBari, and Liliya Abramchayeva Imran Ahmed, Colin Grimes, Edgar Romney, Evan A. Moeller, Jefferey LeMaster, and Michael Mayhew for their able assistance with this project. A previous version of this article appeared in 45 Ariz. L. Rev. 293 (2003; readers should consult that version for a fuller First Amendment analysis).

[1]This was not the first time, in recent history, that the National Association for the Advancement of Colored People (NAACP), at least a local branch, has criticized media portrayals of African Americans. In 1997, three local African American groups led by the Beverly Hills / Hollywood chapter of the NAACP (along with Mothers in Action and the Brotherhood Crusade) launched an attack against television comedies that portray Blacks in a buffoonish manner. The groups targeted eight series that aired on the FOX, WB, and UPN networks (Braxton, 1997). The programs targeted were as fol-

lows: *Martin, Wayan Brothers, The Jamie Foxx Show, Homeboys in Outer Space, Goode Behavior, Sparks, In the House,* and *Malcolm and Eddie*. Billie J. Green, President of the NAACP chapter, stated the following: "I know comedy is comedy, but there's a fine line when people are laughing with you and people are laughing at you. Right now people are laughing at us. What's on these shows is horrible. Parents do not want their kids watching these shows. It is not a fair representation of black America. What we are seeing is like *Amos 'n' Andy* and Stephin Fetchit. In fact, *Amos 'n' Andy* was a better show than what we're seeing now" (quoted in Braxton, 1997, p. A1). The groups did not want the shows canceled; they just wanted the offensive stereotypes removed. The groups backed down due to pressure by the National Association for the Advancement of Colored People.

[2]What is also disturbing, but is not addressed in this chapter, is the stereotyping that occurs on news programs. This stereotyping may be more insidious and pernicious than what occurs in entertainment programming, because people may be more likely to accept news as accurate representations, even if those reports present a skewed picture of reality. See generally Entman and Rojecki (2000). A Pew Research Center survey reported that 64% of the U.S. public relies on local television as its principal source of news, down from 77% in 1993 (Schulze, 1999).

[3]It has been reported that UPN and WB may be moving away from programming Black-themed shows (Hall, 1999).

[4]Lowry, Jensen, and Braxton (1999) note that the "right demographics" usually are "hip teenagers" and 18- to 34-year-old viewers with years of buying power ahead of them. During the sale of advertising for the 1999 to 2000 season, WB saw its sales increase by 50% to $459 million (p. A1). With shows like *Dawson's Creek,* WB aimed directly at this youth market. Advertisers are willing to pay a premium for programs that can attract the "right demographics."

[5]See Mark (1991), discussing that the New South Wales Anti-Discrimination Act was amended to include racial vilification as a ground of discrimination; see also "Sex Role Portrayal for Television and Radio Programming" (1990), a guide for broadcasters to set standards to equalize the portrayal of men and women by broadcasters.

[6]See generally Hazlett (1990), noting that Congress passed the 1926 Radio Act expressly for the purpose of ensuring that no private rights to the broadcast spectrum "would be recognized and requiring that the broadcasters immediately sign waivers giving up their rights and disclaiming any vested interests."

[7]The Federal Communications Commission (FCC) may refuse to renew the license of a broadcaster who fails to serve the public interest. Moreover, the FCC can impose a forfeiture, which is a financial penalty, against a broadcaster who violates a specific rule. Finally, the FCC can grant the licensee a short-term renewal for less than the customary license term, as a sort of probationary period (Communications Act of 1934, Section 307).

[8]The "ordinary viewer test" is borrowed from the "ordinary reader test" for evaluating similar types of discrimination under the Fair Housing Act (Baynes, 2003b).

[9]The Federal Communications Commission has considered this underrepresentation, as evidenced by these reports, in developing its minority ownership policy in 1978 [See State of Policy on Minority Ownership of Broadcasting Facilities, 68 F.C.C.2d 979 (1978)].

[10]For example, consider the colloquy between then-President Bill Clinton and audience member, Mr. Morgan:

> *Mr. Morgan*: I have my own prejudices, whereas if I'm walking downtown on a street and I see a black man walking towards me that's not dressed as well, I might be a little bit scared.
>
> *The President*: Do you think that's because of television crime shows, or because of your personal experience?
>
> *Mr. Morgan*: It would have nothing to do with my personal experience. Just from the media, television shows, and things that I have heard. ("Discussion Remarks in Town Hall Meeting on One America," 1997)

[11]The recent situation involving the possibility that ABC would drop Ted Koppel's *Nightline* for David Letterman's *The Late Show* is a case in point. The actual difference in audience size between *Nightline* and *The Late Show* was not that large; however, *The Late Show* has a younger audience than *Nightline*, for which advertisers were willing to pay a premium (see Holston, 2002a; Winer, 2002). Ultimately, David Letterman decided to stay with CBS, and ABC decided to keep *Nightline* (Gay, 2002).

[12]For example, in the New York, Washington, DC, and Detroit radio markets, the minority-formatted stations reach a larger audience than the other stations because those cities are comprised largely of members of minority groups.

[13]Of course, there might be some justified criticism if the manufacturers of certain potentially unhealthy products focused their advertisements exclusively on African American consumers. But it is still noteworthy that when the advertisers plan to market a supposedly high-end product, they use mostly White models and advertise to largely White audiences.

[14]Justice O'Connor reasoned that "any public entity, state or federal, has a compelling interest in assuring that public dollars, drawn from the tax [dollars] of all citizens, do not serve to finance the evil of private prejudice" (*City of Richmond v. J. A. Croson Co.*, 1989).

[15]Characters on shows like *LA Law, ER, Chicago Hope,* and *Homicide* come to mind.

[16]*The Cosby Show* raises other issues. A study found that many White viewers used the upper-middle-class status of the fictional Huxtable family as proof that Black Americans no longer faced any barriers in the real world (Zurawik, 1995).

[17]The 1997 FOX cancellation of most of this all-minority lineup caused controversy and led to African American protests. As a result of the protests, the television program *Living Single* was saved from cancellation for a few months. *Living Single* revolved around several young, professional Black male and female characters living and working in New York City (Lowry et al., 1999).

[18]The show "spent four of its six prime-time seasons as the highest-rated series on television and never finished lower than third place" (Anderson, 2002).

[19]CNN has a 24-hr network in Spanish. Small nuggets of Spanish dialogue have been incorporated into some mainstream television shows (Dougherty, 1997).

[20]The National Council of La Raza, in making its ALMA awards for film, TV, and music, gives an award each year to a Latino or Latina actor who plays a non-Latino or non-Latina character.

[21]Shows like *Cops* and *America's Most Wanted* are called reality based because they involve "real events." In *Cops,* cameramen shoot footage by traveling with police officers on their activities in a particular city ("Fox Bringing 'COPS' Back for 11th Season," 1998). They move from city to city over the course of the season. *America's Most Wanted* reenacts unsolved crimes and displays photos of the alleged perpetrator in an effort to solicit the public's assistance in catching him or her (see Perkins, 1994).

[22]Latinos and Latinas are America's largest minority (Jones, 2004). Spanish-language cable channels like TeleMundo, Univision, and Galavisin exist, and some Latino-themed shows on cable such as Showtime's *Resurrection Blvd.* exist. However, those cable channels and shows are not free like broadcast television. Moreover, to the extent that the Spanish-language cable channels market solely to Spanish-speaking Latinos and Latinas, they preclude access to non-Spanish-speaking Latinos and Latinas.

[23]Young girls are also influenced by the stereotypes against them. A 1995 Lou Harris survey seems to confirm that girls are strongly influenced by the female characters that they see on television. This influence may confirm Professor Zerbinos's analysis. In the Lou Harris survey, 51% of girls in Grades 3 through 6 acknowledged that they talk like a character they have seen on television, and 41% of girls in Grades 7 through 12 do so (see Walter, 1995). Among the younger girls, 24% wear clothes that they have seen television characters wear, whereas 34% of the older girls do so (Walter, 1995).

[24]Although these statistics deal with Black children, the concepts are probably basic enough to apply to other children of color.

[25]When it airs the program, the broadcaster must identify the program as educational and informational. The program must be listed in the children's report placed in the broadcaster's public inspection files.

[26]To qualify as core programming, the Federal Communications Commission held that "the show must have serving the educational and informational needs of children as a significant purpose" (Federal Communications Commission, 1996, p. 10698).

[27]To establish a race-based affirmative action program, you generally need to show that there is a compelling government interest for the government action and that it is narrowly tailored. Most courts find past discrimination to be a compelling government interest.

REFERENCES

A conversation on race: America, seen through the filter of race. (2000, July 2). *The New York Times,* p. 4.11.

American Association of Retired Persons. (2004). *The Gallup organization, civil rights and race relations.* Retrieved October 27, 2002, from http://www.aarp.org

Adler, R. S., & Pittle, R. D. (1984). Cajolery or command: Are education campaigns an adequate substitute for regulation? *Yale Journal on Regulation, 1,* 171–178.

Anderson, C. (2002). *I love Lucy*. Retrieved October 30, 2002, from http://www.museum.tv/archives/etv/I/htmlI/ilovelucy/ilovelucy.html

Appelbaum, S. (2001, September 3). Spanish flying. *Cablevision,* p. 25.

In re Applications of Alabama Educational Television Commission, 50 F.C.C.2d 461, 465 n.5. (1975).

Aucoin, D. (1999a, July 15). TV networks under fire for diversity gap. *The Boston Globe,* p. A1.

Aucoin, D. (1999b, July 30). NBC pledge on diversity. *The Boston Globe,* p. D1.

Battaglio, S. (1997, December 29). NBC gets nothing from Seinfeld for Christmas: He's reportedly offered $5 mil. an episode. *Hollywood Reporter,* p. 1.

Baynes, L. M. (2000). Life after Adarand: What happened to the metro broadcasting diversity rationale for affirmative action in telecommunications ownership? *University of Michigan Journal of Law Reform, 33,* 87–132.

Baynes, L. M. (2003a). Racial stereotypes, broadcast corporations, and the business judgment rule. *University of Richmond Law Review, 37,* 819–899.

Baynes, L. M. (2003b). Whiteout: The absence and stereotyping of people of color by the broadcast networks in primetime entertainment programming. *Arizona Law Review, 45,* 342–349.

Beale, L. (2003, September 9). A Middle East coup; the part of an Iranian on network TV is a breakthrough worth taking a risk for; *Whoopi* creators say. *Los Angeles Times,* p. E11.

Berkowitz, H. (2001, October 12). Spanish-language Telemundo bought by NBC. *Newsday,* p. A62.

Berson, M. (1994, April 10). Native American images: Stage and screen reflect more Indians, but has picture really changed? *The Seattle Times,* p. F1.

BET reaches syndication deal with paramount TV. (2003, January 8). Retrieved January 5, 2005, from http://www.bet.com/articles/0,,c3gb-5825,00.html

Biddle, F. (1996, August 27). "Homeboys": Lost in outer space? *The Boston Globe,* p. E8.

Braxton, G. (1992, October 4). Where more isn't much better: African Americans are increasingly welcome in prime time, but some observers say the new shows fail to rise above stereotypes. *Los Angeles Times,* p. 3.

Braxton, G. (1994, September 14). It's all in the (ground-breaking) family television: As a sitcom centered on Asian Americans, *All American Girl* is being monitored by advocacy groups concerned about racial stereotypes. Welcome to the pressure cooker. *Los Angeles Times,* p. 1.

Braxton, G. (1997, February 8). Groups call for changes in portrayals of Blacks on TV. *Los Angeles Times,* p. A1.

Braxton, G. (1999, October 9). Survey cites low number of minority writers on series television: NAACP lack of diversity on staff is more blatant than among the casts of new fall series. *Los Angeles Times,* p. F2.

Braxton, G. (2001a, October 17). Mfume appears to delay boycott television: Associates of the NAACP's president say plans to protest a lack of diversity at the major networks may be on hold but not derailed. *Los Angeles Times,* p. F1.

Braxton, G. (2001b, November 25). A Cosby for our time? As far as Damon Wayans is concerned, father really does know best, and he is set to prove it on the hit family comedy "My Wife and Kids." *Los Angeles Times,* p. F8.

Braxton, G. (2002a, January 21). Networks' showcases aim to improve diversity effort; Television* Some in the industry welcome the auditions; others have their doubts. *Los Angeles Times,* p. F1.

Braxton, G. (2002b, January 30). Director diversity seen as lacking; studios and production companies lag in hiring female and minority directors for prime- time shows, a DGA study says. *Los Angeles Times,* p. F1.

Braxton, G., & Lowry, B. (1999, July 23). Small screen, big picture, TV's diversity dilemma. *Los Angeles Times*, p. F1.
Breakdown Services, Ltd. Retrieved April 3, 2003, from http://www.breakdownservices.com
Briefing Notes on Advertising Study. (1998, December 15). Retrieved September 14, 2005, from http://www.fcc.gov/Bureaus/Mass_Media/Informal/ad-study/adver.html
Brown, J. (1997, March 9). Worse by far than Amos 'n' Andy. *The Tampa Tribune*, p. 6.
Brown v. Board of Educ. 347 U.S. 483, 494 n.11 (1954).
Calvo, D. (1999, November 20). The dearth of minority faces on the air begins at the writing and casting phase, where characters are usually assumed to be White. *Los Angeles Times*, p. F1.
Carmody, J. (1998, May 7). The TV column: News channel 8 wins the cable ace awards. *The Washington Post*, p. B09.
Chandrasekaran, R. (1996, November 22). Politics finding a home on the net: Post- election surveys show the web gains influence among voters. *The Washington Post*, p. A4.
Children Now. (2002). Fall colors: Prime time diversity report—2002. Retrieved August 1, 2003, from http://www.childrennow.org/publications.html
Children Now. (2003). Fall colors: Prime time diversity report—2003. Retrieved September 14, 2005, from http://publications.childrennow.org/publications/media/fallcolors_2003.cf m
City of Richmond v. J. A. Croson Co., 488 U.S. 469, 492 (1989).
Civil Rights Act of 1991, Pub. L. No. 102-166, 105 Stat. 1071 (1991).
Communications Act of 1934, Pub. L. No. 416, 48 Stat. 1064 (1934).
Dawidziak, M., & Feran, T. (1999, August 15). Is TV's racism Black and White or just green? Network programmers deal with charges from NAACP that minorities on small screen don't reflect big picture. *Plain Dealer*, p. 1A.
Delgado, R., & Stefanic, J. (1992). Images of the outsider in American law and culture. *Cornell Law Review, 77*, 1258–1297.
de Moraes, L. (2001, November 29). Who wants *Millionaire*? Maybe not ABC. *The Washington Post*, p. C1.
Dowell, P. (1995, January 1). The mythology of the western: Hollywood perspectives on race and gender in the nineties. *Cineaste*, p. P6.
Discussion remarks in Town Hall Meeting on One America—President Clinton's initiative on race. (1997, December 3). *The White House Office of the Press Secretary*. Retrieved September 1, 1998, from http://clinton4.nara.gov/textonly/Initiatives/OneAmerica/1997120427 51.html
Diuguid, L., & Rivers, A. (2000). The media and the Black response. *Annals of the American Academy of Political & Social Sciences, 569*, 120–134.
Dougherty, R. (1997, April 3). When the Spanish language is spoken on prime time TV today, there's no more "splainin" to do: Yiddish already blazed that trail. *Chicago Tribune*, p. 1.
Dreazen, Y., & Porter, E. (2003, September 23). Univision gets FCC clearance for Hispanic broadcasting deal. *The Wall Street Journal*, p. A3.
DuBois, W. E. B. (1997). *The souls of Black folk*. D. Blight & R. Gooding-Williams (Eds.). New York: Bedford/St. Martin's.
Du Brow, R. (1991, November 26). NBC's dramatic surge in quality TV. *Los Angeles Times*, p. F16.
Elber, L. (1999, September 21). Amid Hispanic boycott comes slur on NBC. *Sun-Sentinel*, p. 4E.
Engstrom, J. (1991, July 25). For Elaine Miles, acting is easy—and so is the pay. *Seattle Post-Intelligencer*, p. C1.
Engstrom, J. (1993, March 9). Indians hold negotiations with northern exposure. *Seattle Post-Intelligencer*, p. C5.
Entman R., Melican, D. B., & Munoz, I. (1998). Mass media and reconciliation: A report to the advisory board and staff. Washington, DC: President's Advisory Commission on Race.

Entman, R., & Rojecki, A. (2000). *The Black image in the White mind: Media and race in America*. Chicago: University of Chicago Press.
Farhi, P. (1995, January 8). Amos 'n' standby: Television's dramatic deficit for African Americans. *The Washington Post*, p. C1.
Farhi, P. (1999, November 22). For BET, some static in the picture, Bob Johnson wanted people to turn on his cable network. He got his wish. *The Washington Post*, p. B6.
Farhi, P. (2000, February 13). TV's skin-deep take on race: False harmony, not lack of Black shows, called problem. *The Washington Post*, p. G01.
FCC v. League of Women Voters of California, 468 U.S. 364 (1984).
Federal Communications Commission. (1996). Policies and rules concerning children's television programming, 11 FCC Rcd. 10660.
Feran, T. (1997, February 26). Black, White preferences in viewing vary widely. *Plain Dealer*, p. 5E.
Ferris, S. (1994, September 27). Prime time Latino characters now TV's favorite criminal target. *Chicago Tribune*, p. 5.
Fletcher, M. (1999, July 28). Latinos plan boycott of network TV: Goal of "brownout" is better roles for Hispanics. *The Washington Post*, p. C1.
Fox bringing "COPS" back for 11th season. (1998, April 16). *Chicago Tribune*, p. 9.
Gaiter, L. (1999, August 4). Put to rest the "Spirit of Proposition 209": Racism: Whites like to think they instantly voided their history of prejudice. *Los Angeles Times*, p. B7.
Gardner, N. T. (1985). Cameras in the courtroom: Guidelines for state criminal trials. *Michigan Law Review, 84*, 475–516.
Gay, V. (2002, April 9). Flash/Disney boss finally backs nightline. *Newsday*, p. A12.
Graham, J. (1994, July 18). Who's that "girl"? Press gets a closer look. *USA Today*, p. 3D.
Graves, S. B. (1999). Television and prejudice reduction: When does television as a vicarious experience make a difference? *Journal of Social Issues, 55*(4), 707–708.
Greenberg, B. (1972). Children's reaction to TV Blacks. *Journalism Quarterly, 49*, 5–14.
Grover, R. (2001, September 24). Media giants are glued to Latino TV. *Business Week*, p. 105.
Hall, R. F. L. (1994). The fairness doctrine and the first amendment: Phoenix rising. *Mercer Law Review, 45*, 705–771.
Hall, S. (1999, July 29). Blacklash networks scramble after NAACP criticizes fall lineups for their lack of minority characters. *The Indianapolis Star*, p. E01.
Hazlett, T. (1990). The rationality of U.S. regulation of the broadcast spectrum. *Journal of Law and Economics, 33*, 133–175.
Hevrdejs, J., & Conklin, M. (1995, March 27). Oscar night means plenty of pomp and little happenstance. *Chicago Tribune*, p. 12.
Highest-rated primetime programs—all other homes. (1999–2000). Retrieved April 3, 2003, from http://www.nielsenmedia.com/ethnicmeasure/african-american/programsOther.html
Hispanics now watching more of same hits as other viewers. (1996, October 18). *Houston Chronicle*, p. 5.
Hofmeister, S. (2000, November 4). Viacom expands cable empire with BET purchase. *Los Angeles Times*, p. C1.
Holston, N. (2002a, March 12). What's the bottom line on the news? Networks need more ad dollars, younger viewers. *Newsday*, p. B2.
Holston, N. (2002b, August 25). The color of prime time: When it comes to more and better roles for minorities in drama TV executives deliver little more than snow and static. *Sun-Sentinel*, p. 1D.
H.R. 2700, 107th Cong. (2001).
Ignatiev, N. (1995). *How the Irish became White*. Oxford, England: Routledge.

Jacoby, T. (2000, January 24). Adjust your sets. *New Republic,* p. 21.
James, M. (2001, November 4). Suitors stay tuned for Univision's next media move: Many are eyeing the Spanish language broadcast leader. But acquisition would be costly, analysts say. *Los Angeles Times,* p. C1.
Janison, D. (1998, June 12). NBC: Sorry about Seinfeld: Puerto Rican coalition accepts apology for flag-burning plot. *Newsday,* p. A8.
Jensen, R. (1998, July 19). White privilege shapes the U.S.: Affirmative action for Whites is a fact of life. *Baltimore Sun,* p. 1C.
Jicha, T. (2002, March 27). Comedian's sitcom too short on comedy. *Sun-Sentinel,* p. 3E.
Johnson, S. (1999, July 16). Asia minor: Among TV's neglected minorities, Asian Americans may be the most underrepresented of all. *Chicago Tribune,* p. 1.
Johnson, S. (2002, February 1). Getting color on television: African Americans on TV: A history of talent, ambition and frustration. *Chicago Tribune,* p. 1.
Jones, S. (2004, January 5). Hispanics surpass blacks as growth market for ads. *The Washington Post,* p. E1.
Kennard, W. (1999, November 29). *Statement regarding the NAACP public hearing on diversity in network television.* Retrieved February 24, 2005 from http://www.fcc.gov/Speeches/Kennard/Statements/stwek969.html
Kim, J. (1999, September 23). Just what she wants: Comic-actress Margaret Cho takes control. *Chicago Sun-Times,* p. 50.
Kolker, C. (1999, July 28). Latino groups urge boycott of network TV media: Coalition decries the lack of industry jobs for minorities and the negative portrayals on screen. *Los Angeles Times,* p. A12.
Lafayette, J. (2000, February 7). NBC most upscale: Analysis says peacock network draws richest broadcast viewers. Electronic Media, p. 10.
Lawler, S. (1996, March 17). Irene Ng as Shelby Woo. *The Morning Call,* p. T3.
Littlefield, K. (1999, December 12). Getting the call: What goes on in closed-door casting sessions paints racial mix of prime time. *Orange County Register,* p. F10.
Long, T. (2002, December 11). Networks score poorly in reflecting diverse audience. *The Seattle Times,* p. F5.
Lowry, B. (1999, October 19). If at first you do succeed, write, write again. *Los Angeles Times,* p. F1.
Lowry, B., Jensen E., & Braxton, G. (1999, July 20). Networks decide diversity doesn't pay. *Los Angeles Times,* p. A1.
MacMillan, A. (2002, January 20). All in the familia. *New York Daily News,* p. 3.
Marder, K. (1995, December 31). O.J. Simpson trial verdict top TV moment of year. *Times Union,* p. H1.
Mark, S. (1991). Is conciliation of racial vilification complaints possible? *Without Prejudice, 3,* 3–8.
Massey, D., & Denton, N. (1993). *American apartheid: Segregation and the making of the underclass.* Cambridge, MA: Harvard University Press.
McIntosh, P. (1997). White privilege and male privilege: A personal account of coming to see correspondences through work in women's studies. In R. Delgado & J. Stefancic (Eds.), *Critical White studies: Looking behind the mirror* (pp. 291–299). Philadelphia: Temple University Press.
McKissack, F. (2002, October 15). Black TV families are back. *Madison Capital Times,* p. 1D.
McPherson, J. G. (2001, September 1). Targeting teens. *Hispanic,* p. 3236.
Michaelson, J. (1998, October 11). Morning report. *Los Angeles Times,* p. F2.
Minorities are relatively prevalent on television: Study says. (1999, September 28). *Star Tribune,* p. 8E.

NAACP reports little progress in network diversity. (2001, August 17). *Telegraph Herald,* p. B8.

National Association for the Advancement of Colored People. (2001). Out of focus—out of sync. Retrieved February 1, 2005, from http://www.naacp.org/news/releases/tv2001.pdf

Nielsen ratings: Viewers go eye to eye with CBS' "Survivor." (2002, December 25). *St. Paul Pioneer Press,* p. 4B.

O'Connor, J. (1993, October 11). PBS revives a series on race and America. *The New York Times,* p. C16.

Office of Communication of the United Church of Christ v. FCC (D.C. Cir. 1965). 359 F.2d994.

Open letter to Robert Johnson, CEO, Black Entertainment Television. (2001, November 2). Council of Presidents of African American Greek Letter Organizations.

Out of the Picture: Hispanics in the Media. (1994). Washington, DC: National Council of La Raza.

Overton, S. (2002). But some are more equal: Race, exclusion, and campaign finance. *Texas Law Review, 80,* 987–1056.

Padilla, M. (1997, September 12). Hispanics decry negative image in media stereotypes, causes many Latinos to turn to Spanish-language broadcasts: Leaders say. *Orlando Sentinel,* p. A1.

Patterson, J. (2001, February). Friday review: Hollywood Reporter: Extreme prejudice: Why Bush is bad news for Black people in the media. *The Guardian,* p. 5.

Pattison, K. (1996, June 24). Video producer covers Indian's tales in *Our Own Voices,* voids stereotypes. *Los Angeles Daily News,* p. SV4.

Perigard, M. (1995, April 23). Crossing the border although Desi Arnaz captured America's heart 40 years ago, a new generation of Latino actors is still struggling for acceptance. *Boston Herald,* p. 6.

Perkins, K. (1994, September 9). Love and smaltz: Will viewers cozy up to reality-based romance on TV? *Chicago Tribune,* p. 3.

Petrozzello, D. (2002, April 16). Black–White ratings gap is widening. *New York Daily News,* p. 90.

Pierce, S. D. (2003, September 6). NBC's *Whoopi* is in your face. *Deseret News,* p. E8.

Poindexter, P., & Stroman, C. (1981). Blacks and television: A review of the research literature. *Journal of Broadcasting, 25,* 103–122.

Poniewozik, J. (2001, May 28). What's wrong with this picture? The U.S. Hispanic population has grown 58% in 10 years, to 35 million. On TV Latinos are down 2% of characters. Why the brownout? *Time, 157,* p. 80.

Porter, E. (2002, December 31). Latinos tune in to watch as George Lopez pursues American dream on ABC. *The Wall Street Journal,* p. A9.

Quan, D. (2002, June 30). Kicking the box: Asian actors take stand against stereotypical roles. *Houston Chronicle,* p. 16.

Randolph, L. (1994, May 1). Life after the Cosby Show: Activist-actor celebrates 30 years of wedded bliss: Continues fight against black stereotypes on TV. *Ebony,* p. 100.

Red Lion Broadcast Company v. FCC, 395 U.S. 367 (1969).

Report of the National Advisory Committee on Civil Disorders. (1968). New York: Bantam Books.

Riggs, M. (1986). (Producer & Director). *Ethnic notions.* KQED-TV San Francisco.

Robinson, R. (1995). The racial limits of the fair housing act: The intersection of dominant White images, the violence of neighborhood purity, and the master narrative of Black inferiority. *William and Mary Law Review, 37,* 69–159.

Roman, E. (2000). Who exactly is living la vida loca? The legal and political consequences of Latino–Latina ethnic and racial stereotypes in film and other media. *Journal of Gender, Race & Justice, 4,* 37–68.

Romano, A. (2001, October 1). Checking the census. *Broadcast & Cable,* p. 32.

Ross, T. (1998). Being White. *Buffalo Law Review, 46,* 257–279.
Rubin, E. (1990). Television and the experience of citizenship. *Texas Law Review, 68,* 1155–1168.
Russakoff, D. (2000, September 23). Keeping up with the Garcias: Children's TV leads Latino emergence. *The Washington Post,* p. A1.
Ryan, S. (2002, March 24). Latinos finally beginning to see themselves on television. *The Boston Globe,* p. L8.
Ryan, S. (2004). Now on the small screen: Less diversity, cancellations mean a whiter shade of TV. Retrieved July 3, 2004, from http://www.boston.com/ae/tv/articles/2004/05/30/now_on_the_small_sc reen_le ss_diversity?
Sacks, K. (1997). How did Jews become White folks? In R. Delgado & J. Stefancic (Eds.), *Critical White studies: Looking behind the mirror* (pp. 395–401). Philadelphia: Temple University Press.
Sandell, S. (2002, November 11). Television & radio tuned in: Even a nostalgic guest turn can't help a lackluster "Parkers." *Los Angeles Times,* p. E14.
Sardar, Z. (2000, May 22). China syndrome: Depictions of the Chinese in movies. *New Statesmen,* p. 46.
Schapiro, M. (1992, March 29). Trademarks for offbeat, literary backgrounds mark imaginations of series writers. *Austin-American Statesman,* p. 5.
Schneider, M. (2001, February 12). Blacks and Whites share more TV faves. *Daily Variety,* p. 5.
Schulman, H., Bobo, L., Krysan, M., & Steeh, C. (1997). *Racial attitudes in America: Trends and interpretations.* Cambridge, MA: Harvard University Press.
Schulze, J. (1999). Four model stations. *Columbia Journalism Review, 37,* 74.
Sex role portrayal for television and radio programming. (1990, October 26). Canadian Retrieved October 5, 2004, from http://www.cbsc.ca/english/codes/sexrole.htm
Shin, A. (2004, June 7). Broadcasting company sets its sights high. *The Washington Post,* p. E1.
Signorielli, N., & Kahlenberg, S. (2001). Television's world of work in the nineties. *Journal of Broadcasting and Electronic Media, 45*(1), 4–22.
Snow, S. (1998, June 12). Arts and entertainment reports from the times, national and international. *Los Angeles Times,* p. F2.
Sterngold, J. (1998, December 29). A racial divide widens on network TV. *The New York Times,* p. A12.
Storm, J. (1996, June 19). Why TV comedies are in black and white while dramas come in color. Life is integrated at work: at home, it's not. *Milwaukee Journal Sentinel,* p. 1.
Superville, D. (1996, April 20). Stereotypes of Hispanics still on TV: Study shows. *Fort Worth Star-Telegram,* p. 38A.
Tagney, J., & Feschbach, S. (1988). Children's television-viewing frequency: Individual differences and demographic correlates. *Personality & Social Psychology Bulletin, 14,* 145–158.
Taylor, A. (1993, July 29). *Northern Exposure* unfairly minimizes Alaska Indians' native culture. *Dayton Daily News,* p. 8A.
Taylor, C. (1995, December 31). Stars of '95-TV. *Seattle Times,* p. 3.
The Children's Television Act of 1990, Pub. L. No. 101_437, 104 Stat. 996-1000.
Top primetime programs—African American homes (1999–2000). Retrieved April 3, 2003, from http://www.nielsenmedia.com/ethnicmeasure/african-american/programsAA.html
Turner, R. (1995). Thirty years of title VII's regulatory regime: Rights, theories, and realities. *Alabama Law Review, 46,* 375–485.
Tuv, J. (2002, January 11). Controversial differences. *Indianapolis Reporter,* pp. N2, B5.
Umstead, R. T. (2001a, April 9). Lifetime leads cable ratings rise. *Multichannel News,* p. 3.
Umstead, R. T. (2001b, June 18). BET specials, movies prompt record ratings. *Multichannel News,* p. 46.
Walter, T. (1995, November 2). Girls remake TV in their own image. Project tunes out stereotype messages. *Commercial Appeal,* p. C1.

Watkins, S. C., & Emerson, R. A. (2000). Feminist media criticism and feminist media practices. *Annals of the American Academy of Political & Social Sciences, 571,* 151–166.

When being no. 1 is not enough: The impact of advertising practices on minority- owned and minority formatted broadcast stations. (2002). Retrieved May 3, 2002 from http://www.fcc.gov/Bureaus/Mass_Media/Informal/ad-study

Wilkerson, D. (1996, December). Power beyond the remote control. *Black Enterprise,* p. 75.

Williams, G. (2000). Don't try to adjust your television—I'm black: Ruminations on the recurrent controversy over the Whiteness of TV. *The Journal of Gender, Race & Justice, 4,* 99–136.

Window dressing on the set: Women and minorities in television. (1977). Washington, DC: United States Commission on Civil Rights.

Winer, L. (2002, April 21). Critical mass/age jokes are getting old. *Newsday,* p. D2.

WPBN/WTOM License Subsidiary, Inc. F.C.C.R., 15, 1838–1841 (2000).

Worthy, P. (1996). Diversity and minority stereotyping in the television media: The unsettled first amendment issue. *Hastings Communications and Entertainment Law Journal, 18,* 509–567.

Wu, F. (2002). *Yellow: Race in America beyond Black and White.* New York: Basic Books.

Zoglin, R. (2002). The TV star, Lucille Ball. Retrieved October 15, 2002, from http://www.time.com/time/time100/artists/profile/lucy.html

Zurawik, D. (1995, February 9). Eye on the black experience. *Everyday Magazine,* p. 1G.

12

Serving the Public Interest: Broadcast News, Public Affairs Programming, and the Case for Minority Ownership

Christine M. Bachen, Allen S. Hammond, IV, & Catherine J. K. Sandoval
Santa Clara University

The inadequacy of the media's representation of minorities has engendered a long history of public concern and debate. Mainstream media sources, typically White-owned and mostly White-staffed, have been repeatedly criticized for reporting events or dramatizing life from a predominantly White perspective. The limitations of the White-dominated media prompted people of color to create alternative media outlets where they could be assured of more representative and relevant content. An early example of this can be seen with the first American Black newspaper, *Freedom's Journal,* started by Samuel E. Cornish and John Brown Russwurm before the Civil War as an expression of abolitionist sentiment. In their first edition they wrote, "We wish to plead our own cause. Too long have others spoken for us. Too long has the public been deceived by misrepresentation in things which concern us dearly" (Wilson & Gutiérrez, 1995, p. 181).

Creating alternative print media could be managed on a relatively small budget. For potential broadcasters, the dual constraints of the considerable financial investment required and the competition for space along the broadcast spectrum resulted in a different reality. With the emergence of broadcasting as a "pervasive medium" in American life, shortcomings in representation and coverage of minorities became the impetus for government intervention and the development of regulatory policy. In this chapter, we consider the history and rationales behind the Federal Communication Commission's (FCC's) efforts to address minority representation within the broadcasting industry. We examine the legal history associated with these policies and regulations and the social scientific evidence that addresses the claims and challenges associated with these policies.

OWNERSHIP, PROGRAMMING DIVERSITY, AND GOVERNMENT RESPONSE

The origins of the U.S. government's recognition of the importance of broadcast ownership to diversity of programming may be traced to three critical elements: (a) the FCC's longstanding statutory responsibility to ensure that broadcast licensees use the scarce public airwaves consistent with the public interest, convenience, and necessity; (b) the segregationist editorial activity of the Mississippi Publishers Association, the former broadcast licensee of WLBT-TV in Jackson, Mississippi, that consistently declined to serve the needs and interests of the sizable African American citizenry in the community it was licensed to serve, and denied all of its citizens the opportunity to view news about the civil rights movement; and (c) the publication of the reports of the Kerner Commission and the U.S. Commission on Civil Rights, which confirmed that the biases reflected in the news coverage of WLBT were not local and isolated but national and systemic.

THE PUBLIC'S INTEREST IN DIVERSITY

The FCC is charged with ensuring that those licensed to use the airwaves do so in the "public interest, convenience and necessity" (Communications Act of 1934). In *National Broadcasting Co. (NBC) v. U.S.* (1943), the U.S. Supreme Court recognized the broad powers of the FCC to regulate the use of the airwaves for broadcast radio. The court emphasized that the "public interest" is the interest of the listening public in the "larger and more effective use of radio," especially given the limited amount of radio spectrum available (*NBC v. U.S.*, 1943, p. 216, citing Communications Act of 1934). It added that the aim of the Communications Act of 1934 was to "secure the maximum benefits of radio to all people of the United States" (*NBC v. U.S.*, 1943, p. 217). Thus, the FCC does not merely act as a technical traffic cop, ensuring that those licensed to use the spectrum do not interfere with each other, but can set broad policies to make sure that the radio spectrum is used to serve the public interest.

Red Lion Broadcasting v. FCC (1969) reiterated the premise that the First Amendment's purpose is to preserve an "uninhibited marketplace of ideas," as the foundation of democratic debate and decision making (*Red Lion Broadcasting v. FCC,* 1969, p. 390). Such debate can produce an "informed public capable of conducting its own affairs" (*Red Lion Broadcasting v. FCC,* 1969, p. 392). The Supreme Court emphasized that "speech concerning public affairs is more than self-expression; it is the essence of self-government" (*Red Lion Broadcasting v. FCC,* 1969, p. 390, citing *Garrison v. State of Louisiana,* 1964).

The recognition of the value of diverse speech was affirmed in *Turner Broadcasting v. FCC* (1997), where a 5 to 4 majority of the Supreme Court upheld Congress's regulations requiring cable system operators to carry over-the-air television broadcast signals. The Court emphasized that "promoting the widespread dissemination of information from a multiplicity of sources" was a compelling state interest (*Red Lion Broadcasting v. FCC,* 1969, p. 189). The majority in *Turner Broadcasting v. FCC* stressed the view, rooted in the First Amendment, that "the widest possible dissemination of information from diverse and antagonistic sources is essential to the welfare of the public" (p. 192, quoting *United States v. Midwest Video Corp.,* 1972, in turn quoting *Associated Press v. United States,* 1945).

In its 1965 Policy Statement on Comparative Hearings, which the FCC used to decide who would be awarded a broadcast license, the FCC described two primary selection criteria: the best practicable service to the public and maximum diffusion of control over the mass media (FCC, 1969). The Court of Appeals for the District of Columbia (D.C.) Circuit in *TV 9 Inc. v. FCC* (1974), held that the FCC may take into account a racial or ethnic minority's ownership of stock as part of the determination of which broadcast license applicant would best serve the public interest. The D.C. Circuit in *TV 9 Inc. v. FCC* observed, "When minority ownership is likely to increase diversity of content, especially opinion and viewpoint, merit should be awarded in the licensing process" (p. 938). The Court added that the fact that nonminority owners planned to address minority viewpoints "does not offset the fact that it is upon ownership that public policy places primary reliance with respect to diversification of content, and that historically has proven to be significantly influential with respect to editorial comment and the presentation of news" (*TV 9 Inc. v. FCC,* p. 938). *TV 9 Inc. v. FCC* recognized the link between minority ownership and diverse viewpoints, later examined in *Metro Broadcasting, Inc v. Federal Communications Commission* (1990).

WLBT-TV AND THE EDITORIAL CONTROL OF THE LICENSEE

Television Station WLBT in Jackson, Mississippi, was the first FCC-licensed station in the United States to lose its license for failure to meet the needs of its community, including African Americans. The D.C. Circuit Court of Appeals in *Office of Communication of the United Church of Christ (Office, UCC) v. FCC* (1966) required the FCC to hold an evidentiary hearing concerning allegations that the licensee had engaged in racial discrimination during its broadcasts, and that its news reporting lacked balance. The 1966 UCC case about WLBT also affirmed the right of the public to bring complaints against FCC licensees, and have them heard and considered in the licensing and license renewal process. The D.C. Circuit stressed that, "the interests of the public are dominant," for they are "the owners of the channels of television—indeed, all broadcasting" (*UCC v. FCC,* 1966, p. 1003).

During the FCC proceedings to evaluate whether WLBT should keep its license, the FCC received evidence that WLBT used racially disparaging terms when describing African Americans, and cut off network news programming showing attempts to desegregate lunch counters. UCC argued that in 1955, WLBT, owned by the Mississippi Publishers Corporation, had "deliberately cut off a network program about race relations on which the General Counsel of the NAACP, Thurgood Marshall, was appearing" to discuss the landmark *Brown v. Board of Education of Topeka Kansas* (1955) case which ended legal sanction of racial desegregation in schools (*Office, UCC v. FCC,* 1966, p. 998). WLBT station manager Fred Beard allegedly boasted about deliberately cutting off the Thurgood Marshall program, disguising it as a technical problem by putting up the words "Sorry Cable Trouble" (Fuller, 2005, p. 265). In 1957, WLBT allegedly presented a program urging the maintenance of racial segregation and refused requests for time to present opposing views.

In 1962, the FCC again received complaints that WLBT presented programs concerning racial integration in which only one viewpoint was aired. Viewers complained that during the Civil Rights Movement, if Dr. Martin Luther King, Jr. (Jackson, 2004) was scheduled for a network program, it was not carried on WLBT. As late as 1963, WLBT continued to maintain that it would not air any "inflammatory" programs and that any program dealing with civil rights, racial issues, or integration would not be aired (Thomas, 2004; WLBT and Pro-Segregation TV). Thomas (2004) observed the following: "What WLBT considered 'inflammatory,' the United Church of Christ and African American residents considered educational and news programs in the public interest."

Once desegregation began at the University of Mississippi, WLBT and another station in Jackson, "were accused of helping to foster an atmosphere of violent resistance and encouraging the mob action ... that left two dead and dozens injured" (Thomas, 2004). WLBT broadcast an editorial opposing an

African American student's admission to the University of Mississippi that claimed, "The word of the hour, the word of the day, the word of the year is: Never!" (Thomas, 2004). When the FCC investigated these allegations, it held that only segregationist editorials on the air were under scrutiny, not the news operations and newscasts (Thomas, 2004). On remand to the FCC, the FCC renewed the broadcast license, an action that was later overruled by the D.C. Circuit. (*Office, UCC v. FCC,* 1969).

After analyzing the FCC record regarding the license renewal, the D.C. Circuit noted the FCC hearing examiner's hostility toward the UCC petitioners, and confusion about which party had the burden of proof in the face of evidence of racial discrimination, uncontroverted by the station's licensee (*Office, UCC v. FCC,* 1969). Rather than remand to the FCC for another hearing, the Court in the second WLBT case in 1969 announced, "We are compelled to hold, on the whole record, that the Commission's conclusion is not supported by substantial evidence. For this reason the grant of a license must be vacated forthwith and the Commission is directed to invite applications to be filed for the license" (*Office, UCC v. FCC,* 1969, p. 550).

The WLBT case demonstrates the control FCC licensees have over the content they broadcast, even when they are affiliates of major networks who send them a great deal of programming. Although WLBT's license revocation established a line of public interest service licensees must meet, it also demonstrates the potential for influence over news, public affairs, and other content that a licensee may have.

THE KERNER COMMISSION REPORT

The challenge to the license renewal of WLBT took place during the height of the Civil Rights Movement. The National Advisory Commission on Civil Disorders (what become known as the Kerner Commission) investigated the causes for the urban riots that took place in the summer of 1967 in the United States (Kerner Commission, 1968). Although many causes of the riots were disclosed, one chapter of the report (known as the Kerner Commission Report) focused explicitly on the news media and its coverage of the riots, and more generally, of race. Not only did the Kerner Commission Report (1968) find news media coverage of the 1967 riots lacking, it also critiqued the press for its ongoing failure to depict the conditions of and difficulties of surviving in the Black ghetto. The Kerner Commission concluded that the news was reported mainly from a White perspective and pointed to the paucity (under 5%) of Black journalists in reporting and decision-making roles.

THE FCC RESPONSE

For a decade, the FCC sought to improve broadcaster responsiveness to minority audiences by using race neutral policies. In 1968, as a partial response to the concerns expressed in the Kerner Report, the FCC established policies to address complaints that broadcast licensees engaged in employment practices that discriminated against minorities. In 1969, the FCC adopted rules forbidding licensee discrimination on the basis of race, color, religion, or national origin, and requiring that "equal opportunity in employment ... be afforded by all licensees ... to all qualified persons" (FCC, 1969, p. 248). "Sex" was added as an impermissible basis for discrimination in May 1970 (FCC, 1970). In 1970, the FCC adopted rules requiring licensees to file annual employment reports and a written equal employment opportunity report. In 1975, the FCC reiterated and clarified its policy on employment discrimination, emphasizing that its rules embodied the concepts of nondiscrimination and affirmative action (FCC, 1975). In 1976, the FCC sought to assure that the needs, interests, and problems of a licensee's community (including minorities within that community) are both ascertained and treated in the programming of the licensee. Under the FCC's ascertainment requirements, licensees were required to contact community leaders and members of the general public, including minorities, to obtain information about community interests and to present programming responsive to those interests (FCC, 1976).

Despite its efforts, in 1978, the FCC observed that the views of racial minorities continued to be inadequately represented in the broadcast media (FCC, 1978a). The FCC found the situation detrimental to the entire viewing and listening public. Adequate representation of minority viewpoints in programming serves not only the needs and interests of the minority community but also enriches and educates the nonminority audience. It enhances the diversity of programming which is a key objective not only of the Communications Act of 1934, but also of the First Amendment.

TELEVISION NEWS MEDIA COVERAGE OF RACE: FROM KERNER TO THE PRESENT DAY

Time has not erased the deficits in media coverage of race identified in the Kerner Commission Report. Consistently, studies find that minorities are underrepresented in the media or, when present, are portrayed in limited or stereotypical roles (Poindexter, Smith, & Heider, 2003). Over the years, the nature of the representations has changed to some degree, but limitations persist that have important ramifications for public perceptions of race.

TELEVISION NEWS COVERAGE OF MINORITIES

More Americans use local television news as their primary news medium than any other medium (news audiences increasingly politicized, 2004). Studies of local TV news coverage in Los Angeles (Dixon & Linz, 2000), and Philadelphia (Romer, Jamieson, & deCoteau, 1998) found that crime news—a staple of local newscasts (Gilliam & Iyengar, 2000)—more often features Blacks and Latinos as perpetrators of crimes compared to Whites. Whites—according to findings by Dixon and Linz (2000) and Romer et al. (1998)—were overrepresented as homicide victims compared to crime statistics from their regions, whereas Blacks and Latinos were underrepresented as victims.

In their analysis of just over 3,000 news stories about crime in the Los Angeles area during 1996 and 1997, Gilliam and Iyengar (2000) found that 83% of these were about violent crime. Over 50% of all the crime reports made an explicit visual or verbal reference to the race or ethnicity of the suspect. Fifty-six percent of the suspects in these crime reports were minorities, and when only violent crimes were considered, that proportion rose to 59%. White perpetrators were disproportionately associated with nonviolent crime stories on the news, whereas actual crime statistics for Los Angeles County showed that minorities accounted for the largest share of nonviolent felonies. Instead, local television news emphasized minorities as the principal perpetrators of violent crimes, and thus, may forge a three-way association between crime, violence, and minority status in the mind of the viewer.

Even when Whites are as likely as Blacks to be depicted as perpetrators of violent crimes, a study of local news in Chicago demonstrated that White victims outnumbered Black victims, despite the fact that Blacks in that city were more likely to be victimized (Entman, 1992; Entman & Rojecki, 2000). This misrepresentation is augmented by more subtle differences in how defendants are portrayed: Black defendants are less likely to be identified by name and are more likely to be shown in physical custody by a police officer (handcuffed, grasped, restrained) than White defendants (Entman & Rojecki, 2000).

Poindexter et al. (2003) provide additional support that local news creates a "frame" that links African Americans with crime. News coverage of African Americans, Latinos, Asian Americans, and Native Americans was analyzed in a sample of news stories in local television newscasts from 26 stations in 12 cities from the years 1987, and 1989 through 1998. The researchers noted the race and ethnicity for anchors, reporters, news sources, and perpetrators of crimes. Additionally, they coded the "racial focus" of a story, wherein if more than half of the individuals shown in a news story were of a particular race or ethnic group, that race would be coded as the primary focus. Their examination of crime stories revealed that more than half of the perpetrators were White (51%), compared to 41% Black, 2% Latinos, and 1% Asian. However, in looking at the racial focus of news stories delivered by a reporter, they found that 69% of Black-focused stories were about crime, compared to just 28% of White-focused stories.

The racial or ethnic background of the on-air news staff revealed a consistent pattern of marginalization for the minority reporters and news anchors (Poindexter et al., 2003). In stories delivered by a reporter, most of the reporters were White (73%). Just 16% were African American and 3% Latino (8% of the reporters' race and ethnicity could not be determined). The race or ethnicity of news anchors followed suit, with the majority being White and African Americans the second most common. Looking at the race and ethnicity of anchors according to whether they spoke first or second in the newscast, African American anchors were more likely to speak second than first.

The study also found that the race and ethnicity of sources used in the stories—whether as experts or private citizens—privileged White sources across the board. Only when multiple sources appeared did the numbers of minority sources—almost exclusively African American—increase. Rarely were minorities the first source presented (12% for experts and 14% for private citizens).

Analyses of race representation in network news broadcasts have been fewer, and because crime news tends to be less common as an ongoing topic in network newscasts, network news analyses have tended to focus on other types of content. In doing so, they have revealed other forms of racial or ethnic bias.

Television as an audiovisual medium draws heavily on images to convey the meaning behind certain social problems or issues, including poverty and its symptoms (Entman & Rojecki, 2000). In samples of local and national network news, Entman and Rojecki (2000) found that symptoms associated with poverty could be grouped in two broad categories—where poverty was portrayed as a threat to both the nonpoor and poor through crime, drugs, or gangs, or poverty was portrayed as a source of suffering for the poor. The dominant visual images associated with stories dealing with poverty were those of Black persons in organized activities (such as marches, meetings, or church worship); Black persons milling about in unorganized activities, often along with police officers; urban blight (e.g., boarded up buildings); or Black community leaders or politicians talking with a group. Although some of the coverage could engender pity or compassion about the kind of suffering experienced by those impoverished, in stories on discrimination or economic suffering, television news failed to visually express suffering in a way that could provoke sympathy. Rarely was poverty dealt with explicitly in terms of underlying causes and basic information about income and wealth distribution.

More broadly, in their 1997 study of network news, Entman and Rojecki (2000) demonstrated that the range of topics attributed to Black interviewees was very limited compared to Whites. Out of nearly 1,400 soundbites, only one Black person said anything in an economics-related story, compared with 86 soundbites associated with White speakers. This pattern recurred for foreign affairs coverage, science or technology, health matters, and several other areas that either "invoked the common experiences or interests of Americans as a whole (disasters, foreign affairs, politics, and deaths/rituals) or that involved technical expertise (science, economics)" (Entman & Rojecki, 2000, p. 64). Black voices were more common in stories dealing with entertainment, sports, or discrimination—areas already stereotypically associated with African Americans. Data from transcriptions in which the word "Black" appeared (or other words connoting the group) revealed that Blacks were mentioned in contexts associated with crime (either as perpetrators or victims) or when they require attention from the government (such as affirmative action cases). Although the number of references to Latinos or Hispanics was far fewer than to Blacks, the range of topics associated with them was similarly narrow and stereotypic.

Even news stories that focus on the legislative records of African American members of Congress provide a limited focus on their congressional records, despite the fact that these legislators' agendas are increasingly similar to their non-Black counterparts (Schaffner & Gadson, 2004). Noting White citizens' perception that African American politicians are narrowly focused on minority issues, and thus, may not represent their interests, Schaffner and Gadson's study examined local news coverage for the link between the race or ethnicity of the House member and indicators of whether the subject matter of the story was race-oriented. They examined newscast abstracts of 168 major network affiliates, covering at least part of 370 congressional districts (85% of all districts). Their findings demonstrate that although African Americans legislators received more coverage than their colleagues, this coverage tended to emphasize race-related issues more than other legislative accomplishments. This was especially true in less diverse markets.

One network news study explicitly examined crime portrayals, failing to replicate local news' common depiction of African Americans as more frequent perpetrators of crime than Whites (Dixon, Azocar, & Casas, 2003). Drawing on a representative sample of news programs from ABC, NBC, and CBS from 1994 to 1997 and 2000, they found that Whites were more often portrayed as perpetrators and victims compared to Blacks. However, Whites were overrepresented and African Americans were underrepresented as victims of crimes when compared with actual crime statistics for the relevant period, a pattern that—as previously noted—can reinforce the perception that African Americans are a threat.

Turning to the two dominant Spanish-language television networks (that reach over 90% of Latino households in the United States), Subervi-Vélez (1999) provides a view of national and local news coverage in the area of health. Although the general emphasis on health was comparable to general market television, Spanish-language television stations cast the health news in ways that made it more relevant for the Latino audience through the provision of an expert or local cultural or community angle.

RADIO NEWS MEDIA COVERAGE OF MINORITIES

Much less scrutiny has been given to radio news, either for its coverage about minorities or its ability to shape race-related perceptions of the public. Yet radio news is another important source of news for many Americans. A 2001 study conducted by the Radio and Television News Directors Foundation reported that although television remains the dominant news medium, most people use radio as a news source during the day.

For example, about one third of adults turn to radio for their news when they get up and are getting ready for their day. More than three quarters of commuters rely on radio for news while traveling to and from work—and once there, one third of workers use radio to get most of their news. Listeners surveyed perceived radio as second to local and national TV for providing a lively exchange of opinions on issues, ranking above newspapers for this purpose (Radio and Television News Directors Foundation, 2001).

Indeed, news ranked second—after music—as a reason why people tune into a radio station. The study also found that African American and Hispanic audiences listen to more radio than the general population, and their use of radio as a significant news source continues into the evening. Across all groups, the most popular source of radio news is music stations. Adults ages 18 to 64 spend as much time per weekday listening to news on stations that play mostly music as they do listening to all-news stations, talk-radio, and public radio stations combined.

News coverage, especially that relevant to minority concerns, that is included by other types of radio station formats (e.g., musically focused), remains understudied. Instead, political talk radio has received the most scholarly attention for its ability to garner a large, national audience and the possibility that it persuades listeners to adopt the viewpoints espoused by its hosts (Barker & Knight, 2000).

Although most studies do not provide a systematic analysis of its content, as part of their study on the ability of talk radio to shape public opinion, Barker and Knight (2000) identified the frequency with which certain topics were mentioned during 1993 to 1995 on the Rush Limbaugh program. Statements promoting the virtues of individual initiative, the free market, and the Republican Party were common, as were condemnations of the media, the Clinton administration, and other groups perceived to interfere with economic freedom. Although sexist comments were often expressed, Barker and Knight did not find comments reflecting "overt racism" (p. 154). However, one of the sample messages from the program suggests the presence of racism of the type that Gandy (1998) refers to in his discussion of "modern racism" (p. 219). In discussing a crime bill (one of the frequently mentioned issues on the show), Limbaugh said, "The crime bill is worthless—it contains meaningless policies and programs, such as midnight basketball games in inner cities" (Barker & Knight, 2000, p. 169). Just as Entman and Rojecki (2000) identified ways in which Blacks become associated with crime and violence, and unpopular policies such as welfare and affirmative action in local television news, if one examined Limbaugh's program with a coding instrument tuned to carefully examine race, the biases identified in television news coverage might be replicated in at least some talk radio shows as well.

Talk show programs offer a range of themes to their listeners (Cappella, Turow, & Jamieson, 1996). In a comparison of over 50 programs spanning an ideological spectrum from conservative, moderate, and liberal, the analysis found that foreign affairs and military matters were covered more by moderate and conservative programs than liberal shows that gave priority to family, education, children, prayer, gender roles, and ethics. All types of programs tended to cover human rights and minorities to the same extent (about 10% of their content). In contrast, coverage of crime, punishment, and justice ranged from 14.4% (liberal) to 21.1% (moderate) and 16.2% (conservative). Unfortunately, the analysis focused only on the broad categories of content, not on the nature of the messages within each category.

A Black-owned FM community radio station in South Central Los Angeles (KJLH) was the focus of a case study by Johnson (2004). Johnson notes that, historically, Black radio plays an active role in community affairs, informing and unifying its mostly African American listeners, providing an important forum during times of crisis, and supporting political activism especially through voter registration drives. During the civil unrest following the Rodney King beatings in 1992, for example, an analysis of the "Front Page" program (a 90-min on-air discussion of issues that affect the African American community) showed an emphasis on discussing violence and the Los Angeles Police Department, but also on community unity, empowerment, safety and peace, and economic development (in that Black-owned businesses and media were seen as critical toward meeting the social and political objectives within the community).

THE LINK BETWEEN NEWS MEDIA COVERAGE OF RACE AND PUBLIC ATTITUDES ABOUT RACE

The Kerner Commission was concerned that deficits in news media coverage of minorities was, in part, responsible for the civil unrest that ensued in 1967 (Kerner Commission, 1968). What empirical evidence do we have that news media coverage shapes media consumers' knowledge, attitudes, or behaviors? The findings of several studies confirm that television news constrains White viewers' perceptions and attitudes of minorities, and, more broadly, the policies and programs they are likely to support. Moreover, minority viewers express continued dissatisfaction with the way they are represented in the news.

Gilliam and Iyengar (2000) substantiate that local television news coverage of crime can heighten negative attitudes toward African Americans by White viewers. As one test of the impact of news viewing on attitudes about crime and the link between crime and race, the researchers designed an experiment in which participants viewed a crime story embedded in a 15-min newscast that either featured close-up photos of African American or White male suspects. Findings revealed that when exposed to the story featuring the African American suspect, White participants' negative perceptions of African Americans increased. More White participants believed that crime is caused by individual failings and supported more punitive crime policies. The White participants viewed African Americans more negatively in terms of their perceptions of African Americans as law abiding, intelligent, disciplined, or lazy. These experimental findings were reinforced by survey findings from an annual study of the social and political attitudes of LA county residents. Interviews with 647 participants, where news viewing habits were compared with attitudes toward crime and race, found that more frequent local news viewers were more likely to support punitive remedies and perceive African Americans as less intellectually able.

In a study that compared frequency of TV news viewing with perceptions of race, Busselle and Crandall (2002) found that heavier news viewing was consistent with "modern racism," where these viewers are more likely to believe that lack of job opportunities is not a reason for the relative lack of success among

African Americans than their lesser viewing counterparts, and instead, are more likely convinced that lack of motivation is a reason for lack of success. Busselle and Crandall (2002) conclude the following: "These relationships are consistent with content analyses indicating that Blacks in the news are often portrayed as criminals or as the idle, yet able-bodied, poor" (p. 279).

A further link between news coverage, racial attitudes, and subsequent evaluations of political candidates was documented by Valentino (1999) in his experimental study. A racially and ethnically diverse group of participants in the study were either shown no crime story, a story with nonminority suspects, or a story with minority suspects, and then asked to evaluate presidential candidates Clinton and Dole on a variety of measures, including an overall assessment of the candidates and specific assessments of the candidates' performance in certain issue areas. Valentino found that coverage that portrayed minority suspects was a potent trigger for priming racial attitudes and raising the saliency of crime performance in the overall assessment participants made of the candidates. The findings also demonstrated that one "racially coded" area like crime can prime another racially coded issue like welfare. When shown a minority suspect, White participants were more likely to prioritize their perception of the candidate's concern for Whites as a factor in their overall support.

As an adjunct to their analysis of local and network television, Entman and Rojecki (2000) surveyed White Indianapolis residents about their attitudes toward race. In follow-up interviews with a subset of respondents, they asked specifically about images of Blacks seen on the news. Media images—especially those that associate Blacks with violence and laziness—fueled attitudes about Blacks representing a threat and lacking responsibility. Although these attitudes were especially strong among those not personally acquainted with Blacks, the authors conclude the following: "The power of such forms is evident in the fact that the reality created by news coverage is compelling enough to override lived experience" (p. 44).

In the sphere of radio, several studies attest to the ability of political talk radio to inform and shape attitudes toward political figures (Barker & Knight, 2000; Hall & Cappella, 2002; Lee & Cappella, 2001), although research has yet to examine the impact on racial beliefs or attitudes.

Squires (2000) notes that generally the question of how Black-controlled mass media shape Black public life has not been as rigorously analyzed as White-controlled media on White attitudes toward Blacks. Drawing on ethnographic and survey research for her analysis of listeners to WVON-AM, a Black-owned radio station in Chicago, she found that the station provided a forum for people to talk and connect listeners with other community events of relevance to the Black community. Moreover, WVON sponsored some of these events. Listeners drew comparisons between WVON and White-owned, mainstream media, arguing that WVON gave a fairer view of their communities, and citing the deficiencies of White-owned media. Squires (2000) writes of the bond between fellow listeners and the "larger imagined black community" (p. 91) facilitated by the discussions and other activities made available through the station.

FOUNDATIONS FOR PUBLIC POLICY

The deficiencies in the news media's coverage of minorities identified by the Kerner Commission Report in 1968 have not been rectified. Coverage of racial or ethnic groups other than African Americans by the news media is relatively infrequent. The coverage that does occur—and this is documented more clearly for African Americans than other groups—reflects a limited range of activities, concerns, and accomplishments, and tends to support a view of ethnic minorities as a threat or social burden. The concern, also identified by the Kerner Commission, that news portrayals shape the attitudes, beliefs, and actions of the public, has been supported by theoretical and empirical analysis in the ensuing years. Indeed, a demonstrated link between television news media coverage of race (whether cast as news or entertainment) and public perceptions of race does exist.

The Kerner Report identified a corrective measure: integrate more journalists of color into key decision-making roles. Many minority journalists believe that change should begin at the head of the media operation. In a survey of nearly 800 minority broadcast and print journalists, respondents agreed that minority executives would cover more stories about all minority groups and generally improve the coverage of minorities by being more sensitive to racism (Rivas-Rodriguez, Subervi-Vélez, Bramlett-Solomon, & Heider, 2004).

The FCC applied various race-neutral policies to address, whether directly or indirectly, the issue of minority underrepresentation or misrepresentation in the media. One is license revocation, as in the WLBT case, for failure to serve the needs of the community, a rarely used remedy. Another was the Fairness Doctrine, which required balance in news reports. Under the Fairness Doctrine, broadcasters were required to devote a reasonable percentage of air time to issues of public concern, and to provide an opportunity for contrasting views (FCC, 1949). The FCC repealed that requirement during the Reagan Administration, arguing that the market would best achieve the viewpoint competition the First Amendment contemplates (Complaint of Syracuse Peace Council Against Television Station WTVH, 1987; FCC, 1987). A third approach was the development of policies based on antidiscrimination and ascertainment requirements. The FCC found these policies insufficient to address the problem and they were later repealed relying instead on a general obligation broadcasters have to address "issues of concern to their community of license" (FCC, 1983, p. 1420). A final response was to use race conscious policies to promote minority ownership, both to increase diffusion of control over the media and to encourage the likelihood that programming responsive to minority community needs would be aired.

The next section examines the historical and legal underpinnings of minority ownership policies. It examines recent studies exploring the correlation between minority ownership and programming. It also discusses the relevance of these studies to judicial inquiries about the constitutionality of programs to encourage minority ownership.

MINORITY OWNERSHIP POLICIES

The FCC's minority ownership policies have their origin in the FCC's initially ineffective responses to segregationist broadcast licensee WLBT's refusal to fairly respond to the needs and interests of the African American community, and the community as a whole, in Jackson, Mississippi, the area it was licensed to serve. Neither the station nor the FCC adequately responded to the Kerner Commission's findings that the broadcast media portrayed African Americans in a stereotypic, racially insensitive manner. As discussed earlier, in the face of evidence that WLBT refused to carry programming about the Civil Rights Movement, the FCC renewed WLBT's license. On appeal, the Circuit Court for the District of Columbia overturned the renewal in *Office, UCC v. FCC* (1969), finding that the record of the licensee's consistent refusal to carry any programming dealing with civil rights, racial issues, or integration while advocating a segregationist perspective and engaging in derogatory stereotyping of African Americans did not justify renewal. The WLBT decision represented a turning point in recognizing that serving the whole community, including its racial and ethnic minority members, was crucial to determining whether broadcasters were serving the public interest.

In response to the Kerner Commission findings that the broadcast media's unbalanced portrayals of African Americans contributed to the civil unrest in 1967 following the assassination of Martin Luther King, the FCC instituted anti-employment discrimination policies and equal employment guidelines for broadcast licensees. In addition, the FCC established community ascertainment requirements for broadcast licensees. Licensees were required to contact community leaders and members of the general public to obtain information about community interests and to present programming responsive to those interests.

The FCC developed a broadcaster community leader checklist consisting of 20 groupings or institutions found in most communities. The FCC required that licensees specifically contact and interview minorities in the community, both as a distinct grouping or institution, for example, the NAACP (among the 20 groupings outlined by the FCC) and within the 19 "nonminority" institutions or groupings. Licensees were required to present lists of ascertained needs and interests and responsive programs as part of their applications for renewal of their licenses. The ascertainment requirements were abolished in 1981 (*UCC v. FCC*, 1983, p. 1421).

Despite the FCC's antidiscrimination, equal employment, and ascertainment requirements, in 1977 the U.S. Commission on Civil Rights reported that minorities remained unfairly portrayed and substantially underrepresented in the media. The findings of the report, entitled "Window Dressing on the Set: Women and Minorities in Television," were based on employment data obtained from 40 commercial and public television stations, programs broadcast between 1969 and 1974 and on news programs broadcast between March 1974 and February 1975. The Civil Rights Commission report asserted that broadcasters misrepresented the extent of their compliance with antidiscrimination and equal employment opportunity rules. The report also castigated the FCC for allowing broadcasters to police themselves regarding the portrayal of minorities in news, public affairs, and entertainment programming. The FCC defended its Equal Employment Opportunity policies and argued that any attempt on its part to directly regulate content would run afoul of censorship prohibitions in the Communications Act of 1934.[1]

However, in its Policy Statement on Minority Ownership, the FCC (1978b) concluded that despite its race neutral efforts to enhance diversity of viewpoint via its equal employment opportunity and community ascertainment requirements, the views of minority Americans remained inadequately represented in the broadcast media, and that inadequacy adversely affected the American public's right to diversity. Faced with the documented inadequacy of minority portrayals and representation in broadcasting, mindful of the statutory prohibition against government censorship of broadcast speech, and cognizant of the editorial control vested in the broadcast licensee, the FCC implemented several minority ownership policies to enhance broadcast diversity.

In its competitive process for the award of initial broadcast licenses, the FCC gave a "plus" to applicants that were in part or whole, minority owned or managed.[2] Under its distress sale policy, the FCC allowed a broadcast licensee that had been designated for hearing because of an issue that disqualified it from controlling a license, to sell its license to a minority owned firm to avoid the loss of value of the license (FCC, 1978a, p. 983; *Metro Broadcasting, Inc. v. FCC*, 1990). In addition, under its tax certificate policy, the FCC awarded a certificate allowing capital gains taxes to be deferred when a broadcast or cable system owner elected to sell their license to minority owned or controlled entities or entrepreneurs.[3] The FCC also continued its antidiscrimination and equal employment opportunity policies for broadcast licensees.

From 1978 to 1990, the FCC's minority ownership policies were a critical catalyst in the increase of minority-owned broadcast stations. According to government sources, from 1978 to 1990 minority ownership of the roughly 12,000 radio and 1,200 television stations increased from approximately 1% to 3.5% (Gerard, 1990). However, the modest growth in minority broadcast ownership was accompanied by challenges to the ownership policies and questions about whether minority ownership of broadcast stations increased program diversity.

MINORITY OWNERSHIP AND DIVERSITY AS A COMPELLING STATE INTEREST

In 1990, in *Metro Broadcasting, Inc. v. FCC*, two of the FCC's policies, minority enhancement in comparative licensing and the distress sale transfer to a minority owned enterprise, were challenged as violations of the equal protection requirements of the Fifth Amendment.[4] The policies under review were challenged in separate proceedings and consolidated for consideration by the Supreme Court.

In one case, Metro Broadcasting sought review of decisions by the FCC and the D.C. Circuit Court of Appeals awarding a new television station to Rainbow Broadcasting Company (Rainbow) in a comparative hearing. In that case, the Circuit Court affirmed the FCC's determination that Rainbow's minority ownership was a decisive factor in awarding the license to Rainbow rather than Metro Broadcasting (*Winter Park Communications, Inc. v. FCC*, 1989). In the second case, a different panel of the D.C. Circuit overturned an FCC order approving Faith Center, Inc.'s distress sale of its broadcast license to minority-owned Astroline Communications, Inc. the Circuit Court panel ruled that the FCC order allowing the distress sale deprived Shurberg Broadcasting of its right to equal protection under the Fifth Amendment (*Shurberg Broadcasting of Hartford, Inc. v. FCC*, 1989).

A majority of the Supreme Court held that the FCC's policies did not violate equal protection. They offered three reasons. First, it was determined that the comparative plus and distress sale policies were the result of express congressional policy and FCC expertise to which the Court accorded deference.

Second, it was noted that the policies were based on empirical evidence of a nexus between minority ownership and broadcast diversity. Finally, the majority determined that the policies were substantially related to the achievement of the federal government's interest in broadcast diversity and were limited and properly tailored remedies that did not place undue burdens on nonminorities (*Metro Broadcasting, Inc. v. FCC,* 1990). In reaching its conclusions, the Court majority explicitly stated the following:

> The FCC's conclusion that there is an empirical nexus between minority ownership and broadcasting diversity is a product of its expertise, and we accord its judgment deference ... [T]he FCC's reasoning with respect to the minority ownership policies is consistent with longstanding practice under the Communications Act. From its inception, public regulation of broadcasting has been premised on the assumption that diversification of ownership will broaden the range of programming available to the broadcast audience. Thus, "it is upon ownership that public policy places primary reliance with respect to diversification of content, and that historically has proved to be significantly influential with respect to editorial comment and the presentation of news. (*Metro Broadcasting, Inc. v. FCC,* 1990, pp. 570–571, citing *TV 9 Inc. v. FCC,* 1973, p. 938)

Increasing the number of minority viewpoints by increasing minority ownership of media was found to be important to achieving the government's First Amendment goal of diversifying control over broadcast media. The goal of diversification was deemed to be of critical importance because the right to speak (the right to create, select, and edit what may be said over the public airwaves) is vested in the broadcast station owner (Hammond, 1991).

By contrast, the dissent challenged the existence of a nexus between minority ownership and programming diversity. The dissent further argued that even if there were a nexus, the requirements of the marketplace would constrain minority station owners' program selection.

The Court majority did not find the dissent's arguments to be persuasive. Instead, the Court found that although "station owners are guided to some extent by market demand in their programming decisions, Congress and the Commission have properly determined that there may be important differences between the broadcasting practices of minority owners and those of their nonminority counterparts" (*Metro Broadcasting, Inc. v. FCC,* 1990, p. 580). Moreover, the Court held that the conclusion of Congress and the FCC that there is a nexus between minority ownership and broadcasting diversity was "corroborated by a host of empirical evidence" that "minority-owned stations tend to devote more news time to topics of minority interest and to avoid racial and ethnic stereotypes in portraying minorities" (*Metro Broadcasting, Inc. v. FCC*, 1990, pp. 580–581).

The Court cited the findings of the Congressional Research Service (CRS; 1988) study of the nexus between minority broadcast station ownership and broadcast programming. In its report, the CRS analyzed data from a survey commissioned by the FCC in which approximately 8,720 FCC-licensed radio and television stations were queried about programming practices. The CRS found that although only 20% of stations with no African American ownership responded that they attempted to direct programming at African American audiences, 65% of stations with African American ownership reported that they did so. Although only 10% of stations without Hispanic ownership stated that they targeted programming at Hispanic audiences, 59% of stations with Hispanic owners said they did. These findings led the CRS, and consequently the Court, to conclude that there was a strong correlation between minority ownership and diversity of programming (*Metro Broadcasting, Inc. v. FCC*, 1990). This conclusion was later corroborated by a second subsequent analysis of the same data (Dubin & Spitzer, 1995). The Court also cited studies showing that "a minority owner is more likely to employ minorities in managerial and other important roles where they can have an impact on station policies"(*Metro Broadcasting, Inc. v. FCC*, 1990, p. 583, no. 34, citing Wimmer, 1986, p. 426, no. 516).

In addition, the Court majority cited findings of other studies that the minority status of an owner influences a station's selection of topics for news coverage and the presentation of editorial viewpoint, especially on matters of particular concern to minorities. "Minority ownership does appear to have specific impact on the presentation of minority images in local news," the Court noted, "inasmuch as minority-owned stations tend to devote more news time to topics of minority interest and to avoid racial and ethnic stereotypes in portraying minorities"[5] (*Metro Broadcasting, Inc. v. FCC*, 1990, p. 581).

The constitutional jurisprudence on which the *Metro Broadcasting, Inc. v. FCC* (1990) decision was based was short lived, however. In *Adarand Constructors v. Pena* (1995), a subsequent Supreme Court held that the intermediate scrutiny standard of review employed by the Court in *Metro Broadcasting, Inc. v. FCC* was inappropriate and overruled the *Metro Broadcasting, Inc. v. FCC* decision with regard to the standard. The 1995 *Adarand Constructors v. Pena* Court majority stated the following:

> All racial classifications, imposed by whatever federal, state, or local governmental actor, must be analyzed by a reviewing court under strict scrutiny. In other words, such classifications are constitutional only if they are narrowly

> tailored measures that further compelling governmental interests. To the extent that *Metro Broadcasting* is inconsistent with that holding, it is overruled. (p. 227).

A narrow reading of the *Adarand Constructors v. Pena* (1995) holding regarding the *Metro Broadcasting, Inc. v. FCC* (1990) precedent would support a conclusion that only the standard of review was at issue. At least one appeals court has argued that as a result of the decision in *Adarand Constructors v. Pena*, the *Metro Broadcasting, Inc. v. FCC* Court finding that broadcast diversity was a compelling government interest also had been overturned (*Lutheran Church-Missouri Synod v. FCC*, 1998).[6] Taken a step further, it could be argued that diversity in a pluralistic society was no longer deemed a compelling government interest.

In this context, the Supreme Court's 2003 decision in *Grutter v. Bollinger* is of particular importance. The *Grutter v. Bollinger* majority opinion establishes that diversity is a compelling state interest for purposes of determining the constitutionality of race-based governmental action in the context of equal protection jurisprudence.[7] Although *Grutter v. Bollinger* was decided in the context of graduate school admissions, its application is not necessarily limited to the higher education context. The Supreme Court in *Grutter v. Bollinger* held that race may be a factor in admitting law students to promote diversity in the educational setting and better prepare students for the workforce and the world ahead. This forward-looking compelling state interest, promoting diversity of dialogue, is fundamental to the purpose of broadcasting.[8] The Supreme Court in *Red Lion Broadcasting v. FCC* (1969) emphasized the role of broadcasting in serving as a forum for the "marketplace of ideas," central to our democratic society. *Grutter v. Bollinger* answered in the affirmative the question of whether the forward-looking purpose of promoting diversity can be a compelling state interest.

The *Metro Broadcasting, Inc. v. FCC* (1990), *Adarand Constructors v. Pena* (1995), and *Grutter v. Bollinger* (2003) opinions may be read as establishing that any government use of race-based remedies must be examined and pass muster under strict scrutiny analysis, and that diversity remains a compelling state interest. However, given Justice O'Connor's *Metro Broadcasting, Inc. v. FCC* dissent and the circuit court opinion in *Lutheran Church-Missouri Synod v. FCC* (1998) overturning the FCC's Equal Employment Opportunity rules, the question remains as to whether the Court would consider the government interest in facilitating broadcast station ownership diversity to be compelling. Justice O'Connor, the author of the *Grutter v. Bollinger* majority opinion affirming diversity as a compelling interest, is also the author of the dissenting opinion in *Metro Broadcasting, Inc. v. FCC* challenging the government's assertion that its interest in broadcast station ownership diversity is compelling.

THE DISSENT IN METRO BROADCASTING

In her *Metro Broadcasting, Inc. v. FCC* (1990) dissent, Justice O'Connor argued that under strict scrutiny, only the compelling government interest of remedying past discrimination could support the government's use of racial classifications. However, the FCC did not institute the minority ownership policies to remedy past discrimination. Despite the absence of a remedial intent, Justice O'Connor sought to hold the policies to the strict scrutiny (remedial) standard. Under the standard, the government's interest in program diversity had to be "sufficiently specific and verifiable" to support the use of the race-based minority ownership policies (*Metro Broadcasting, Inc. v. FCC,* 1990 p. 613). She argued that the government's interest did not meet the test because the interest was too amorphous. According to Justice O'Connor, the government had not established how one would define or measure a particular viewpoint that might be associated with race, or even how one would assess the diversity of broadcast viewpoints. Consequently, the interest could not be compelling. In her opinion, the government had failed to identify and quantify the existence of such race-based viewpoints. From this, Justice O'Connor concluded that the equation of race and ethnicity with viewpoint rested on an assumption that a particular viewpoint is held by particular racial or ethnic groups and that a particular applicant, solely by virtue of her race or ethnicity, is more likely to provide that desired viewpoint. Such an assumption, according to Justice O'Connor, constituted constitutionally impermissible racial stereotyping.

Justice O'Connor speculated that the minority ownership policies would include many members of a particular racial or ethnic group that would have no interest in advancing the views the FCC believed to be underrepresented. At the same time, the policies would not award a preference to individuals of other racial or ethnic groups who might be particularly well versed in and committed to presenting those views. Consequently, the policies excluded nonminority groups from favor, regardless of whether the particular viewpoints were held. Thus, for instance, persons who do not get a comparative "plus" for minority ownership in the competitive licensing process may claim that they have been judged according to their race rather than on a relevant criterion.

Justice O'Connor also challenged Congress's and the FCC's assumption that a strong correlation existed between a station owner's race and broadcast programming. She questioned the proposition that the absence of minority views was directly correlated to the absence of sizable numbers of minority-owned stations. She asserted that the "assumption is correct only to the extent that minority-owned stations provide the desired additional views, and that stations owned by individuals not favored by the preferences cannot, or at least do not, broadcast underrepresented programming" (*Metro Broadcasting, Inc. v. FCC,* 1990, p. 618).

Finally, Justice O'Connor questioned whether a broadcast station owner's ethnically or racially motivated preferences would prevail against an owner's personal inclinations to realize a profit or a market that might demand programming expressing different viewpoints.

JUSTICE O'CONNOR'S ANALYSIS IN *GRUTTER v. BOLLINGER* (2003)

In contrast to her *Metro Broadcasting, Inc. v. FCC* 1990 dissent, Justice O'Connor's majority opinion in *Grutter v. Bollinger* (2003) establishes that diversity is a compelling state interest for purposes of determining the constitutionality of race-based governmental action in the context of equal protection jurisprudence. The *Grutter v. Bollinger* opinion demonstrates that the application of strict scrutiny is not necessarily fatal to efforts by the government to consider race.[9] Moreover, the Court majority also made it clear that remedying past discrimination is not the only permissible justification for race-based governmental action.

In concluding that the University of Michigan law school could have a compelling state interest in student body diversity, the Court states that it deferred to the school's assessment that student diversity will yield substantial educational benefits. However, the Court stressed the importance of the significant factual substantiation submitted by the school and its amici. According to the proffered evidence, the benefits of a diverse student body include the following: the facilitation of "cross-racial understanding" that helps to break down racial stereotypes and "enables [students] to better understand persons of different races" (*Grutter v. Bollinger,* 2003, p. 321).

Educational diversity also promotes "positive learning outcomes, better prepares students for an increasingly diverse workforce and society, and better prepares them as professionals" (*Grutter v. Bollinger,* 2003, p. 321). These assertions were reiterated and substantiated by major American businesses and the United States military, which emphasized that diversity was necessary to global competitiveness and national security. The Court itself acknowledged the importance of educational diversity to effective participation in the civic life of the nation.

There is a significant relationship between these educational goals and broadcasting's broader mission of promoting the marketplace of ideas. Broadcasting shapes cross-racial and ethnic understanding and may expose the American public to the existence of an increasingly diverse society and world. The Supreme Court has recognized broadcasting as a "prime source of national cohesion" (*Red Lion Broadcasting v. FCC,* 1969, p. 387, no. 15) and a "uniquely pervasive presence" in American life (*FCC v. Pacifica Foundation,* 1978, p. 748).

Although it may be properly argued that the government has a compelling interest in broadcast diversity just as it does in educational diversity, evidence that establishes the compelling nature of the interest in broadcast diversity is of critical importance to a finding that minority broadcast station ownership policies further broadcast diversity. Such evidence must address the nexus questions raised in Justice O'Connor's dissent.

THE DEFINITION, MEASUREMENT, AND ASSESSMENT OF VIEWPOINT DIVERSITY

Justice O'Connor's *Metro Broadcasting, Inc. v. FCC* (1990) dissent raised five nexus questions: (a) Do station owners' race or ethnicity influence how their stations are run and what is broadcast, and how close that correlation is for purposes of determining whether the remedy of preference "fits" the categorization? (b) Are race and ethnicity associated with viewpoints or is the assertion of a relationship an unsupported racial generalization or stereotype? (c) Do minority owners provide views that are not provided by majority owners? (d) Do station owners' race or ethnicity prevail against personal inclinations or market forces to influence the expression of a racial or ethnic perspective in the broadcast market? (e) Do owners have much control over content, justifying preferences based on ownership?

Several recent studies have provided data that inform these questions. As discussed in more detail later, the studies show that minority ownership makes a difference to the type and amount of programming targeted at minority communities. This is also true for news and public affairs, where minority owners were more likely to tailor their stories to the interests of minority communities. These studies support the conclusion that there is a nexus between minority ownership and diversity supporting the compelling state interest to remedy the dearth of that diversity.

STUDIES ON THE NEXUS BETWEEN MINORITY OWNERSHIP AND BROADCAST DIVERSITY

In 1997, the FCC put out a request for empirical research on the impact of minority ownership on programming in an effort to build on and address the weaknesses of the CRS study conducted in 1988 (and reanalyzed by Dubin & Spitzer in 1995). One study funded in part by the FCC but independently conducted by researchers from Santa Clara and Stanford universities, was an effort to address a number of the concerns raised in Justice O'Connor's *Metro Broadcasting, Inc. v. FCC* (1990) dissent (Bachen, Hammond, Mason, & Craft, 1999; see also Mason, Bachen & Craft, 2001). Specifically, this study addresses the O'Connor dissent's concerns about how to measure viewpoints, as well as the nexus between race or ethnicity of the station owner and content. Given the First Amendment values behind the diversity rationale, the research focused on speech that courts have held to be at the core of the First Amendment's protections: news and public affairs programming. In this regard, the study also examines whether the race or ethnicity of station owners affects the quantity of news and public affairs programming and whether it impacts the likelihood of stations to cover particular issues of interest to racial or ethnic minorities.

News or public affairs programming directors from minority-owned and nonminority-owned (hereafter, "majority-owned") stations were interviewed about several areas of programming and station characteristics. These included the amount and type of news and public affairs programming broadcast; their efforts to find a local news angle on a state, national, or international news story, especially when attempting to meet the needs of a particular audience; how a station distinguishes itself from its perceived primary competition, and whether these efforts reflect an attempt to meet the needs of a particular audience; and how a station defines and assesses the needs of its intended audience. The final sample included interviews from 99 news directors from minority-owned television and radio stations and 112 from majority-owned stations. Researchers controlled for market characteristics by pairing a minority-owned station with a majority-owned station within the same market.

The findings revealed that minority-owned stations, especially radio stations, differed in several ways from their majority-owned counterparts in decisions made about programming and news focus. Minority-owned radio stations were significantly more likely to choose a program format that appealed to a minority or ethnic audience and to provide news and public affairs programming of particular concern to minority or ethnic audiences. They were also more likely to tailor their news stories to minority community concerns.

The staff compositions of the stations differed as well: although majority-owned stations tended to have larger staffs, the proportion of minority staff persons was higher in minority-owned stations. Involvement by owners in news-related activities was also greater in the minority-owned stations compared with their majority-owned counterparts, although in a multivariate analysis with other measures including owner race or ethnicity and the percentage of minorities on the staff, owner involvement failed to be a significant predictor.

Additional analyses from the same data set by Craft (2003) attempted to clarify the nature of owner involvement in minority-owned and majority-owned stations. Craft concluded that owner involvement affects news and public affairs programming diversity through indirect means. Findings showed that when owners are perceived to be more involved in the day-to-day news and public affairs programming activities, broadcast station employees are more likely to perceive their values to be similar to the values of the station owner and to agree that the owner is the primary communicator of news values to employees.

Importantly, the study by Bachen et al. (1999) found that minority- and majority-owned stations did not differ on certain dimensions, such as the total amount of news broadcast. The significant differences emerged when the focus of the news story was considered. A higher percentage of minority-owned stations offer public affairs programming than do majority-owned stations. Connected with this finding is that minority-owned stations paid greater attention to ethnic and minority audiences' needs and interests and tended to program with those needs and interests in mind.

These findings dovetail with the results of several studies discussed earlier in the chapter. Subervi-Vélez (1999) found that health news broadcast by the major U.S. Spanish-language networks and their respective local stations, although similar on many dimensions to general-market television, was tailored to the Latino audience in ways that made the news more relevant to them. The examples of African American–owned radio stations KJLH-FM in Los Angeles (Johnson, 2004) and WVON-AM in Chicago (Squires, 2000) also demonstrate the greater attention given to issues that can impact minority listeners and communities. Both created forums for minority communities to discuss critical issues, an especially important resource as the Johnson (2004) study found during troubled times such as the uprising in Los Angeles following the Rodney King verdict. They also encouraged political participation through voter registration. As discussed earlier, Squires's (2000) study found that WVON listeners believed that station presented a fairer view of their communities than the White-owned, "mainstream" media.

Justice O'Connor also questioned whether the absence of minority views was directly correlated to the absence of sizeable numbers of minority-owned stations. She asserted that the "assumption is correct only to the extent that minority-owned stations provide the desired additional views, and that stations owned by individuals not favored by the preferences cannot, or at least do not, broadcast underrepresented programming" (*Metro Broadcasting, Inc. v. FCC,* 1990, p. 619).

In the studies reviewed earlier, we have seen evidence that minority-owned stations do indeed provide "desired additional views" and that majority-owned stations are less likely to broadcast "underrepresented programming." Thus far, the emphasis has been on data gathered from specific stations, noting differences between minority-owned and majority-owned stations when such comparisons are possible. Siegelman and Waldfogel (2001) look at the availability of minority programming and how that is linked more broadly to characteristics of the marketplace. They raise the question about whether small groups with distinct preferences—such as might be the case with racial and ethnic minorities—might be underserved by the radio market because the economic forces will favor stations that can deliver large numbers of people with similar preferences.

Drawing on data for commercial radio stations in 244 markets in 1993 and 1997, the researchers examined owner race, programming format, and total listening according to listeners' race and ethnicity for over 5,000 stations at each time period. Analyses demonstrated that preferences for programming among minorities and Whites are quite distinct. The amount of minority-targeted programming depends on the size of the minority population in that geographical area. Although the majority of stations targeting Blacks and Hispanics were White-owned, they found that minority ownership increases the net amount of minority-targeted programming. Markets with more minority-owned stations also have more minority-targeted stations. Most minority-owned stations do in fact broadcast minority-targeted programming; accordingly, these stations do add to the total programming available to minority listeners. Siegelman and Waldfogel (2001) conclude that "policies promoting minority ownership seem like a plausible method for increasing welfare by correcting inefficient underprovision" (p. 25).

Television programming preferences also differ sharply between Blacks and non-Blacks, and between Hispanics and non-Hispanics (Waldfogel, 2004). In a study that examined programming offerings and viewer data from 66 large television markets, the pattern found in radio repeated: the targeting of local programming to minority viewers is much greater in markets with larger minority populations. Additionally, the quantity of locally controlled minority-targeted television draws minority viewers. Some of this programming is linked to station ownership—for example, the study found that Spanish-language stations are much more likely to be present in markets that have larger

Hispanic populations. This means Hispanic viewers will encounter more group-targeted programming because there are more Spanish-language stations.

In *Metro Broadcasting, Inc. v. FCC* (1990), Justice O'Connor questioned whether the government could adequately define or measure a viewpoint associated with race or adequately assess the diversity of broadcast viewpoints generally. If it could not be measured, there would be no way to determine whether the asserted interest was warranted or for how long a policy based on the interest would be justified. She also questioned whether the assumption of a racial "viewpoint" that underlies the policy of taking race or ethnicity into account for the purpose of promoting broadcast viewpoint diversity, was based on stereotypes or assumptions about the correlation between race and viewpoint.

An analysis of studies published from 1999 to the present did not identify any study specifically defining and analyzing "minority" or "ethnic" viewpoints per se, rather, most researchers have identified minority preferences (demand side) for particular types and formats of programming. Minority and ethnic preferences have historically been founded on the prominence of minority cast members, hosts, reporters, or news anchors in programming; the prominence of identifiable minority artists and their works; the absence of offensive or misleading stereotypes; and the articulation of minority perspectives on current events and issues of public importance. The latter preference may in fact be one for the articulation of viewpoints resonant with those of the audience.

On the supply side, minority and ethnically owned stations were more likely to provide a program format attractive to minority or ethnic audiences, were more likely to present a diversity of on-air talent, were more likely to provide news and public affairs programming on events of particular concern to minorities and ethnic audiences, and were more likely to tailor news stories to address minority concerns (Bachen et al., 1999)

The National Telecommunications and Information Administration (NTIA) study of minority-owned broadcast stations reports that 75% of stations owned by minorities responding to the Department of Commerce's survey broadcast in formats targeted at minorities (Ofori, 1999). The study of minority-owned and minority-targeted radio stations and advertising industry practices commissioned by the FCC reported that in 1999, three-quarters of all stations reporting to the NTIA as minority-owned broadcast in formats focused on the minority community. The authors also point out that some station owners avoid format names or labels associated with minorities such as "Urban" or "Black" because of discrimination they encounter in the advertising marketplace. Thus, many of the minority-owned stations with formats not "labeled" as minority-owned are probably still targeting minorities and have large minority audiences, but are trying to escape negative market practices which reduce their revenues and opportunities to compete for advertising (Ofori, 1999).

Siegelman and Waldfogel (2001) found that there is a nexus between the race or ethnicity of broadcast licensees and the content of the programming their stations provide. Their study highlights that most minority owners broadcast in a minority-oriented format, providing evidence that counters Justice O'Connor's concern in *Metro Broadcasting, Inc. v. FCC* that the FCC's association of minority ownership with minority programming is a stereotype.

The research suggests that Justice O'Connor misperceives the fundamental gist of what minority ownership can be expected to achieve. Rather than seeking to assure the existence of a particular race-based viewpoint on the part of the station owner, what is in fact realized is a sensitivity to and appreciation for minority or ethnic preferences and viewpoints that allows for their articulation as part of the marketplace of ideas. Justice O'Connor also questioned whether an owner's ethnically or racially motivated preferences would prevail against an owner's personal inclinations or market forces.

Siegelman and Waldfogel (2001) hypothesize that the willingness to accept smaller returns could explain why greater Black ownership increased Black-targeted programming: additional Black owners were willing to enter low-profitability market niches. However, there was insufficient station profit data available to allow an examination of the thesis. The Ivy Planning Group (2000) study, "Whose Spectrum Is It Anyway? Historical Study of Market Entry Barriers, Discrimination and Changes in Broadcast and Wireless Licensing, 1950 to Present," provides anecdotal evidence of the commitment of minority owners to provide content responsive to their communities, even when they have more lucrative offers to sell their stations.

The O'Connor dissent also states her view that "station owners have only limited control over the content of programming" (*Metro Broadcasting, Inc. v. FCC*, 1990, pp. 626–627). This assertion is unsupported by any evidence or analysis. The control the WLBT television station owners had over programming, although they were an NBC affiliate, demonstrates the potential for owner involvement in editorial decisions about what to broadcast and what opinions will or will not be aired.

Two recent examples of broadcast owner exercise of editorial control lend further support to this observation. During the 2004 presidential campaign, the owners of the Sinclair Broadcasting group ordered their 62 television stations to preempt regularly scheduled programming and air a film highly critical of presidential candidate Senator John Kerry's antiwar activities 30 years ago (Rutenberg, 2004). The owners ultimately elected to air a portion of the controversial film despite running a significant financial and political risk (Holman, 2006). Sinclair's initial decision alienated some advertisers, enraged consumer and media watchdog groups who vowed to challenge its station licenses when they come up for renewal, and unnerved some analysts and investors considering the company's financial outlook (Carter, 2004). Nevertheless, the broadcaster persisted in presenting the programming.

The radio boycott of the Dixie Chicks after one of the group's members criticized the President's decision to go to war with Iraq is another example (Chonin, 2003; Staples, 2003). In that case, Cumulus Media, the second largest owner of radio broadcast stations in the United States, made a corporate decision to ban the airing of the music of the Dixie Chicks on its 42 country music stations for 30 days after lead singer Natalie Maines criticized President Bush for the war in Iraq (Saldana, 2003; Turner, 2004). The corporate broadcast owner's decision generated significant ire and concern in the music community and earned sharp rebukes from members of the United States Senate (Bachman, 2003; "Dixie Chicks Ban," 2003; Seiberg, 2003). Cox Radio, another broadcast group owner also established a ban on the Dixie Chicks.

The broadcasters defended their ban by stating that they were responding to public sentiment, some of which clearly disfavored Maines' statement. Yet, despite the ban and perhaps in reaction to it, the Dixie Chicks, one of the most popular country western and pop groups, have continued to perform in sold out and nearly sold out venues (Saldana, 2003; Williamson, 2003). Thus, contrary to Justice O'Connor's surmise, broadcast owners currently can and do exercise editorial control over content in ways that may be inconsistent with the dictates of the market.

Several commenters in the FCC's 2002 review of broadcast regulations submitted evidence of the influence of owners on content. In that proceeding, the UCC cited a Pew Research Center study of television journalists and executives that found nearly one quarter of journalists purposefully avoid newsworthy stories and nearly as many soften the tone of stories to benefit the interest of their news organizations. The UCC also cited a 2002 study finding that outlets included more references to their own products and services and treated those items more favorably than others, thus exhibiting a synergy bias (*Prometheus v. FCC,* 2004, fn. 26). The Consumer Federation of America (CFA), in its comments on the FCC's 2002 broadcast ownership review, cited a 2002 study finding that election information on news pages was slanted in favor of candidates endorsed on the editorial page. CFA also referred to a 2001 survey of news directors finding that media owners and sponsors pressure reporters to slant the news (*Prometheus v. FCC,* 2004, fn. 26).

In the *TV 9 Inc. v. FCC* case in 1974, the D.C. Circuit emphasized that public policies rely upon "ownership ... with respect to diversification of content" (*TV 9 Inc. v. FCC,* 1974, pp. 937–939). The Court noted that historically ownership has influenced "editorial comment and the presentation of news" (*TV 9 Inc. v. FCC,* 1974, p. 938). The Supreme Court in *NBC v. U.S.* (1943) emphasized that the licensee must have primary control and responsibility for the license and broadcast content (*NBC v. U.S.,* 1943, pp. 205–206). Thus, there is both legal precedent and empirical evidence of the importance of ownership to broadcast content.

We have presented compelling evidence that minority owners affect the type, quality, and extent of programming offered to audiences. Evidence shows minority-owned stations tailor programming to take into account the interests and concerns of minority communities. Minority owners also promote more programming addressing minorities whether through their own content or the marketplace response. Thus, in order to foster diversity of viewpoints in the marketplace, it is appropriate to look to minority ownership policies.

FCC REVIEW OF BROADCAST OWNERSHIP RULES

The FCC has a timely opportunity to consider the evidence of the positive impact of minority ownership on program diversity. The Telecommunications Act of 1996 required the FCC to review the broadcast ownership rules every 2 years. As part of this process, the FCC considered whether it should raise the cap on the number of stations a radio broadcast owner could control in a geographic market, and whether to raise the number of television stations an entity could control nationally (FCC, 2003). After the FCC raised the television station national ownership limits and changed a number of other rules, the Third Circuit Court of Appeals in *Prometheus Radio Project v. FCC* (2004), overruled a number of the FCC's decisions as lacking a rational basis. Rational basis is the lowest standard of review, but requires that there be sufficient evidence in the record to support the governmental body's decision, in this case, the FCC. The Third Circuit found that evidentiary basis lacking on a number of counts.

Notably, the FCC had eliminated the Failed Station Solicitation Rule (FSSR), which required a television license or construction permit holder to provide notice of the sale to potential out-of-market buyers before it could sell the failed, failing, or unbuilt television station to an in-market buyer (*Prome-*

theus Radio Project v. FCC, 2004, p. 420). The rule was designed to reduce information barriers (and "old boy" network barriers) that kept potential minority buyers from learning about a license for sale.

The FSSR arose out of the FCC's 1999 Television Rules Review, and was created to "ensure that qualified minority broadcasters had a fair chance to learn that certain financially troubled—and consequently more affordable—stations were for sale" (*Prometheus Radio Project v. FCC*, 2004, p. 420).[10] In the study commissioned by the FCC of historical market entry barriers and discrimination in broadcast and wireless licensing, the authors found that restricted access to information and opportunity was a barrier to minority ownership. One African American broadcaster interviewed for the study observed the following: "minorities are often the last to know about broadcast deals because they are not part of the network; and that by the time minorities find out, the deals have become public and the negotiations have already taken place" (Ivy Planning Group, 2000, p. 57). The FSSR rule was a race-neutral means to address this information barrier regarding possible broadcast license acquisition opportunities.

The Third Circuit concluded that the FCC's failure to mention anything about the effect this change would have on potential minority station owners evidenced a lack of reasoned analysis. The Third Circuit noted that although the FCC had promised in 1999 to "expand opportunities for minorities and women to enter the broadcast industry," the FSSR remained its only policy specifically aimed at fostering minority television station ownership (*Prometheus Radio Project v. FCC*, 2004, p. 420). The opinion stated that:

> in repealing the FSSR without any discussion of the effect of its decision on minority television station ownership (and without ever acknowledging the decline in minority station ownership notwithstanding the FSSR), the Commission entirely failed to consider an important aspect of the problem, and this amounts to arbitrary and capricious rulemaking. (*Prometheus Radio Project v. FCC*, 2004, p. 420)

The Third Circuit found the FCC's repeal of the FSSR inconsistent with the FCC's obligation to make the broadcast spectrum available to all people "without discrimination on the basis of race" (*Prometheus Radio Project v. FCC*, 2004, p. 420, citing Communications Act of 1934). In its order, the FCC reaffirmed its goals of competition, diversity, and localism. The Third Circuit noted that "(i)n setting its licensing policies, the Commission has long acted on the theory that diversification of mass media ownership serves the public interest by promoting diversity of program and service viewpoints, as well as by preventing undue concentration of economic power" (*Prometheus Radio Pro-*

ject v. FCC, 2004, p. 383, citing FCC, 1978b). The repeal of the FSSR with little comment or support seems inconsistent with those goals.

The Third Circuit noted that the FCC deferred consideration of the Minority Media and Telecommunications Council's (MMTC) other proposals for advancing minority and disadvantaged business and for promoting diversity in broadcasting. They required that the FCC's rulemaking process in response to the Third Circuit remand address MMTC's minority ownership and diversity proposals at the same time.

In the face of the FCC's past findings about the dearth of minority ownership, limited access to information about potential deals, capital barriers, and other factors, *Prometheus Radio Project v. FCC* (2004) requires FCC consideration of the impact of broadcast regulations on this population. This is significant because the *Prometheus Radio Project v. FCC* decision suggests that it would be "arbitrary and capricious" to fail to take into account the effect of regulatory changes on minority ownership and diversity. A race-based remedy would be subject to strict scrutiny under *Adarand Constructors v. Pena* (1995). However, *Prometheus Radio Project v. FCC* suggests that the FCC must consider the effect of race-neutral regulations on minority ownership to avoid being "arbitrary and capricious."

CONCLUSION

Broadcast television and radio are primary sources of news and public affairs information for American society. As a result, they have the potential power to produce national cohesion and reflect the diversity of American voices in the marketplace of ideas. To date, broadcasting has failed to live up to that potential. Nearly 50 years after WLBT blacked out pro-integration reports of the Civil Rights Movement and its leaders, and broadcast stereotypical portrayals of African Americans, minorities still occupy secondary, often nonmanagement, broadcast positions, and are too often misportrayed as criminals or otherwise absent from coverage. Although there have been some improvements in coverage and portrayals, the overall picture remains blurred at best for minorities, blank at worst.

In examining solutions, it appears that the FCC's policies to encourage minority ownership of broadcast facilities did work to diversify programming, including news and public affairs. The studies discussed show that minority owners program their shows differently, tailoring news and public affairs to the interests of minority audiences. Their presence in the marketplace also encourages more programming targeted at minority audiences. Contrary to Justice O'Connor's concerns expressed in her *Metro Broadcasting, Inc. v. FCC* (1990) dissent, minority owners introduce greater diversity to the content we see and hear, a fundamental goal of the First Amendment. There is indeed a nexus between minority ownership and programming diversity. By contrast, the race neutral policies implemented by the FCC to date have been far less successful in increasing broadcast program diversity.

As the FCC examines broadcast ownership regulations in the wake of the remand of the *Prometheus Radio Project v. FCC* (2004) decision, it has the opportunity to review the lengthy record on the effectiveness of race-based and race-neutral ownership policies. In the wake of the *Grutter v. Bollinger* (2003) decision, the FCC can properly acknowledge the compelling state interest at stake in its promotion of the First Amendment value of viewpoint diversity. Finally, as the studies establish, there is a nexus between minority ownership and broadcast program diversity. The nexus is established both by the absence of such diversity in the absence of minority ownership and its significant increase where minority ownership is present. In short, both recent court rulings and social science evidence supports a move by the FCC to establish meaningful minority ownership policies in broadcasting.

NOTES

[1]Section 326 of the Communications Act of 1934 states the following: "Nothing in this chapter shall be understood or construed to give the Commission the power of censorship over the radio communications or signals transmitted by any radio station, and no regulation or condition shall be promulgated or fixed by the Commission which shall interfere with the right of free speech by means of radio communication" (47 USC §326).

[2]In comparative proceedings for a new broadcast license, the FCC considered the extent of minority ownership in a license applicant's ownership structure as one of many factors in determining which potential licensee would best serve the public interest and therefore was most deserving of the license (FCC, 1978a).

[3]If the seller reinvested the proceeds from the sale into another broadcast property or other property similar or related in purpose, the sale to the minority owner was treated as an involuntary conversion and the gain was not taxable until the replacement property was sold (FCC, 1978a, p. 983).

[4]The Equal Protection clause of the Fourteenth Amendment states the following in relevant part: "No state shall make or enforce any law which den(ies) to any person within its jurisdiction the equal protection of the laws" (U.S. Constitution, Amendment 14, §1). Thus, the Fourteenth Amendment prohibits state (and local) governments from denying any individual "equal protection of the law." The Due Process clause of the Fifth Amendment has been interpreted by the Supreme Court as applying the requirements of equal protection of the laws to actions of the federal government as well (*Bollinger v. Sharpe*, 1954, pp. 498–500).

[5]*Metro Broadcasting, Inc. v. FCC,* 497 U.S. 546, 581 (1990), citing, Fife (1986a); see also M. Fife (1986b).

[6]"[T]he [Metro] majority's analysis of the government's 'diversity' interest seems very much tied to the more forgiving standard of review it adopted" (*Lutheran Church-Missouri Synod v. FCC,* 1988, p. 354).

[7]The Supreme Court in *Grutter v. Bollinger* (2003) stated the following: "We first wish to dispel the notion that the Law School's [diversity] argument has been foreclosed, either expressly or implicitly, by our affirmative-action cases decided since Bakke. It is true that some language in those opinions might be read to suggest that remedying past discrimination is the only permissible justification for race-based governmental action. But we have never held that the only governmental use of race that can survive strict scrutiny is remedying past discrimination" (p. 328).

[8]A forward-looking purpose serves a compelling state interest such as promoting diversity of dialogue, whereas a remedial purpose compensates for past discrimination.

[9]Strict scrutiny is not "strict in theory, but fatal in fact" (*Adarand Constructors v. Pena,* 1995, p. 237). Although all governmental uses of race are subject to strict scrutiny, not all are invalidated by it. When race-based action is necessary to further a compelling governmental interest, such action does not violate the constitutional guarantee of equal protection so long as the narrow-tailoring requirement is also satisfied.

[10]See FCC (1999, pp. 13–14, 74).

REFERENCES

Adarand Constructors Inc. v. Pena, 515 U.S. 200 (1995).

Associated Press v. United States, 326 U.S. 1 (1945).

Bachen, C., Hammond, A., Mason, L., & Craft, S. (1999). *Diversity of programming in the broadcast spectrum: Is there a link between owner race or ethnicity and news and public affairs programming?* (Report submitted to the Office of Communications Business Opportunities, Federal Communications Commission). Washington, DC: Federal Communications Commission.

Bachman, K. (2003, July 14). 180 degrees of separation: NAB does an about-face on TV ownership caps: McCain blasts radio. *Mediaweek* [online]. Retrieved May 12, 2005, from http://wwwfcc.gov/opportunity/meb_study/content_ownership_study.pdf

Barker, D., & Knight, K. (2000). Political talk radio and public opinion. *Public Opinion Quarterly, 64,* 149–170.

Bollinger v. Sharpe, 347 U.S. 497 (1954).

Brown v. Board of Education of Topeka, Kansas, 349 U.S. 294 (1955).

Busselle, R., & Crandall, H. (2002). Television viewing and perceptions about race differences in socioeconomic success. *Journal of Broadcasting and Electronic Media, 46,* 265–282.

Cappella, J., Turow, J., & Jamieson, K. (1996). *Call-in political talk radio: Background, content, audiences, portrayal in mainstream media.* Philadelphia: The Annenberg Public Policy Center of the University of Pennsylvania.

Carter, B., (2004, October 18). Risks seen for TV chain showing film about Kerry. *The New York Times,* p. C1.

Chonin, N. (2003, April 9). Musicians make peace with the Net: Anti-war songs change online music delivery. *San Francisco Chronicle,* p. D1.

Communications Act of 1934, 47 U.S.C. §§151, 301, 326 (1934).

Complaint of Syracuse Peace Council Against Television Station WTVH, 2 FCC Rcd 5043 (1987), aff'd sub nom.

Congressional Research Service. (1988). *Minority broadcast station ownership and broadcast programming: Is there a nexus?* Washington, DC: Library of Congress.

Craft, S. (2003). Translating ownership into action: Owner involvement and values at minority- and non-minority-owned broadcast stations. *Howard Journal of Communications, 14,* 147–158.

Dixie Chicks ban draws Senate concern on radio consolidation. (2003, July 9). *Communications Daily,* p. 3.

Dixon, T, L., Azocar, C. L., & Casas, M. (2003). The portrayal of race and crime on television network news. *Journal of Broadcasting and Electronic Media, 47,* 498–523.

Dixon, T. L., & Linz, D. (2000). Race and the misrepresentation of victimization on local television news. *Communication Research, 27,* 547–573.

Dubin, J., & Spitzer, M. L. (1995). Testing minority preferences in broadcasting. *Southern California Law Review, 68,* 841–884.

Entman, R. M. (1992). Blacks in the news: Television, modern racism and cultural change. *Journalism Quarterly, 69,* 341–361.

Entman, R. M., & Rojecki, A. (2000). *The black image in the white mind: Media and race in America.* Chicago: University of Chicago Press.

Federal Communications Commission. (1949). Editorializing by Broadcast Licensees, 13 F.C.C. 1246.

Federal Communications Commission. (1965). Policy Statement on Comparative Hearings, 1 F.C.C.2d 393.

Federal Communications Commission. (1969). Nondiscrimination Employment Practices of Broadcast Licensees, 13 FCC 2d 240.

Federal Communications Commission. (1970). Nondiscrimination Employment Practices of Broadcast Licensees, 23 FCC 2d 430.

Federal Communications Commission. (1975). Nondiscrimination in the Employment Policies and Practices of Broadcast Licensees, 54 FCC 2d 354, 357.

Federal Communications Commission. (1976). Ascertainment of Community Problems by Broadcast Applicants, 57 FCC 2d 418.

Federal Communications Commission. (1978a) Statement of Policy on Minority Ownership of Broadcasting Facilities, 68 F.C.C.2d 979.

Federal Communications Commission. (1983). Deregulation of Radio, 84 F.C.C.2d 968, aff'd in part, remanded in part sub nom. *Office of Communication United Church of Christ v. FCC,* 707 F.2d 1413, 1420 (D.C. Cir. 1983).

Federal Communications Commission. (1987). Inquiry into Section 73.1910 of the Commission's Rules and Regulations Concerning Alternatives to General Fairness Doctrine Obligations of Broadcast Licensees, 2 FCC Rcd 5272.

Federal Communications Commission. (1999). Television Rules Review, 14 F.C.C.R. 12,903.

Federal Communications Commission. (2003). Report and Order and Notice of Proposed Rulemaking, 18 F.C.C.R. 13,620.

Federal Communications Commission v. National Citizens Commission for Broadcasting, 436 U.S. 775 (1978b).

Federal Communications Commission v. Pacifica Foundation, 438 U.S. 726 (1978).

Fife, M. (1986a). The impact of minority ownership on minority images in local TV news. In O. H. Gandy (Ed.), *Communications: A key to economic and political change. Selected proceedings from the 15th annual Howard University Communications Conference* (pp. 99–125). Washington, DC: Center for Communications Research, Howard University.

Fife, M. (1986b). *The impact of minority ownership on broadcast news content: A multi-market study.* (Report submitted to the National Association of Broadcasters). Washington, DC: National Association of Broadcasters.

Fuller, L. (2005). WLBT news in the deregulation era: Modern racism or representative picture? *Journal of Black Studies, 35,* 262–292.

Gandy, O. H., Jr. (1998). *Communication and race: A structural perspective.* New York: Oxford University Press.

Garrison v. State of Louisiana, 379 U.S. 64 (1964).

Gerard, J. (1990< August 1). Minority role in broadcasting yields far bigger effect on radio than TV. *The New York Times,* p. 6.

Gilliam, F. D., Jr., & Iyengar, S. (2000). Prime suspects: The influence of local television news on the viewing public. *American Journal of Political Science, 44,* 560–573.

Grutter v. Bollinger, 539 U.S. 306 (2003).

Hall, A., & Cappella, J. N. (2002). The impact of political talk radio exposure on attributions about the outcome of the 1996 U.S. Presidential election. *Journal of Communication, 52,* 332–350.

Hammond, A. (1991). Diversity and equal protection in the marketplace: The Metro Broadcasting case in context. *Arkansas Law Review, 44,* 1063–1106.

Holman, D. (2006, May). Kerry yellow: The windsurfer of 2004 has taken up swiftboating. *The American Spectator* [online]. Retrieved July 24, 2006 from http://www.spectator.org/dsp_article.asp?article_id=9897

Ivy Planning Group. (2000, December). Whose spectrum is it anyway? Historical study of market entry barriers, discrimination and changes in broadcast and wireless licensing, 1950 to present. Retrieved May 13, 2005, from, http://ftp.fcc.gov/opportunity/meb_study/historical_study.pdf

Jackson, B. P. (2004, December 5). *The ghost of WLBT: History repeats itself with UCC ad controversy.* Retrieved March 11, 2005, from http://www.ucc.org/justice/witness/wfj120504.htm

Johnson, P. (2004). Black radio politically defined: Communicating community and political empowerment through Stevie Wonder's KJLH-FM, 1992–2002. *Political Communication, 21,* 353–367.

Kerner Commission. (1968). *Report of the U.S. National Advisory Commission on Civil Disorders.* Washington, DC: U.S. Government Printing Office.

Lee, G., & Cappella, J. N. (2001). The effects of political talk radio on political attitude formation: Exposure versus knowledge. *Political Communication, 18,* 369–394.

Lutheran Church-Missouri Synod v. Federal Communications Commission, 141 F.3d 344 (D.C. Cir. 1998).

Mason, L., Bachen, C. M., & Craft, S. L. (2001). Support for FCC minority ownership policy: How broadcast station owner race or ethnicity affects news and public affairs programming diversity. *Communication Law and Policy,* 6(1), 37–73.

Metro Broadcasting, Inc. v. Federal Communications Commission, 497 U.S. 547, rehearing denied 497 U.S. 1050 (1990).

National Broadcasting Co. v. U.S., 319 U.S. 190 (1943).

News audiences increasingly politicized: Online news audience larger, more diverse (Section I., Where Americans Go for News). (2004, June 8). *The Pew Research Center for the People and the Press.* Retrieved July 7, 2006, from http://people-press.org/reports/display.php3?PageID=833.

Office of Communication of the United Church of Christ v. Federal Communications Commission, 359 F.2d 994 (D.C. Cir. 1966).

Office of Communication of the United Church of Christ v. Federal Communications Commission, 425 F.2d 543 (D.C. Cir. 1969).

Ofori, K. A. (1999). *When being number 1 is not enough: The impact of advertising practices on minority-owned and minority-formatted broadcast stations.* Retrieved May 16, 2005, from http://www.civilrightsforum.org/fccadvertising.htm

Poindexter, P. M., Smith, L., & Heider, D. (2003). Race and ethnicity in local television news: Framing, story assignments and source selections. *Journal of Broadcasting, 47*, 524–536.

Prometheus Radio Project v. Federal Communications Commission, 373 F.3d 372 (3rd Cir. 2004).

Radio and Television News Directors Foundation. (2001). *The American radio news audience survey: Examining the use, perception, and future of radio news.* Retrieved March 15, 2005, from http://www.rtnda.org/radio/

Red Lion Broadcasting v. Federal Communications Commission, 395 U.S. 367 (1969).

Rivas-Rodriguez, M., Subervi-Vélez, F. A., Bramlett-Solomon, S., & Heider, D. (2004). Minority journalists' perceptions of the impact of minority executives. *Howard Journal of Communications, 15*, 39–55.

Romer, D., Jamieson, K. H., & deCoteau, N. J. (1998). The treatment of persons of color in local television news. *Communication Research, 25*, 286–305.

Rutenberg, J., (2004, October 11). Broadcast group to pre-empt programs for anti-Kerry film. *The New York Times*, p. A19.

Saldana, H., (2003, July 27). Chick flak: Experts say country music can't afford to lose the Dixie Chicks. *San Antonio Express-News*, p. 1J.

Schaffner, B. F., & Gadson, M. (2004). Reinforcing stereotypes? Race and local television news coverage of Congress. *Social Science Quarterly, 85*, 604–623.

Seiberg, J. (2003, July 9). Dixie Chicks trip up radio titans. *Daily Deal/The Deal* [online]. Retrieved July 9, 2003, from http://www.legs.com/research/retrieveframes?_m=517836ac7c9697oda3901428767002eb&csvc=blicform=bool&_fmtstr=full&docnum=1&startdoc=1&wchp=dglbvlb_zskak&_md5=ef6faa5728b013235780f3296292a78f1

Shurberg Broadcasting of Hartford, Inc. v. Federal Communications Commission, 876 F.2d 902 (D.C. Cir. 1989).

Siegelman, P., & Waldfogel, J. (2001). *Race and radio: Preference externalities, minority ownership and the provision of programming to minorities.* Retrieved March 1, 2005, from http://www.fcc.gov/ownership/roundtable_docs/waldfogel_c.pdf.

Squires, C. R. (2000). Black talk radio: Defining community needs and identity. *Harvard International Journal of Press/Politics, 5*, 73–95.

Staples, B. (2003, June 8), Driving down the highway, mourning the death of American radio. *The New York Times*, p. 12.

Subervi-Vélez, F. A. (1999). Spanish-language television coverage of health news. *Howard Journal of Communications, 10*, 207–228.

Syracuse Peace Council v. FCC, 867 F2d 654 (D.C.C.R. 1989), cert. denied, 493 U.S. 1099 (1990).

Telecommunications Act of 1996, Pub. L. No. 104–104, 110 Stat. 56 § 202(h) (1996).

The Hotline.

The Pew Research Center for the People and the Press. (2000, June). *Internet sapping broadcast news audience.* Retrieved April 8, 2005, from http://people-press.org/reports/display.php3?ReportID=36

Thomas, W. G., III. (2004, November 3). *Television news and the civil rights struggle: The views in Virginia and Mississippi. Southern Spaces.* Retrieved March 11, 2005, from http://www.southernspaces.org/contents/2004/thomas/4a.htm

Turner Broadcasting v. Federal Communications Commission, 520 U.S. 180 (1997).

Turner, T. (2004, July 1). Break up this band! How government protects big media—and shuts out upstarts like me. *Washington Monthly, 36,* 30–36.

TV 9 Inc. v. Federal Communications Commission, 495 F.2d 929 (D.C. Cir. 1974), cert. denied, 419 U.S. 986 (1974).

U.S. Commission on Civil Rights. (1977). *Window dressing on the set: Women and minorities in television: A report of the United States Commission on Civil Rights.* (No. CR 1.2:W 72). Washington, DC: Author.

United States v. Midwest Video Corp., 406 U.S. 649 (1972).

Valentino, N. A. (1999). Crime news and the priming of racial attitudes during evaluations of the president. *Public Opinion Quarterly, 63,* 293–320.

Waldfogel, J. (2004). Who benefits whom in local television markets? *Brookings-Wharton Papers on Urban Affairs,* 257–305. Retrieved May 3, 2006 from http://muse.jhu.edu/journals/brookings-wharton_papers_on_urban_affairs/v2004/2004.1waldfogel.html

Williamson, N. (2003, August 22). Free the Dixie three. *The Guardian,* p. 6.

Wilson, C. C., II., & Gutiérrez, F. (1995). *Race, multiculturalism, and the media* (2nd ed.). Thousand Oaks, CA: Sage.

Wimmer, K. A. (1986). Deregulation and the market failure in minority programming: The socioeconomic dimensions of broadcast reform. *Communications/Entertainment Law Journal, 8,* 329–480.

Winter Park Communications, Inc. v. Federal Communications Commission, 873 F.2d 347 (D.C. Cir. 1989).

IV

Contextualizing Media Diversity and Localism: Audience Behavior and New Technologies

13

Diversity of Exposure

James G. Webster
School of Communication, Northwestern University[1]

Policymakers have wrestled with the concept of media diversity for decades. Typically, their attention has focused on either the diversity of sources or the diversity of content available to the public. While these are important considerations, they ignore a crucial question. What do audience members do with the media options they have? Do they consume a varied diet of program types and ideas, or binge on the equivalent of junk food? Is there diversity of exposure? The data and methodological tools needed to answer these questions in a nonconjectural way already exist. Those answers could provide a useful "reality check" as we consider the meaning of diversity in the new media environment.

TYPES OF DIVERSITY

Napoli (1999) has suggested a useful framework for thinking about media diversity. He argues that the concept can be understood as having three component parts: (a) source diversity, (b) content diversity, and (c) exposure diversity. There is an extensive literature on the first two types of diversity (e.g., Einstein, 2004), but, as Napoli notes, the latter has been largely neglected. This chapter comments briefly on the first two, and then expands on the idea of diversity of exposure.

Source diversity can include ownership diversity or workforce diversity. In the current media environment, it's hard to argue that there is not at least a numerical diversity of sources. Over 80% of U.S. television households subscribe to some sort of "alternative delivery system" providing programming above and beyond local broadcast outlets. Indeed, Nielsen Media Research has reported that the average U.S. home receives over 100 channels of programming (Nielsen Media Research, 2004). Obviously the Internet and DVDs offer the public even more choices. Of course, a single corporation can control multiple outlets and multiple owners can replicate content, so having many sources is largely meaningless if there is no corresponding diversity of content across those channels of communication.

Content diversity can include differences in program types, a demographic diversity of the characters represented in media, and, perhaps most important for First Amendment purposes, a diversity of ideas or viewpoints. Many policymakers would content themselves with an empirical demonstration that the public had access to diverse content offerings. Frankly, in a world with hundreds of TV channels and millions of Web sites from which to choose, even the more elusive content diversity would be hard to avoid. What is most interesting, and critical to understanding the diversity question, is how people do or do not make use of that universe of content.

This brings us to the concept of "diversity of exposure," the forgotten stepchild of the policy debate. Napoli (1999) categorized diversity of exposure into two types: horizontal and vertical. The former refers to the distribution of audiences across content options or channels. This is akin to the concept of audience fragmentation that so occupies the attention of media industries. The latter refers to the diversity of content consumed by individuals. This is related to a feature of mass behavior called "audience polarization" (Webster & Phalen, 1997). Evidence of polarization is much harder to come by, although it can be extracted from the data routinely collected by audience measurement companies like Nielsen and Arbitron. Getting a handle on both types of exposure diversity is essential to completing the picture on media diversity.

OUR HOPES AND FEARS

Before jumping into a study of what media people actually consume, it's worth reflecting on what patterns of exposure may be welcome or worrisome. There are four scenarios that should be considered. Each has strong normative overtones.

One Generalist

One possibility, at least in theory, is that everyone attends to one general interest source of content. This is consistent with the notion of a common "public sphere" (Habermas, 1991), and is a model that seems to underlie much First

Amendment theory. Here, citizens participate in a public forum where diverse ideas can be circulated and weighed. In the end, consensus, or perhaps even the truth, may emerge. This is rather like the old world of Israel's publicly owned broadcast monopoly, wistfully described by Katz (1998):

> Television controlled by the Broadcasting Authority was the only show in town. Within two years of its inauguration, almost all households owned television sets, and almost everybody watched almost everything on the one monopolistic channel. From the beginning, strong emphasis was placed on news and public affairs. (p. 105)

In such a media environment, no horizontal diversity of exposure is possible because only one channel is available. Vertical diversity—the diet of content that each individual consumes—is essentially a function of what is served up by the monopolist.

Even if such a common sphere existed at some point in history—and there is reason to doubt it did (Schudson, 1992)—it is certainly long gone from the modern media marketplace. Still, it serves as a useful model against which other possibilities can be judged.

Generalists With Many Specialists

A second scenario is that general interest media are augmented by many more specialized sources of content. The latter would cater to smaller communities of interest—or what Sunstein (2001) called "enclaves." This is the model that Katz (1998) identified as the democratic ideal:

> If one were designing a participatory democracy, one would make provision for a central space in which all citizens could gather together and for dispersed spaces in which they could meet in smaller, more homogeneous groups. Ideally, the agenda would be agreed upon in the central space (forum, agora, town meeting), mulled over in the dispersed spaces (café, salon, club, trade union hall, party headquarters), and returned for debate and decision to the central space. In the era of mass society and mass communication, these spaces would be served, even cloned, by generalized media dedicated to the polity as a whole, and specialized media dedicated to the citizens' need to know what like- or right-minded others are thinking. (p. 99)

This is an appealing model similar to Sunstein's (2001) blend of enclaves and "general interest intermediaries," and Fraser's (1992) description of "subaltern counterpublics" within the larger public sphere. Here, horizontal diversity is achieved because the audience is spread across both types of content. Under this model we would expect to see people watching special interest programming but spending considerable time with general interest fare.

Specialists Without Polarization

Another possibility worth considering is that the new media environment will be populated exclusively by special interest media. This would mean the end of general interest outlets, or, less kindly put, programming aimed at "the lowest common denominator." Under this scenario, the media, in effect, offer a vast buffet of exotic foods including many local delicacies, and we discover that people are inclined to sample a little of each. Here the audience is not polarized into exclusive communities of interest, but exhibits more catholic tastes. Of course, much of what we know about human behavior, and our penchant for selective exposure, suggests we will do otherwise. Still, there is some evidence that social elites are becoming more "omnivorous" in their consumption of cultural products (Holt, 1998; Peterson & Kern, 1996).

In such a world, there is considerable horizontal diversity, as the mass audience is distributed across a multitude of offerings, and there is vertical diversity, because everyone consumes a varied diet.

Specialists With Polarization

The very idea of specialized media, however, suggests a degree of polarization. Such materials are designed to appeal to some while being ignored by others. It's quite possible, then, that each specialized outlet will create an enclave of loyalists who attend to "like-minded" speech, whereas the rest of the public remains either uninterested or uninvited. Although this kind of world might pass muster with those who advocate consumer sovereignty and a "market economics" view of policymaking, it is a troubling prospect for those who advocate a social values approach (Entman & Wildman, 1992; Sunstein, 2001).

It's in this spirit that Sunstein (2001) warns of new media that filter content and the consequent rise in "group polarization":

> An understanding of group polarization casts light on the potential effects not only of the Internet but also of radio and television, at least if stations are numerous and many take a well-defined point of view. Recall that mere exposure to the positions of others creates group polarization. It follows that this effect will be at work for nondeliberating groups, in the form of collections of individuals whose communications choices go in the same direction, and who do not expose themselves to alternative positions. (p. 73)

In much the same vein, Turow (1997) sees technology and advertiser-driven programming dividing America into the equivalent of "gated communities," and Gitlin (1998) suggests that the public sphere is being broken into "sphericules."

Superficially, this world looks rather like the scenario of specialists without polarization. That is, in either case, the mass audience is distributed across a variety of specialized content options, each winning a tiny share of the market. However, beneath this veneer, there is no vertical diversity because each person consumes an unvaried, and presumably unhealthy, diet.

MEASURING DIVERSITY OF EXPOSURE

How best to measure exposure diversity? It is useful to consider three potential units of analysis: (a) viewer-centric measures, (b) content-centric measures, and (c) channel-centric measures. The focus here is on the medium of television, although the same conceptual framework might be applied to other media. I'll also address behavioral measures that could be constructed from the databases created in the day-to-day business of audience measurement. In the case of U.S. television, this would be the data collected by Nielsen in either its national (NTI) or local (NSI) samples. Exploiting existing data has two important advantages: first, the cost of collecting the data has already been incurred so a secondary analysis should, in theory,[2] be relatively inexpensive; and second, Nielsen methods and numbers are well understood in media industries, and so have a degree of credibility that is difficult to match in customized studies.

Viewer-Centric Measures

The most obvious way to measure vertical diversity is to track the consumption patterns of individuals over time. We know, for example, that of the 100+ channels available in a typical home, an average household actually views fewer than 15 in a typical week (Nielsen Media Research, 2004). People maintain surprisingly small "repertoires" even in the face of great numerical abundance (e.g., Ferguson & Perse, 1993; Heeter, 1988; Neuendorf, Atkin, & Jeffres, 2001). Aside from these averages, we know relatively little about factors associated with the size of people's repertoires. Similarly, we know little about the substantive content of repertoires. For example, are there viewers who never see local news or public affairs? Who are they? How much time do different kinds of people spend with these and other program types?

Content-Centric Measures

One could also consider audience shares for programs of a type (e.g., Napoli, 1997). This addresses the concept of horizontal diversity. For instance, what percentage of all the time spent viewing is devoted to the local news, or programs owned by a particular entity? Or, to take a more global perspective, what percentage of all time spent watching is devoted to imported versus domestically produced programming (Curran, 1998)? Vertical diversity might be examined by looking at "audience duplication" across pairs of programs to identify patterns of program-type loyalty. This would enable us to say that the audience for "60 Minutes" also watches "20/20," or that network news viewers also tend to watch local news.

Channel-Centric Measures

Channels are an interesting unit of analysis because newer networks tend to specialize in a type of content (Turow, 1997; Webster, 1986, 2005). Returning to our buffet analogy, they are food stations offering one specialty item, or at least catering to one kind of diner. Furthermore, channels are generally owned by a single entity so measures of attendance can indicate a corporation's actual share of audience across channels. Such behavioral measures might be a more useful metric than simply noting the percentage of households capable of receiving a signal. It's also possible to assess channel-centric polarization. What percentage of the audience watches a channel? What percentage avoids it? Among those who watch, how much time do they spend viewing? Even a network with a tiny overall share of the audience might have loyal viewers. For example, do the viewers of FOX News or MTV or Black Entertainment Television (BET) watch those networks to the exclusion of other more mainstream fare? Do they constitute the worrisome case of "specialists with polarization"? Inventive uses of existing data can provide answers.

If we are serious about understanding diversity in an age of media abundance, we need to be serious about diversity of exposure. We might begin with an assessment of the current state of affairs. Knowing what use the audience actually makes of the media environment could help us craft sensible policy prescriptions.

A CASE STUDY IN DIVERSITY OF EXPOSURE TO TELEVISION

What follows is a brief case study illustrating how commercial audience measurement can give us insights into diversity of exposure. It is based on an analysis of data collected in the first week of February 2003 by Nielsen Media Research using its national peoplemeter sample. These are the kinds of data on which virtually all national TV media buys, and many programming decisions, are based. Peoplemeters are electronic devices that monitor the behavior of all TV sets in sample households and are designed so that individual members of the household can signal their presence to the meter. Nielsen places meters in homes using a probability sampling procedure. At the time, Nielsen had a national sample of just over 5,000 households, including almost 13,000 individuals. Over any measurement period, the actual number of homes providing useful information is somewhat less than the total installed base. For a more complete description of Nielsen's methods, see Webster, Phalen, and Lichty (2006).

The centerpiece of the analysis is a rather large table (see Table 13.1) that describes each of 62 national networks on five dimensions. These are the most widely viewed networks in the country and serve as the study's units of analysis. Hence, this is an example of a channel-centric study. The first column of data is the universe of households in which each network can be received, expressed as a percentage of total TV households (TVHH). The next two columns of data report the size of each network's audience. They offer ways to assess horizontal diversity. The first is the network's overall share of audience. That is, of all the viewing done by adults during the week, what percentage of the total number of "man-hours" is attributable to a particular network. The second is the network's cumulative audience (i.e., the "cume" or reach) expressed as the percentage of all persons 18+ who have viewed for at least 1 min during the week. The remaining two columns of data are measures of audience polarization. They offer a picture of vertical diversity. These metrics are less familiar than "ratings" and "shares" and so deserve a few words of explanation.

Nielsen Media Research sells a service to clients called "NPower." It allows those clients to access the Nielsen database so they can produce customized analyses. One reason polarization is not well documented in the academic literature is because it's a form of cumulative audience behavior (see Webster et al., 2006) that is not routinely described by Nielsen in published reports. NPower, however, is capable of tracking individuals over time, and producing a number of such measures. I am using two closely related measures.

The first is "time-spent-viewing" (TSV). This is a simple metric, directly analogous to the measures of time-spent-listening common in radio research. It is the average number of minutes per week spent viewing the network in question, among those who tuned in for at least a minute (i.e., those in the cume). So, in the case of a broadcast network with a large cume, it's based on a large number of people. In the case of a cable network with a smaller cume, it's based on a smaller sample size. It is the total amount of time that people who used the network actually spent watching that network, whether in multiple viewing sessions or just one.

The second measure is "share-within-cume." This is an unconventional measure. Simple TSV can be hard to interpret without reference to the total amount of time a channel's users spend watching television. This measure adjusts for that by representing TSV as the percentage of total TV-viewing time. In other words, among those who watched the network (the cume), what share of their time did they spend watching? As with TSV, it is based on samples that vary with the size of the cume.

Horizontal Diversity of Exposure

The first question deals with how the mass audience is distributed across channels. Are general interest intermediaries (e.g., the broadcast networks) holding their own? Table 13.1 presents the results of the analysis. Networks are listed down the left-hand side. To make the table easier to evaluate, I organized these as either broadcast or cable networks and, within each grouping, sorted them by the average time-spent-viewing.

TVHH Universe describes the percentage of all television households, an estimated 106.7 million at the time of this survey, capable of receiving the network signal in question. This is a powerful structural constraint that circumscribes a network's ability to serve as a common public forum. As would be expected, the older broadcast networks had near universal penetration of the market, with coverage that ranged from 99% to 95% of all TVHH. The newer broadcast networks (i.e., FOX, UPN, WB, and PAX) had somewhat reduced coverage ranging from 93% to 85%. The most successful advertiser-supported cable networks generally covered 80% to 70% of the market, whereas newer or more regional services had considerably less coverage. Premium cable services (e.g., HBO, Showtime, and Cinemax) that charge an additional fee to subscribers had smaller coverage still. Because there are 339 national cable networks (National Cable & Telecommunications Association [NCTA], 2004), there were over 270 services not included in Table 13.1. These would, undoubtedly, be at the lower end of the coverage spectrum. As such, they could scarcely serve as a national public forum.

Share of total audience viewing expresses how large a "piece of the pie" each network gets. If all sources of programming were listed, the numbers would add up to 100%. In the case of Table 13.1, the column total is 65. In other words, 35% of all the television viewing done in this week in February

TABLE 13.1

Diversity of Exposure Across Television Networks

	Structure	Horizontal Diversity		Vertical Diversity	
Network	*TVHH Universe*	*Share of Total Audience Viewing*	*Weekly Cume*	*Average Time Spent Viewing Per Week*	*Share Within Cume*
Broadcast Networks					
CBS	95%	6.3	65%	189	7.9
NBC	95%	5.9	67%	173	7.4
ABC	97%	5.1	66%	152	6.4
PBS	99%	2.0	45%	89	3.7
FOX	93%	1.9	47%	78	3.3
WB	90%	0.8	25%	59	2.4
PAX	85%	0.4	15%	55	2.0
UPN	86%	0.4	18%	46	1.7
Cable Networks					
HBO	33%	2.0	20%	196	8.0
FOX News Channel	77%	2.7	27%	193	7.5
Lifetime Movie	34%	0.6	7%	167	5.5
Cinemax	20%	0.7	9%	159	6.3
SHOWTIME	21%	0.6	9%	146	5.5
Turner Network Television (TNT)	81%	2.3	34%	134	5.0
Lifetime	81%	1.9	28%	130	4.8
Game Show Network	47%	0.4	6%	128	4.4
TV Land	73%	1.1	16%	127	4.2
CNN	81%	2.1	35%	118	4.7
Nickelodeon	81%	1.5	25%	117	4.6
TBS Superstation	82%	2.3	39%	116	4.5
SOAP Network	27%	0.1	2%	115	4.0
Hallmark Channel	47%	0.5	9%	110	3.7
Court TV	71%	0.8	16%	103	3.6
Home & Garden TV	75%	1.0	20%	97	3.8
USA Network	81%	1.6	34%	95	3.6
Cartoon Network	77%	0.7	15%	95	3.7
SCI-FI Channel	75%	0.8	17%	87	3.0
The Movie Channel	19%	0.2	5%	86	3.0
ESPN	81%	1.1	25%	85	3.4
History Channel	77%	1.0	23%	85	3.4
A&E	81%	1.1	26%	85	3.1
MSNBC	73%	0.9	23%	76	2.9
Food Network	73%	0.7	17%	75	2.9
Black Entertainment TV (BET)	70%	0.5	14%	75	2.7
Toon Disney	35%	0.1	3%	72	2.6
The Learning Channel	79%	1.1	30%	71	2.8
American Movie Classics	79%	0.9	25%	71	2.5
Disney Channel	76%	0.6	18%	70	2.7

(continued)

TABLE 13.1 *(continued)*

	Structure	Horizontal Diversity		Vertical Diversity	
Network	TVHH Universe	Share of Total Audience Viewing	Weekly Cume	Average Time Spent Viewing Per Week	Share Within Cume
Cable Networks (con't.)					
FX	75%	0.9	26%	66	2.6
WGN Superstation	53%	0.6	17%	64	2.3
Animal Planet	76%	0.7	21%	63	2.3
Discovery	81%	0.9	29%	59	2.3
MTV	80%	0.7	26%	55	2.3
Comedy Central	77%	0.6	22%	53	2.2
CNN Headline News	78%	0.7	25%	51	2.0
Spike TV (TNN)	81%	0.7	26%	51	1.9
CNBC	79%	0.4	14%	51	2.0
Weather Channel	80%	0.6	24%	50	1.9
Speed Channel	52%	0.1	6%	48	1.8
Discovery Health	39%	0.1	5%	45	1.7
Country Music Television (CMT)	62%	0.3	12%	43	1.6
ESPN2	79%	0.4	21%	41	1.6
ABC Family	80%	0.5	23%	40	1.6
Woman's Entertainment (WE)	47%	0.2	8%	38	1.3
Bravo	65%	0.3	14%	36	1.3
Entertainment TV (E!)	75%	0.5	25%	36	1.5
Travel Channel	66%	0.3	16%	36	1.3
VH1	78%	0.4	23%	34	1.4
TV Guide Channel	53%	0.3	19%	32	1.2
National Geographic	39%	0.1	5%	31	1.1
Outdoor Life	47%	0.1	5%	28	1.0
FUSE	28%	0.0	2%	16	0.6
TOTAL		65.0			

Note. From Webster (2005), Beneath the Veneer of Fragmentation: Television Audience Polarization in a Multichannel World, *Journal of Communication,* Blackwell Publishing. Used by permission.

was attributable to sources not on the table. This would include individual stations broadcasting syndicated or locally produced programming (e.g., the local news) as well as those 270 missing national networks. I should also note that this method of calculating share of total audience assumes each network is feeding programming 24 hr a day. For all broadcast networks and some cable-only services, that was not the case. Hence, their shares of total viewing may seem rather low. By way of contrast, if shares were calculated only during those times when each broadcast network was actually on the air, their numbers would be significantly higher (e.g., ABC was 9.1, CBS was 10.8, FOX was

8.4, NBC was 11.3, UPN was 2.4, and WB was 3.1). These are closer to the audience shares most often reported in the popular and trade press.

Of course, most of the networks in Table 13.1 are owned by a parent company that has other networks in its portfolio. As corporate entities, then, they occupy a larger space in the lives of viewers than individual network shares would suggest. For example, Viacom, Disney, and Time Warner each enjoyed a double-digit share of the audience (13.3, 13.0, and 12.5, respectively). To achieve those combined shares, however, a corporation is likely to offer diverse services. The News Corp portfolio, for instance, includes FOX News, which appeals to a relatively old, politically conservative audience; the FOX television network, which appeals to a relatively young, urban audience; and the Speed Channel, which appeals to NASCAR dads. All this bespeaks the rather murky relationship between ownership and content diversity (Napoli, 1999).

That said, audience shares capture rather well the phenomenon of audience fragmentation, and offer a nice snapshot of the state of horizontal diversity. The big-three networks have roughly twice the audience of their nearest competitors. But in absolute terms, they now occupy just a sliver of the time people spend watching TV. Beyond them, viewing is widely distributed.

Unfortunately, shares don't tell us much about the intensity of channel use. Small numbers could mean that everyone watches just a little, which would be consistent with the "specialists without polarization" hypothesis. Or it could mean that a handful of viewers spend long periods of time with the channel, whereas others ignore it altogether. That would be consistent with the "specialists with polarization" hypothesis.

Weekly cumes provide a different and somewhat more revealing measure of audience size. They describe the percentage of the adult population that watched each network at least once. Obviously, the flip side of the cume is the percentage of the population that never watched the network. So here we get our first glimpse of the number of viewers who anchor one end of what may be a polarized distribution. As with audience shares, the big-three networks (i.e., ABC, CBS, and NBC) had the largest audiences. Each one was viewed by approximately two thirds of the audience during the week. Of course, that means that one third of the adult population didn't watch ABC or CBS during a time of particularly heavy television viewing. Beyond the major broadcast networks, audience cumes dropped off rather quickly. Even among networks that had a substantial potential universe, cumes were quite low. For example, UPN was receivable in 86% of all TVHHs, yet it had a weekly reach of just 18% of adults. This suggests that most viewers hadn't included UPN in their channel repertoires, a fate that was characteristic of many smaller networks.

Both total audience shares and weekly cumes, which are themselves highly correlated ($r = .883$, $p < .01$), show considerable horizontal diversity of exposure across television networks. The cume data also provide a partial answer to the question of vertical diversity. Once we get beyond the major broadcast networks, a great many people who could use the remaining networks never do. They sit at the pole of nonuse. What these measures fail to reveal is how much time the users of a network actually spend in attendance. We need different metrics to see the rest of the distribution.

Vertical Diversity of Exposure

The two remaining columns add to the picture on vertical diversity. Average TSV gives us a sense of the intensity of channel use among a network's viewers. Each of the big-three networks continued to do well, being viewed for 2½ to 3 hr a week. But the networks wracking up the largest TSV were HBO and the FOX News Channel. Each was watched for over 3 hr a week. Premium cable channels and networks specializing in movies were also watched for relatively long periods of time. Beyond that, an odd collection of networks with otherwise small audience shares were high on the list.

Share-within-cume expresses TSV as a percentage. So, for example, although HBO was viewed by just 20% of the adult population (i.e., the cume), those people spent 8% of their time watching HBO. The overall pattern of results for share-within-cume was quite similar to TSV ($r = .988$, $p < .01$). HBO, FOX News, and the big-three networks again posted the highest values. Interestingly, these measures of the intensity of channel use were unrelated to the channel's universe. So the most available channels were not necessarily the ones that drew the heaviest use.

We've seen that the direst predictions for the new media environment envision very little vertical diversity of exposure. In this world, the mass audience is broken into enclaves that consume a steady diet of like-minded speech and very little else. The marketplace of ideas, our common public sphere, becomes many sphericules (e.g., Gandy, 2001; Gitlin, 1998; Sunstein, 2001). Turow (1997) has offered the most extensively developed of these portraits of the television audience. He sees advertisers and new media technologies breaking America into the equivalent of gated communities:

> Once the emerging system is solidified, it will not be easy to change. Media technologies and formats that have been shaped by the values of social division will reinforce those values even when leaders in their rhetoric are trying to bring people together. Like heavy gates separating one community from another, the very structure of the American media world will drive people apart for a long time to come. (p. 200)

Measures of polarization offer a way to assess how much time people spend behind those gates. Consider three networks that cater to specific segments of the audience: BET, MTV, and FOX News. BET provides "... entertainment, music, news and public affairs programming for the African–American audience" (NCTA, 2004, p. 53). MTV targets 12- to 34-year-olds with music videos and many regularly scheduled series ranging from news to animation. FOX News claims to offer "fair and balanced coverage of the day's events," but is widely regarded as appealing to a politically conservative viewership. Each reached a modestly sized audience, with weekly cumes of 14%, 26%, and 27%, respectively. Those who tuned into BET or MTV spent less than 3% of their time with those channels. Even the audience for FOX News, with its high TSV, spent 92.5% of its time watching something else on television. If these viewers live in cloistered communities, they clearly spend a good deal of time out on the town.

A Closer Look at FOX News Viewers

Of course, it might be instructive to know what other media the viewers of any particular channel consume. Here, too, the Nielsen data can provide an answer (as least as far as their television viewing goes). Table 13.2 offers a comparison on how the viewers of FOX News allocate the rest of their viewing in comparison to nonviewers.

TABLE 13.2

FOX News Viewer's Allocation of Time Across Selected Sources

	Reach Among Fox	*Audience Shares*	
Source	*News Viewers*	*Viewers*	*Nonviewers*
NBC Affiliates	85%	9.42	12.53
CBS Affiliates	84%	8.79	12.08
ABC Affiliates	84%	8.11	10.81
FOX News Channel	100%	7.47	—
FOX Affiliates	78%	4.77	7.31
CNN	68%	2.88	1.62
WB Affiliates	54%	2.07	3.58
HBO	25%	1.80	2.10
MSNBC	55%	1.63	0.47
History Channel	46%	1.62	0.76
A&E	47%	1.45	1.03
Home & Garden TV	39%	1.43	0.75
PBS Affiliates	57%	1.41	2.34
UPN Affiliates	44%	1.18	2.34
CNBC	35%	0.65	0.23

As we've seen, FOX News viewers spent 7.5% of their time watching that network. However, roughly 85% of them watched at least one of the big-three affiliates, and, on average, they spent more time watching those sources.[3] Most FOX News viewers also watched PBS, although it occupied less than 2% of their time. It would be interesting to know just what programs they watched on these affiliates. Was it, for instance, something that might challenge or reinforce a particular world view? This could be answered with "program-centric" analyses. For the time being, however, it appears that this audience is not just a polarized enclave, but a group that spends considerable time with general interest programming. The same can be said of all of the 62 networks (Webster, 2005).

CONCLUDING THOUGHTS

This quick look at diversity of exposure to television offers a number of insights. There is great horizontal diversity. The mass audience is widely distributed across several dozen national networks. In fact, this is a more egalitarian distribution than what we find in Web use, where the audience tends to concentrate on the most popular offerings (e.g., Adamic & Huberman, 1999; Hindman & Cukier, 2003; Webster & Lin, 2002).

Of course, this means that the big-three networks—which would probably qualify as general interest intermediaries—no longer dominate the nation's attention. Over the years, they have clearly lost ground to the competition (Webster, 2005). For social theorists like Katz (1998) and Sunstein (2001), this is a troubling development. Nonetheless, they occupy a special place in the media landscape. Most Americans still watch them at length. The same cannot be said of any other networks.

Whether the big-three networks will continue to hold that privileged position is an interesting question. In many ways, they look like anomalies. Will they remain as "outliers" or eventually regress toward the mean? Although there is no way to know for certain, social scientists often study younger cohorts to anticipate change (e.g., Putnam, 2000; Rahn & Rudolf, 2001). Assessing the behavior of young adults (e.g., 18- to 24-year-olds) might offer a glimpse into the future of broadcast television, and with it the future of our last great cultural forums.

The preliminary indications on vertical diversity of exposure are, I think, rather hopeful. The mass audience certainly has not devolved into myriad enclaves, each attending to one or two sources of content. Some networks, like FOX News, do enjoy relatively high levels of loyalty among their viewers, but even these people seem to consume a varied diet of programming—at least as far as channel-centric analyses allow us to see. As a rule, viewers appear to use a mix of general interest and specialized media. These findings are consistent with studies of Internet usage. According to Neuman, "research thus far on Web behavior reveals diverse personal interests but a surprising balance among specialized and 'mainstream' sites among new and experienced users" (2001, p. 311). Even in the smaller arena of overtly political speech, Internet users seem to seek out at least some diversity of expression (Horrigan, Garrett, & Resnick, 2004). Perhaps, instead of binging on one type of content, American media users are, indeed, more omnivorous (Holt, 1998; Horrigan et al., 2004; Peterson & Kern, 1996).

At least two cautions are in order. First, the technology for delivering television and most other media is undergoing constant change. Digital video recorders and video on demand are currently on the verge of widespread adoption. These will undoubtedly make it easier for viewers who are so inclined, to see what they want to see. Second, no matter what patterns of exposure emerge, we should be careful not to equate TSV with effect. It may be that even a little exposure to politically or culturally extreme materials leads to the kind of social divisiveness or group polarization many fear (e.g., Gitlin, 1998; Sunstein, 2001; Turow, 1997).

Even so, studying diversity of exposure would represent an important, nonconjectural, and eminently feasible step forward in our understanding of media diversity. It would move us beyond our preoccupation with the character of the media environment, toward an appreciation of how diversity is, or is not, realized in the lives of people who inhabit that environment.

NOTES

[1]The author thanks Nielsen Media Research for making the necessary data available and Turner Broadcasting for executing the NPower analyses The author also thanks Eszter Hargittai, Philip Napoli, Robert Verbanac, Jack Wakshlag, and Steve Wildman for their valuable comments and contributions. Parts of this chapter have appeared in Webster (2005), Beneath the Veneer of Fragmentation: Television Audience Polarization in a Multichannel World, *Journal of Communication,* Blackwell Publishing.

[2]Nielsen provides access to its database through a facility called "NPower. " Two limiting factors need to be considered. First, Nielsen sells this service to clients and pricing may not reflect the actual cost of incremental analyses. Second, analyses are typically limited by the software Nielsen provides. Not everything that can be imagined in theory can be constructed with Nielsen programs.

[3]In the comparison of FOX News viewers and nonviewers, network viewing totals are to all programming feed by affiliates, not just the network feed as is the case in Table 13.1

REFERENCES

Adamic, L. A., & Huberman, B. A. (1999). *The nature of markets in the World Wide Web*. Palo Alto, CA: Xerox Palo Alto Research Center.

Curran, J. (1998). Crisis of public communication: A reappraisal. In T. Liebes & J. Curran (Eds.), *Media, ritual and identity* (pp. 175–202). London: Routledge.

Einstein, M. (2004). *Media diversity: Economics, ownership, and the FCC.* Mahwah, NJ: Lawrence Erlbaum Associates.

Entman, R. M., & Wildman, S. S. (1992). Reconciling economic and non-economic perspectives on media policy: Transcending the "marketplace of ideas." *Journal of Communication, 42*(1), 5–19.

Ferguson, D. A., & Perse, E. M. (1993). Media and audience influences on channel repertoire. *Journal of Broadcasting & Electronic Media, 37,* 31–47.

Fraser, N. (1992). Rethinking the public sphere: A contribution to the critique of actually existing democracy. In C. Calhoun (Eds.), *Habermas and the public sphere* (pp. 109–142). Cambridge, MA: MIT Press.

Gandy, O. H. (2001). Dividing practices: Segmentation and targeting in the emerging public sphere. In W. L. Bennett & R. M. Entman (Eds.), *Mediated politics: Communication in the future of democracy* (pp. 141–159). Cambridge, England: Cambridge University Press.

Gitlin, T. (1998). Public sphere or public sphericules? In T. Liebes & J. Curran (Eds.), *Media, ritual and identity* (pp. 168–174). London: Routledge.

Habermas, J. (1991). *The structural transformation of the public sphere: An inquiry into a category of bourgeois society.* Cambridge, MA: MIT Press.

Heeter, C. (1988). The choice process model. In C. Heeter & B. Greenberg (Eds.), *Cable-viewing* (pp. 11–32). Norwood, NJ: Ablex.

Hindman, M., & Cukier, K. N. (2003, December). *Measuring media concentration online and offline.* Paper presented at the conference on Media Diversity and Localism: Meaning, Metrics, and the Public Interest, New York.

Holt, D. B. (1998). Does cultural capital structure American consumption? *Journal of Consumer Research, 25,* 1–25.

Horrigan, J., Garrett, K., & Resnick, P. (2004, October). *The Internet and democratic debate.* Washington, DC: Pew Internet & American Life Project.

Katz, E. (1998). And deliver us from segmentation. In R. G. Noll & M. E. Price (Eds.), *A communications cornucopia: Markle Foundation essays on information policy* (pp. 99–112). Washington, DC: Brookings Institute.

Napoli, P. M. (1997). Rethinking program diversity assessment: An audience-centered approach. *Journal of Media Economics, 10,* 59–74.

Napoli, P. M. (1999). Deconstructing the diversity principle. *Journal of Communication, 49*(4), 7–34.

National Cable & Telecommunications Association. (2004). *Cable developments 2004.* Washington, DC: Author.

Neuendorf, K. A., Atkin, D. J., & Jeffres, L. W. (2001). Reconceptualizing channel repertoire in the urban cable environment. *Journal of Broadcasting & Electronic Media, 45,* 464–482.

Neuman, W. R. (2001). The impact of the new media. In W. L. Bennett & R. M. Entman (Eds.), *Mediated politics: Communication in the future of democracy* (pp. 299–320). Cambridge, England: Cambridge University Press.

Nielsen Media Research. (2004). *Television audience 2003.* New York: Author.

Peterson, R. A., & Kern, R. M. (1996). Changing highbrow taste: From snob to omnivore. *American Sociological Review, 61,* 900–907.

Putnam, R. (2000). *Bowling alone: The collapse and revival of American community*. New York: Simon & Schuster.

Rahn, W. M., & Rudolph, T. J. (2001). National identities and the future of democracy. In W. L. Bennett & R. M. Entman (Eds.), *Mediated politics: Communication in the future of democracy* (pp. 452–467). Cambridge, England: Cambridge University Press.

Schudson, M. (1992). Was there ever a public sphere? If so, when? Reflections on the American case. In C. Calhoun (Ed.), *Habermas and the public sphere* (pp. 143–163). Cambridge, MA: MIT Press.

Sunstein, C. (2001). *Republic.com*. Princeton, NJ: Princeton University Press.

Turow, J. (1997). *Breaking up America: Advertisers and the new media world.* Chicago: University of Chicago Press.

Webster, J. G. (1986). Audience behavior in the new media environment. *Journal of Communication, 36*(3), 77–91.

Webster, J. G. (2005). Beneath the veneer of fragmentation: Television audience polarization in a multi-channel world. *Journal of Communication, 55*(2), 366–382.

Webster, J. G., & Lin, S. F. (2002). The Internet audience: Web use as mass behavior. *Journal of Broadcasting & Electronic Media, 46,* 1–12.

Webster, J. G., & Phalen, P. F. (1997). *The mass audience: Rediscovering the dominant model.* Mahwah, NJ: Lawrence Erlbaum Associates.

Webster, J. G., Phalen, P. F., & Lichty, L. W. (2006). *Ratings analysis: The theory and practice of audience research* (3rd ed.). Mahwah, NJ: Lawrence Erlbaum Associates.

14

A Mile Wide and an Inch Deep: Measuring Media Diversity Online and Offline*

Matthew Hindman†
Arizona State University

Of the many changes that have altered the American media landscape in the last decade, the growth of the Internet is arguably the most significant. In the early 1990s, less than a million Americans were online; by late 2004, that number had risen to 120 million, a solid majority of the U.S. adult population. Seventy million Americans now log on to the Internet in a typical day, reading news, checking e-mail, and engaging in a host of other online activities.[1] Although the number of Americans online is now expanding only slowly, after the rapid growth of the late 1990s, the importance of Internet content in the American media diet continues to grow. Broadband penetration in America is still expanding at an exponential rate (Horrigan, 2004); among the highly educated and the young, heavy Internet use is now the rule.

A focal point of this volume is understanding and measuring diversity in the contemporary media landscape. If we want to gauge media diversity more broadly, we need to understand the large and increasingly important contribution that the Internet makes to that diversity. Yet the nature of the Internet makes discussions of online diversity more difficult than similar discussions about other media. Other chapters in this volume have forced us to distinguish between diversity of outlets, and diversity of usage—between the number of media voices that are theoretically available, and the number of voices that citizens actually hear. This distinction is particularly important in the online world. The central argument of this chapter is that, although the range of online content is vast, the range of sites that users actually visit is small. In fact, the diversity of media outlets that citizens use may be smaller online than in traditional media.

Media diversity online is paradoxical. On one hand, no other medium can compare with the indescribably vast range of content available on the World Wide Web. As of this writing, Google claims to index more than 8 billion web pages, and even this number represents only a fraction of the total content available. In addition to the large amount of content produced by corporations, governments, and organizations, tens of millions of individual citizens have personally posted online content; 8 million Americans have created their own blogs (Ranie, 2005). Content creation on the World Wide Web is decentralized, and anyone with Internet access can contribute. The result is a cornucopia of information on nearly every conceivable topic.

Academic and popular observers have long assumed that this vast amount of content online would diffuse the attention of the public away from a few mainstream media outlets, and toward countless small-scale Web sites. The Internet, everyone seemed to agree, was a "narrowcasting" or "pointcasting" medium. Prominent scholars found it easy to imagine that the Internet would make broadcasting "largely a thing of the past" (Sunstein, 2001, p. 3). Many could not resist invoking Gutenberg; just as the printing press had fueled the reformation and the political liberalization of Europe, they argued that the Internet would have dramatic effects on politics and culture (Barlow, Birkets, Kelly, & Slouka, 1995; Hewitt, 2005). More recently, the highly celebrated growth of blogs has convinced even many skeptics that these early claims about the Internet have been fulfilled. Media elites such as Tom Brokaw have declared that blogs represent "a democratization of news," amplifying the voice of ordinary citizens (Guthrie, 2004, p. A2).

Beliefs that the Internet and other new technologies (such as satellite and cable television) have created a dramatically more fractured media environment seem to have also influenced American communications policy. In 2003, with the Federal Communications Commission (FCC) set to relax longstanding restrictions on media ownership, FCC Chairman Michael Powell declared that new technologies ensured diversity in the content that citizens saw. As Powell explained, "What's happening now is that technology creates many different platforms and means of distributing news and content in a way that's more dynamic and diverse, as opposed to [a time] when I say to my kids, 'Sit down at 7 p.m., turn on Walter Cronkite, we'll get our news and go to bed'" (Manjoo, 2003, p. 3).

This chapter argues against much of the contemporary consensus about the Internet as a "narrowcasting" medium, and offers a very different perspective on the amount of diversity that the Internet adds to the larger media environment. Online diversity is astonishingly shallow. Despite the vastness of online content—or, more accurately, because of it—Web users cluster tightly around a small number of successful sites. In almost every niche, a handful of Web sites get more traffic than all of the rest combined. Everyone knows that Amazon dominates online bookselling, and eBay dominates online auctions. But many have failed to recognize that these sorts of winners-take-all patterns show up in nearly every aspect of online life—including online outlets for politics, news, and entertainment. This fact naturally changes our assessment of what the Internet means for politics and culture.

The rest of this chapter is organized in a straightforward fashion. First, I begin by outlining why online audience concentration matters. As I show, different assumptions about audience concentration lead to different conclusions about the Internet's impact on politics and society.

Next, I identify metrics with which we can compare concentration in the online and offline worlds. For the purposes of this analysis, we use the Hirschman-Herfindahl Index (HHI) and the Gini Coefficient, the two metrics for concentration most commonly used by regulators and social scientists. We also use the Noam Index, a recent metric proposed by Eli Noam, which attempts to balance the market power of the largest players with the number of media "voices" that reach a nontrivial audience.

I use these metrics to compare a series of nationwide data sets on audience concentration within various different forms of media. This analysis demonstrates that across all the different metrics, Internet content produces levels of audience concentration greater than those in traditional media. This comparison is particularly striking with regard to newspapers, where the same news articles are distributed both in print and on the World Wide Web. The Web content produces far greater levels of audience concentration.

Although many causes may contribute to online concentration, I conclude by highlighting a few particularly important factors. First, the vastness of online content makes navigational aids critical. In particular, hyperlinks and search engines play a key role in funneling Web users to a handful of sites.

Second, I suggest that the Internet disadvantages local content providers. This fact can be seen with particular clarity in the newspaper market. Most newspapers in United States are small, local monopolies; yet online, these news organizations compete for the attention of the public with hundreds of other news outlets from around the country and around the world. I argue that there may be a trade-off between the number of choices available to individual citizens and media diversity at the national level. Ironically, more choice for individuals may make the small number of prominent national news outlets even more important.

DIFFERENT VISIONS OF THE INTERNET: WHY ONLINE CONCENTRATION MATTERS

In laying out the argument of this chapter, we should begin by considering a very basic question: why is online concentration worth measuring in the first place? Why should we care if Internet users get most of their news and information from 2 sites, 20 sites, or 200 sites?

One part of the answer is provided by the other chapters of this volume. Since the beginning of the American republic, there has been a broad public understanding that media diversity is an essential part of democratic politics. American public policy from the founding onward fostered a media environment less concentrated than that in Canada, England, or continental Europe (Starr, 2004). As Justice Hugo Black famously declared in *Associated Press v. U.S.* (1945), the American Constitution and the general welfare of the public require "the widest possible dissemination of information from diverse and antagonistic sources" (p. 1424). As the Internet becomes an increasingly large part of the American media landscape, it is important to measure its impact on this broad public goal.

Information on online concentration raises another set of questions as well. Since the advent of the World Wide Web, broad democratic concerns have been tied to debates about the "nature" of the Internet. For many, it seemed obvious that Internet users would spread their attention across a broader array of outlets than television watchers or newspaper readers. Previously, the argument went that citizens were limited by the small number of broadcast channels or local publications available in their local area; with these limits removed, and with the ability to publish no longer limited to those with a printing press, the public would consume a much wider array of content. Some viewed this change positively, arguing that "the universe of permissible opinions will expand, unconstrained by the prejudices, tastes or interests of the old media elite" (Last, 2002, p. 1). Others worried that the same process would balkanize public discourse, destroy public trust, and empower extremists (e.g., Sunstein, 2001). The recent explosion of blog readership has led many to reiterate these arguments. Some have celebrated the "democratizing" potential of blogs, whereas others have worried that blogging lacks the checks and balances of traditional journalism and gives too much power to "a guy sitting in his living room in his pajamas" (Yeager, 2004, p. 17).

Debates about whether the Internet is improving or degrading public discourse are unlikely to be settled anytime soon. Yet some researchers have questioned the central assumption of these debates: the claim that Internet users will be exposed to a wider range of content than those who use other communications media. Some skepticism has come from social scientists, who have highlighted social barriers that constrain Internet use. By the mid-1990s, much research on the digital divide showed that traditionally disadvantaged groups lagged in their access to the Internet; although some of these gaps have subsequently narrowed, important disparities remain.[2] In addition to gaps in Internet access, other scholars showed that many users were unskilled and unsophisticated (Hargittai, 2003). With political content in particular, some claimed that few citizens were motivated to take advantage of new online sources of political information (Norris, 2001). As traditional news outlets and interest groups moved online, some scholars concluded that the Internet would merely support "politics as usual" (Margolis & Resnick, 2000; see also Davis, 1998).

Still, on the issue of online diversity, the most fundamental challenge has come not from social scientists but from computer scientists and applied physicists. These researchers began by searching for statistical regularities in the structure of the World Wide Web and in the surfing habits of users. What they found was initially surprising. To begin with, researchers looked at the distribution of hyperlinks among different Web sites. In theory, Web sites can link to any other site on the World Wide Web equally; real-world data, however, showed a pattern of links that was anything but equal. Over the entire World Wide Web, researchers found that the distribution of both inbound and outbound hyperlinks followed a power law or "scale-free" distribution (Barabási & Albert, 1999; Barabási, Albert, Jeong, & Bianconi, 2000; Kumar, Raghavan, Rajagopalan, & Tomkins, 1999). More precisely, the probability that a randomly selected Web page has K links is proportional to $K^{-\alpha}$ for large K.

Data follow a power law distribution when the size of an observation is inversely and exponentially proportional to its frequency. Pareto's (1897) "80/20 rule"—where 20% of the population controls 80% of the wealth—is an example of a power law distribution. Within the social and natural sciences, many other phenomena obey this statistical pattern: from earthquakes to intracell protein networks, from the size of firms to the size of cities, from the severity of wars to the distribution of human sexual contacts (Cederman, 2003; Huberman, 2001; Krugman, 1994; Liljeros, Edling, Nunes Amaral, Stanley, & Aberg, 2001).

As the examples illustrate, many different processes can generate a power law distribution. But in every case, a power law distribution leads to remarkably inegalitarian outcomes. To get a sense of just how extreme these results can be in practice, imagine a hypothetical community where wealth is power law distributed. At one end of the spectrum, there is 1 millionaire, 10 individuals worth at least $100,000, a hundred people worth $10,000, and a thousand people worth at least $1,000. At the opposite end of the spectrum, 1,000,000 people have a net worth of $1. In this hypothetical community, wealth is distributed in proportion to the function $K^{-\alpha}$, where $\alpha = 1$.

Studies have found the online environment to be far more concentrated even than the hypothetical example shown earlier, generating values of $\alpha \approx 2.1$ for inbound hyperlinks, and $\alpha \approx 2.7$ for outbound hyperlinks (Barabási et al., 2000; Faloutsos, Faloutsos, & Faloutsos, 1999; Kumar, Raghavan, Rajagopalan, & Tomkins, 1999). Importantly, research has shown that the number of hyperlinks a site receives is closely correlated with its traffic (Hindman, 2003). Traffic, like link structure, follows a power law distribution with roughly the same parameters (Adamic & Huberman, 2000; Huberman, Pirolli, Pitkow, & Lukose, 1998). A few popular sites (such as Yahoo, AOL, or Google) receive a large portion of the total traffic; less successful sites (such as most personal Web pages) receive no traffic at all.

Over the entire World Wide Web, then, there is strong evidence that traffic and links follow strict winners-take-all patterns. Similar patterns of concentration can also be found at a microlevel. Researchers have shown that highly concentrated patterns of links exist among sites dedicated to a wide array of commercial activities (Huberman, 2001; Pennock, Flake, Lawrence, Glover, & Giles, 2002). And commercial sites are not the only subcategories of Web content that follow these highly skewed distributions of links and traffic. Fears about media concentration have often been grounded in concern for the diversity in the political information and viewpoints to which citizens are exposed. Political Weblogs also demonstrate highly skewed patterns, with most of the links and traffic accruing to a small set of "A-list" bloggers (Shirky, 2004). Previous research by the author shows that these patterns are particularly strong among community Web sites focused on political topics. Across a wide array of different political communities—from gun-control sites to sites on the U.S. presidency, sites on Congress to sites on abortion, death penalty sites to sites about general politics—a small set of sites receives more links than all the rest put together (Hindman, 2003).

All of these data on online concentration return us to the central question with which we began this section. On the one hand, the Internet allows citizens to choose from a far broader set of sources than was possible a generation ago. At the same time, much evidence suggests that online diversity is far narrower in practice than it is in theory. These strict hierarchical patterns of online traffic force us to think differently about the "openness" of the Internet. Yet for both policymakers and scholars, the central concern is this: how does the concentration that exists online compare to the concentration we are used to in traditional media?

Answering this question requires two things. First of all, it requires data on audience concentration across different media. Second, it requires that we choose measures of concentration that make cross-media comparison possible. The next section offers both data and metrics.

COMPARING ONLINE AND OFFLINE CONCENTRATION

This analysis places online concentration alongside newspaper circulation, magazine circulation, and radio station listenership. Any study of this kind has limitations. First, none of these media are exactly comparable with the World Wide Web, or with each other. A Web site is not interchangeable with a radio station or a newspaper. Cross-media comparison can indeed end up comparing apples and oranges, and this must be acknowledged from the start.

Second, much of the concern about media diversity has focused on patterns of ownership within and across different media types. Ownership patterns are undeniably important, and diverse research has shown the effects of ownership on the content that media outlets carry.[3] Yet this study takes a different focus, counting different outlets of the same media parent company as different voices. Two different radio stations owned by the Clear Channel Corporation, for example, are considered separately.

There are several reasons for this approach, but the most important rationale concerns the role geographic barriers—or lack thereof—may play in supporting online concentration. As the title suggests, this volume is particularly concerned with the fate of local content and local media sources in the 21st century. In most areas of traditional media, a given media outlet only reaches a small part of the country. This is not true of the magazines included in our study; publications such as *Newsweek* and *The New Yorker* are distributed nationwide. However, it is largely true of newspapers: only *The New York Times, The Wall Street Journal,* and *USA Today* have significant national circulations. Radio stations similarly can be heard only within a small region.

This chapter looks at media concentration from a national perspective. The FCC, in its creation of a "diversity index" to guide regulatory policy, has explicitly limited itself to local media markets. If one is interested in the number of choices that any given citizen can choose, this focus makes sense. Yet if we want to ask a different and broader question—namely, the diversity of media sources consumed over the nation as a whole—the methodology I propose is preferable.

The limitations of the study should thus be borne in mind. Yet if we should be cautious in interpreting the results, the larger patterns are difficult to ignore. Viewed from the national level, the concentration of audience share we see online seems at least as great as that found in the offline world.

DATA

The data analysis in this chapter is separated into two parts. In the first part, I gather a diverse group of data sets for online and offline content, trying to provide an overview of concentration across different media types. In the second part, I look at a smaller data set, trying to isolate the effects of media type on audience concentration. Both parts of this analysis suggest that, all else being equal, online audiences are more concentrated than those for offline content.

For the broad survey of concentration in different media types, I first examine data on radio station listenership. I compile a national-level data set using Arbitron corporation ratings data on all commercial radio stations, both AM and FM, within the top 50 radio markets of the United States. These 50 markets serve 128 million people age 12 or older, roughly half of the nation's total 12-and-older population. This data set covers 1,289 commercial stations, and it was the most recent public data available through Arbitron's Web site as of December 2003.

Second, I look at data on print media, both newspapers and magazines. In both cases, nationwide circulation data come from the Audit Bureau of Circulations (ABC). The ABC data include circulation figures for 653 magazines and 1,058 newspapers nationwide, as of early 2004.

I weigh these data on radio and print against data sets on online concentration. First and foremost, I look at the traffic patterns among the 100 most visited English-language Web sites, according to March 2005 traffic data from Alexa.com.[4] I also look at traffic among blogs, where the common use of the SiteMeter.com service provides us with a consistent data on traffic to these sites. In this case, I use information drawn from N.Z. Bear's Weblog Ecosystem project, which aggregates the SiteMeter data; I use the traffic ranking of the 5,000 top blogs tracked by the Ecosystem project, as of March 2005. In the blog data, the most heavily trafficked site receives more than 300,000 visits daily, whereas the least popular sites receive 10 visits a day.

The second part of the analysis is narrower, looking at the area where online and offline content is arguably most comparable. The overwhelming majority of American newspapers now have official Web sites that offer online versions of their print content. This fact allows me to isolate the effect that the distribution mechanism—in this case, print versus World Wide Web—has on the level of audience concentration. Print circulation numbers again come from the ABC, as of March 2005. Traffic data for these newspaper Web sites comes from Alexa.com, as of March 2005. To ensure comparability across data sets, the analysis of this second section is limited to the top 150 newspapers in the country, as determined by the ABC. This limitation is largely for practical reasons: Alexa provides publicly available traffic data only for the top 100,000 Web sites by traffic rank. Although all of the top 150 newspapers are in this category, the list of the top 250 or top 500 newspapers would include numerous publications that do not meet the threshold. Last, this second section also includes March 2005 traffic data from the top 150 blogs, again from N.Z. Bear's web site.

METRICS FOR CONCENTRATION

With these data sets in hand, we must consider what sort of measures can fruitfully be used to illustrate disparities in concentration. I choose to adapt two commonly used metrics from other areas of the social sciences to provide benchmarks of concentration across mediums. In addition, I also use the Noam Index, a recently proposed measure intended specifically to assess diversity in media markets.

The first of these metrics is the Gini coeffient. Originally developed in the early 20th century to measure income inequality, the Gini coefficient can be used, as Corrado Gini (1921) himself declared, to calculate relative inequality for almost any resource. The Gini coefficient is the mean difference across all observations between the Lorenz curve and the line of perfect equality.[5] Stated formally, if y is a vector of incomes, with extreme values of y_{min} and y_{max}, a mean of m, and a cumulative distribution of $F(y)$, the Gini coefficient can be calculated as follows:

$$G = \frac{\int_{\min}^{\max} F(y)[1 - F(y)]}{\mu}$$

The Gini coefficient produces possible values between 0 and 1.

The second measure of inequality that we adapt for these purposes is the HHI. Originally developed to measure firm power within industries, the HHI is calculated by taking an observation's total resource share expressed as a percentage, squaring it, and taking the sum across all observations. Expressed more formally, the HHI can be calculated as:

$$HHI = \sum_{1}^{N} P_i^2$$

In this case, P_i is the percentage of total audience attracted by the ith media outlet or Web site. HHI has possible values between 0 and 10,000. In the context of the federal antitrust law, market segments with an HHI of less than 1,000 are considered unconcentrated, an HHI of between 1,000 and 1,800 denotes a moderately concentrated market, and markets above 1,800 are considered highly concentrated (DOJ & FTC, 1997).

Third, we employ the Noam Index, a measure recently proposed by Eli Noam specifically to capture diversity in media markets. Noam argues that "one should not have to choose between a measure of market power (the HHI) or of pluralism (the number of voices) but ought to incorporate both" (Noam, 2004, p. 2). Noam's solution to this problem is straightforward: to take the HHI and divide it by the square root of the number of media "voices" in a given market. The Noam Index is thus derived from the following equation:

$$Noam = \sum_{1}^{N} \frac{P_i^2}{\sqrt{N}}$$

where P_i is the percentage of total audience attracted by the ith media outlet, and N is the number of outlets. Only those voices that achieve some minimal level of audience share are counted in the metric. Noam includes all voices with more than 1% of the total market in the index: "One per cent seems a reasonable floor: small but not trivial" (Noam, 2004, p. 3). As with the HHI, the Noam Index provides possible scores between 0 and 10,000, although all non-monopoly markets will score lower on the Noam Index and they do on the HHI.[6]

The HHI and the Gini coefficient are the most commonly used metrics of inequality or concentration in the social sciences; the Noam Index is so new that it has yet to see much use. These are hardly the only the only possible choices for concentration metrics, however, so it is worth taking a moment to consider the reasons these measures are attractive in this context.

HHI and the Gini coefficient are each representative of other, substantively similar metrics.[7] The two measures differ radically in their emphases, and the relative weight they afford to observations large and small. The HHI focuses on the observations with the very highest values. Smaller players receive almost no weight in calculating the final statistic, and consequently adding additional observations with a tiny share of total resources has negligible effect on the HHI. (The Noam Index, which is derived from the HHI, shares the same property for all sources below the 1% threshold.) The Gini coefficient, by contrast, is a just a mean—the mean difference between the Lorenz curve and the line of perfect equality—and as such it is drawn equally from all observations in the data. Adding a large number of observations with tiny values raises the Gini coefficient dramatically.

The Gini coefficient and the HHI scale differently with the size of the populations they measure. Imagine two villages with identical distributions of wealth, one 5 times the size of the other. These two towns would have identical Gini coefficients; however, the larger town would have an HHI one-fifth that of the smaller community. In general, the Gini coefficient will produce substantively similar results to other metrics, such as the uncertainty ratio, which also looks at how equally resources are distributed across the broad population. The HHI will generally produce a similar assessment of concentration to other metrics that focus on the power of the largest players, such as CR4 or CR8 (Yim, 2003). As is seen later, in the markets we examine, the Noam Index produces results nearly identical to the HHI.

In short, then, the HHI, the Noam Index, and the Gini coefficient provide very different measures of concentration. Their agreement in this case thus adds to the robustness of the findings.

RESULTS

Having discussed both the data sources and the different metrics, it is time to put them to the test. The results of this analysis highlight just how profound online concentration appears. By these metrics, audiences on the World Wide Web appear even more tightly focused than those of more traditional media. Although these results need to be supplemented by additional research, they do show convincingly that the structure of online attention is hardly a radical break with the broadcast model. Readership comparisons between the online and print versions of newspapers are particularly dramatic. All else being equal, the World Wide Web seems to promote consumption concentration patterns more extreme than those in traditional media.

First, it is worth considering the broad outlines of concentration across a variety of different types of content. Table 14.1 lays out these results in detail. The first four rows present levels of concentration among the nation's top 100 radio stations, magazines, and newspapers, along with audience concentration among the top 100 English-language Web sites. In every case, Web site traffic is far more concentrated than that found in more established media outlets. First, consider the Gini coefficient. By this measure, the nation's top 100 newspapers and top 100 magazines look significantly more concentrated than

TABLE 14.1

Concentration Across Media

	Gini Coefficient	*HHI*	*Noam Index*	*Top 10*
Radio—Top 100 stations	.21	118	19	20%
Print—Top 100 newspapers	.40	189	34	32%
Print—Top 100 magazines	.44	262	55	39%
WWW—Top 100 sites	.66	721	180	62%
Radio—Stations in top 50 markets	.53	19	*	7%
Print—All U.S. newspapers	.69	73	18	19%
Print—All U.S. magazines	.70	123	34	27%
WWW—All Weblog traffic	.89	221	61	38%

Note. This table presents data on the level of concentration across different media types. Online audiences appear dramatically more concentrated than offline audiences. (The Noam Index could not be calculated for the national radio listenership, because not a single station reached the 1% threshold for inclusion in the metric.) HHI = Hirschman-Herfindahl Index; WWW = World Wide Web.

listenership on the nation's 100 most popular radio stations. Yet Web traffic is more concentrated still: magazine circulation produces a Gini coefficient of .44, whereas patterns of Web traffic generate a Gini coefficient of .66.

Similar results can be seen with the HHI. Web traffic produces an HHI of 721, dramatically more concentrated than any other medium. Moreover, Web traffic produces a Noam Index of 180, three times higher than that for magazines, the next most concentrated type of content. In one sense, this result is surprising. As Noam explains it, the Noam Index should account not just for the market power of the top content producers, but also for the number of distinct outlets in a media market. In terms of the raw number of voices available, the World Wide Web greatly exceeds that of other media. Newspapers, magazines, and radio stations number in the hundreds or the low thousands nationwide, whereas Web sites number in the tens of millions. But by setting a minimum audience threshold to be included in the measure, the Noam Index consistently finds a larger number of voices in traditional media than it does on the World Wide Web.

Leaving aside these metrics, and looking just at the percentage of the total audience accounted for by the top 10 outlets, also reinforces the conclusion that online content is more concentrated than content in traditional media. In this sample, the top 10 outlets in radio and print garner between 20% and 39% of the total audience for their respective media. On the World Wide Web, the top 10 sites account for 62% of total traffic.

Ideally, this analysis would be repeated looking not just at the top 100 sites, but at all outlets within these different media types. Unfortunately, such analysis goes beyond the limits of recent, publicly available data. However, there is strong reason to believe that similar results would be found at any level of analysis. First of all, as was noted earlier, we know what the distribution of traffic looks like over the entire World Wide Web. According to the Alexa data, the 100th ranked English-language Web site receives roughly 1% of the traffic that Yahoo, the top site, receives. Nonetheless, if we believe the host of studies that have found Web traffic to be power law distributed, we know that this 100th ranked Web site receives an order of magnitude more traffic than sites an order of magnitude below it in the rankings. In short, these winners-take-all patterns are so extreme that expanding the number of outlets included cannot add enough traffic to change the substantive conclusions.

There is another line of analysis which also supports the idea that, over the entire World Wide Web, site traffic is more concentrated than radio listenership or print readership. As noted earlier, blog readership, just like overall Web traffic, follows a power law distribution. Moreover, the power law patterns which govern blog links and blog traffic are actually less extreme than those which govern traffic on the broader World Wide Web (Adamic & Glance, 2005; Adamic & Huberman, 2000; Shirky, 2004). Because of the common use of the SiteMeter service to track site visitors across different blogs, Weblogs are one area of the World Wide Web where there is consistent and reasonably comprehensive traffic data.

If we compare the relatively complete data on blog traffic with the broader data sets on radio listenership and print circulation, the results show that online content again looks more concentrated than offline content. The Gini coefficient, the HHI, and the Noam Index all point to this conclusion. The top 10 Weblogs in our sample account for 38% of the total traffic, a substantially larger portion than the top 10 outlets account for in other media.

There is thus little evidence that the Internet has led to the diffusion of citizens' attention away from a few important outlets. As noted earlier, many observers have suggested that the Internet will be bad news for general interest intermediaries—that the Internet will naturally lead to a far more fractured media environment. Yet the empirical evidence which should support this claim runs in exactly the opposite direction. The more choices that citizens have, it seems, the more they have converged on the same few outlets of information.

Nonetheless, one might object to this analysis on the grounds that any comparison of this kind is only partially valid. This section began by noting that cross media studies can often result in comparing apples and oranges. For the sake of argument, let us grant that this is true—perhaps a Web site and a radio station are so different that the earlier comparison has little meaning. Ideally, we would like to examine identical content both online and offline, and see if the method of distribution makes a difference in audience concentration.

There is one obvious area in which such a comparison is possible. Of the nation's top 150 newspapers by circulation, 149 run news Web sites, either by themselves or in partnership with other news organizations (typically a local television station). Thanks to the ABC and Alexa.com, both the circulation figures for these newspapers and the traffic figures for the corresponding Web sites are easily available.

Newspaper content allows us to isolate the effect of the distribution medium from a host of potentially confounding variables. Printed newspapers and newspaper Web sites are run by the same organizations—written by the same staff, in the same building, with the same resources. The newspaper content available online is usually identical to articles in the print editions.

Table 14.2 presents this analysis in detail. Across every measure, newspaper readership online is substantially more concentrated than newspaper readership in print. Online readership patterns produce an HHI 2½ times that found in these newspapers' print versions; the Noam Index is nearly 3 times higher. In this sample, the nation's top 10 newspapers account for 30% of the total print readership. By contrast, the top 10 newspaper sites account for more than half of newspaper readership online.

Given that the content being compared here is mostly identical, these results are striking. Yet the point is further reinforced by comparing online newspaper traffic with traffic in other areas of the World Wide Web. The third row of Table 14.2 presents data on traffic within the top 150 Weblogs. The content found in these blogs is very different than the content found in a typical newspaper. Yet the patterns of concentration we see in blogs and newspaper Web sites are almost identical. In terms of audience concentration, the medium by which content is distributed seems to matter more than the content itself.

TABLE 14.2

Newspaper Audiences, Online and Off

	Gini Coefficient	*HHI*	*Noam Index*	*Top 10*
Newspapers: Print circulation (top 150)	.47	165	34	30%
Newspapers: Web readership (top 150)	.69	426	98	52%
Blog readership (top 150)	.65	426	100	53%

Note. This table looks at audience concentration among newspaper readers, looking at newspaper readership both in print and on the World Wide Web. For purposes of comparison, it also presents data on concentration among those who read Weblogs. Although the online and offline newspapers mostly provide identical content, online readers are far more concentrated. Blog readers and online newspaper readers, by contrast, have nearly identical patterns of concentration. HHI = Hirschman-Herfindahl Index.

THE TOP OF THE OCEAN

The previous section has offered a comparative perspective on media concentration. It has argued against visions of the Internet as a radically decentralized medium where large media outlets are unimportant. It is undeniably true that there are billions of Web pages on the open Internet, offering a plethora of possible information choices for citizens. Yet the data presented earlier suggest that expanding the number of options available to citizens has not had the expected effects. More choice has meant more concentration.

From satellite radio to cable television, many media are expanding greatly in the number of channels or outlets from which citizens can choose. Unsurprisingly, diversity of usage has not increased as a linear function of the number of channels and outlets available. The Internet provides an extreme example of this phenomenon—as well as a profound demonstration that all media outlets are not created equal. Others in this volume have argued persuasively that the FCC's effort at a diversity index, which is based on the principle of counting the number of media voices, is ill-suited to measuring real diversity. If counting the number of voices fails to capture diversity in traditional media markets, this technique makes even less sense online. In theory, the number of voices available online seems nearly infinite. However, most of these voices are heard by only a trivial audience.

For some observers, these data may be a puzzle. At first glance, it is indeed counterintuitive to believe that the Internet will concentrate, rather than diffuse, the attentions of the broader public. There is much that we still do not know about the underlying causes of audience concentration online. Nonetheless, several important factors clearly contribute to this result. This section outlines a few of these factors. Taken together, these dynamics make online concentration seem not just expected, but even overdetermined. We need to move beyond generalizations about the "openness" of the Internet, and consider instead the structural factors that constrain the possibilities of media diversity online. The Internet may work differently than traditional media, but obstacles to diversity remain.

First, one obstacle is the structure of the World Wide Web itself. Much talk about the Internet as an accessible medium has highlighted its unusual, "end-to-end" architecture. In theory, any computer on the Internet can retrieve information from any other. Yet this is true of only one layer of the Internet's architecture; other integral parts of the medium—such as the patterns of links which weave the World Wide Web together, or the search engines which filter online content—actively promote concentration.

Everyone agrees that the Internet is big. From the perspective of the average consumer, the size of the Internet is a difficulty as well as a blessing. A citizen might spend his or her entire life online and not see more than a tiny fraction of the billions of available Web pages. Sorting through that body of content is a task so large that every user must take cognitive shortcuts to simplify the process.

It is for this reason that the highly concentrated, winners-take-all patterns in the link structure of the Internet are so important. Both directly and indirectly, the number of links pointing to a site is a powerful determinant of the traffic that site receives. In the direct sense, links are important because people follow them. The more links there are to a Web site, the more likely it is that users will click on these links. Moreover, all modern search engines emphasize this link structure in ranking their search results (Brin & Page, 1998; Ding, He, Husbands, Zha, & Simon, 2002; Marendy, 2001). Although the underlying ranking algorithms may be somewhat more complex, in practice the sites that receive the highest rankings and the most traffic are those that receive the most links. This makes search engines into a popularity contest. That may make it easier to find quality content, but it also makes online audiences more concentrated.

In comparing online content producers with traditional media outlets, there are additional reasons why we might expect the Internet to be more concentrated than its offline brethren. The Internet dramatically changes the cost of distributing content, but it has done little to change the costs of producing content in the first place. Consider the case of newspaper publishing. In the Internet age, it is cheaper to pay for Web servers and bandwidth costs than it is to pay for printing presses, ink, paper, and delivery vans. Yet at the same time, most other costs of producing a newspaper have hardly budged. Journalists still need offices, telephones, computers, and salaries. Introductory economic textbooks have long cited the economies of scale available in newspaper publishing as an invitation to local monopoly. High fixed costs, combined with low marginal costs, have usually led one publication to dominate local markets: once the first copy of a newspaper is produced, the cost of printing a second one is negligible. Yet the marginal costs of distributing content are even lower online. Presumably, the economies of scale available online are larger as well.

This fact forces us to pay greater attention to the role of geography in promoting media diversity. In the newspaper market, for example, geographic barriers have played a key role in protecting local monopolies from competition. On the Internet, these local barriers are removed—and the economies of scale which have allowed most local newspapers to force out their competitors now operate to the disadvantage of local content producers.

To understand what this may mean in practice, consider a hypothetical newspaper reader. Let us call her Cheryl, and presume that she is an avid Web surfer who lives in Walla Walla, Washington. If Cheryl is most interested in local news, the online and print versions of the *Walla Walla Union-Bulletin* may continue to be attractive. If Cheryl is mostly interested in international affairs or national politics, however, there is little reason for her to continue reading the local paper, online or off. Dozens of newspaper and news Web sites offer more extensive coverage of national and international news than the *Union-Bulletin* does. Switching costs are low: all Cheryl has to do is to stumble across one of these Web sites once, and then bookmark it so that the site is easy to return to later. Rather than paying to have the *Union-Bulletin* delivered to her doorstep, Cheryl can access most news and newspaper Web sites for free. For a resident of a small agricultural town with a population of 30,000, this is an enormous expansion beyond what was available a decade ago.

From the perspective of democratic theory, people like Cheryl suggest a trade-off between competing democratic values. On the one hand, we would ideally like to provide every citizen with as many media choices as possible. If free flow of information is the lifeblood of democracy, more information from more outlets is an obvious good. In the words of Justice Black cited earlier, democratic theory seeks "the widest possible dissemination of information from diverse and antagonistic sources" (*Associated Press v. U.S.*, 1945, p. 1424). As the 21st century opens, citizens with the necessary motivation and skills can reach thousands of online news outlets based in every corner of the globe.

On the individual level, then, there's no question that the number of choices available has expanded. But consider again the case of Cheryl. What if she, and millions of other people in her position, make the same choices? What if they all focus their online news readership on *The New York Times* and *The Washington Post*? What if expanding the number of choices actually means that fewer outlets reach a substantial portion of the public?

The data sources discussed earlier suggest that this is exactly what is happening. *The New York Times*' share of online newspaper traffic is 3.5 times its share of the print newspaper market; *The Washington Post* online likewise earns nearly 3 times its offline share. *The Boston Globe,* the *San Francisco Chronicle,* and the *Washington Times* also have online audience shares more than double their share of print circulation. At the other end of the scale, 126 of the 150 newspapers attract a smaller portion of online newspaper traffic than they do print circulation. It is overwhelmingly local, smaller-circulation papers which are weaker online than offline. We want citizens to have access to the nation's best newspapers, no matter where they live. At the same time, it is increasingly clear that geographic barriers, which used to limit the media in most communities to a handful of broadcast stations and a single local paper, have also meant a less concentrated and more diverse media environment at the national level.

Ultimately, the link structure of the World Wide Web, and the economies of scale available in online publishing, are characteristics of online content that have important implications for the fate of diversity on the World Wide Web. These factors should provide a counterweight to persistent talk about the "openness" of the Internet. Certain aspects of the Internet's architecture are remarkably open, and rightly celebrated. But the Internet is more than just the TCP/IP protocol, or the open standards that allow the creation of documents in HTML. If we think more broadly about what citizens need to find and use online information, other limits to diversity become highly salient.

CONCLUSION

In the 1989 movie *Field of Dreams,* an Iowa farmer played by Kevin Costner begins to hear voices in his cornfields. These voices repeat a simple but compelling message: "if you build it, they will come." In the past decade, much that has been said and written about the Internet has been based on a similar philosophy. It remains common to read about how the Internet will send citizens to a broader set of sources than they would visit in traditional media. Although millions of sites have been built in the past decade, for most the traffic has not come. The result has been a small handful of sites that reach a significant portion of the online audience, and millions of sites that reach almost no one at all.

The focus of this chapter has been to place online concentration in a broader comparative perspective. Our goal has been to develop both data sets and metrics that make cross-media comparison possible, to view the patterns we see on the World Wide Web alongside the more familiar patterns of concentration in the traditional media marketplace.

The results of this analysis are striking. Audience concentration over the entire World Wide Web seems to exceed that in newspapers, magazines, and radio listenership. Even when the content distributed is largely identical to traditional media content, the World Wide Web produces profound patterns of concentration. In comparing newspaper circulation with readership of online newspaper Web sites, we find concentration is far greater online than off.

The World Wide Web is a critical part of the media environment. It is now the largest public information source ever assembled by humankind, comprising innumerable terabytes of data—more than one could explore in many lifetimes. Yet in talking about the diversity available on the World Wide Web, we must confront a central contradiction. Online, a smaller number of outlets have consistently garnered a larger share of the total audience. It may be true that every web site has a voice—but most speak in a whisper and a powerful few have a megaphone.

That the World Wide Web may exacerbate, not remedy, long-standing concerns over media concentration contradicts commonly held notions of the Internet as an informational nirvana. Yet just as people have evolved their thinking about what the "dot-com" world means for business after an initial period of overexcitement, scholars and regulators need to reconsider their assumptions about what the World Wide Web means for media diversity. High levels of audience concentration must be acknowledged as a central feature of the online landscape. Diversity on the Internet may be broad, but it is also remarkably shallow.

NOTES

*Early versions of this chapter were prepared for presentation at the Ford Foundation conference on media diversity in December of 2003, as well as the CITI conference on online media concentration in April 2004. I offer sincere thanks to the conference participants for their comments and criticism. This work was supported in part by a doctoral fellowship from the National Center for Digital Government, at Harvard's John F. Kennedy School of Government, under National Science Foundation Grant No. 0131923.

†Political Science Department, Arizona State University (ASU Box 873902, Tempe, AZ 85287-3902. E-mail: hindman@asu.edu).

[1]All figures are from Ranie (2005); on differing accounts of how many Americans are online, see Bimber (2003).

[2]For the best early surveys of the digital divide, see NTIA (1995, 1998). For more recent assessments, see NTIA (200) and Hoffman, Novak, and Schlosser (2001).

[3]Examples of recent research on this topic include Gilens and Hertzman (2000) and Curtin (2000).

[4]Alexa measures the surfing habits of millions of individuals worldwide who have installed Alexa's toolbar or related software. Although Alexa also provides rankings of the top 10,000 or 100,000 Web sites, it charges a substantial fee for this proprietary data.

[5]The Lorenz curve can be obtained by plotting the cumulative distribution function of the resource in question against the cumulative distribution of the population possessing the resource. In a population governed by perfect equality, the Lorenz curve is a perfectly straight line: 30% of the population owns 30% of the wealth, 75% of the population owns 75% of the wealth, and so forth.

[6]As a rough guideline, Noam suggests we should consider markets with an index of 300 or lower to be unconcentrated, those between 300 and 500 moderately concentrated, and markets with a score above 500 highly concentrated.

[7]On this point, see the discussion in Yim (2003).

REFERENCES

Adamic, L., & Glance, N. (2005). *The political blogosphere in the 2004 U.S. election: Divided they blog.* Retrieved February 11, 2005, from http://www.hpl.hp.com/research/idl/papers/politicalblogs/

Adamic, L. A., & Huberman, B. A. (2000). The nature of markets on the World Wide Web. *Quarterly Journal of Economic Commerce, 1,* 12.

Associated Press v. U.S., 326 U.S. 1 (1945).

Barabasi, A.-L., & Albert, R. (1999). Emergence of scaling in random networks. *Science, 286,* 509–512.

Barabasi, A.-L., Albert, R., Jeong, H., & Bianconi, G. (2000). Power law distribution of the World Wide Web. *Science, 287,* 12–13.

Barlow, J. P., Birkets, S., Kelly, K., & Slouka, M. (1995). What are we doing online? *Harper's, 291,* 35–46.

Bimber, B. (2003). Notes on the diffusion of the Internet. Retrieved March 31, 2005, from University of California at Santa Barbara Web site: http://www.polsci.ucsb.edu/faculty/bimber/Internet-diffusion.htm

Brin, S., & Page, L. (1998). The anatomy of a large scale hypertextual Web search engine. *Computer Networks and ISDN Systems, 30,* 107–117.

Cederman, L.-E. (2003). Modeling the size of wars: From billiard balls to sand piles. *American Political Science Review, 97,* 135–150.

Curtin, M. (2000). Gatekeeping in the neo-network era. In M. Suman & G. Rossman (Eds.), *Advocacy groups and the entertainment industry* (pp. 65–76). Westport, CT: Praeger.

Davis, R. (1998). *The web of politics.* London: Oxford University Press.

Department of Justice & Federal Trade Commission. (1997). *Horizontal merger guidelines. Issued April 2, 1992; revised April 8, 1997.* Retrieved October 2, 2004, from http://www.usdoj.gov/atr/public/guidelines/horiz_book/hmg1.html

Ding, C., He, X., Husbands, P., Zha, H., & Simon, H. (2002). *PageRank, HITS, and a unified framework for link analysis* (Tech. Rep. No. 49372). Berkeley, CA: Lawrence Berkeley National Laboratory.

Faloutsos, M., Faloutsos, P., & Faloutsos, C. (1999). On power-law relationships of the internet topology. *SIGCOMM, X,* 251–262.

Gilens, M., & Hertzman, C. (2000). Corporate ownership and news bias: Newspaper coverage of the 1996 Telecommunications Act. *Journal of Politics, 62, 369–386.*

Gini, C. (1921). Measurement of inequality of incomes. *The Economic Journal, 31,* 144–126.

Guthrie, J. (2004, October 3). Fellow anchors defend Rather on forged papers. *San Francisco Chronicle,* p. A-2.

Hargittai, E. (2003). *How wide a Web?: Inequalities in accessing information online.* Unpublished doctoral dissertation, Princeton University, Princeton, NJ.

Hewitt, H. (2005). *Blog: Understanding the information reformation that's changing your world.* Nashville, TN: Nelson Books.

Hindman, M. (2003). *'Googlearchy': How a few heavily linked sites dominate politics online.* Unpublished manuscript.

Hoffman, D. L., Novak, T. P., & Schlosser, A. E. (2001). The evolution of the digital divide: Examining the relationship of race to Internet access over time. In B. M. Compaine (Ed.), *Digital divide: Facing a crisis or creating a myth?* (pp. 47–98). Cambridge, MA: MIT Press.

Horrigan, J. (2004, April). *55% of adult Internet users have broadband at home or work* (Data memo). Washington, DC: Pew Internet and American Life Project.

Huberman, B. A. (2001). *Laws of the Web*. Cambridge, MA: MIT Press.

Huberman, B. A., Pirolli, P. L. T., Pitkow, J. E., & Lukose, R. M. (1998). Strong regularities in world wide web surfing. *Science, 280,* 95–97.

Krugman, P. (1994). Complex landscapes in economic geography. *American Economic Review, 84,* 412–416.

Kumar, R., Raghavan, P., Rajagopalan, S., & Tomkins, A. (1999). Trawling the Web for emerging cyber-communities. *Computer Networks, 31,* 1481–1493.

Last, J. V. (2002, March 14). *Reading, writing and blogging*. Retrieved October 13, 2005, from http://www.weeklystandard.com/Content/Public/Articles/000/000/001/009flofq.asp

Liljeros, F., Edling, C. R., Nunes Amaral, L. A., Stanley, H. E., & Aberg, Y. (2001). The web of human sexual contacts. *Nature, 411,* 907–908.

Manjoo, F. (2003, May 21). Can the Web beat big media? *Salon*. Retrieved June 30, 2003, from http://archive.salon.com/tech/feature/2003/05/21/web_vs_big_media/

Marendy, P. (2001). A review of World Wide Web searching techniques, focusing on HITS and related algorithms that utilise the link topology of the World Wide Web to provide the basis for a structure based search technology (technical report). North Queensland, Australia: James Cook University.

Margolis, M., & Resnick, D. (2000). *Politics as usual: The cyberspace 'revolution.'* New York: Sage.

Noam, E. (2004, September 7). How to measure media concentration. *Financial Times* [online]. Retrieved October 13, 2005, from www.ft.com

National Telecommunications and Information Administration. (1995). Falling through the 'net: A study of the "have nots" in rural and urban America. Washington, DC: Author.

National Telecommunications and Information Administration. (1998). Falling through the 'net II: New data on the digital divide. Washington, DC: Author.

National Telecommunications and Information Administration. (2002). A nation online: How Americans are expanding their use of the Internet. Washington, DC: Author.

Norris, P. (2001). *Digital divide*. New York: Cambridge.

Pareto, V. (1971). *Manual of political economy*. (A. S. Schweir, Trans.; A. S. Schweir & A. N. Page, Eds.). New York: A. M. Kelley.

Pennock, D. M., Flake, G. W., Lawrence, S., Glover, E. J., & Giles, C. L. (2002). Winners don't take all: Characterizing the competition for links on the Web. *Proceedings of the National Academy of Sciences, USA, 99,* 5207–5211.

Ranie, L. (2005). The state of blogging (Data memo). Washington, DC: Pew Internet and American Life Project.

Shirky, C. (2004, January 24). *Inequality in the weblog world* (Seminar presentation). Berkman Center for Internet and Society, Harvard University, Cambridge, MA.

Starr, P. (2004). *The creation of the American media: The political origins of modern communications*. New York: Basic Books.

Sunstein, C. (2001). *Republic.com*. Princeton, NJ: Princeton University Press.

Yeager, H. (2004, September 24). Blogs bias and 24-hour news: How a fragmented media are shaping the US election. *The Financial Times*, p. 17.

Yim, J. (2003). Audience concentration in the media: Cross-media comparisons and the introduction of the uncertainty measure. *Communications Monographs, 70,* 114–128.

15

Content Diversity Online: Myth or Reality?

Eszter Hargittai
Northwestern University

THE IMPORTANCE OF STUDYING "EXPOSURE DIVERSITY"

A vast amount of material is available to users of the World Wide Web. Search engines index the contents of billions of pages—by last reports one of the most widely used search engines, Google, claims to index over 8 billion—yet they admittedly only cover a fraction of all available content (Sullivan, 2005). Unlike with other media, once content on the Web is publicly available, anyone with knowledge of its Web address can access it. This has led to much enthusiasm regarding the medium, including justification for media deregulation by former Federal Communications Commission Chair Michael Powell (Manjoo, 2003). But does the Web really offer a panacea to concerns about diversity in the media landscape? In addition to looking at what is theoretically available to users, I argue that we must also consider what is realistically within their reach (Hargittai, 2000). To understand realistic accessibility as opposed to mere availability, we must consider what factors influence the types of material that people are most likely to retrieve online. In this chapter, I argue that the way content is organized on Web sites and users' ability to navigate the Web both influence what material is most easily accessible.

Napoli (1999) outlines a helpful framework for approaching questions about media diversity by identifying three different types: (a) source diversity, (b) content diversity, and (c) exposure diversity. Webster (this volume) offers a helpful summary of this approach and points out the dearth of research on "exposure diversity." His chapter explores the viewing habits of TV audiences in a multichannel environment. In a similar vein, this chapter looks at the actual online actions of Internet users to shed light on whether the promises of the Internet for content diversity are realized when it comes to average users' utilization of the medium.

To explore this question I look at the options for, and processes of, finding information about local cultural events online. The availability of local content is of particular interest for discussions about media diversity as local content can easily be the first to disappear when national media buy up local media outlets. It is cheaper to syndicate a centrally-created program than to run local versions across numerous outlets. However, this may be to the detriment of local information. Can the Web act as an alternative source of information about local events?

I use several methodologies to investigate what options are most realistically accessible to Internet users when it comes to locating information about local cultural events. In the next section, I describe the methods used in the study on which I base the findings in this chapter. Then I look at how content about local cultural events is presented on the most popular Web sites, portals, or "point-of-entry" sites. Next, I discuss findings from the study in which I conducted in-person observations of 100 randomly sampled adult Internet users' online experiences. Results suggest that the factors traditionally responsible for how people are able to access information about movies and other local cultural events are very much mirrored online.

STUDYING PEOPLE'S ONLINE INFORMATION-SEEKING BEHAVIOR

The findings in this chapter are based on an in-depth study of 100 adult Internet users' online information-seeking behavior. In this section, I briefly describe the methods of data collection and analysis. For more details about the methodology, including sampling procedure, recruitment, the interview protocol, particulars about the in-person observations, and description of the coding and classification scheme, please see Hargittai (2002, 2004).

To gain a thorough understanding of people's online information-seeking behavior, I collected data through in-person observations and interviews with randomly selected adult Internet users between the summers of 2001 and 2002 in a New Jersey county. The response rate for participation was 54%, considerably high given that respondents were asked to come to a university location, traveled up to a half hour each way to the study location, and spent on average an hour and a half with the researcher. Study participants reported information about their Web and other media uses on a questionnaire and also supplied basic demographic information.

The main component of the study session involved sitting at a computer and looking for various types of material online. Respondents chose the computer platform and browsing software of their preference. They were then asked to find information ranging from local cultural events to tax forms, information about political candidates, health material, and other content. The questions were presented in sequence one at a time and participants were given unlimited amounts of time to work on each task. The participants were not offered any advice on how to look for content; they had to rely on their existing know-how and experiences. They started out with a blank homepage and it was up to them to find their way to a search engine or any other Web site on which they proceeded to find the requested material. For example, a user may have gone to a search engine and typed in a query to find information. Alternatively, others went directly to a Web site about which they had previous knowledge. A third popular option was to click on links on portal sites and follow the Web site recommendations on the proceeding pages.

Respondents represented a diverse group of Internet users ranging from salespeople to administrative assistants, students to teachers, military personnel, architects, and retired people. They ranged in age from 18 to 81; half were women (51%), and the median level of education was a college degree. Table 15.1 presents specifics about the demographic background of sample respondents. Regarding their Internet experiences, most participants can be considered veterans as the median number of years people had been using the medium was 6 years. Nonetheless, the sample also includes some novice users, with 13% having gone online 2 years within the time the study took place. Participants differed considerably in the amount of time they spent surfing the Web weekly. Although some respondents only went online for a few minutes daily, others were constantly connected, with up to 30 hr of Web use each week. Such diversity among study participants allows us to gain an idea of average users' online experiences instead of limiting findings to a very particular online population. Moreover, we are able to explore the relationship between users' demographic characteristics, their experiences, and their online abilities.

To understand what types of information sources adult Internet users are most likely to consult on the Web, I analyzed participants' online actions. I developed a coding scheme for classifying each move a user can make to go from one Web page to the next. Hargittai (2004) describes this method in detail. The resulting summary documents of people's online actions include every move

TABLE 15.1

Descriptive Statistics about Sample Participants

	Mean	*SD*	*Median*	*Minimum*	*Maximum*
Age	42.96	15.86	42	18	81
Education	16.21	2.72	College	Less than high school	PhD
Family income	$98,394	$57,452	$84,500	$18,250	> $250,000
Number of years since first use of the Internet	6.28	3.38	6	0	16
Number of hours browsing the Web weekly	8.62	9.39	7	8 min	70 hr

participants made with information about the Web sites they visited, how they got there, and how much time they spent on each page. These data allow us to aggregate information about the types of Web sites people visit during their online sessions and how they seek various types of material on the Web. I draw on this nuanced coding of the data to explore later how users look for information about local cultural events online.

In addition to the data described earlier—demographics, user experience, and online actions—I also aggregated information about how much time people spent looking for content and whether they were able to complete tasks successfully. I coded the sessions for completion rate of each task and amount of time spent on each query measured in seconds. These measures reflect people's online abilities and comprise the dependent variable in the analyses shown later. Before presenting the results of the statistical analyses, in the next section I discuss how information about cultural events is organized online.

THE AVAILABILITY OF CULTURAL EVENT INFORMATION ONLINE

Information about movies is quite easily accessible on the Web. Several portal sites have movie links directly on their homepage.[1] In contrast, information about other types of entertainment is much less prominent on the welcome pages of such aggregator sites.

Consider, for example, the layout of categories on Yahoo's homepage as shown in Fig. 15.1. Although there is a "Movies" link right on the homepage, there is no equivalent direct link for those seeking information about theaters or orchestra performances.[2] If a user is looking for movie information, he or

Figure 15.1. Yahoo's directory categories containing movie and theater information, 2001 (time of study). (Arrow and circle added to point out relevant sections of the image.)

she is given the link quite prominently on the homepage. This is the case on other portals used by study respondents as well (e.g., att.net or excite.com). In contrast, those looking for theater information on Yahoo's homepage would have to know that it is located under the directory heading "Arts & Humanities." Moreover, it is not enough to click on that link to access the "Theater category." It takes one more click on the link "Performing Arts" to finally see a link labeled "Theatre."

On one of New Jersey's regional portals, www.nj.com, the "Movies" and "Theater" link were featured at the same level at the time of the research project. This site was popular with several participants of the study. Nine of them used it for finding various types of content. On www.nj.com, both "Movies" and "Theater" links were prominently visible when one clicked on the "Entertainment" link on the homepage (see Fig. 15.2 for details). However, once a user clicked on the "Movies" link she was taken directly to a search engine for movie listings (see Fig. 15.3 for a copy of what the user saw on the resulting

Figure 15.2. The entertainment category links on local Web portal nj.com.

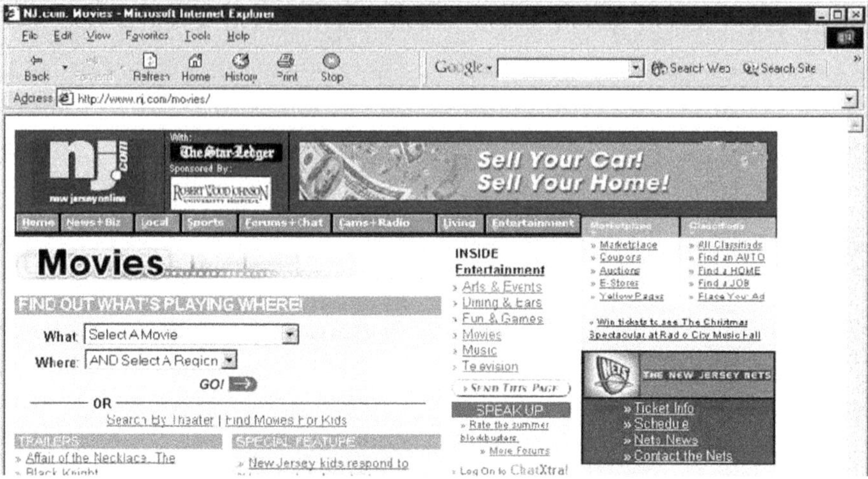

Figure 15.3. Nj.com's Movie search page (2001).

Web page). In contrast, if she clicked on the "Theater" link, she had to guess the next step, because there was no obvious schedule information on the resulting page. If she guessed "right" (picked the second link shown on Fig. 15.4) then she was finally on a page where she could look for theater performance schedules (see Fig.15.5 for the resulting page).

Figure 15.4. The page that comes up after a user clicks on Theater on nj.com's homepage (2001). Circle added for emphasis.

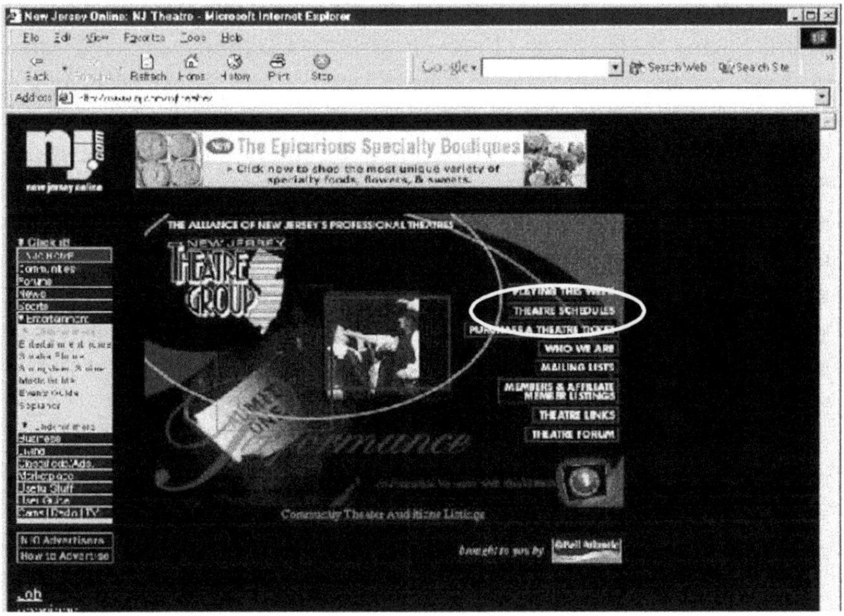

Figure 15.5. Nj.com's Theater page (2001) white circle signaling the "Theatre Schedules" link. Circle added for emphasis.

It is curious that www.nj.com had decided to make it so difficult to get to this page when, in fact, the directory structure of their site as per the page's URL suggests that it was quite high in the directory hierarchy (http://www.nj.com/njtheatre). That is, the fact that "njtheatre" is immediately after the domain name "www.nj.com" signals that the theater directory is a top directory on the www.nj.com site similarly to the movie directory. Again, these images are copies of what users saw in the study in 2001.

A look atwww. nj.com in 2005 shows similar organization of content although a link to theater schedule information is no longer available anywhere on the Web site, making that material even harder to access. The heading "Movies" and "Theater" are still accessible at the same level. However, it is no longer possible to find a page—no matter how far down one tries to drill in the site—that gives the user the option of searching for theater show times in the area. The one seemingly relevant link is specified as an advertisement and links to a page with show times for Broadway musicals. A user may be led to believe that there are no theater performances available in Central New Jersey. This is an incorrect assumption because such award-winning theaters as the McCarter Theatre in Princeton put on performances regularly. Moreover,

McCarter Theatre and other local arts establishments have Web sites of their own publicizing their events. However, without a central searchable repository, they are harder to reach than sites of large venues whose performances are aggregated in large databases.

Another hurdle to finding certain types of content online concerns one's geographical location. Some Web services offer information about events by localities but only aggregate content for metropolitan areas. For example, America Online (AOL) offers localized listings but only for certain metro areas. On the main welcome screen of AOL's interface under the heading "My Places," the user has the option of clicking on the link "Local News" (see Fig. 15.6). The destination page (replicated in Fig. 15.7) shows the list of possible Local News locations. If a user is looking for information about Central New Jersey, then he or she must choose from among New York, North Jersey, or Philadelphia (indicated on the figure with circles). There is, however, no local events page for Central New Jersey.

Although the organization of movie content and information about other cultural events may simply mirror the organization of these cultural industries in the offline world, it is important to recognize that content organization and presentation on the Web for the most part mirror existing industrial organization instead of offering alternative avenues for reaching audiences and al-

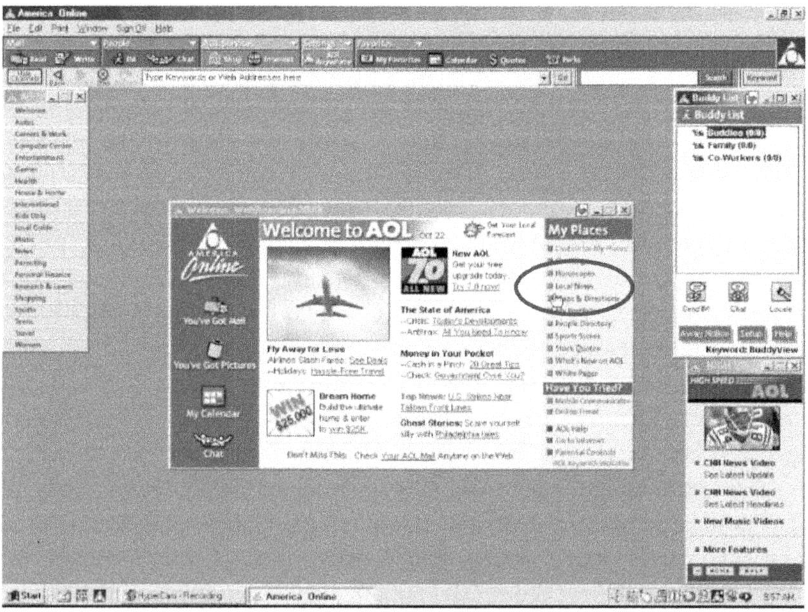

Figure 15.6. AOL's welcome screen with the "Local News" link designated by the circle (added for emphasis).

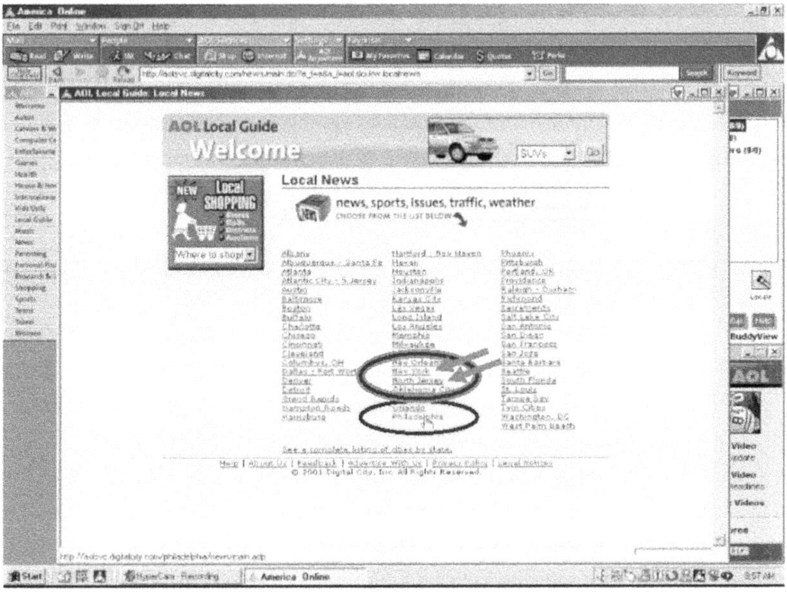

Figure 15.7. AOL Local News options (circles and arrows added for emphasis).

lowing them to find detailed local content. Theoretically, there is no reason why a large online database about all national theatrical or symphony performances cannot exist and offer a one-stop access to such information. However, there is no such service and finding information about such cultural events is just as disparate in the online landscape as it is through more traditional methods.

Even if a user knows what steps to take on the portal sites described earlier, he or she is not presented with a national database of theater information in the end. Unlike movie schedules that are aggregated nationally, other types of performances are harder to find online. Users looking for jazz or orchestra performances are also left without a central database to offer information. In the next section, I present the results of an empirical study testing whether the aforementioned differences in how cultural event information is organized online influences people's ability to find local event information.

ACCESSING CULTURAL EVENT INFORMATION ONLINE

The aforementioned description of how cultural information is organized online suggests that movie information may be easier to access than other performances due to its more centralized system. Thanks to the research project described earlier regarding users' online information-seeking behavior, it is possible to test this hypothesis empirically. In one of the tasks, respondents were asked to look for information about local cultural events, in particular, the schedule for a movie or theater performance. It was up to participants to decide whether they would look for a movie listing or another type of cultural event such as theater and orchestra performances, symphony or jazz concerts. These specifics were not imposed on participants to explore a task reflective of their own interests.

In the aggregate, 85% of the 100 respondents in the study were able to complete this task successfully. On average, they spent a little more than 2 min on the task. Those who were successful averaged less than 2 min, with the unsuccessful searchers spending over 4 min on this task on average. According to the survey that participants filled out about their earlier Web-use experiences, 61% had looked at a movie or TV Web site in the previous 30 days and 64% had looked at a Web site for music or concert information, so the task was not completely foreign to the majority of users.

Were participants in the sample who looked for movie listings more successful in their quest to find relevant information than those who looked for other types of local cultural events? Results indicate that 9% of those who looked for movie information were unable to find it whereas 33% of those who looked for other types of material were unsuccessful. It seems that indeed, movie information is easier to find online.

More refined analyses are necessary to draw a link between content organization and accessibility of content to users. It may be that certain types of people are more likely to look for movies than others, and those may be the people who are better at searching for online material in the first place. It is indeed the case that older people were less likely to search for movie listings. We know from research exploring age differences among Internet users that older adults spend less time online (Loges & Jung, 2001) and are less likely to find various types of material (Hargittai, 2003). Other demographic characteristics and previous experience with this particular task may also influence people's success with this task, so it is important to account for them when analyzing predictors of task completion.

To test whether it is really the case that movies are easier to find online than other types of local entertainment, I turn to statistical analyses of the data I collected in my study about how users find information regarding local cultural events. I ran a discrete-time logit on hazard for completion of the task (Allison, 1985). I created a person-record file using 10-sec intervals. This new data set allows us to take into account how long people took to complete tasks in addition to information about whether they were successful in finding the requested information. The following is the model specification:

$$\mathbf{Log\,(p/1{-}p) = \beta_0 + \beta_1 log(t) + \Sigma\beta_j x_j} + \varepsilon$$

I use an approximation of Weibull hazard [logged time indicated as log(t) in the model] because theoretically it makes the most sense to assume that there is a log-linear increase in the hazard across time for completing a task (whether that be successful completion or giving up on a task). The model predicts the likelihood of having completed the task in any one time interval.

The model includes information about user demographics, presence of children in the household, quality of equipment, social support networks, autonomy of use, and experience using the Web. There is also a variable controlling for recent experience with this particular task ("looked at movie site"). Additionally, I added a variable signaling whether the respondent had looked for movie time listings as compared to details about other local cultural events. There are two additional dummy variables. They indicate whether the respondent's first move when working on this task was to go directly to a movie site or a theater site. Also, to account for any system-wide changes in the Web during the course of the study, I include a control variable for the amount of time—measured in days—that had elapsed since the first respondent's study session.

The findings presented in Table 15.2 suggest that, controlling for individual characteristics and the conditions of one's use and experience with the task, those who looked for movie listings in response to this task were statistically significantly more likely to complete the task successfully in any one time interval than those who looked for other types of local cultural events. In short, users do a better job in finding movie schedules online than other types of cultural event information. Moreover, those who typed in the URL of a movie site also had a higher rate of completion. In this analysis, I also controlled for having typed in the URL of a theater. This variable, however, does not show any relationship with ability to complete this task. The reason for this may be that theater sites are not always as user-friendly and scheduling information is not as readily available, as on the aggregated movie sites.

Is it generally the case that the traditional outlets are the first point-of-entry for users seeking content online? More than with most other tasks administered in the study, many respondents' first reaction was to look for this type of information in traditional media sources such as the online version of their local newspaper. Among those who looked for movie information in response to seeking local cultural events, 16% of respondents used moviefone.com, 10

TABLE 15.2

Discrete-Time Logit Predicting Hazard for Completion of Task for Finding Information About Local Cultural Events (Standard Errors in Parentheses)

Female	**–0.809****	(0.254)
Age	**–0.035***	(0.014)
Education	0.079	(0.047)
Black	–0.714	(0.429)
Family income	0.115	(0.213)
Child in household	–0.330	(0.314)
High speed	–0.029	(0.332)
Social support	0.042	(0.023)
Net advice	**–0.174***	(0.068)
Free Internet use at work	0.473	(0.266)
No. of Access locations	**1.125****	(0.383)
Time on World Wide Web per week	0.088	(0.201)
Use years	0.203	(0.337)
Looked at movie site	0.242	(0.360)
Movies for task	**0.924***	(0.433)
Direct movie site URL	**0.744***	(0.301)
Direct theater site URL	0.942	(0.750)
Time into study	0.004*	(0.002)
Weibull hazard	0.834***	(0.184)
Intercept	–9.390***	(2.840)
N	1,405	

***$p < 0.001$; **$p < 0.01$; *$p < 0.05$, two tailed.

turned to AMC Theatre's Web site, and seven went to Hollywood.com. That means that over a third of all respondents or 43% of those looking for movies went to a large commercial aggregator site. A surprising number of people looked for such information using local sources. Nine percent of users went to the New Jersey portal www.nj.com, five tried to access the information through the Princeton Packet's online presence, and some tried using a local university's homepage.

CONCLUSION

Although the Internet is undoubtedly a medium like no other in terms of the amount of diverse content it makes available to users, sources closely tied to traditional media and organization of content remain the most easily accessible even in this new environment. In particular, local content that is hard to aggregate into national databases seems to be considerably less within the reach of users than content that is packaged for widespread consumption. The observations presented based on average Internet users' online experiences suggest that mere presence of content diversity online does not guarantee its ease of accessibility.

One possible explanation for how users access content online given the vast amounts of resources is to assume that they gravitate toward their preferences. Given the myriad of information sources online, we may expect that users choose whatever they deem most relevant. If this is the case, then users are simply exercising their choice by going to sites that mirror traditional media. However, it would be wrong to assume that the content users access is necessarily a reflection of their preferences. Several factors such as online content organization and user skill are at work when users browse material on the Web and these influence what content people are more or less likely to access.

The most popular portal sites represent enormous media companies (Manjoo, 2003). Although it is not necessarily the case that they are all owned or affiliated with big traditional media companies, they are certainly parts of significant ventures. The amount of advertising and resources that go into these services allows them to far surpass what a small unaffiliated Web site can achieve in popularity and exposure. Another factor that influences what types of content users reach concerns their online abilities. Users differ considerably in how well they are able to navigate online materials. Those who are more skilled will be more likely to find the types of content of direct relevance to their interests. However, others will be more dependent on the information presented on easily accessible sites such as big portals.

Overall, it would be wrong to assume that the mere presence of diverse material on the Web will result in users accessing a smorgasbord of content. As presented in this chapter, an interplay of many factors determines what information is most realistically within the reach of users. It is important to draw a distinction between available and accessible content online. When we assess the state of online content diversity, we must rely on data about users' actual behavior in addition to considering what content exists on the Web. As shown in this chapter, Internet use can reflect offline content utilization regardless of what is theoretically available to users.

NOTES

[1]By "portal sites" I refer to point-of-entry sites such as Yahoo! or MSN that often are set as default browser pages by Internet service providers and constitute the first page users see when they go online.

[2]The illustrations shown in this chapter are from the time of the study, 2001 to 2002, to reflect what study respondents saw when they participated in the study. Yahoo's

Web site directory today, in 2005, also prominently displays a "Movies" category right on the homepage while continuing to have no direct link called "Theater."

REFERENCES

Allison, P. (1985). *Event history analysis.* Thousand Oaks, CA: Sage.

Hargittai, E. (2000). Open portals or closed gates? Channeling content on the World Wide Web. *Poetics, 27,* 233–253.

Hargittai, E. (2002). Beyond logs and surveys: In-depth measures of people's Web use skills. *Journal of the American Society for Information Science and Technology Perspectives, 53,* 1239–1244.

Hargittai, E. (2003). *How wide a web? Inequalities in accessing information online.* Unpublished doctoral dissertation, Princeton University, Princeton, NJ.

Hargittai, E. (2004). Classifying and coding online actions. *Social Science Computer Review, 22,* 210–227.

Loges, W. E., & Jung, J.-Y. (2001). Exploring the digital divide: Internet connectedness and age. *Communication Research, 28,* 536–562.

Manjoo, F. (2003). Can the web beat big media? *Salon.* Retrieved November 20, 2004, from http://www.salon.com/story/tech/feature/2003/054/21/web-vs-big-media/ index-np.html

Napoli, P. (1999). Deconstructing the diversity principle. *Journal of Communication, 49*(4), 7–34.

Sullivan, D. (2005, January 28). Search engine sizes. *Search Engine Watch.* Retrieved October 13, 2005, from http://searchenginewatch.com/reports/article.php/2156481

16

Proactive Media Policy in an Age of Content Abundance

Ellen P. Goodman
Rutgers–Camden School of Law

Imagine a mediascape in which public appetites for video programming were completely satisfied. There was enough video on demand, broadband videocasting, peer-to-peer distributed video, as well as scheduled cable, satellite, and broadcast programming to satisfy the tastes of most every audience member, whether those tastes ran to conservative commentary, Spanish-language dramas, reality programming, or local news. Would this be a mediascape in which the aims of media policy were satisfied?

The central question in media policy debates today is how digital networks and consumer technologies affect the pursuit of traditional policy goals like localism and diversity. With such an abundance of media content available over cable, satellite, and the Internet, and with increased consumer control over access to such content, is government intervention in media markets still necessary?

For the most part, policymakers and advocates begin to address this question from a seductively uncontroversial premise: that the goal of media policy is to protect public access to a diversity of speech, including "local" and noncommercial content (Owen, 2003). It is from this premise that arguments typically flow about media concentration, public interest obligations, and the need for public broadcasting. So framed, these arguments turn on disputes about how well media markets function—essentially, about the responsiveness of these markets to smaller taste and geographic communities.

This emphasis on consumer satisfaction is misleading. It suggests that the goals of media policy are satisfied once consumers have a sufficiently large (however measured) choice of media products. And yet, media critics have long been concerned with more than just the mere availability of diverse content. They have also recognized the importance of exposure to both a diversity of voices and to particular programming, like public affairs, that has positive externalities for civil society (Baker, 2002). Democratic theorists from different traditions seem to agree that even if audience members do not demand the variety of content that is important for a robust democracy, they should be exposed to it (Baker, 2002; Entman, 1989; Sunstein, 1993).

Exposure can bring audience members to new and challenging content, and perhaps most importantly, to shared content, in either case generating social good by improving citizen contributions to democratic debate. To support this kind of exposure, government intervention in media markets must do more than simply increase the responsiveness of media markets to consumer demand. Such intervention must influence demand, cultivating public tastes in ways that support democratic ideals. It follows that a media policy that takes on the challenge of exposure in this sense must be proactive as well as reactive.

This chapter explores the proactive element of media policy in the context of digital innovations. In the bygone era of analog communications, it was possible to achieve proactive media policy goals just by increasing market responsiveness to niche audiences. This was because content was scarce and attention abundant. A public hungry for content was likely to be exposed to whatever was on offer with just a few revolutions of the television dial. Policy initiatives that increased the diversity of media content would simultaneously satisfy audiences that demanded such content, and expose audiences that did not.

In the digital mediascape, the ratio of viewer attention to video content has flipped. It is attention that is now scarce and content that is abundant. Audiences bombarded with information coursing through digital networks are much more likely to filter out content they do not seek, channeling their media selections into specialized cable outlets, weblogs, DVDs, and video-on-demand. As a result, they can more easily avoid content that they do not initially demand, but might consume if enticed. Policies focused almost entirely on correcting the failures of markets to give underserved audience segments what they want will have less and less impact on the complementary goal of exposure.

If media policies are to effectuate proactive goals in the digital era, what is required is a new emphasis on content consumption, as opposed to mere content availability. The regulatory models of the past, like restrictions on the ownership of broadcast outlets and broadcast content requirements, are essentially reactive policies aimed at increasing the representation of underproduced content. There is nothing wrong with this in theory, but these regulatory policies cannot contend with the digital filters that reduce exposure to the very content that policy enables. Subsidies offer a more promising policy tool for a reconstructed public service media. Policymakers and theorists ought to focus on the use of subsidies for a new brand of digital media that not only supply programming, like public broadcasting does today, but also engage a distracted and atomized audience in content that furthers longstanding media policy goals.

NARROW AND BROAD MARKET FAILURES

Before we can understand this policy proposal, we must understand the nature of the goal it is meant to further. There is clearly a tension between the reactive policy goal of increasing the availability of content and the proactive policy goal of increasing exposure to content. It is a tension apparent in the metaphor that dominates communications policy: the marketplace of ideas (*Abrams v. United States,* 1919; *Lamont v. Postmaster General,* 1965). This metaphor appeared in early 20th-century First Amendment jurisprudence in response to government attempts to suppress speech for furtherance of asserted public interests. No, said the Supreme Court, the public's interest is in truth, and the way to truth is through the competitive struggle of bad speech with good, of popular with unpopular ideas (*Whitney v. California,* 1927). The ideology behind the marketplace metaphor was that speech markets should be thrown open to the people as sovereign consumers rather than regulated by the sovereign.

By the mid-20th century, a metaphor first deployed to fend off government regulation had morphed into a defense of regulation. Both courts and the Federal Communications Commission (2003a and 2003b; Napoli, 2001) began to use the metaphor of a competitive speech market to justify government intervention in electronic media markets to preserve choice in the marketplace of ideas (*Fox Television Stations, Inc. v. Federal Communications Commission,* 2002).

The main intervention was to prevent excessive media consolidation, which was thought to reduce the range of ideas that compete for acceptance in the market. Of course antitrust law is government's customary tool to preserve consumer choice and competition. Special media-specific rules to limit concentration, increase access, or promote diverse speech are premised on the notion that speech markets should provide more choice than ordinary product markets because diverse speech is so central to democratic governance (Krotoszynski & Blaiklock, 2000; Stucke & Grunes, 2001).

The pursuit of a more robust speech market through media policy has met with two principal difficulties. Theorists and policymakers have struggled to determine whether the appropriate focus of policy is on speakers (i.e., who owns media outlets) or on speech (i.e., what types of programming is available) (Federal Communications Commission, 2003a; *Metro Broadcasting, Inc. v. Federal Communications Commission,* 1990). They also have struggled to find a methodology distinct from antitrust analysis by which to assess the diversity of speech markets (*Sinclair Broad. Group Inc. v. FCC,* 2002).

Related to these two conceptual challenges are even more fundamental questions. What is the cause of the diversity deficit that media policy seeks to remedy? If the deficit results from failures of the market to deliver expressive goods to audiences that demand them, then the policy response to these market failures—what I call narrow market failures—is reactive. It seeks to identify and then react to unmet consumer demand by increasing opportunities for consumer satisfaction.

But perhaps the diversity deficit has another source, namely the failure of consumers to demand the range of expressive goods that democracy requires. If so, the reason that media outlets provide so much programming about plastic surgery and so little about local politics is not because of structural impediments to alternative programming, but because of demand side deficits. In this case, if there is a market failure, it is a broad failure of markets to do what markets are not designed to do: produce goods for which there is insufficient consumer demand, but important civic value (Fiss, 1987). The appropriate policy response to this kind of market failure is proactive, in that it seeks to expose people to content that they do not, at least initially, demand.

Although American media policy does not clearly identify the source of the diversity deficit, policy enactments have been largely reactive and dominated by the rhetoric of narrow market failure. These are policies that emphasize the role of government in perfecting market responsiveness to consumer demand. Take, for example, the localism policy by which the Federal Communications Commission (FCC) regulates the ownership of local broadcast stations to increase the "local" character of the electronic media. This policy is premised on the failure of the unregulated market to respond adequately to the "needs and interests" of the local community (Federal Communications Commission, 2003a; *Federal Communications Commission v. Pottsville Broad. Co.,* 1940; *NBC v. United States,* 1943). Policy posits consumer demand for programming that is produced locally and deals with local interests. It further posits that this demand would not be satisfied without government intervention to reduce media concentration and proscribe duties of local service because centralized media find it more profitable to serve the needs and interests of the national audience. American media policy, like political theory, has endorsed the notion that dispersed power increases the responsiveness of institutions to public desires—an essentially reactive goal (Price, 1995; Starr, 2004).

The ongoing and passionate debates about media deregulation mirror this emphasis on consumer satisfaction. In 2003, the FCC significantly relaxed the restrictions on media consolidation in local markets (Federal Communications Commission, 2003a). The large media companies that supported increased consolidation argued that market forces were sufficient to ensure their responsiveness to local consumer demand for products like local news, which are highly profitable (Fox Entertainment Group, 2003). Opponents of deregulation fought on the same ground, arguing that consolidation makes it harder for broadcasters to make programming choices that are responsive to local viewers, as opposed to the interests of centralized management (National Association of Broadcasts and Network Affiliated Stations Alliance, 2002). The FCC itself underscored the primacy of satisfying consumer demand by looking to the ratings for local news in gauging the health of localism. In other words, the agency identified localism policy with the provision of programming that has popular appeal within a local market (Federal Communications Commission, 2003a).

Public concern over Clear Channel's aggressive move to consolidate ownership of radio stations nationwide and in local markets provides another example of the emphasis on consumer satisfaction shared by those on both sides of the consolidation debate. Critics of consolidation say that Clear Channel's ownership of some 1,200 radio stations has decreased diversity by expunging local talent and diverse playlists (Copps, 2003). Clear Channel responds that the efficiencies of concentration have allowed it to better satisfy public appetites for the genres that independently owned competing stations were unwilling to risk (Prindle, 2003). Although some listeners might miss the idiosyncratic voice of an independent station, most listeners are better satisfied. Here again, both critics and champions of consolidation identify consumer satisfaction as the goal, differing only in the way that they define consumer wants.

Of course the pursuit of consumer satisfaction and the correction of narrow market failures is a natural and appropriate goal in a market economy. The problem is that a theory of government intervention in media markets centered exclusively on the goal of increasing consumer choice does not really capture the marketplace of ideas ideal, and media policy shows it. For a marketplace of ideas to function in the way that democratic theorists envision, content must not only be diverse. It must be shared. Central to different strains of democratic theory is the notion that a heterogeneous citizenry must be exposed to the tastes and views of others (Baker, 1998; Meiklejohn, 1948; Sunstein, 1997). A trade of ideas, like any other trade, requires exchange. Rational exchange requires that individuals be exposed in common to the abundance of ideas the marketplace yields. To extend the marketplace metaphor, the ideal speech market is not an agglomeration of specialty shops, each with an inventory that perfectly satisfies a narrow palette. Rather it is more like a big box retail outlet that attracts a varied public with a wide range of products, inviting comparisons between the known and the unknown and delighting with serendipitous discovery. According to this view, the object of diversity is to increase exposure to, as well as satisfy demand for, differentiated speech (Postman, 1985; Sunstein, 2001).

It is not just in theory, but in policy too, that one can discern the limitations of an emphasis on consumer satisfaction as the basis for government intervention in media markets. This is most evident, not surprisingly, in the policies that foster a noncommercial alternative to consumer-driven media. Congress created the public broadcasting system in the mid-1960s in part as an expression of reactive policy objectives. The new service was to serve unmet demand for certain kinds of media content, thereby satisfying "unserved and underserved" audiences (47 U.S.C. § 396(a)(6), 2000). At the same time, an enduring aim of public broadcasting is much more proactive—to bring people to content that bolsters democratic aspirations (Rowland, 1993). This content consists of "high quality" programming, marked by creative risks and innovation that is not in sufficient demand to be produced commercially.[1] Public broadcasting's mandate to expose as well as satisfy reflects the insight that Cass Sunstein (2000) has put so well: that there "is a large difference between the public interest and what interests the public" (p. 501). Government interventions like subsidies for noncommercial media can be seen as attempts to alleviate the broad failures of markets to expose people to content they do not initially demand.

This proactive policy thrust, most explicit in public broadcasting, is also faintly discernible in diversity and localism policies. Both sets of policies, although focused largely on the correction of narrow market failures, have to varying degrees over the decades been concerned with public exposure as well as public satisfaction. Erstwhile localism policies, for example, required broadcasters to actively identify community needs instead of merely relying on market signals or regulated industry structure to set the programming agenda (Federal Communications Commission, 1971).[2] This recognition that there might be community needs unexpressed even in a regulated market with increased sensitivity to the demands of local audiences is a nod in the direction of broad market failures. Old localism policies went even further in establishing "guidelines" concerning the "major elements usually necessary to meet the public interest" (Federal Communications Commission, 1960, p. 2314). Other policy interventions supported the production of local content for which there was negligible or at least insufficient demand (Federal Communications Commission, 1979).[3] Although this kind of regulation went by the boards during the deregulation of the 1980s and 1990s, there appears to be renewed interest in policies that reach beyond narrow market failures and the goal of improving responsiveness to consumer demand (Federal Communications Commission, 2004a).

In diversity policy too, we may be seeing new sensitivity to the role of media exposure and demand in the marketplace of ideas. For the most part, as noted earlier, the rhetoric and implementation of diversity policy has been reactive. The objective has been "to ensure that citizens in all areas of the country have a diverse array of media outlets available to them" (Federal Communications Commission, 2003b, p. 2). Until recently, the FCC measured diversity by counting the stalls in the marketplace. The speech market in a given community would be considered satisfactorily diverse if consumers could choose from among a sufficient number of independent media "voices," without regard to audience exposure to each voice (see Owen, 2004). An alternative method would be to assess diversity by the content that people actually consume, focusing on exposure in addition to mere availability (Napoli, 1999).

The FCC (2003a) in 2003 combined these two approaches in a "Diversity Index," which it developed to gauge the relative robustness of local speech markets in a consolidating media industry. In large part, the Diversity Index developed out of the reactive notion that policy should ensure choice. That is, it assessed the diversity of speech within a particular medium (e.g., television, radio, cable) by counting the number of distribution outlets available to consumers. But in assessing the importance of each different medium to the marketplace of ideas, the Diversity Index looked to actual audience usage, recognizing that the availability of diverse viewpoints on cable channels, for example, is of limited value if citizens are not actually exposed to these viewpoints (Federal Communications Commission, 2003a). An appeals court found this hybrid approach to be unreasonable (*Prometheus Radio Project v. FCC*, 2004), and scholars have criticized it variously for giving too little weight to actual consumption patterns (Napoli & Gillis, 2005), or too much weight (Owen, 2004). What is interesting for our purposes is that the hybrid approach revealed even a deregulatory FCC's dissatisfaction with a purely reactive media policy that deals only in the potential for consumer satisfaction and not in the actuality of consumer exposure.

NEW TECHNOLOGIES, CONTENT ABUNDANCE, ATTENTION SCARCITY

The choice between a reactive policy that corrects narrow market failures to better satisfy consumers, or a proactive policy that tackles broad market failures to better engage citizens, was not terribly significant in the analog world. There were limited content options available through the mass media. Audiences were captive to, and hungry for, the limited fare on offer. Thus, any policy that increased the availability of content demanded by some would have the effect of increasing exposure to shared content for most. When public television broadcast a documentary or when commercial stations held political debates, a good number of viewers who did not initially demand the content would nonetheless stumble across it. To the extent that local stations identified community needs, and made programming decisions in response to these needs, the resulting programming was guaranteed an audience. Digital innovations fundamentally change the relationship between the audience and content, putting pressure on policymakers and theorists to recognize the differences between narrow and broad market failures and refine the objectives of media policy. Today, the scarce resource is attention, not programming. Media policies designed to improve market reactions to existing consumer demand will not necessarily advance, and indeed may frustrate, proactive policy goals of exposure. The supply of programming for which there is limited demand, but anticipated public value, is unlikely to reach viewers who are otherwise committed.

Before discussing the policy implications of the digital mediascape, I want to highlight two digital innovations that are most significant to the availability and consumption of electronic media content. These are developments in the network infrastructure that delivers video content, and devices that facilitate consumer participation in the production and selection of such content.

Cable, satellite, and broadcasting all use, or are transitioning to, digital networks, and have been joined by telephone companies delivering video over fiber networks. The first salient feature of these networks is that they feature digital compression technologies that dramatically increase the capacity of traditional video providers to deliver content (Federal Communications Commission, 2004b). At the same time, as broadband access to the Internet proliferates, the Internet becomes a video distribution platform, providing vast new capacity for content to reach consumers. Video can be streamed over virtual channels or downloaded through file transfer protocols. In addition, software programs like BitTorrent make it possible for individuals to share video files through distributed software, much as they have shared music files for the past several years (Werbach, in press). This explosion in distribution capabilities will allow individuals to construct video packages from a wide array of choices and amass huge libraries of video content.

The second important feature of digital networks is that they are interactive and invite consumer participation. Interactivity allows consumers to become producers, uploading and widely distributing video content of many sorts, such as relatively polished productions, video weblogs, or collaborative works that mix professionally produced programming with amateur input.

Even when consumers are merely consumers, interactivity changes the way they consume video and the response of video producers to consumer demand signals. For example, interactive digital technologies permit substantial disintermediation of video content by allowing consumers to select programming on a per-program basis, instead of relying on network programmers to bundle video content (Federal Communications Commission, 2005). Although centralized firms still will be responsible for making investment decisions about what kinds of content to develop, interactivity increases the chances that consumers will be able to signal their preferences on a program-by-program basis, and therefore, the likelihood that media markets will satisfy individual preferences (Yoo, 2003a).

As content options increase, it becomes more important for audiences to be able to navigate easily among media offerings. Digital technologies respond to this need by providing tools for audience control over the selection and timing of media experiences. Such technologies include search engines, like digital electronic program guides, that allow the viewer to filter out content. They also include digital video recorders or other digital storage devices that enable viewers to record and replay video on their own schedules (Federal Communications Commission, 2004b).

It is not clear what the impact of this newfound audience control over media experiences will be on content consumption, but one can reasonably forecast that viewers will manage video consumption like they now manage Internet content consumption. Indeed, the choice of distribution technology used to deliver video programming, whether it is the Internet or cable, or wireless broadband, is fast becoming irrelevant. In the digital mediascape, the use of "favorites," "bookmarks," and search functions almost certainly will come to be the way that viewers select programming over all platforms.

Digital technology calls into question the goals and methods of American media policy. At first blush, it might appear that the new abundance of distribution channels, combined with consumer control, will increase consumer satisfaction in a more diverse array of video content. I have argued elsewhere that content abundance will not necessarily overcome narrow market failures because some kinds of content are likely to be underproduced even as the opportunities for distribution dramatically expand (Goodman, 2004).

Indeed, the very proliferation of content may well reduce the critical audience mass that is necessary to support many types of programming. As a result, there will continue to be demand for certain media products that media producers will fail to satisfy, notwithstanding the explosion of media distribution channels. But even if content abundance did correct narrow market failures, there would be the problem of broad market failures. With respect to these, digital networks and filtering tools are likely to reduce audience exposure to the array of content that is important for vibrant democratic discourse.

Policy interventions to correct broad market failures have sought to increase the availability of certain types of content, such as noncommercial programming, on the unstated assumption that such content would be consumed even if not initially demanded (Tracey, 1998). The policies relied on a kind of "content drift" whereby, under conditions of channel scarcity and attention abundance, audiences would come across and ultimately coalesce around the content on offer (Katz, 1998). The increase in content options over digital media, by fragmenting the audience and fraying attention, reduces audience exposure to products responsive to broad market failures (Ang, 1991; McQuail, 2003).

Content abundance and consumer control in the digital era undermine content drift as an instrument of media policy in two ways. Digital innovations in distribution, production, and selection make attention scarce, drawing eyes away from content responsive to proactive media policy goals and diluting the quality of attention even when the audience is "tuned in" (Gitlin, 2003). Consumers taking advantage of interactive tools or distracted by a multitude of video options can easily choose not to be exposed to content that a proactive media policy advances, such as community-oriented or noncommercial programming. A number of scholars worry that Internet services reduce exposure to media experiences that would build solidarity (Sunstein, 2001) or enhance political discourse (Cooper, 2004). Others have observed that digital video recorders and program guides operating in traditional television media reduce the likelihood that consumers will be exposed to media content they do not seek or will converge on the same programming in a democratically significant way (Napoli, 2003; Webster & Phalen, 1994).

Recent scholarship on what is known as "social software" suggests that consumers may increasingly filter media choices through screens they build with like-minded peers by rating content and directing each other to programming they have selected (Hunter & Lastowka, 2004). The result will be a highly personalized media environment that reinforces existing perspectives and predilections—extremely satisfying for the consumer, but not necessarily conducive to a trade in ideas. Given the tools of consumer control and the quantity of content to be controlled, there is no reason to think that citizens caught up in the digital flow of bits will engage in the shared informational experiences that are important to careful deliberation in a democracy.

Even if some degree of unsought exposure to different perspectives takes place in the digital mediascape, there is a second feature of digital media that tends to undermine proactive media policy goals. This is the quality of audience attention, which may be so poor in a state of information overload that audience exposure is not meaningful.

Overload can be expected in a media environment in which the simultaneous usage of video is increasing along with the absolute consumption of video. For example, average television viewing increased between 1998 and 2001 from 1,551 to 1,661 hrs. per year. Over the same period, average annual consumer Internet usage increased from 54 to 134 hrs. and average annual video game usage increased from 43 to 78 hrs. (U.S. Census, 2004). Some of the gain in screen time came at the expense of other leisure activities and because of a net increase in screen time, but much of the increase was due to simultaneous usage of video media (U.S. Census, 2004).[4] This amount of total and simultaneous screen time tends to result in an information flow that "exceeds the interpretative capacity of the subject" (Stevenson, 1995, p. 157). In other words, an overexposed and restless audience, even in the currents of content drift, may not be reached in a meaningful way (Baudrillard, 1990).

It is not just the amount of information that is taxing, but also the degree to which viewers are responsible for the critical functions once exercised by content providers. Viewers click remote control devices between 36 and 107 times an hour and three quarters of younger Americans watch the news with a remote in hand (Gitlin, 2003). It is hardly a surprise that, knowing the fragility of their audience's attention, entertainment and news producers emphasize sex, violence, and speed, sometimes at the expense of the more enduringly provocative (Croteau & Hoynes, 2001; Sabato, 1991). The toll of attention scarcity is perhaps greatest on news. In both the gathering and presenting of news, producers rush to get stories into the flow of information, without thoroughness or nuance (Gans, 2003; Gitlin, 2003). In this way, raw information floods information networks, often in a fairly undigested form, burdening the audience's already strained attention to process the information received.

NEW DIRECTIONS

Recognizing that digital technology undermines content drift as a means for pursuing a proactive media policy agenda, policymakers and theorists must begin to test interventions in media markets against the facts of content abundance and audience control. They should consider not only what market structures and public service obligations will promote programming that supports democratic culture, but also how policy can bring the public to such programming.

Regulatory strategies are handicapped in promoting consumer participation in diverse and local media products for two reasons. Most fundamentally, regulation cannot, in a liberal democracy, force viewers to consume media products they do not think they want in the name of the public interest. Of course, a regulatory regime might try to increase consumer exposure to particular content without going so far as to mandate exposure. In a sense, the FCC's Fairness Doctrine, which at one time required television stations to present opposing sides of controversial issues, did something like this and some have advocated like regimes for digital content.[5] Similarly, commercial channels of communication, whether they are television or Internet-based, might be required to include public service media content, as they have been obliged to do in the U.K. (Scannell, 1995). Given the proliferation of consumer filtering and choice, these kinds of interventions are of questionable efficacy. Consumers equipped with digital selection and filtering tools are likely to avoid content they do not demand no matter what the regulatory efforts to force exposure (Hunter, 2002).

Even if effective, these kinds of rules are problematic from a legal standpoint. They almost certainly would be held to be unconstitutional in the United States as applied to any medium other than broadcasting (*Reno v. ACLU*, 1997). Even as to broadcasting, the rationale that has justified a greater degree of regulation—the scarcity of the airwaves—is moribund and most commentators believe it is only a matter of time before broadcast regulations are invalidated on First Amendment grounds.[6]

Media subsidies provide a more promising avenue for advancing media policy in the digital environment. As an initial matter, the government has far greater leeway to subsidize media than it does to impose regulations under First Amendment jurisprudence (Goodman, 2002). Subsidies for the development of particular content genres or perspectives do not abridge freedom of speech unless the recipient of the funds is compelled to sacrifice a constitutional right to obtain the benefit (Sullivan, 1989). To be sure, government can abuse its power to subsidize by influencing the coverage of current events or otherwise surreptitiously injecting particular government-generated viewpoints into the marketplace (Barstow & Stein, 2005; Goldstein, 2004). The risk of such influence has been mitigated in the past by interposing institutional buffers, like the Corporation for Public Broadcasting, between producers and government. Nevertheless, the inherently political process of subsidizing media will always put these buffers under pressure, and make transparency concerning the use of funds essential.

The more pressing question for media policy is not what can go wrong with subsidies in the digital era, but what can go right? What is it that subsidies might be able to achieve that a regulatory policy of content drift cannot? Media subsidies have the potential to advance both proactive and reactive policy agendas, by boosting consumption of, and critical engagement with, the content they support. A number of scholars recognize the increased importance of subsidies to a democratic media in the digital era (Baker, 2002; Shapiro, 1999; Sunstein 2001). What few have focused on, however, is the relationship between subsidies and the new dynamics of content abundance and attention scarcity. Public broadcasting, reliant as it is on supply side content drift, and an outdated broadcast distribution platform, cannot be the sole repository of media subsidies. Subsidized content must reach consumers over all media platforms, like broadband networks, cable, and satellite.

More importantly, for subsidized content to have any impact on broad market failures, it must work to promote demand as well as supply. In a sense, this is what public broadcasting has tried to do with "copycat programming" created to siphon audiences away from commercial platforms—a strategy that has drawn considerable criticism (Ledbetter, 1997). As columnist George Will has acidly commented, if noncommercial media does nothing than offer more of what commercial media provides, it will be like "the body politic's appendix: ... vestigial, purposeless and occasionally troublesome" (Will, 2005, p. A-25).

What if, instead, a more robust incarnation of public service media operated on multiple fronts to attract the public to programming that neither commercial nor amateur media provided—high cost content with positive democratic externalities? Subsidies might support noncommercial search engines that brought consumers to public service media, toward the production of interactive noncommercial media content like virtual reality games, or the sponsorship of peer-produced content. In addition, subsidies might promote the integration of media content with real space encounters and community activities that would engage the public.

The public journalism movement supplies some early thinking about an engaged response to the blizzard of digital content. In the early 1990s, print journalists began to develop a theory of journalism that challenged the conception of journalists as dispassionate observers. Instead, what came to be called civic or public journalism vested journalists with a responsibility to promote deliberation over issues of common concern and enhance the problem-solving capabilities of citizens (Friedland & Nichols, 2002). According to Jay Rosen, a journalism theorist, the movement was "about forming as much as informing a public" (McMasters, 1997, p. 191). In what others have called an effort to increase "social capital," those engaged in public journalism sought further exposure to difference and consensus over the common (Brookes, 2004). In so doing, public journalism pioneered the use of digital tools and real space events to capture audience attention (Friedland & Nichols, 2002).

Public broadcasting, although limited by insufficient funding and the broadcast distribution medium, embarked on similar projects on a small scale in the early 2000s. These methods included community outreach, widespread talent development and exploitation, synergistic partnerships with other nonmarket actors, the leveraging of content over multiple platforms, and, perhaps most importantly, a focus on media consumption as well as production. The following are some examples.

- *Breaking the Cycle,* a documentary on the working poor, used a multimedia, multi-institutional approach to video programming. Producers developed a sophisticated outreach program in connection with the film to target families, workers, and employers, to offer workplace training, and to provide media resources in family leadership and economic development. In addition, national and local partners, including the Children's Defense Fund and the Urban Institute, lined up to provide resources "to strengthen community and neighborhood services for low income workers to improve their job skills" (National Center for Outreach, 2004, p. 1).
- In Kentucky in the spring of 2001, a public broadcasting station encouraged all readers in the state to consume and discuss the same book, Kentucky author Barbara Kingsolver's *The Bean Trees.* More than 130 educational institutions, bookstores, schools, businesses, media outlets, and civic and social service organizations participated. Materials about the book and promotions were distributed through book club electronic networks, and the public station devoted a month to the book, offering a profile of the author, live call-in programs, and an on-air panel discussion. Public radio stations simulcast or repeated the programming. In the end, the book was distributed throughout classrooms and adult education centers, bookstores and libraries, and close to 10,000 readers registered to participate in online discussions.

- In Minnesota, public television's efforts to leverage its own technology and resources to partner with local organizations resulted in distinctly local content and community-oriented public service. A Minneapolis public station has dedicated a substantial part of its broadcast channel to an initiative called the Minnesota Channel Partners' Collaborative, which produces, promotes, and broadcasts nonprofit partners' most valuable content. The partners help provide the content and pay production costs, but the station provides production assistance and quality control, assuring that the product is of high quality. The content is frequently used in community events, performances, and presentations.
- WNYE-TV, a public station owned by the New York City Department of Education, used just $750,000 to create School Night, a weekly prime-time program engaging more than 3,000 public school students in the production of programming geared to their peers. The station produced 78 programs, including a quiz show combining academic knowledge and street smarts. It enlisted a prominent local documentary filmmaker to help more than 150 New York City public school kids to produce and narrate their own documentaries. Exploiting other local talent, the station employed more than 3,000 students in creating a talk show, featuring famous graduates from New York City high schools, including Tim Robbins, Al Sharpton, Harvey Keitel, astronauts, and physicists (Kandel, 2003).

Digital media and the citizen participation it enabled took public journalism to another level. Public engagement could similarly transform public service media. By seeding and nurturing public participation on new digital platforms and with new content formats, media policy might go much further in forging exposure to content in the service of proactive media policy goals.

At the cutting edge of such efforts are the steps the BBC and, to a lesser extent, American public television entities have taken to make content available to the public to consume and manipulate. In 2004, the BBC launched its open archiving program whereby it allows viewers to access content on the Web under permissive copyright policies. The public can then remix, comment on, and integrate content into their own expression. This kind of expressive freedom is designed to both attract viewers to the public media content and give new life to that content (BBC, 2004).[7] American public television is in the early stages of implementing similar programs (Open Media Network, 2005).[8] It is too early to tell whether these innovations will increase engagement with public media content, but without such innovations that seek out audience connection and participation, public service media will be of diminishing value in the digital era.

CONCLUSION

Digital media demand new thinking about how to achieve policy goals amid content abundance and attention scarcity. A vast array of content channels in the digital era may well reduce the need for reactive media policies aimed at consumer satisfaction. By contrast, the proactive goals of exposure are in jeopardy. The marketplace of ideas metaphor that guided media policy through the 20th century was premised not only on an abundance of consumer choice, but on shared consumption and exposure to difference. Individuals who did not choose to be exposed could hardly help it in media markets with four or five video channels.

Theories about the democratic significance of media that are premised on audience exposure must contend with an overexposed and discriminating audience. Digital networks and consumer devices make proactive media policy far more difficult to implement because choice and control support the atomized consumption of media and the unchallenged filtering of content. Unless media policy is able to address media consumption patterns in the public interest, the focus of policy will necessarily be limited to narrow market failures and the provisioning of stalls in the marketplace as opposed to a robust exchange of ideas. Changes in the dynamics of media production, distribution, and consumption suggest a new direction for a proactive media policy. The direction is toward heavier reliance on subsidies as opposed to regulation, and not just for public broadcasting, but for a new array of noncommercial content delivered over all digital platforms. It is content that ought to be coupled with efforts to engage citizens in both production and consumption in furtherance of democratic media policy goals.

NOTES

[1]See 47 U.S.C. § 396(g)(1)(A), authorizing the Corporation for Public Broadcasting to facilitate the transmission of "programs of high quality, diversity, creativity, excellence, and innovation, which are obtained from diverse sources." See also Carnegie Commission (1967).

[2]The ascertainment policy required broadcasters to follow procedures in ascertaining from community leaders and other members of the public what kind of programming would best serve the needs and interests of the community. The ascertainment requirement was later eliminated (Federal Communications Commission, 1984).

[3]This approach is evident in rules that protect local broadcasters' contractual rights to exclusive transmission of syndicated programming within their local markets (Federal Communications Commission, 1979).

[4]Video game usage and Internet usage are projected to increase by about 40% and 60%, respectively, in 2006. Even television viewing is expected to increase along with the total number of hours per person per year devoted to media consumption (U.S. Census Bureay, 2004).

[5]One proposal is to revive and extend defunct broadcast regulations, like the Fairness Doctrine, into cyberspace, for example, by requiring linking to contrasting perspectives (see Sunstein, 2001, pp. 186–189).

[6]The First Amendment exceptionalism for broadcasting has been criticized in both the courts and the academic literature. See, for example, *Federal Communications Commission v. League of Women Voters* (1984) and *Time Warner Entertainment Co. v. FCC* (1977). See also Fowler and Brenner (1982), Krattenmaker and Powe (1985), and Yoo (2003b).

[7]BBC, Building Public Value: Renewing the BBC for the Digital World at 60-63, June 2004, available at http://www.omn.org/press/pubbroadcast0805.htm, retrieved April 5, 2006.

[8]Open Media Network, http://www.omn.org/press/pubbroadcast0805.htm, retrieved April 5, 2006.

REFERENCES

Abrams v. United States, 250 U.S. 616, 630 (1919).

Ang, I. (1991). *Desperately seeking the audience.* New York: Routledge.

Baker, C. E. (1998). The media that citizens need. *University of Pennsylvania Law Review, 147,* 317–408.

Baker, C. E. (2002). *Media, markets, and democracy.* New York: Cambridge University Press.

Barstow, D., & Stein, R. (2005, March 13). "Under Bush, a new age of prepackaged news." *The New York Times,* p. A1.

Baudrillard, J. (1990). Mass media culture. In P. Foss & J. Pefanis (Eds.), *Revenge of the crystal: Selected writings on the modern object and its destiny: 1968–1983* (pp. 63–97). London: Pluto Press.

Brookes, M. (2004). Watching alone: Social capital and public service broadcasting. Retrieved February 5, 2005, from http://www.bbc.co.uk/info/policies/pdf/watching_alone.pdf

Carnegie Commission. (1967). *Public television: A program for action.* New York: Harper & Row.

Cooper, M. (2004). *Media ownership and democracy in the digital information age.* Palo Alto, CA: Stanford Center for the Internet and Society.

Copps, M. (2003). Dissent to 2002 biennial regulatory review—Review of the Commission's broadcast ownership rules and other rules adopted pursuant to Section 202 of the Telecommunications Act of 1996. Retrieved February 5, 2005, from http://hraunfoss.fcc.gov/edocs_public/attachmatch/FCC-03-127A5.pdf

Croteau, D., & Hoynes, W. (2001). *The business of media: Corporate media and the public interest.* Thousand Oaks, CA: Pine Forge Press.

Entman, R. M. (1989). *Democracy without citizens: Media and the decay of American politics.* New York: Oxford University Press.

Federal Communications Commission. (1960). Report and statement of policy re: Commission en banc programming inquiry, 44 F.C.C. 2303.

Federal Communications Commission. (1971). Primer on ascertainment of community problems by broadcast applicants, 27 F.C.C.2d 650.

Federal Communications Commission. (1979). Cable television syndicated program exclusivity rules, 71 F.C.C.2d 1004.

Federal Communications Commission. (1984). Revision of programming and commercialization policies, ascertainment requirements, and program log requirements for commercial television stations, 98 F.C.C.2d 1075.

Federal Communications Commission. (2003a). 2002 biennial regulatory review—review of the Commission's broadcast ownership rules and other rules adopted pursuant to Section 202, report and order and notice of proposed rulemaking, 18 F.C.C.R. 13,620.

Federal Communications Commission. (2003b). *FCC sets limits on media concentration: Unprecedented public record results in enforceable and balanced broadcast ownership rules*. Retrieved February 5, 2005, from http://hraunfoss.fcc.gov/edocs_public/attachmatch/DOC-235047A1.pdf

Federal Communications Commission. (2004a). Broadcast localism, notice of inquiry, 19 F.C.C.R. 12,425.

Federal Communications Commission. (2004b). FCC annual assessment of the status of competition in the market for the delivery of video programming, tenth annual report, 19 F.C.C.R. 1606.

Federal Communications Commission. (2005). Annual assessment of the status of competition in the market for the delivery of video programming, eleventh annual report. Retrieved October 14, 2005, from http://hraunfoss.fcc.gov/edocs_public/attachmatch/FCC-05-13A1.pdf

Federal Communications Commission v. League of Women Voters, 468 U.S. 364 (1984).

Federal Communications Commission v. Pottsville Broad. Co., 309 U.S. 134 (1940).

Fiss, O. (1987). Why the state? *Harvard Law Review, 100,* 781, 788–794.

Fowler, M. S., & Brenner, D. L. (1982). A marketplace approach to broadcast regulation. *Texas Law Review, 60,* 207–257.

Fox Entertainment Group. (2003). Comments in 2002 biennial regulatory review—Review of the Commission's broadcast ownership rules and other rules adopted pursuant to section 202, MB Docket No. 02–277.

Fox Television Stations, Inc. v. Federal Communications Commission, 280 F.3d 1027 (D.C. Cir. 2002).

Friedland, L. A., & Nichols, S. (2002). *Measuring civic journalism's progress: A report across a decade of activity.* Retrieved April 5, 2006, from http://www.pewcenter.org/doingcj/research/measuringcj.pdf

Gans, H. J. (2003). *Democracy and the news.* New York: Oxford University Press.

Gitlin, T. (2003). *Media unlimited: How the torrent of images and sounds overwhelms our lives.* New York: Owl Books.

Goldstein, A. (2004, May 20). "GAO says HHS broke laws with Medicare videos." *The Washington Post,* p. A1.

Goodman, E. P. (2002). Bargains in the information marketplace: The use of government subsidies to regulate new media. *Journal of Telecommunication & High Technology Law, 1,* 217–292.

Goodman, E. P. (2004). Media policy out of the box: Content abundance, attention scarcity, and the failures of digital markets. *Berkeley Technology Law Journal, 19,* 1389–1472.

Hunter, D. (2002). Philippic.com. *California Law Review, 90,* 611–671.

Hunter, D., & Lastowka, F. G. (2004). Amateur-to-amateur. *William & Mary Law Review, 46,* 951–1030.

Kandel, N. (2003, December). Presentation delivered at the Media Diversity and Localism: Meaning, Metrics, and the Public Interest Conference, Donald McGannon Communication Research Center, Fordham University, New York.

Katz, E. (1998). And deliver us from segmentation. *Annals of the American Academy of Political and Social Science, 456,* 22–33.

Krattenmaker, T. G., & Powe, L. A., Jr. (1985). The Fairness Doctrine today: A constitutional curiosity and an impossible dream. *Duke Law Journal, X,* 151–176.

Krotoszynski, R. J., Jr., & Blaiklock, R. M. (2000). Enhancing the spectrum: Media power, democracy, and the marketplace of ideas. *Illinois Law Review, 2000,* 813–885.

Lamont v. Postmaster General, 381 U.S. 301 (1965).
Ledbetter, J. (1997). *Made possible by ...: The death of public broadcasting in the United States*. New York: Norton.
McMasters, P. (1997). A First Amendment perspective on public journalism. In J. Black (Ed.), *Mixed news: The public/civic/communitarian journalism debate* (pp. 188–195). Mahwah, NJ: Lawrence Erlbaum Associates.
McQuail, D. (2003). *McQuail's mass communication theory* (4th ed.). Thousand Oaks, CA: Sage.
Meiklejohn, A. (1948). *Free speech and its relation to self-government*. New York: Harper Brothers.
Metro Broadcasting, Inc. v. Federal Communications Commission, 497 U.S. 547 (1990).
Napoli, P. M. (1999). Deconstructing the diversity principle. *Journal of Communication, 48*, 7–34.
Napoli, P. M. (2001). *Foundations of communications policy: Principles and process in the regulation of electronic media*. Cresskill, NJ: Hampton.
Napoli, P. M. (2003). *Audience economics: Media institutions and the audience marketplace*. New York: Columbia University Press.
Napoli, P. M., & Gillis, N. (2005, November). *Reassessing communications research's potential contribution to communications policy: The case of media ownership and the diversity index*. Paper presented at the annual meeting of the National Communication Association, Boston.
National Association of Broadcasters and Network Affiliated Stations Alliance. (2002). Comments filed in 2002 biennial regulatory review—Review of the Commission's broadcast ownership rules and other rules adopted pursuant to Section 202, MB Docket No. 02-277, 39-40.
National Center for Outreach. (2004). Outreach pipeline. Retrieved October 16, 2004, from http://www.nationaloutreach.org/PIPELINE/Pipeline.pdf
NBC v. United States, 319 U.S. 190 (1943).
Owen, B. M. (2003). Regulatory reform: The Telecommunications Act of 1996 and the FCC media ownership rules. *Michigan State University/Detroit College of Law Review, X*, 671–700.
Owen, B. M. (2004). *Confusing success with access: "Correctly" measuring concentration of ownership and control in mass media and online services*. Unpublished manuscript. Retrieved February 10, 2005, from http://ssrn.com/abstract=54302
Postman, N. (1985). *Amusing ourselves to death: Public discourse in the age of show business*. New York: Penguin.
Price, M. E. (1995). *Television, the public sphere, and national identity*. New York: Oxford University Press.
Prindle, G. M. (2003). No competition: How radio consolidation has diminished diversity and sacrificed localism. *Fordham Intellectual Property, Media & Entertainment Law Journal, 14*, 279–325.
Prometheus Radio Project v. FCC, 373 F.3d 372 (3d Cir. 2004).
Reno v. ACLU, 521 U.S. 844 (1997).
Rowland, W. D., Jr. (1993). The institution of U.S. public broadcasting. In E. M. Noam & J. Waltermann (Eds.), *Public television in America* (pp. 113–144). Gutersloh, Germany: Bertelsmann Foundation.
Sabato, L. (1991). *Feeding frenzy: How attack journalism has transformed American politics*. New York: Free Press.
Scannell, P. (1995). Britain: Public service broadcasting, from national culture to multiculturalism. In M. Raboy (Ed.), *Public broadcasting for the 21st century* (pp. 23–41). Luton, England: University of Luton Press.
Shapiro, A. L. (1999). *The control revolution: How the Internet is putting individuals in charge and changing the world*. New York: Public Affairs.
Sinclair Broad. Group Inc. v. FCC, 284 F.3d 148 (D.C. Cir. 2002).

Starr, P. (2004). *The creation of the media: Political origins of modern communications.* New York: Basic Books.
Stevenson, N. (1995). *Understanding media cultures: Social theory and mass communication.* London: Sage.
Stucke, M. E., & Grunes, A. P. (2001). Antitrust and the marketplace of ideas. *Antitrust Law Journal, 69,* 249–302.
Sullivan, K. M. (1989). Unconstitutional conditions. *Harvard Law Review, 102,* 1415–1506.
Sunstein, C. R. (1993). *Democracy and the problem of free speech.* New York: Free Press.
Sunstein, C. R. (1997). *Free markets and social justice.* New York: Oxford University Press.
Sunstein, C. R. (2000). Television and the public interest. *California Law Review, 88,* 499–564.
Sunstein, C. R. (2001). *Republic.com.* Princeton, NJ: Princeton University Press.
Time Warner Entertainment Co. v. FCC, 105 F.3d 723, 724 n.2 (D.C. Cir. 1997)
Tracey, M. (1998). *The decline and fall of public service broadcasting.* New York: Oxford University Press.
Turner Broad. Sys., Inc. v. FCC, 512 U.S. 622 (1994).
U.S. Census Bureau. (2004). *Department of Commerce, Statistical Abstract of the United States, Section 24: Information and Communications.* Retrieved February 22, 2005, from http://www.census.gov/prod/2004pubs/03statab/inforcomm.pdf
U.S. Code, Title 47, Section 396(a)(6) (2000).
Webster, J. G., & Phalen, P. F. (1994). Victim, consumer, or commodity? Audience models in communications policy. In J. S. Ettema & D. C. Whitnsey (Eds.), *Audiencemaking: How the media create the audience* (pp. 19–37). Thousand Oaks, CA: Sage.
Werbach, K. (in press). The implications of video P2P on network usage in video peer to peer. In E. Noam & D. Gerbarg (Eds.), *Peer to peer as a distribution medium.*
Whitney v. California, 274 U.S. 357 (1927).
Will, G. F. (2005, March 3). "Cut Buster loose." *The Washington Post,* p. A25.
Yoo, C. S. (2003a). Rethinking the commitment to free, local television. *Emory Law Journal, 52,* 1579–1717.
Yoo, C. S. (2003b). The rise and demise of the technology-specific approach to the First Amendment. *Georgetown Law Journal, 91,* 245–356.

Author Index

F

G

H

T

U

V

W

Subject Index

B

C

For Product Safety Concerns and Information please contact our EU
representative GPSR@taylorandfrancis.com
Taylor & Francis Verlag GmbH, Kaufingerstraße 24, 80331 München, Germany

www.ingramcontent.com/pod-product-compliance
Ingram Content Group UK Ltd.
Pitfield, Milton Keynes, MK11 3LW, UK
UKHW022114190926
475702UK00013B/1436
9780415650038